Turkey

Fodor's 90

Turkey

FODOR'S TRAVEL PUBLICATIONS, INC.
New York & London

ISBN 0–679–01838–7

Fodor's Turkey

Editor: Richard Moore
Assistant Editors: Caz Philcox, Barbara Vesey
Area Editor: Linda Stout
Editorial Contributor: Peter Sheldon
Drawings: Lorraine Calaora
Cartography: C.W. Bacon, Brian Stimpson, Swanston Graphics
Cover Photograph: Robert Frerk/Woodfin Camp

Cover Design: Vignelli Associates

Special Sales

Fodor's Travel Publications are available at special discounts for bulk purchases (100 copies or more) for sales promotions or premiums. Special editions, including personalized covers, excerpts of existing guides, and corporate imprints, can be created in large quantities for special needs. For more information, write to Special Marketing, Fodor's Travel Publications, 201 East 50th Street, New York, NY 10022. Enquiries from the United Kingdom should be sent to Fodor's Travel Publications, 30–32 Bedford Square, London WC1B 3SG.

MANUFACTURED IN THE UNITED STATES OF AMERICA
10 9 8 7 6 5 4 3 2 1

CONTENTS

FACTS AT YOUR FINGERTIPS

Planning Your Trip. What It Will Cost 1; When to Come 1; Special Events 2; Sound and Light 3; Official Holidays 3; The Highlights of Turkey 3; Suggested Itineraries 4; Tour Information 4; Sampling the Tours 5; Travel Documents 5; What to Take 6.

Getting to Turkey. By Air—From The U.S. 7; From the U.K. 7; By Sea 8; By Train 8; By Car 9; By Bus 10.

Arriving in Turkey. Customs 11; Money 11.

Staying in Turkey. Hotels 11; Student Travel and Youth Hostels 12; Club Méditerranée 13; Thermal Resorts 13; Camping 13; Restaurants 13; Tipping 14; Shopping 14; Closing Times 14; Mail 14; Telephones 15; Museums and Archeological Sites 15; Interpreter Guides 15; Medical Treatment 15; Electricity 15; Drinking Water 16; Pollution Report 16; Convenient Conveniences 16; Photography 16; Reading Matter 16; Sports 16; Winter Sports 17.

Traveling in Turkey. By Air 17; By Ship 17; By Train 18; By Bus 18; By Car 18; By Taxi 20.

Mythology and Archeology. The Gods 20; Greco-Roman Archeological Outline 21; Key to Historical Sites 22.

Leaving Turkey. Turkish Customs 24; Customs on Return 24; Duty Free 25.

EXPLORING TURKEY

CONTENTS

FOREWORD

East is East and West is West—but Turkey is something else. This proud and popular assertion has never been truer. After breaking with the Islamic Orient that it had dominated for so long to join the 20th-century Occident, Turkey has reverted to the role which geography has so obviously meant it to play. Inspired by East and West alike, the country is now finding, with a new self-assurance, its own cultural and political solutions. With the experience of millennia to draw on, Turkey naturally insists on working out its own destiny, rejecting any imposed foreign models that have proved unsuitable.

After suffering countless invasions of all kinds down the centuries, Turkey is now handling an unprecedented tourist invasion successfully. The boom in tourism has been one of the world's most staggering during the last few years—and rightly so. Visitors can enjoy standardized modern comforts in the large towns, the main sites and along the west and south coasts in a unique diversity of art and nature. If there's one regret, it is the population explosion that made the towns grow too quickly—often at the expense of the old picturesque individuality for the sake of dreary architectural sameness. The coastal beauty spots are becoming as crowded as anywhere on the Mediterranean, but there are still many solitary coves and empty beaches. Away from the scary traffic of the major towns, endless miles of roads provide easy driving through a magnificent variety of scenery, with the two coastal highways north and south unrivaled anywhere.

Turkey revels in contrasts. Except for the U.S.S.R. it is the only country to straddle two continents, 97% of its land mass extends over Anatolia, while the rest provides a foothold in Europe. Guardian of the Bosphorus, Turkey is the eastern anchor of N.A.T.O., yet it maintains a strong presence in the Middle East. It is in its present secular form one of the newest countries, lying over the relics of the world's oldest. Remains of four great civilizations—Hittite, Hellenistic, Byzantine, and Turkish—to mention only the most imposing—are scattered throughout the country. Crossing the road may bridge thousands of years back into antiquity or the Middle Ages. Subtropical beaches are within easy driving distance from ski resorts.

And, best of all, the Turks have not yet been spoiled by their tourist boom. Despite the language barrier they are most helpful everywhere, while traditional hospitality can be experienced with the old warmth in Eastern Anatolia by the more adventurous travelers. For the more demanding, conducted tours are the safest bet in those regions where accommodations fail to equal the friendly welcome.

For the traveler who is always on the lookout for the new and strange, Turkey in many ways represents one of the world's last frontiers.

*

We would like to express our gratitude to Mr. Y. Emcan, former General Director of Information, the Ministry of Culture and Tourism, Ankara, for his help and interest in our work. We would also like to thank Jean Stern, James Farrant, Eris and Nisan Akman, Metin Denisloz, Andrew Lee, Nigel Seidelin, Chris Slade, Lynn Jackson, and Gill Williams, as well as Selami Karaibrahimgil of the Turkish Tourist Office in London.

*

While every care has been taken to assure the accuracy of the information in this guide, the passage of time will always bring change, and consequently the publisher cannot accept responsibility for errors that may occur.

All prices and opening times quoted in this guide are based on information available to us at press time. Hours and admission fees may change, however, and the prudent traveler will avoid inconvenience by calling ahead.

Fodor's wants to hear about your travel experiences, both pleasant and unpleasant. When a hotel or restaurant fails to live up to its billing, let us know and we will investigate the complaint and revise our entries where the facts warrant it.

Send your letters to the editors of Fodor's Travel Publications, 201 E. 50th Street, New York, NY 10022.

FACTS AT YOUR FINGERTIPS

FACTS AT YOUR FINGERTIPS

Planning Your Trip

WHAT IT WILL COST. Turkey is still the cheapest country in the Mediterranean, but on two very different levels. The western-style hotels and restaurants, especially those dealing mainly with package tours, offer roughly the same amenities as those in rival touristic countries at a certain discount. But simple establishments—and simple is the key word despite the private showers almost everywhere and cleanliness—are staggeringly cheap, even in the main towns and resorts, let alone the remoter places. Likewise, genuine Turkish food, so infinitely preferable to the inadequate imitations of international cuisine in more pretentious places, can be enjoyed for less than the price of junk food, which is also available.

Though the rate of inflation is still over 50%, compensatory devaluations keep prices fairly stable as measured against foreign currencies. We continue, therefore, to quote prices in U.S. dollars, a practice now followed by some of the leading establishments, sightseeing tours, etc. But price adjustments are not automatic; public transport and museum charges, for instance, have lagged a long way behind. This might, however, change gradually.

Hotels, restaurants, nightclubs and campgrounds are all classified, and the price ranges for each category are set by the Ministry of Tourism and must be posted in each room. There are considerable variations within each category; prices are higher in the two main towns and along the Bosphorus. For large parts of the interior there often is nothing other than the inexpensive level in both quality and price. We give our price grading in the sections following under *Hotels* and *Restaurants.*

Some miscellaneous prices: barber, $1.50–$8; small bottle of beer, 60¢–$2; minibus in city, 20¢; sandwich, 30¢–$1. Coffee, 30¢–$2, depending on whether it is Turkish or American. Tea (home-grown) is now the national drink, 15¢–50¢. Soft drinks, 75¢–$1.80.

WHEN TO COME. The climate in Turkey varies a good deal according to time and place. On the Anatolian plain, summer is hot and dry (up to 102° Fahrenheit) but with cool nights, and winter snowy and cold (down to 2°F below zero). The Black Sea coast is mild and damp, with a rainfall of 90 inches a year, while the Mediterranean coast has a moderate climate the year round, with an average of 75°F.

The tourist season lasts from the beginning of April to the end of October, and is at its height in July and August. The best time of the year is

1

from April to June or during September and October inland and for sightseeing. Swimming is enjoyable only from May through October on the Black Sea and Mediterranean coasts, where the winters are mild, but wet. In central and eastern Anatolia the cold winters are not recommended for travel.

Average early afternoon temperatures in Fahrenheit and Centigrade—

	Jan.	Feb.	Mar.	Apr.	May	June	July	Aug.	Sept.	Oct.	Nov.	Dec.
Istanbul												
F°	45	47	52	61	68	77	81	81	75	67	59	51
C°	7	8	11	16	20	25	27	27	24	19	15	11
Ankara												
F°	39	42	51	63	73	78	86	87	78	69	57	43
C°	4	6	11	17	23	26	30	31	26	21	14	6

Average Sea Water Temperatures—

	Jan. C°	Apr. C°	July C°	Oct. C°
Marmara Region (Istanbul)	8	10	23	17
Aegean Region (Izmir)	11	15	26	21
Mediterranean Region (Antalya)	17	18	26	24
Black Sea Region (Trabzon)	10	10	24	19

SPECIAL EVENTS. Some events have variable dates from year to year, so check in advance. **January:** Camel Wrestling, Selçuk, 2 days in midmonth. **February:** Folkdance Festival, Ankara, for 3 days at the end of the month. **April:** Traditional Mesir Illuminations, Manisa, 4 days; Nyassa Festival, near Sultanhisar, 3 days.

May: Festival of Ephesus for a week at start of month—first of many theater, music and folklore festivals set in antique Greek theaters; Festival of Silifke, for a week towards end of month; Festival of Bergama, last week of May.

June: Rose Festival, Konya, beginning of month; Music and Water Sports Festival, Foça, second week; Istanbul Arts Festival, Turkey's outstanding cultural happening, with Turkish and foreign companies performing music and theater at St. Irene in the Topkapı Palace, the Yedikule Fortress, Rumeli Hisar, and the Atatürk Cultural Palace, starting mid-June for 4 weeks.

July: Turkish Wrestling Matches, Kırkpınar, Edirne, one week; Apricot Festival, Malatya; Folk Dance Festival, Samsun, throughout the month; Sea Festival, Çeşme, 5 days; Nasreddin Hoca Celebrations, Akşehir; Folklore Festival, Bursa, 3 weeks; International Festival, Ayvalık, 3 days.

August: Trojan Horse Festival, Çanakkale, second week of month; Assumption, Mass celebrated by Archbishop of Izmir in the "House of the

Virgin Mary" at Ephesus, on 15th; Commemoration Feast of Haci Bektaş, 14th-century founder of Bektaşi order of Dervishes, at Niğde on 19th; International Fair at Izmir, Aug. 20 to Sept. 20.

September: Ahi Evran Memorial Celebrations at Kırşehir, 4 days; Hittite Festival at Çorum, 4 days, mid-month; Cappadocian Grape Harvesting Festival at Ürgüp; Watermelon Festival at Diyarbakır, 4 days; Culture and Art Festivities, Adana; Tuvana Festivities, Ereğli, 2 days.

October: Art and Culture Festival, Antalya, one week; Carpet Festival, Manisa, 2 days; Folk Poets Contest, Horse Races and Javelin Games, at Konya, 10 days.

December: St. Nicholas celebrations, at Demre, 4th to 8th; Mevlana Commemoration celebrations with Rites of the Whirling Dervishes, at Konya, 13th to 16th. (Book tickets well in advance through travel agent.)

Sound and Light—Son et Lumière. **May** through **October:** Sound and Light spectacle in front of Sultan Ahmet Mosque in Istanbul. **August** and **September:** at Atatürk Mausoleum in Ankara.

Official Holidays. January 1, New Year's Day. April 23, National Independence and Children's Day. Sunset April 24 to sunset April 27, Şeker Bayram, Ramadan Feast. May 19, Atatürk Commemoration, Youth and Sports Day. July 1–5, Kurban Bayram, Sacrifice Feast. August 30, Victory Day. October 29, Republic Day, parades in Ankara and Istanbul.

THE HIGHLIGHTS OF TURKEY. You cannot hope to see a country as large as Turkey in one visit. Air travel, of course, allows you to cover great distances in a short time, and the Turkish inland airlines are well run; but it gives at best only a fleeting knowledge of the country and its people. The few, very roundabout railway lines are complemented by a network of fast and very comfortable buses to all towns, while ships call at the ports of both coasts.

Cars are, of course, the best means to get to know the out-of-the-way sights, though roads often leave a lot to be desired. Most drivers enter Turkey through *Edirne.* The first look at the Selimiye mosque, and the street life, is unforgettable. Of course, no traveler would think of going to Turkey without a long stay in *Istanbul.* The old town, its countless mosques and palaces and museums, the network of its streets, the modern town overlooking the Bosphorus, one of the most beautiful waterways in the world, and the Golden Horn, form a whole that delights the most hardened globe-trotter.

Bursa is worth a day's outing for its monuments, its atmosphere, and its position at the foot of Mount Uludağ, the Olympus of Bithynia. It is within easy reach of Istanbul, as are the beaches of Kilyos and of Şile on the Black Sea, the Princes' Islands, Çanakkale (by boat from Istanbul), and the ruins of Troy for lovers of antiquity. Historic Nicaea (Iznik) is also nearby.

Towards *Ankara,* via Abant and Bolu. Ankara itself is a green oasis in a near-desert landscape, with its modern architecture and its Museum of Anatolian Civilizations, the last an indispensable preparation for sightseeing in Boğazkale.

On the west coast of the Mediterranean, *Izmir* is the best starting point for excursions to the ancient Greek towns of *Pergamon, Ephesus, Didyma, Priene,* and so on. The whole region is full of interest to art lovers. *Pamuk-*

kale, near Denizli, has one of the wonders of nature: its splendid petrified waterfalls. On the southern coast, *Antalya* is a popular holiday resort: beaches and mountains as far as Alanya, and mild weather even in winter.

To the south and southeast of Ankara, the Seljuk towns of *Konya* and *Kayseri,* and the extraordinary stone outcroppings of *Göreme* and *Ürgüp,* are part of a separate itinerary. The region of *Antakya* (the old Antioch) and its port *Iskenderun,* on the way to Syria and Lebanon, is mostly of historical interest.

To the northeast, on the *Black Sea,* the coastline from Sinop to Trabzon is just being discovered. Best see it by boat, a 6-day cruise leaving from Istanbul.

The east of Turkey is touristically little developed. To the southeast of Erzurum, the Lake Van region is stark and beautiful, and has some interesting ruins. Archeologists will find the valley of the Euphrates (Firat) of great interest, but everyone will admire the astonishing memorial of Antiochus Commagenes on Nemrut Dağ.

Some of the most renowned *Christian sites* are in Turkey, such as the Virgin Mary's house in Ephesus, St. Peter's cave in Antakya (the old Antioch), the Basilica of St. John at Ephesus, and at Demre, the church of St. Nicholas (near Finike). Going back to Biblical times, some 40 placenames in the New Testament alone are now within Turkey's borders. The "Seven Churches of Asia" on the route of St. Paul's momentous journeys, are all here.

Two suggested itineraries depend on the length of time available as well as on the stamina of the sightseer.

1) The short tour: Istanbul–Yalova–Bursa–Manisa–Izmir–Ephesus–Izmir–Pergamon–Troy–Çanakkale–Istanbul. About 2,000 km. (1,250 miles) in 5 or 6 days.

2) The devotee's tour, with varying degrees of discomfort and language difficulties: Istanbul–Ankara–Boğazkale–Amasya–Tokat–Sivas–Malatya–Adiyaman (Nemrut Dağ)–Gaziantep–Adana–Kayseri–Cappadocia (valley of Göreme–Ürgüp–Nevşehir)–Konya–Beyşehir–Antalya   Burdur–Pamukkale–Aydın–Ephesus–Kuşadası–(Prince–Miletus–Didyma)–Izmir–   Pergamon–Edremit–Troy–Bursa–Istanbul. Almost 6,000 km. (3,730 miles) in one month.

Without a car, a pleasant alternative is a cruise from Istanbul along the Aegean, Mediterranean or Black Sea coasts, with stopovers at main ports.

TOUR INFORMATION. Even experienced travelers will find it advantageous to employ a travel agent. For package tour bookings and transportation reservations his charge to you will be the same as you would pay direct, as he receives a commission from carriers and tour operators. If he works out an individual itinerary for you, he will make a service charge on the total cost of your trip—usually 10 to 15 percent. If in doubt, consult the *American Society of Travel Agents,* 1101 King St., Alexandria, VA 22314 or the *Association of British Travel Agents,* 55–57 Newman St., London W1 (tel. 01–637 2444).

Turkish Tourist Offices: **In the U.S.:** 821 U.N. Plaza, New York, NY 10017 (tel. 212–687–2194); 2010 Massachusetts Ave., N.W., Washington,

DC 20036 (tel. 202–429–9844). **In the U.K.:** 170–173 Piccadilly, London W1V 9DD (tel. 01–734 8681, 01–355 4207). Also in most European capitals, Kuwait and Tokyo. Within Turkey, offices in some 50 towns and resorts.

Sampling the Tours. U.S. Travel Agents offering tours to Turkey include:

American Express Co., Travel Division, 822 Lexington Ave., New York, NY 10021 (tel. 212–758–6510).

Persepolis Travel Ltd., 501 Fifth Ave., Suite 1414, New York, NY 10017 (tel. 212–972–1333).

In the U.K.: *Serenissima Travel Group,* 21 Dorset Sq., London NW1 6QG (tel. 01–730 9841).

Simply Turkey, 486 Chiswick High Road, London W4 57T (tel. 01–747 1011).

Turkish Connections, Golden House, 29 Great Pulteney St., London W1R 3DD (tel. 01–439 7406).

Turkish Delight Holidays, 164B Heath Rd., Twickenham, Middlesex TW1 4BN (tel. 01–891 5901).

Package tours to Turkey tend to be of three kinds. The first is primarily a cruise among the Greek islands, touching at only a few points on the Turkish coast—usually to visit Ephesus—for a few hours. The second type of tour includes from one to several days in Istanbul, but rarely anything else in Turkey. The third type attempts to give you some idea of what this large, ancient, and extraordinarily varied country has to offer usually in the form of Special Purpose Tours and organized coach tours.

From the U.S.: *Persepolis Travel, Ltd.,* 501 Fifth Ave., Suite 1414, New York, NY 10017, features a 10-day tour that centers on Istanbul, Ankara and surrounding areas, for about $1,585.

Sobek Expeditions, P.O. Box 1089, Angels Camp, CA 95222, offers the excitement of rafting safaris down the Coruh River. This 16-day adventure costs $1,875 (including meals but not including airfare), and is an amalgam of boats, rafts, hiking and generally exploring the fascinating countryside that the river passes through.

Mountain Travel Inc., 6420 Fairmount Ave., El Cerrito, CA 94530-3606, organizes a 13-day hiking tour up Mount Ararat for $1,925 plus airfare.

From the U.K.: *Turkish Connections,* Golden House, 29 Great Pulteney St., London W1R 3DD (tel. 01–439 7406) has tours to Cappadocia and western Turkey and resort holidays.

Turkish Wildlife Holidays, 8 The Grange, Elmdon Park, Solihull, West Midlands B92 9E1 (tel. 021–742 5420) specializes in four-wheel-drive tours to remoter parts.

Serenissima (see above) has lecture tours to east and west Turkey, as well as cruises aboard the *Serenissima Tura.*

TRAVEL DOCUMENTS. To visit Turkey all you need is a valid national passport. **U.S. residents** should apply several months in advance of expected departure date. Apply in person to the U.S. Passport Agencies, local County Courthouses or selected Post Offices nationwide. If you have a passport issued within the past 12 years you may also apply by mail. In addition to the completed application (Form DSP-11), new applicants will need (1) Proof of citizenship, such as a birth certificate; (2) two identical photographs, two inches square, in black and white or color, on nonglossy paper and taken within the past six months; (3) $35 for the passport itself plus a $7 processing fee if you are applying in person (no processing fee when applying by mail) for those 18 years and older; or if you are under 18, $20 for the passport plus a $7 processing fee if you are applying in person (again, no extra fee when applying by mail); (4) proof of identity that includes a photo, such as a driver's license, previous passport, or any governmental ID card. Adult passports are valid for 10 years, others for five years. When you receive your passport, write down its number, date and place of issue separately. The loss of a valid passport should be reported immediately to the local police and to the Passport Office, Department of State, 1425 K St. NW, Washington, DC 20524; if your passport is lost or stolen while abroad, report it to the local authorities and apply for a replacement at the nearest U.S. embassy or consular office.

Canadian citizens should apply in person to regional passport offices, post offices or by mail to Bureau of Passports, External Affairs, Ottawa, Ontario K1A 0G3. A $25 fee, a guarantor, two photographs and evidence of citizenship are required. Canadian passports are valid for five years and are nonrenewable.

British subjects. Apply to your travel agency or main post office. The application should be sent or taken to the passport office for your area (as indicated on the guidance form). Apply at least five weeks before the passport is required. The regional passport offices are located in London, Liverpool, Peterborough, Glasgow, and Newport. The application must be countersigned by your bank manager or by a solicitor, barrister, doctor, clergyman, or Justice of the Peace who knows you personally. You will need two full face photos. The fee is £15 for a 10-year passport.

British Visitor's Passport. This simplified form of passport has advantages for the once-in-a-while tourist to European countries. Valid for one year and not renewable, it costs £7.50. Applications must be made in person at a post office, Monday to Friday, and identification plus two passport photographs are required—no other formalities.

Health Certificates. Not required for entry into Turkey for visitors arriving from the United States, Canada and Europe. We suggest that you consult your doctor or travel agent for advice on which—if any—inoculations you should have for your own protection.

WHAT TO TAKE. The first principle is to travel light, using strong, lightweight luggage, and dripdry, crease-resistant fabrics for clothing. If you plan to fly, you have a real incentive to stay below the first-class transatlantic limit of 66 pounds and economy limit of 44 pounds; each pound overweight costs extra money. Moreover, most bus lines as well as some international trains place limits on luggage weight (usually 55 pounds) or bulk.

Even if you are traveling by ship, resist the temptation to take more than two suitcases per person in your party, or to select luggage larger than you can carry yourself. Porters are increasingly scarce in many parts of Europe, though *not* in Turkey itself, and you will face delays every time you change trains (or hotels), go through customs, or otherwise try to move about. Motorists should limit their luggage to what can be locked into the trunk or boot of their car during daytime stops. At night, everything should be removed to the hotel room.

Consider the season of the year and the altitude at which you plan to stay. Sea level resorts may be fine for summer wear, but warmer evening clothes are essential for places only a few miles inland at a higher altitude. Most hotels offer laundry facilities, but results vary considerably.

Turkey is an informal country, where one rarely dresses for dinner outside Ankara, Istanbul and Izmir. In summer men wear lightweight slacks, open-neck shirts and sandals; women cotton dresses or slacks. Winters on the Mediterranean coast are mild, less so on the Marmara and Black Sea, and grim indeed in the interior. So fit your wardrobe to your destination. Take sturdy, comfortable shoes for visiting archeological and historical sites, sunhats for protection in summer, and headscarves for women to wear when visiting mosques.

Turkey is a Moslem country, and while bikinis and too brief beachwear may pass in the major international resorts, don't offend local susceptibilities by walking in the street of a small town in "undress" or by entering religious establishments or mosques in shorts or attire exposing too much of the body. Show the same respect you would in a cathedral or synagogue.

Towels, soap, and toilet paper are supplied in all hotels, except out-of-the-way establishments. But the toiletries may not be up to home standards. In major towns and resorts you can generally get European brands of medicines, suntan lotions, toothpaste, and razor blades. Coffee is obtainable in most hotels, often at an additional charge; for the outback bring your own. Prescriptions for special medicines can rarely be filled. Earplugs and eyeshades come in handy.

Getting to Turkey

BY AIR. From the U.S. Unfortunately there are no nonstop services from the U.S. direct to Turkey; however, many major international carriers fly from North America to Turkey (usually Ankara or Istanbul) with stopovers (and a change of planes) in various European cities, including *Pan Am, Alitalia, KLM, Lufthansa,* and *Pakistan Airlines. Turkish Airlines* flies weekly services from New York via Brussels.

Fares. New York to Istanbul at press time (and therefore subject to increase) round trip first-class fare was about $5,078 and the round trip business fare was about $2,960. There are various excursion fares available as we go to press, although, with further changes in the fare structure pending, the following can only be a general guide. The most convenient is APEX (advance booking by 21 days, minimum stay seven days, maximum six months). This costs between $934 and $1,102 (round trip).

From the U.K. From London Heathrow in high summer there are two direct flights daily to Istanbul by *THY Turkish Airlines* and *British Airways.* The flying time is around 3 hrs. 45 mins. Fares are not cheap. Expect to pay £986 round trip in First class, £606 Economy, and £342 for an APEX round trip in high summer. Also book well in advance as demand for seats often outstrips supply.

In many cases it is cheaper to book a complete package holiday than to pay the full air fare. Turkey's increasing popularity has encouraged some charter operators to sell seats direct to the public at lower rates.

Charter airlines flying from London's Gatwick airport or Manchester include *Air Europe, British Airtours, British Island Airways, Dan Air,* and *Orion,* which fly to Istanbul, Izmir, Dalaman, and Antalya. Most travel agents sell seat-only charter flights. Fares range from around £120–£175.

Flight bargains in the form of unfilled holiday seats are often available to late bookers so scan the classified advertising columns of newspapers such as the London *Evening Standard, The Times, Sunday Times,* and the *Mail on Sunday.* Now some words of warning: always ask what the price being quoted includes—airport tax?, currency surcharge?, fuel surcharge? The price may not be quite as cheap as it seemed at first. Always ring all the companies and compare quotes, remembering that the fares shown in the ad usually carry restrictions. In the U.K. always pay by credit card in order to give yourself protection against default or fraud by the agent when buying over the phone.

BY SEA. The only passenger line still regularly sailing the Atlantic is Britain's *Cunard*—and they only sail to France and Britain, albeit on the *Queen Elizabeth 2.* Details can be had from Cunard Line Ltd., 555 Fifth Ave., New York, NY 10017 (tel. 212–880–7500).

However, it is possible to sail the Atlantic, and to a wide range of destinations, on a cargo ship, many of which carry a limited number of passengers. Bear in mind though that this is surprisingly popular and waiting time is now around two years. But if you're interested, call *Freighter World Cruises, Inc.* (tel. 818–449–3106) and order their biweekly newsletter *Freighter Space Advisory* at $27 a year.

There is a greater choice in the Mediterranean. *Turkish Maritime Lines (Denizyollari)* liners make regular runs from Cyprus, Ancona, Venice, Alexandria, Haifa, and of course, all around the Turkish coasts. Reductions are available on round-trip tickets, cruises, and to students, journalists, families, and groups. The same line has summer car ferry services from Venice and Ancona to Izmir and Istanbul. Journey time is about 3 days and apart from passengers, the ferries also carry up to 100 cars. Arriving in Turkey by this line entitles you to reductions on the inland services. The fares in both first and tourist class vary according to season on most lines. Ferries run between Greece and Turkey from May through September: Chios to Çeşme, Samos to Kuşadası, Kos to Bodrum, Rhodes to Marmaris. There are daily ferries from Famagusta (in Turkish Cyprus) to Mersin, and a hovercraft service between Famagusta and Taşucu.

Royal Cruise Line, 1 Maritime Plaza, Suite 660, San Francisco, CA 94111, includes stops in Turkey on its trans-Mediterranean cruises.

BY TRAIN. The most convenient route from London is via Ostende and Cologne (sleeping cars and couchettes available), arriving in Munich around 4 the following afternoon. The connecting service, the *Istanbul Express,* leaves Munich early evening (giving time to stock up with provisions!) and travels through Yugoslavia the next day and Bulgaria the following night to reach Istanbul mid-morning—*if* the train is on time. Couchettes (wagons-lits sleepers available to Belgrade) must be booked in advance and visas will be needed. There is a buffet-refreshment service in Turkey. The second-class round trip fare is around £290; for the sake of comfort, consider traveling first class.

From Venice there is a service via Belgrade and Sofia to Istanbul (second-class couchettes available), taking about 40 hours.

If money is no object there is the *Nostalgic Orient Express,* operated by Intraflug A.G. of Zurich. This magnificent train is composed of original 1920s coaches (so do not expect air-conditioning, etc.) and runs a couple of times a year from Zurich to Istanbul.

For planning your rail journey to Turkey the *Thomas Cook European Timetable* is essential reading. For planning rail travel within Turkey buy their *Overseas Timetable.* Both are available by mail; in the U.K. from *Thomas Cook,* Timetable Publishing Office, P.O. Box 36, Peterborough PE3 6SB (also over-the-counter at any branch of Thomas Cook); in the U.S.A. from *Stephen Forsyth Travel Library,* 9154 West 57th Street, Shawnee Mission, KS 66203.

BY CAR. From London, you must count on an average of 4 to 5 days, depending on the speed of your car, to cover the 3,000 km. (1,870 miles) to Istanbul. The *American Automobile Association,* in addition to supplying motorists with useful information, will help arrange travel in (and tours of) Turkey. Check with their offices in the U.S. at 1000 AAA Drive, Heathrow, FL 32746 (tel. 800–336–4357); or with the British *Automobile Association,* Fanum House, 5 New Coventry St., London W1V 8HT (tel. 01–749 9911).

The shortest route from **Great Britain,** if you want to drive all the way, is via Ostende–Frankfurt–Munich–Salzburg–Klagenfurt to Ljubljana in Yugoslavia, then along that country's only through highway to Belgrade. This two-lane *Autoput* is straight, but rather monotonous, bumpy and crowded with trucks. An alternative route from Frankfurt is via Nürenberg–Linz–Vienna–Budapest–Belgrade. The four-lane motorway through Belgrade is being extended to Nis, but speed limits are strictly enforced, as they are on the narrower 87 km. (54 miles) to Dimitrovgrad and the Bulgarian border. No visa needed for Yugoslavia for U.K. citizens; Americans require a transit visa, obtainable at the border. Both U.S. and U.K. citizens require transit visas (valid for 30 hours only) to drive through Bulgaria. These must be obtained beforehand. If you plan to stay more than 30 hours in Bulgaria, you must have an entry visa. This too must be obtained beforehand. In the U.S., contact the *Bulgarian Embassy,* 1621 22nd St., NW, Washington, DC 20008; in the U.K. contact the *Bulgarian Legation,* 186 Queen's Gate, London, SW7 5H1.

From there, it is on to Sofia, Plovdiv, Haskovo, Svilengrad, and the Turkish border; most green cards are valid only for European Turkey, so check before continuing on to Edirne and Istanbul.

If you prefer to bypass Bulgaria, you drive from Nis to Skopje and on an all-too-narrow road sometimes cut through rock to the Greek border. Then you can enjoy the motorway to Thessaloniki, but slow down again on the narrower road to Kavala, Komotini, Alexandroupolis, the Ipsala Bridge (Turkish frontier), Tekirdağ and Istanbul. The detour around Bulgaria through Greece adds about 450 km. (280 miles).

Car-sleeper expresses and car ferries. Some 1,320 km. (825 miles) and two or three days of tiring driving can be saved by crossing from Sheerness to Vlissingen and boarding the *summer* motorail from 's-Hertogenbosch to Ljubljana; or Dover to Ostende and car-sleeper from Brussels to Ljubljana. While the cost of the train is high, it must be offset against the expenses of hotels and gasoline. This is a limited summer service (once-weekly) and can be booked through *DER Travel Service,* 18

Conduit St., London W1R 9TD (tel. 01–408 0111). A round-trip ticket gives significant reduction. Ask about inclusive car ferry and motorail fares from the U.K.

Driving may be further reduced (but not costs or time) by using the car ferries from Italy to Turkey. *Turkish Maritime Lines* sails in 48 hours from Ancona to Izmir (summer only): for details contact their agents, *Sunquest Holidays,* Aldine House, 9–15 Aldine Street, London W12 8AW (tel. 01–749 9911). *Libra Maritime Lines* sails weekly June to September from Piraeus to Izmir in 17 hours. *British Ferries'* ship *Orient Express* sails weekly May through October from Venice to Istanbul and Kusadaşı via Piraeus, and takes 3 days: a round trip for two people with car will be about £1,500.

Driving license. An international driving license is needed for hiring a car; a national driving license is in theory sufficient for driving your own car, but in case of accidents—and they are frequent—an IDL will be of advantage. The *green insurance card* has to be endorsed for European and Asiatic Turkey. Otherwise short-time Turkish insurance, third party only, must be taken out at the border; this is incredibly cheap, but better not tried out.

BY BUS. There is one main bus service during the summer months from London to Istanbul run by a group of reputable companies under the banner of *National Express-Eurolines.* Their twice-weekly service runs from London Victoria Coach Station to Munich, from where there is a weekly connecting service to Istanbul run by *Bosfor/DTG.* An adult round trip works out at around £200, with slight reductions for students. Details from National Express-Eurolines, The Coach Travel Centre, 13 Regent St., London SW1Y 4LR (tel. 01–730 0202), or from most travel agents. Note these services are operated by several different companies so expect to change buses en route. It is advised that the outward and return journeys are booked at the same time. As with rail travel it is essential to ensure that valid visas are carried for all countries to be passed through. Various services are operated from Austria, France, and West Germany to Turkey at lower prices, primarily for guest workers returning home. However, many of these are run by small companies with poor standards of maintenance and safety and are best avoided.

Arriving in Turkey

CUSTOMS. Turkish customs officials are lenient with travelers and rarely look through their luggage. You are allowed your personal belongings, sporting, camping, and photographic equipment, 1.5 kg. of coffee or tea, 2.5 liters of alcohol, 400 cigarettes, 50 cigars. Purchases up to a value of $1,000 can be exported on production of a currency exchange slip. For new carpets the limit is $3,000, while old ones require a special permit. Weapons, ammunition and narcotics are forbidden. There are severe penalties for attempting to export antiques without prior authorization.

MONEY. There are no restrictions on foreign currency brought into the country, but only up to U.S. $3,000 in foreign (i.e.: non-Turkish) currency may be exported. Tourists may export only the equivalent of U.S. $1,000 in Turkish currency. Banknotes and traveler's checks can be exchanged at banks, travel agencies and major hotels at the official rate of exchange.

Although there is no shortage of banks in Turkey, most accept only the best-known traveler's checks; (L) and (E) hotels are more accommodating, but might charge more for the service. Traveler's checks issued by *American Express, Bank of America* and *Citibank* and by *Thomas Cook & Son* and the major British banks are well known and widely accepted.

At press time the exchange rate was approximately 2,000 TL to the U.S. dollar, 3,300 TL to the pound sterling. To reconvert any remaining Turkish money into foreign currency, it is important to retain your original exchange slips.

The monetary unit is the *lira* (TL). There are banknotes of 100, 500, 1,000, 5,000, 10,000 and 20,000. Although there are coins of smaller denominations, they are seldom used.

Devaluation-Inflation. With inflation in 1989 hovering between 50% and 70%, prices in this guide are still quoted in dollars. Constant adjustments in the exchange rate correspond to the inflation rate, so that prices are relatively stable in dollars but not in Turkish lira.

Credit Cards. Credit cards are not accepted very often outside Istanbul and Ankara. In those two cities the major hotels will take them, some shops, a few restaurants, and large international concerns. But you should plan on not being able to use your cards much in Turkey. This will mean carrying more cash with you and keeping an eye open for banks and exchange bureaux in case of need.

Staying in Turkey

HOTELS. The adoption of the star system from one to five in 1987 simplified the official Turkish classifications. But there are also motels, M1 and 2, pensions, P, as well as a handful of rather expensive mountain inns, O for *oberj* (from the French *auberge*). Differences in this nomenclature are rather in the mind of the classifying power than visible to the naked eye! To complicate matters further, Turkish-operated holiday villages (TK for *tatil köyü*) are classed 1 and 2. Then there is the much larger number of locally licensed establishments, not included in the official list, though often just as good. Their names can be obtained only from local tourist offices. Neither price nor comfort justify this tangle, as the criteria are somewhat arbitrary, lack of a restaurant or even a bar automatically relegating the establishment to the bottom.

We have, therefore, adopted our usual categories: Deluxe (L), Expensive (E), Moderate (M) and Inexpensive (I). The American chains are represented so far only by Hilton and Sheraton in Ankara and Istanbul, Ramada in Istanbul, and a Holiday Inn which is due to open in Istanbul in 1990. The Turkish chains, Dedeman, Emek, Etap, Turban, and Tusan, guarantee the standards of their respective categories. Luxury hotels are to be found only in and around big cities like Ankara, Istanbul, and Izmir, but some expensive establishments, modest by western standards, have been opened in coastal resorts where the moderate category on the whole predominates. Inland it is mostly inexpensive, without restaurants. The two top categories are air-conditioned, with radio and optional T.V., but all rooms in the hotels listed in the regional chapters have private showers at least, unless stated otherwise. But plumbing is almost universally a weak point, in western- and eastern-style toilets alike, while the whole concept of comfort leaves much to be desired. Hardly any establishment below expensive features shutters or blinds, so that the sunlight competes with an infinite variety of noises to wake you at dawn, while at night the corridor lights shine through the glass panes above all-too-many doors. Hence the need for earplugs and eyeshades. Before deciding on your room check if shower, toilet, light switches, doorlock all work (from moderate down a rare combination) so that you won't have to change rooms after unpacking.

Off the tourist beat there are often only hotels which have not been granted a rating; though not necessarily unclean or badly run, these rightly unclassified hotels have only the rock-bottom price to recommend them.

It is advisable to book rooms in advance, especially during the season. Beach hotels close October through April. Hotels down to (M) have restaurants, (I) hotels only when stated. Telephone numbers are usually given for the two upper categories and for those where English is likely to be understood by the switchboard.

The following table gives prices in mid-1988 for rooms with bath, including taxes and service charges.

Hotel Prices (in U.S. dollars)

	Deluxe (L)	Expensive (E)	Moderate (M)	Inexpensive (I)
Single	90–150	50–90	20–50	5–20
Double	110–250	50–110	25–50	10–25
Suites	—	150–3000	38–150	—

STUDENT TRAVEL AND YOUTH HOSTELS. Those listed as students or teachers on their passports and holders of International Youth Hostel cards or International Student Conference cards are entitled to use the Kadırga Student Hostel, Cömertler Sok. 6, Kumkapı, Istanbul (tel. 528 2480) and several other hostels. A full list is supplied by the Ministry of Information and Tourism. For an International Youth Hostel card apply to: *American Youth Hostels, Inc.,* PO Box 37613, Washington, DC 20013 (tel. 202–783–6161); or *Canadian Hostelling Association,* 18 Dyward Market, Ottawa, Ont. K1N 7A1 (tel. 613–230–1200).

Students may also obtain a "yellow card" from the organizations listed below, entitling them to reductions of 40% on the Turkish railways, 15% to 50% on Turkish Maritime Lines, 10% on domestic flights and 60% on the international routes of Turkish Airlines.

For detailed information, write to *TMGT* (Turkish National Youth Organization), Tünel, Istiklal Cad. 471/2, Istanbul, or *Ermek Iş Hani,* Kizilay, Ankara; or *TOGTO* (Turkish Tourism Organization of Students and Youth), Samanyolu Sok. 62/8, Şişli, Istanbul.

These organizations also arrange excursions in Istanbul and throughout Turkey. Sample tour: 5 days to Bursa, Troy, Pergamon, Izmir and Ephesus.

CLUB MED. Club Med has four holiday villages in Turkey which are by the sea and offer scuba diving, waterskiing and sailing as well as their distinctive—and very French—Club Méditerranée flair. **In the U.S.,** their address is 3 E. 54th St., New York, NY 10022 (tel. 212–750–1687); **in the U.K.,** 106 Brompton Rd., London SW3 (tel. 01–581 1161); **in Turkey,** Akdeniz TTAS, Büyükdere Cad., Beytam Han Kat: 11 Şişli, Istanbul.

Foça, 250 concrete bungalows grouped in two small hamlets, one on a hill, the other in an olive grove.

Kemer, on the coast road 42 km. (26 miles) from Antalya. In a bay surrounded by pine forests.

Kuşadası, very comfortable bungalows on a secluded promontory.

Palmiye, 56 km. (35 miles) from Antalya, opened in 1987.

THERMAL RESORTS. There are over 1,000 hot springs in Turkey, most of them not yet therapeutically exploited. Leading centers, both for recreation and for medical treatment, are Bursa, Çeşme, Gönen, Pamukkale and Yalova.

CAMPING. The organized campsites along the main roads in western, southern and central Turkey are open April or May through October. The Ministry of Tourism and Information issues a brochure, *Camping in Turkey,* giving time of year when open, location, facilities and so on. Outstanding are the ten *Kervansaray-Mocamps,* near B.P. filling stations, which all have electricity, running water, and some a swimming pool. You will find main camping grounds listed, with their capacity, in the regional chapters.

Mocamp rates are low and, at some camps, bungalows can also be rented. For further details, write *Türk Touring Travel Agency,* Şişli Meydani 364, Istanbul.

RESTAURANTS. The three official classifications are Ö (Özellik Special Site), 1 and 2. They correspond only roughly with our categories—Expensive (E), Moderate (M), and Inexpensive (I). In terms of U.S. dollars, for lunch or dinner per person (without wine), expect to pay around 20–30 in an (E) restaurant, 10–20 in an (M) restaurant, and 5–10 in an (I) establishment. The corresponding rates for breakfast would be 8–12 (E), 5–8 (M), 2–5 (I).

Reservations can normally be made by telephone only for (E) and (M) restaurants in Ankara and Istanbul.

There are few recommended restaurants in the regional chapters, for the simple reason that outside the three main towns and some fish restaurants in the seaside resorts, none deserve to be singled out. Avoid the international-style restaurants, especially in the motels, where the food is indifferent—to please all comers, no doubt—and so pleasing nobody; go to Turkish restaurants, where you will be served tasty and unusual meals. You will pay far less, and be made welcome by a restaurant-keeper willing to face the language problem. The bill of fare is usually written in Turkish only, but you can point out your chosen dish, either among those on display behind glass or by going into the kitchen to choose among those simmering on the stove—except in deluxe restaurants, or those so-called, you are welcome to go into the kitchen and choose your own food. The service is among the fastest in the world. Leave a 10% tip for the waiter and something for the boy who brings the wine, even if service is included in the bill. In some Turkish restaurants, a bowl of water and scent will be brought after the meal.

In small towns, you will only find *lokanta* (taverns). These are often discouraging to look at, but though the food is simple, it is tasty more often than not and usually incredibly cheap. Nevertheless, check your bill, even though it is brought folded up with only the total on the outside.

TIPPING. In hotels not listed by the tourist authorities a tip of 10% to 15% would be gratefully received. In all others, 15% for service is put on the bill, but this is unlikely to find its way to the right pocket. If you have received good service (and service in Turkey is often outstanding) give some recognition to those who have helped to make your stay pleasant. Waiters should be given at least 10% on top of the so-called "service charge" and the chambermaid should receive not less than 50 cents a day. Altogether, reckon a further 15% in all on your hotel bill in "personal" tips.

For taxis, round off the fare to the nearest 100TL to include the tip.

Reckon on 20% at men's barbershops and a bit more at ladies' hairdressers. Porters expect about 50 cents per bag, washroom attendants 30 cents, chambermaids about 75 cents a day.

SHOPPING. For those used to price-tag shopping, Turkish *bedestan* (bazaars) have a somewhat disconcerting way of doing business. If you are nonetheless willing to undertake the endless *pazarlık* (bargaining), try matching your wits against the charming shopkeepers of Istanbul's renowned covered bazaar. Keep in mind that it is both bad manners and bad business to underbid grossly. A bid of half the price asked is fair enough; the haggling can begin around that sum, within reason, sometimes over a cup of coffee on the house, if it's a big item. Old as it is, the trick of not seeming to care what or whether you buy still works.

Whether you have plenty of money to spend or not, there is such a wide range of Turkish handicraft—the best buys are leather coats and jackets, copper and brassware, rugs and embroideries, meerschaum pipes and ornaments—that nobody need leave empty-handed. Carpets are certainly a bargain, but try to carry any you may buy with you rather than arrange for it to be shipped, as shipping can take up to a year. Also beware of "antiques," whose provenance is not even doubtful in most cases, while the genuine article is not allowed to be exported (prison penalties for contravention).

CLOSING TIMES. The day of rest in Turkey is Sunday, but banks also close Saturdays. Many shops in resorts and a few banks stay open on these days. Banks are open weekdays from 8.30–12 and 1.30–5, and most shops from 9–1 and 2–7, closed Sundays. In resort areas some shops stay open late.

MAIL. Post Offices are recognizable by the yellow *PTT* sign, which stands for Post, Telephone and Telegraph. Rates are frequently adjusted to keep up with inflation. Ask your hotel porter for the latest ones. Post Offices in the main towns are open from 8 A.M. to 9 P.M., Monday to Saturday, and 9–7 on Sundays. A Poste Restante service is available in the larger Post Offices. *Istanbul,* Central Post Office, Yeni Postante Cad., Sirkeci; *Ankara,* Central Post Office, Atatürk Bul., Ulus; *Izmir,* Atatürk Cad.

TELEPHONES. Telephone calls are very cheap, though it can sometimes take a long time to get through. Turkey is 7 hours ahead of U.S. Eastern Standard Time and 3 hours ahead of Britain. You should, however, beware of making long-distance calls from your hotel, as these will carry huge mark-ups, as they do in nearly every country.

Pay telephones operate with tokens *(jeton)* that can be purchased at Post Offices and street kiosks. Numbers change frequently, as digits are constantly added in expanding networks.

MUSEUMS AND ARCHEOLOGICAL SITES. Entrance fees vary, but all are low. At most museums there is an extra charge for taking in a camera. Some of the more remote ancient sites are not yet fenced in. Most sites and museums are usually open Tues. to Sun., 9.30–4.30. Some museums and palaces in Istanbul close also a second day or on Tues. instead of Mon. Palaces, open the same hours, are closed Thurs. For details see pp. 101–2. See also the *Key to Historical Sites,* pp. 23–4.

INTERPRETER GUIDES. The Ministry of Tourism, as well as travel agencies, have professional interpreter guides. In large cities, guides for small groups are paid from $7 an hour. Guides for individual tourists are the cream of the profession and slightly more expensive. Special *Tourist Police,* speaking English, French and German, are on duty in Istanbul, Ankara, and Izmir.

MEDICAL TREATMENT. Free treatment is available at the various national hospitals. There is an American hospital in Istanbul at Güzelbahçe Sok. 20, Nisantasi (tel. 131 40 50). Dial 077 for an ambulance.

The *IAMAT* (International Assoc. for Medical Assistance to Travelers) offers you a list of approved English-speaking doctors who have had postgraduate training in the U.S., Canada or Great Britain. Membership is free; the scheme is worldwide with many European countries participating. For information apply in the U.S. to 417 Center St., Lewiston, NY 14092 (tel. 716–754–4883); in Canada, 40 Regal Rd., Guelph, Ont. N1K 1B5; in New Zealand, Box 5049, Christchurch 5; in Europe, 57 Voirets, 1212 Grand-Lancy-Geneva, Switzerland. In Turkey, *IAMAT* has correspondents in Adana, Ankara, and Istanbul. Many other forms of insurance and medical assistance are available; check with your travel agent.

In Great Britain, *Europ Assistance,* 252 High Street, Croydon, Surrey, provide comprehensive medical insurance for a small premium for inclusive coverage. Their services are highly recommended, now also to U.S. travelers via *Europ Assistance Worldwide Services Inc.,* 1133 15th St., NW, Suite 400, Washington, DC 20005 (tel. 800–821–2828). Note, they split Turkey between two of its zones—the European and the Asian sections.

Remember that first aid stations, ambulances, hospitals, nursing homes and so on, do not have a red cross on a white background to distinguish them in Turkey, but a red *crescent* on a white background.

ELECTRICITY. Turkey generally runs on 220 volts, but occasionally, particularly in the older parts of Istanbul, 110 volts. Voltage is marked on hotel power points. The eastern provinces of Turkey often suffer from breaks in electricity service, so it is best to keep a flashlight handy in case the streetlights suddenly fail.

DRINKING WATER. Tap water is supposedly safe to drink in all main cities and resorts as it is heavily chlorinated. However, bottled mineral water (*maden suyu*) is readily available and tastes better.

POLLUTION REPORT. Most of the thousands of miles of the crystal-clear Mediterranean and the less translucent Black Sea coast are blissfully unpolluted, though the occasional slick of tar might be washed ashore even on the remotest beaches. The Bosphorus, despite its closeness to Istanbul, is surprisingly clean, because of the strong current from the north; but the Marmara Sea near the town is better avoided for quite a distance: though not necessarily noxious, it remains an uninviting muddy gray. Nor would anyone want to bathe in the big ports like Izmir, where pollution has spread over most of the bay, with clean beaches only quite a way out.

Air pollution in Istanbul is due to the numerous small craft workshops, domestic heating and industry. The problem has been faced more success-fully in Ankara, where all heating systems are strictly controlled. On wind-less summer days, however, the sun still retires behind exhaust fumes. Dust is prevalent in the dry interior.

CONVENIENT CONVENIENCES. Except at air terminals and railway stations hardly any, and those for men only. You may try the better restau-rants; the simpler ones are very simple indeed, of the no-seat variety.

PHOTOGRAPHY. Turkey, beautiful and strange, is a photographer's paradise. However, country people are camera shy, and though unposed snapshots are more exciting, you may get some very unexpected excite-ment if you don't ask. Never lose sight of the fact that you are in an Islamic country, where the age-old taboo against portraying a human image still lingers, especially in out of the way places. Major brands of film are avail-able everywhere.

READING MATTER. *The Daily News,* the only English daily, contains some useful local information. Like the foreign papers it's available only in main towns and major beach resorts.

SPORTS. **Water sports,** of course, are popular all along the coasts, es-pecially on the splendid beaches of the Aegean and Mediterranean.

Fishing. Some areas prohibit fishing, while others require a permit. Check with the tourist office. Good catches of red mullet, bass, tunny, and grouper in the sea, and in the Anatolian rivers and lakes, carp, pike, sheat-fish and, near the head-water, trout.

Snorkeling. Unpolluted waters round much of the country's coastline make Turkey an exceptionally good place for scuba diving and snorkeling. This is particularly true of the coast round Anatolia, where the water is fabulously clear. The cliff faces here descend abruptly into the sea and are pitted with grottos of extraordinary size. And apart from fish of all kinds, the waters hold a treasury of historical remains awaiting the adventurous diver, but it is illegal to take any ancient souvenirs from the sea. Permits for scuba diving must be obtained from the directorate of the harbor and from the directorate of the ministry of tourism; a diving guide must accom-pany you.

Yachting. On entering Turkish waters yachts must proceed to one of the ports listed below to obtain a transit log. The main marinas are at Bodrum and Kuşadası, but there are mooring facilities and supply stations at Istanbul and the major Mediterranean ports, where yachts can also be hired. The government has set up customs houses in the following ports for private boats: Akçay, Anamur, Antalya, Alanya, Ayvalık, Bandirma, Bodrum, Çanakkale, Çeşme, Datça, Dikili, Fethiye, Finike, Güllük, Iskenderun, Istanbul, Izmir, Kaş, Kemer, Kuşadası, Marmaris, Mersin, Samsun, Taşucu and Trabzon.

Hunting. Almost all the countryside is open to sportsmen, but tourists may hunt only in parties organized by Turkish travel agencies authorized by the Ministry of Forestry. Hunting by private individuals in Turkey is strictly forbidden. You must have your national permit stamped by the Turkish consulate or the Tourism and Information Offices in your country, or at a local town hall in Turkey. Only members of an organized hunting party may bring in one nonrifled gun and 100 rounds of ammunition.

At present, only wild boar may be hunted. The best areas for this are in the Taurus Mountains, around Tarsus in southern Turkey and around Muğla and Marmaris in the southwest. All other game and birds are protected.

Two travel agencies—*Van der Zee*, Cumhuriyet Cad. 16, and *Cem*, Harbiye Halaskar Gazi Cad. 68—both in Istanbul, organize hunting and shooting parties for small groups.

WINTER SPORTS. The most popular **skiing** resort is on Uludağ, by cable car from Bursa. Less developed are Erzurum; Elmadağ, 19 km. (12 miles) from Ankara, and Erciyes Dağ, near Kayseri. Saklikent, 42 km. (26 miles) from Antalya, is being developed into the biggest center. In March and April, skiing can be combined with bathing in the warm Mediterranean.

Traveling in Turkey

BY AIR. As Asiatic Turkey is an extensive and—to a considerable extent—a mountainous area, flying is the easiest way by far for getting about, even between places which seem comparatively close on the map. *Turkish Airlines (THY)* flies an extensive network of internal routes, the busiest being between Istanbul and Ankara, Istanbul and Izmir and Ankara and Izmir. There are also regular services to some 15 provincial cities. Tickets are 15%–20% cheaper if bought in Turkey rather than abroad. Airports are congested. Arrive at least 45 minutes before your flight because security checks, which are rigidly enforced, can be time-consuming.

BY SHIP. Main towns on both coasts can be reached by *Turkish Maritime Lines (Denizyollari)*. The Black Sea line *(Karadeniz)* sails weekly all year from Istanbul to Samsun and Trabzon; the six-day trip is, however, intended more for locals than tourists. From May through September a weekly 6-day cruise goes as far as Rize. Boats also stop at small ports all along the west coast up to Abana and beyond.

The Mediterranean line *(Akdeniz)* sails from Istanbul to Izmir, Kuşadası, Marmaris, Bodrum, Fethiye, Finike, Antalya, Alanya, Mersin and Iskenderun in 10 days. There are also 12-day cruises from Istanbul from May through September, calling at 15 ports. There are many local runs in the Sea of Marmara, to Mudanya and Gemlik, to Çanakkale and the islands of Gökçe and Bozcaada. Ferryboats cross the Dardanelles from Lapseki to Gelibolu and Çanakkale to Eceabat ten or more times daily.

Though the cruises are geared to the tourist market, fares are very low, but there is little luxury even in the luxury class. 50% discount, both on single and roundtrip fares, is available on internal services for visitors arriving from abroad on a Turkish Maritime Line vessel. Standard discounts include: 10% for roundtrip, 10% to 25% for students (depending on class); children 4 to 12 half fare.

Aegean cruises (which can be combined in a fly/cruise package) take in Istanbul, Izmir, Kuşadası, and Marmaris and are more comfortable and up-to-date (but also more expensive) than the Turkish boats.

BY TRAIN. Turkish Railways *(TCDD)* are state-owned, and have a network of 8,300 km. (5,160 miles) connecting all principal towns but leaving large stretches on both coasts unserved. Although the system is slowly modernizing, travel is slow: lines twist and turn along the valleys to avoid mountains and include widely scattered towns. Trains are often very late and on the branch lines there may be a service on only a couple of days a week. The train journey from Istanbul to Ankara takes 9½ hours (580 km. (360 miles) as against 440 km. (273 miles) on the highway). The luxury "Blue Train" *(Mavi Tren),* daily from Istanbul (Haydarpasa) cuts this time to 7½ hours. There are lines from Istanbul (Haydarpasa) to Kars, via Ankara, Kayseri and Erzurum; to Tehran in Iran when services are not suspended as a result of the war between Iran and Iraq; and to Adana and Aleppo in Syria.

Fares are inexpensive enough to travel first class; second is quite grim. It's best to take the expresses or one-class diesel trains, and avoid traveling by night unless by sleeper. There is a reduction of 10% on a roundtrip fare, and groups of 24 or more get a 30% discount, up to 40% for students.

The Turkish railway timetable, *Yolcu Rehberi,* is obtainable only in Turkey and can be difficult to find. For advance planning use the Thomas Cook Overseas Timetable (details in *How to Get There, By Train* earlier in this section).

BY BUS. There are good bus services connecting the major towns and cities, with private companies running frequent and inexpensive trips night and day. In Turkey the roads are often more direct than the railways. However, it is impossible to obtain advance information as buses are run by a multiplicity of companies large and small. On arrival in large towns simply ask for the central bus terminal or *otogar,* and make your way to the central square in smaller towns. There the operators' booking clerks shout their wares from rickety kiosks—just like a market! On popular routes the stiff competition will result in a very good service.

Refrigerated bottled water is generally available without charge.

BY CAR. Driving is to the right of the road, and cars are overtaken on the left, but in the towns, and above all in Istanbul, best be on the lookout. However, as nobody drives very fast there is time to brake. Attention to traffic lights is strictly enforced. In their absence, police direct traffic with shrill whistle blasts.

Parking is a problem in the bigger towns. Avoid the many small one-way streets; in Istanbul it is safer to drive along the big modern thoroughfares: even if longer, you will find your way more easily and lose less time in the long run.

Turkish driving conforms to Mediterranean customs, not precluding overtaking on a curve or on the top of a rise. The vehicle ascending steep narrow gradients has priority, as the usually overloaded trucks often stall when stopped, and you might receive an excellent lesson in Turkish invective. Carts might be driven on the left the better to see the coming cars; also bicycles, which rarely feature any lights. Watch out for peasant carts: a small flickering lantern is the only tail light, when there is one at all. Trucks and farm machines are the worst offenders, hurtling along at a speed to which neither they nor their drivers are attuned.

You might remember that Turkey has one of the highest accident rates proportionate to the number of cars.

Car Hire. The bulk of hired cars are locally made Fiats and Renaults. Self-drive rates are reasonable, starting at around $30 a day, plus 30¢ per km., or $90 a day with unlimited mileage—minimum two days' hire.

Extension of the European Road System. E5 entering from Bulgaria near Edirne is joined by E25 from Greece on the coast of the Sea of Marmara, which it follows to the Atatürk airport, starting point of the six-lane Istanbul bypass over the Bosphorus bridge. From there E5 is a toll road to Izmit, where it reverts to a modest two lanes. Widening again well before the Ankara ringroad, four lanes continue to the Aksaray junction, then again two lanes most of the way to Adana and Antakya to the Syrian border at Yayladağı. E24 branches off E25 in Thrace, crosses the Dardanelles (ferry) more or less following the coast to Izmir, striking inland at Kuşadası to Denizli and Burdur to meet the Mediterranean again at Antalya for the spectacular coastal stretch to Mersin. Here starts Turkey's second toll road, linking up with E5 halfway to Adana, but soon again on its own, running due east to Gaziantep. Narrowed to two lanes, E24 passes Urfa on the way to the border crossings at Şenyurt or Nusaybin south of Mardin. It then continues along the Syrian border to Cizre, where E26 branches south into Iraq. E24 keeps on the eastward course, but there is a gap of 80 km. (50 miles) to the Esendere crossing into Iran, which can only be reached from Van. E23 connects Izmir with Ankara to continue via Sivas and Erzurum to the crossing into Iran at Gurbulak. E390 from Trabzon meets E23 before Erzurum.

Car Transportation from the Turkish Coast to the Greek Islands. Drivers starting out from Istanbul can shorten or vary the return home by using the car ferries that ply between the Turkish coast and the Greek islands, just opposite. The boats are small and relatively expensive. The main crossings are: 1 Cesme to the island of Chios (Sakiz in Turkish); 2 Dikili (94 km., 58 miles north of Izmir) to Lesbos (Midilli); 3 Kuşadası to Samos (Sisam); and occasionally also from Bodrum to Kos (Istanköy) and Marmaris to Rhodes (Rodos). Larger ferry boats take cars and passengers from each of the above islands to the Greek port of Piraeus, outside Athens.

State of the Roads. There are 40,000 km. (25,000 miles) of highways surfaced with rough asphalt, giving a good grip to tires. The ▓▓r- or six-lane bypasses, usually divided by trees and flowerbeds, are a w▓▓e relief from the jammed main arteries through the bigger towns. R▓▓ repairs cover the width of the road—the sight of a bulldozer means tr▓ble. The 20,000 km. (12,500 miles) of secondary roads marked on maps as "stabilized (unsurfaced) roads" are best avoided, unless you have good springs, a high-slung car to negotiate pot-holes and stones, and windows that shut tight against the dust. The local roads are mere tracks, washboard ruts in summer, mud in the rainy season.

Road Signs. In accordance with European practice, warning signs are red and white, information signs blue and white. YAVAŞ means slow; DUR, stop (and stop at once . . .); DIKKAT in a white rectangle, watch out, drive with care. There are milestones every 10 km. (6.2 miles). Entry and exit in the four big cities are clearly indicated, but street names are often difficult to discern; signposts outside even the smallest town indicate beside the name the *nüfus* (population) and *rakim* (altitude). A clearly discernible and comprehensible distinction is between the blue on white signs for place names and black on yellow for sites of interest to tourists.

Road Maps. The official map revised by the Ministry of Tourism every year for free distribution is fairly reliable, if somewhat over-optimistic as to completion of works. All major roads carry three-digit numbers, which are also indicated at all road junctions.

Repairs. Turkish mechanics usually manage to get you going again, at least until you reach a big city for full repairs.

In larger cities whole streets are given over to car repairs, one shop repairs radiators, another electric fittings, another steering wheels, yet another brakes. Each workshop is run by an expert with a team of boys. The prices are not high. Give the boy a small tip. If you are not in the workshop during the repairs, usually done while you wait, don't leave the car papers in the car.

There are Road Rescue Services at six places along the Edirne–Ankara road, the E-5.

Gasoline. B.P., Mobil and Shell, as well as two Turkish oil companies, have filling stations throughout the country. At press time, the cost was the equivalent of about 45 cents per liter (1.76 pints) for *süper* and about 40 cents per liter for regular (normal in Turkish); Motorin (diesel) about two-thirds regular. Super is not always available off the beaten track, so fill well up as the regular is very hard on the car.

Windscreen will be wiped reluctantly after request. Filling stations on the main highways are often advertised a few miles in advance by billboards, and are open 24 hours; others are open from 6 A.M. to 10 P.M. Oil is about $1.90 per liter.

Spare Parts. They are hard to find outside the big towns. Best take a spare-part kit along. Most of the big makes of cars have agents in the main cities of Turkey. For the addresses of foreign car representatives, ask your car salesman for the booklet *After-sales service in Europe*.

BY TAXI. Beside the TAKSI sign on the roof, the numerous taxis are distinguished by a black-and-yellow-checkered band round the middle. Charges are very reasonable. Private minibuses operate effectively and cheaply along fixed routes with frequent stops in all major towns; likewise between towns from special termini.

Mythology and Archeology

THE GODS. The forces of nature that science could not explain at the time appeared to the Greeks as the work of superhuman beings, interpreted into the deeds of man. They set up gods in whom power, wisdom, and eternal youth could not perish. They lived, under the rule of Zeus, on Mount Olympos. Rivalries and intrigues existed in their relationships and marriages, and they often associated with mortals, their offspring becoming demi-gods or heroes. The stories about their adventures forms the mythology of Greece.

The Romans, influenced by the arts and letters of Greece, often identified their gods with the divinities of Greece, with the result that the Greek gods were given Latin names as well.

The 13 chief gods formed the elite of Olympos. Each represented one of the forces of nature and a human characteristic, interpreted by sculptors in their statues of the gods. The following are the 13 main gods, with their descriptive characteristics.

Name		Natural and human characteristics	Attributes
Greek	*Latin*		
Zeus	Jupiter	sky, supreme god	scepter, thunder
Hera	Juno	sky queen, marriage	peacock
Athena	Minerva	wisdom	owl, olive
Artemis	Diana	moon, chastity	stag
Aphrodite	Venus	love, beauty	dove
Dionysos	Bacchus	revels, intoxication	vine, ivy
Demeter	Ceres	earth, fecundity	sheaf, sickle
Hestia	Vesta	hearth, domestic virtues	eternal fire
Apollo	Phoebus	sun, music and poetry	bow, lyre
Ares	Mars	tumult, war	spear, helmet
Hephaestos	Vulcan	fire, industry	hammer, anvil
Hermes	Mercury	trade, eloquence	caduceus, wings
Poseidon	Neptune	sea, earthquake	trident

GRECO-ROMAN ARCHEOLOGICAL OUTLINE. Mycenaean civilization, at its peak c. 1400 to 1200 B.C., disappeared with the arrival of the Dorians whose architecture was born of a combination of solemn Nordic inspiration, measured Mycenaean layout and of Oriental influences in decoration. The Doric style (800–450 B.C.) was characterized by severe simplicity; the flowering of the Ionic style lasted until the period of Macedonian hegemony (338 B.C.), branched out into the more florid Corinthian style and persisted under the Roman domination (146 B.C.–A.D. 395)

Greek sculpture played an important role in the ornamentation of temples but it was also an independent art. The most important periods of its evolution were: the *Archaic* (700–500 B.C.), characterized by a columnlike rigidity of its subjects; the *Classic* period, attaining the summit of corporeal harmony (500–130 B.C.). The most outstanding artists of this epoch were Phidias, Praxiteles, and Skopas. Alexander the Great and his armies introduced Greek art in the eastern Mediterranean and this era (338 to 146 B.C.), typified by an opulent anatomy and by Asiatic influences, is known as the *Hellenistic* period.

The Greek temple, open mainly to priests but sometimes to prominent citizens, was the home of the Divinity, and more often than not it was of small proportions. Rare exception to the oblong, rectangular layout is the *tholos,* a round temple with circular colonnade. Iktinos, Kallicrates, and Mnesikles were among the most outstanding architects.

Secular architecture consisted of open-air theaters, stadiums and of the *agora,* the city's commercial and civic center. The *acropolis,* a citadel, usually enclosed all the sanctuaries. The Greek cities were surrounded by ramparts, the walls of which varied with the epoch (Cyclopean, Pelasgic, Trapezoidal, etc.).

Archeological terms:

Amphora vase, jug

Apse semicircular part of an edifice

Basilica rectangular, oblong edifice

Bouleuterion senate house

Capital uppermost part of a column, usually decorated

Caryatid sculpture of maiden, replacing a column

Hieron scared enclosure

Megaron reception hall in Mycenaean palace

Metope plain or carved panel on temple's frieze

Naos sanctuary of temple

Odeion roofed edifice for artistic performances

Peristyle inner or outer colonnade

Pinacotheca picture gallery

Plinth rectangular base of a column

Pronaos vestibule of sanctuary

Propylae gate to monumental sites

Stele upright, decorated tombstone

Stereobate substructure of a temple

Stoa roofed building, supported by frontal columns, usually a business center

Stylobate foundation platform of a temple

KEY TO HISTORICAL SITES

Turkish place names often bear little or no resemblance to antique names. This key should help in placing the historical sites by the nearest town or village.

Classical Name	Present Name	Classical Name	Present Name
Abidos	Abide	Aspendos	Serik
Adrianople	Edirne	Assos	Behramkale
Aesani	Çavdarhisar	Attalia	Antalya
Amisos	Samsun	Baris	Isparta
Ankyra (Angora)	Ankara	Byzantion	Istanbul
Antiochia (Antioch)	Antakya	(Byzantium, (Constantinople)	
Antiochia of Pisidia	Yalvaç	Caesarea (Eusebeia)	Kayseri
Antiphellos	Kaş	Daphne	Harbiye nr. Antakya
Aphrodisias	Geyre nr. Karacasu	Didyma	Didim
Apollonia, Simena	Uçagiz nr. Finike	Edessa (Antiochia on Kalliroë)	Urfa
Arkadiopolis	Lüleburgaz	Ephesos (Ephesus)	Efes nr. Selçuk
Arsamia	Eski Kahta		

Classical Name	Present Name	Classical Name	Present Name
Filyos	Hisarönü	Nikomedia	Izmit
Gallipolis	Gelibolu	(Nicomedia)	
Gordion	Yassihöyük	Nyssa	Sultanhisar
	nr. Polatlı	Oenae	Unye
Halikarnassos	Bodrum	Olba–	Uzuncaburç
Hattushash	Boğazkale	Diocaesarea	
	nr. Sungurlu	Pergamon	Bergama
Heraklea of	Ereğli	Perge	Aksu
Kappadokia		Philadelphia	Alaşehir
Heraklea of	Ereğli	Philomelion	Akşehir
Pontus		Phokea	Foça
Heraklea by	nr. Milas	Phoenikos	Finike
Latmos		Physkos	Marmaris
Hierapolis	Pamukkale	Pompeiopolis	Viranşehir
Ikonion	Konya	(I)	nr. Mersin
(Claudiconium)		Pompeiopolis	Taşköprü
Issos	Dörtyol	(II)	
Kanesh	Kültepe	Priene	nr. Söke
Kargamish	nr. Birecik	Prusa	Bursa
Kerasous	Giresun	Rodestos	Tekirdağ
(Pharnikia)		Rosos	Uluçinar
Klaudiopolis	Mut	Samasota	Samsat
Klaros and	Değirmendere	Sagalossos	Ağlasun
Kolophon	nr. Izmir	Sardis	Sart nr.
Knidos	nr. Datça		Sahlili
Kommageni	Nemrut Dağ	Seleukia	Silifke
Funeral Mound		Smyrna	Izmir
Kotyora	Ordu	Syllion	nr. Aksu
Kybira	Gölhisar	Telmessos	Fethye
Lampsakos	Lapseki	Teos	Seferihisar
Laodikea	Denizli		nr. Izmir
Larisa	Menemen	Termessos	nr. Korkuteli
Magnesia by	Manisa	Theodosiopolis	Erzurum
Sypilos		Thyatira	Akhisar
Magnesia on	Ortaklar	Tralles	Aydın
Meander		Trapezos	Trabzon
Miletos	Akköy nr.	(Trebizond)	
(Miletus)	Söke	Tripolis on	Buldan
Mylasa	Milas	Meander	
Myra	Demre	Tripolis	Tirebolu
Neo-Caesarea	Niksar	Troy (Ilion)	Truva
Nikea (Nicaea)	Iznik	Xanthos	Kınık

Greek names were frequently latinized during the 500 years of Roman domination which was, however, only an interlude between 1,000 years of city states and Hellenistic kingdoms before and another 1,000 of the Byzantine empire after, both using Greek. The anglicized forms are based on Latin, which is not only often anachronistic but also contrary to the Turkish tourist handouts and signposts. It would, therefore, be unnecessarily confusing to refer to Pergamum, for example, when the site is marked Pergamon. Exceptions are made for the most familiar names, as it seems somewhat pedantic to talk of Kappadokia, Konstantinopolis, Maeandros, etc. Likewise, references to well-known historical events are made in the accepted anglicized form—e.g., Council of Nicaea. Common sense rather than consistency has been the determining consideration.

Leaving Turkey

TURKISH CUSTOMS. Exporting antiques from Turkey is strictly prohibited and the penalties for attempting to do so without authorization are severe.

One final point: keep hold of some TL, as there is an airport tax equivalent to about $11 that is payable on checking in for departure.

CUSTOMS ON RETURN. If you propose to take on your holiday any *foreign-made* articles, such as cameras, binoculars, expensive time-pieces, and the like, register them at the airport or local custom houses in major cities before departure. The registration is valid once and for all. Otherwise, on returning home, you may be charged duty.

U.S. citizens who are out of the United States at least 48 hours and have claimed no exemption during the previous 30 days are entitled to bring in duty free up to $400 worth of articles for bona fide gifts or for their own personal use. The value of each item is determined by the price actually paid (so save your receipts). Every member of a family is entitled to this same exemption, regardless of age, and the allowance can be pooled. Above the basic exemption, the duty is now a flat 10% on everything in the next $1,000, regardless of the kinds of goods assessed.

Do not bring home foreign meats, fruits, plants, soil, or other agricultural items when you return to the U.S. To do so will delay you at the port of entry. It is illegal to bring in foreign agricultural items without permission because they can spread destructive plant or animal pests and diseases. For more information, write to: Quarantines, U.S. Department of Agriculture, Federal Building, Hyattsville, MD 20782.

Not more than 200 cigarettes or 100 cigars may be imported duty free per person, nor more than one liter of wine or liquor (none at all if your passport indicates you are from a "dry" state, or if you are under 21 years of age).

Gifts valued at less than $50 may be mailed to friends or relatives at home, but not more than one per day of receipt to any one addressee and not to include perfumes costing more than $5, tobacco, or liquor.

If your purchases exceed your exemption, list the items that are subject to the highest rates of duty under your exemption and pay duty on the items with the lowest rates. Any article you fail to declare cannot later be claimed under your exemption. To facilitate the actual customs examination, it's convenient to pack all your purchases in one suitcase.

Purchases intended for your duty-free quota must accompany your personal baggage. Turkey has been designated a developing country under the Generalized System of Preferences plan. Under this plan, some 2,700 items may be imported duty free into the U.S. However, since both the countries and the items covered are revised annually, check with the Dept. of Treasury, U.S. Customs Service, Washington, DC 20229. Ask for the pamphlet *GSP and the Traveler.*

Canadian Citizens. Residents of Canada may claim an exemption of $300 a year plus an allowance of one liter of liquor, 50 cigars, 200 cigarettes and one kilo of tobacco. Personal gifts should be mailed as "Unsolicited Gift—Value under $40." For details, ask for the Canada Customs brochure *I Declare.*

British Residents. There are two levels of duty-free allowance for people entering the U.K; one, for goods bought outside the EEC or for goods bought in a duty-free shop within the EEC; two, for goods bought in an EEC country but not in a duty-free shop.

In the first category you may import duty free: 200 cigarettes or 100 cigarillos or 50 cigars or 250 grammes of tobacco (*Note* if you live outside Europe, these allowances are doubled); plus one liter of alcoholic drinks over 22% vol. (38.8% proof) or two liters of alcoholic drinks not over 22% vol. or fortified or sparkling or still table wine; plus two liters of still table wine; plus 50 grammes of perfume; plus nine fluid ounces of toilet water; plus other goods to the value of £32.

In the second category you may import duty free: 300 cigarettes or 150 cigarillos or 75 cigars or 400 grammes of tobacco; plus 1½ liters of alcoholic drinks over 22% vol. (38.8% proof) or three liters of alcoholic drinks not over 22% vol. or fortified or sparkling or still table wine; plus five liters of still table wine; plus 75 grammes of perfume; plus 13 fluid ounces of toilet water; plus other goods to the value of £250. (*Note* though it is not classified as an alcoholic drink by EEC countries for Customs' purposes and is thus considered part of the "other goods" allowance, you may not import more that 50 liters of beer).

In addition, no animals or pets of any kind may be brought into the U.K. The penalties for doing so are severe and are strictly enforced; there are *no* exceptions. Similarly, fresh meats, plants and vegetables, controlled drugs and firearms and ammunition may not be brought into the U.K. There are no restrictions on the import or export of British and foreign currencies.

DUTY FREE is not what it once was. You may not be paying tax on your bottle of whiskey or perfume, but you are certainly contributing to somebody's profits. Duty-free shops are big business these days and markups are often around 100 to 200%. Turkish lira are not accepted, only convertible currencies. So don't be seduced by the idea that because it's duty free it's a bargain. Very often prices are not much different from your local discount store and in the case of perfume or jewelry they can be even higher.

As a general rule of thumb, duty-free stores on the ground offer better value than buying in the air. Also, if you buy duty-free goods on a plane, remember that the range is likely to be limited and that if you are paying in a different currency from that of the airline, their rate of exchange often bears only a passing resemblance to the official one.

Duty-free shops are open for arriving visitors on international flights at all of Turkey's international airports. They are cheaper than European or on-board rates.

TWO WORLDS IN ONE

An Approach to Turkey

Though Turkey is two worlds culturally, economically and historically, and many more geographically and climatically, Asia Minor has, during a remarkably long recorded history, hardly ever been uncompromisingly Asian and even less entirely European, but has fulfilled its geographic function as bridge between Occident and Orient.

The goal of innumerable migrations and the favorite battlefield of countless conquerors, in 1922 Turkey became almost wholly identified with Asia Minor. Excepting some extensions northwest and south, for the first time one country coincided with this clearly defined region which, throughout the millennia, had been either fragmented or part of larger empires. The eternal meeting and melting of different ways of life, cultures and religions finally achieved a unity that recognized its debt to the past, but insisted on its own individuality.

The Setting

The diversity of landscape and climate provide the fitting background for an equal variety of art and architecture. Of Turkey's 779,452 sq. km. (301,380 sq. miles) 97 percent are contributed by the Anatolian peninsula, separated in the northwest by the Sea of Marmara between its gateways—the Bosphorus and the Dardanelles—from the remaining 23,764 sq. km. (9,070 sq. miles) in Thrace. This European part is likewise a peninsula,

27

between the Aegean and the Black Sea, bordering in the west on Greece
(269 km., 167 miles) and Bulgaria (269 km., 167 miles). Proceeding clockwise from the Black Sea coast (1,695 km., 1,053 miles) in the north to the
U.S.S.R. (610 km., 379 miles) and Iran (454 km., 282 miles) east, Iraq
(331 km., 206 miles), Syria (877 km., 545 miles) and the Mediterranean
coast (1,577 km., 980 miles) south, the Aegean coast (2,805 km., 1,744
miles) extends in the west back to the Dardanelles. The Anatolian plateau's average altitude of 1,100 meters (3,609 feet), rises towards the east
to the highest peaks, Ağrı Dağ (Mount Ararat, 16,946 feet), and Süphan
Dağ (4,434 meters, 14,547 feet). To the south the Ala Dağ rises (3,734
meters, 12,240 feet); Ericyes (3,916 meters, 12,848 feet) near Kayseri in
Central Anatolia; Uludağ looms high in the Marmara area, and Honaz
(2,528 meters, 8,294 feet) looms on the Aegean coast. In the west, the highlands slope on the whole gently to the fertile valleys, promontories and
inlets of the Aegean coast, while the Mediterranean coast is more abrupt.
The wall of the Toros (Taurus) Mountains runs like an unbroken bastion
above the southern shores, with only a few passes. The two coastal plains,
ancient Pamphylia and Kilikia (Cilicia), are watered by the Ceyhan and
Göksu, and fringed by sandy beaches. The Black Sea is separated from
the plateau by the two chains of the North Anatolian Mountains (Pontic
Range), the lower Giresun Dağları in the center and the Karadeniz Dağları with lofty Kaçkar (3,937 meters, 12,917 feet) east.

The famed rivers of Mesopotamia, the Euphrates (Fırat) and Tigris
(Dicle), emerge in East Anatolia, near Erzurum and Elazig respectively.
The huge Keban Dam, the world's fourth largest, has spread the waters
of the Fırat in a vast artificial lake near Elazig. Two major dams are under
construction downstream, before the Fırat enters Syria after 971 km. (603
miles). The Toros Mountain barrier allows only a few rivers to reach the
Mediterranean, swift streams whose alluvial deltas sustain intensive agriculture. The largest rivers emptying into the Aegean—the Büyük Menderes and the Gediz—gradually silted up, spelling the doom of once great
ports, like Miletos and Ephesos. Turkey's principal rivers flow into the
Black Sea, after winding tortuously through countless gorges in the arid
steppe. The longest are the Kızılırmak (Red River) (1,355 km., 842 miles)
in the center, and the Sakarya (824 km., 512 miles) in the west, like most
rivers repeatedly dammed up for hydroelectricity and irrigation.

These artificial lakes, though huge, are dwarfed by nature's own, especially Lake Van far east, covering 3,738 sq. km. (1,443 sq. miles) with
brackish water in a veritable inland sea. Other lakes are likewise on an
outsize Asiatic scale, Tuz (1,500 sq. km., 580 sq. miles), supposedly saltier
than the Dead Sea, in Central Anatolia; Beyşehir (656 sq. km., 244 sq.
miles) and Eğridir (468 sq. km., 181 sq. miles) in South Anatolia.

As for the bad news, provided records going back to the year zero can
be called that. All of Turkey, including the European part, is prone to violent earthquakes. In the reign of Augustus, Tralles (Aydın) was destroyed;
in A.D. 17 twelve cities were swallowed in one night; Antioch was flattened
under Trajan; Rhodes and the whole western peninsula were shaken in
A.D. 145. 238, 244, 262 and 300 were all earthquake years. In 354 it was the
turn of Nikomedia (Izmit), Constantinople in 400; in 544 an earthquake
lasted for forty days and for ten in 557, when Constantinople was partly
destroyed and St. Sophia badly damaged. These seismic disasters have continued down the ages and, with eastern Anatolia becoming more accessi-

ble, the score on the Richter scale increased and so did the number of victims. Nobody troubles any longer to wonder *whether* an earthquake will happen, the only question is *where*. No wonder columns lie like sausages cut into slices all over Asia Minor. They proved very handy when one religion took to building with the abandoned materials of another—the church from the temple and the mosque from the church.

Climate, Flora and Fauna

Turkey is blessed with four different types of climate: oceanic, Mediterranean, continental, and mountainous. The Black Sea coastal area is a temperate zone (same latitude as Rome), with a mean winter temperature of 43°F., rising to 68 and 77°F. in the summertime. It has abundant year round rainfall. This area is renowned for its forests of leaf-bearing and coniferous trees, and for the apples, pears, cherries, hazelnuts, mandarin oranges, and tea that are grown there.

The Straits area marks a transition from the Mediterranean climate that prevails along most of the Aegean coast; here, there is plenty of rain, particularly at the end of autumn, and the region enjoys mild winters and hot summers (in Izmir, the temperature can drop to 48°F. in January and range up to the low 80's in summer). The well-irrigated plains produce a variety of crops, including corn, tobacco, and cotton.

Along the Mediterranean shores, summer can be sweltering (sometimes above 100°F.), but the temperature seldom dips below 50°F. in winter. The local vegetation is tropical, with flourishing banana trees, palm trees, citrus trees, sugar cane and cotton.

Though occasional cold and wet spells as late as March restrict the bathing season to May through October, the Mediterranean coast presents a dramatic contrast with the central plateau of Anatolia, where the altitude seldom descends below 1,100 meters (3,609 feet), and where the scattered valleys lying to the north and south are barely passable. The land to the west has variegated relief. Mountains shoot up abruptly above the water's edge, and are divided by deep clefts that allow the balmy Aegean breezes to blow in toward the interior of the mountain chain. Central Anatolia is a region of plateaus and depressions, with occasional bodies of water. Its climate is affected by its remoteness from the sea, and offers many contrasts: it is dry and salubrious, and can be torrid in summer, but becomes freezing in winter. Although there is a certain amount of humidity near the mountains, which allows the forests (coniferous trees, oak, breech and junipers) to thrive, the remainder of the plateau is more reminiscent of a subdesert or a steppe.

The mountain air becomes progressively colder going in an eastward direction and is accompanied by frequent rainfall. North of Mount Ararat, near the Russian border, mean winter temperatures are below 50°F. and snow is plentiful. However, even in these continental regions, winter in the valleys is severe, with extremely hot summers. The latter foster a Mediterranean type of vegetation wherever enough water is available.

Turkey is the habitat of the same animals as are found in the European countries, plus camels (which are becoming ever scarcer) and buffaloes. There is no shortage of sheep and goats, nor of cattle. Wild boar rove in abundance, as well as bears, lynx, all species of rodents, and even leopard.

History Begins in Paradise

The Garden of Eden is supposed to have been in Mesopotamia, the Country Between the Rivers. With very little exercise of the imagination, one could extend the Garden northward into Turkey, where the Euphrates and Tigris flow parallel less than 100 km. apart. In summer that makes climatic sense—about winter it might be preferable to keep quiet.

The second biblical beginning is less controversial. After the Deluge, Noah's ark landed on Mount Ararat in northeast Anatolia. His Paleolithic descendants emerged from the mists of Time and left axe heads and flint stones on the Upper Euphrates, in the vicinity of Ankara, as well as in caves near Antalya and Tokali. Neolithic man spread his tools even further and moved from hunting to farming, living in stone houses as at Cayonu near the headwaters of the Tigris. Obsidian, sharp volcanic rock, was exported as early as 8300 B.C. from the Konya plain, where Çatalhöyük grew into Anatolia's first town from 7000 B.C. on. There was ample space and no competition, but it was too good to last and mankind's happiness declined as the Neolithic period retreated.

Agriculture triumphed over hunting in the sixth millennium. The first fortifications appeared in numerous centers of the Chalkolithic (Bronze Age) throughout Anatolia, which was crisscrossed by more tribes than could possibly have been healthy. Many settlements rose and a few fell, the southern region was conquered by King Sargon of Akkad (2334–2279 B.C.), and history had made its regrettable entrance.

Divided They Fall

Hatti princes united and quarreled in Central Anatolia, where Assyrian Trade Colonies gave their collective name to the period round 2000 B.C. The Indo-European Hittites began their ascent, kingdoms grew into empire which in turn declined into scattered principalities that survived into the eighth century B.C. The Mitanni in the south, the Hurri and Urartians in the east made brief attempts to hold the stage, which was at last—and most unpleasantly—filled by the Phrygians after the Great Migration in c. 1200 B.C.

The curtain raiser to the doom and destruction of the old order in Anatolia was the Trojan War (c. 1230–20 B.C.), the first of the endless ding-dong contests between Asia and Europe fought near the straits separating the two continents. The Phrygians, allies of the Trojans, advanced inland to sack and burn the Hittite Empire on whose ruin they raised an ephemeral kingdom. Not all Achaean Greeks returned home from the opposing camp, some founded cities along the hospitable shores of Asia Minor, later joined by Ionian refugees from the Dorian invasion of Greece. Karians "uncouth of speech" (Iliad II)—the original "barbarians"—swooped further along the coast, to mix beyond any disentangling with the native Leleges, as well as with the Ionian Greeks, especially at Hallikarnassos.

After a procession of dominations—Phrygia following the collapse of the Hittites, only to be replaced by the Cimmerians—the Lydians' last king, Croesus, was deposed by Cyrus the Great (549–29 B.C.) who, for the first time, united the whole of Anatolia. Darius I briefly extended Persian sovereignty into Europe, but though the Greek coastal towns soon regained their independence, most of Anatolia was ruled by Persian satraps.

Alexander and His Successors

After crossing the Hellespont (Dardanelles) at the head of 40,000 Macedonians and Greeks in the spring of 334 B.C., the 22-year-old King Alexander of Macedonia started a triumphal march, unequalled in history, by defeating the Persians and their Greek mercenaries on the Granikos (the Can Çayı near Biga). By cutting the Gordion knot he fulfilled the oracle predicting mastery of Asia and quickly conquered all the lands down to Kilikia. After his victory at Issos, he marched eastwards, out of Anatolia to ever greater fame till his death in Babylon in 323.

His generals, the warring Diadochs (Successors) were Alexander written small, though that was still considerably taller than any rival pretender. Those who succeeded in surviving 42 years of bloody fighting founded three kingdoms that epitomized the Hellenistic Period. Only Antigonos I Monophthalmos (the One-Eyed) might have preserved Alexander's Empire intact, but he was defeated and killed in the Battle of the Kings at Ipsos in Phrygia in 301. Seleukos I Nikator (the Conqueror) gained most of Anatolia, but paid for the elephants that won the victory by ceding his eastern provinces to an Indian king. His fellow victor, Lysimachos, added Bithynia to his Thracian kingdom. Inevitably, the two allies, both aged over 80, fell out, and in 281 Lysimachos was defeated and killed at the battle of Korupedion in Lydia. Seleukos was assassinated in the same year.

Asia Minor became the battleground in the century-long struggle between the Seleukids and the Egyptian Ptolemies, the descendants of Seleukos and Ptolemy. The latter supported Hellenized native dynasties in the regions the Great Alexander had bypassed—Bithynia and Pontos (Pontus) in the north, Kappadokia (Cappadocia) in the southeast. Nikomides I of Bithynia introduced yet another formidable element by inviting the warlike Gauls from Thrace. After much destruction and fighting, they were defeated by Antiochos I Soter (the Savior) in 275 and Attalos I of Pergamon in 230, to be confined to Galatia in central Anatolia.

Antiochos III the Great (223–187) almost succeeded in uniting Asia Minor, but finally unified his rivals, who appealed to the rising power of Rome. Defeated in Greece and at Magnesia by Sipylos (Manisa), Antiochos III ceded all lands west of the Taurus by the Treaty of Apamea in 188. The Hellenistic kings were reduced from allies to vassals, to whom Rome awarded the conquered territories. Eumenes II, another Soter, received the lion's share, and the last of his dynasty, Attalos III in 133 bequeathed his enlarged kingdom to Rome, which thus gained the fabulously wealthy province of Asia. This useful method of territorial expansion was rudely interrupted by the Pontic King Mithridates VI Eupator (120–63) who, despite his gentle epithet of Father-loving, ordered some memorable massacres. It took 20 years for three outstanding Roman generals to drive him by a judicious admixture of diplomacy and the sword out of Greece, western Asia Minor, back to Pontus and into suicide.

In 68 B.C. Pompey became Proconsul of Asia and reorganized the East. Western Pontus was combined with Bithynia, which had been left to Rome by Nikomedes IV in the approved testamentary fashion in 74. The last Seleukid, Antiochus VII Euergetes (the Benefactor), an alcoholic, was unable to halt the decline of his kingdom which ended in 63 as the Roman province of Syria. Armenia survived as a protectorate or buffer state for another millennium, but the rest of Asia Minor was divided into Roman provinces.

Pax Romana and Pax Byzantina

The peace of Rome was effective, and so there was no notable history to record for a long and happy period. The peace of Byzantium was intermittent, plagued by religious as well as military strife. At the end of the third century A.D., the Emperor Diocletian chose Nicomedia (Izmit) as the main imperial residence, in recognition of the power shift to the East. Several persecutions of Christians and even more civil wars later, Constantine the Great (306–37) transferred the capital from Rome to Byzantium and adopted Christianity as state religion. Yet this essential new bond was immediately weakened by the quarrels at the First Ecumenical Council at Nicaea (Iznik) in 325. These altercations became matters of state, when Constantine's three sons encouraged rival creeds in the parts of the Empire they governed. Theodosius the Great (378–95) reunited Christianity and the Empire, but because he combined both spiritual and temporal government as regent of the Church on earth, competing sects inevitably came to oppose both authorities. In the final division between his two sons, Arcadius became the ruler of the much more important Roman Empire of the East, from which Theodosius II (408–50) and his successors proved powerless to prevent the dismemberment of the western half by Germanic tribes.

When Rome itself fell in 476, the Empire was reduced to its Eastern half. There the Hellenistic heritage had maintained Greek as the second language, and it gradually resumed the first place. Latin faded away and the Roman interlude for all practical purposes had run its 500-year-long course. Yet to the very end emperors and citizens alike maintained the fiction of a continuous Roman Empire so successfully that until the dissolution of the Turkish Empire its Christian subjects were called Rumi (Romans). The term Byzantine was only introduced by historians in the 18th century.

The Eastern Empire reached its zenith under Justinian I (527–63), who drained the manpower and treasure of the provinces to reconquer North Africa and Italy. Under his successors the Persian Sassanids overran the south, welcomed by the disaffected Monophysite and Nestorian sects. No sooner had Emperor Heraklios (610–41) saved his capital from a combined Avar-Persian attack and restored the frontier, than both weakened imperial powers were assailed by the Arabs, forged by Islam into a seemingly invincible force. By 636 the southern provinces were again lost, this time for good. Persia fell the following year. The Arabs reached the Bosphorus in 663 and besieged Constantinople by land and sea from 673 to 678.

A new, energetic dynasty drove the invaders back to the Taurus Mountains, which became the backbone of a fluctuating frontier that divided Anatolia more decisively than ever before, but on a local scale of raids and counter-raids, not unlike the English-Scottish border wars. But if the Isaurians restored the military situation, they also plunged the Empire into yet another disastrous religious conflict by forbidding any visual representation of the Divine. Basic to Judaism and Islam, and later embraced by Western Christian sects, this puritan fanaticism rent the Empire for centuries. The Ikonoklasts shattered priceless art treasures until two Empress-

Regents restored the images: Irene through the Seventh Ecumenical Council in 787, after she had blinded her own son to prolong the regency, which failed to prevent a later male relapse; and Theodora who—according to a contemporary chronicle, listing her virtues and praising her piety— ordered "the hanging, decapitation and burning of 100,000 Manicheans."

Her son, Michael the Drunkard, was murdered in 867 by his groom and favorite, who as Basil I founded the Macedonian dynasty. For a change Christianity became a useful tool of the state, when the brothers (later Saints) Cyril and Methodius spread Orthodoxy in the Balkans and Russia. There were early conflicts with the resuscitated Holy Roman Empire in the West, but in compensation the Byzantine fleet wrestled mastery of the sea from the Arabs. Under Basil II (the Bulgar-slayer) the Empire knew a final age of greatness that carried over into the reigns of his nieces, Zoe and Theodora, who maintained the dynasty till 1056 by marrying victorious generals and powerful feudatories.

Schism and Seljuks

In 1054 Michael Cerularius, Patriarch of Constantinople, broke with Rome in a flurry of dogmatic argument about the nature of the Holy Ghost, spiced with quarrels over precedence and church observance. Though he was deposed five years later, the schism between Eastern and Western Christianity was never healed, despite repeated attempts by emperors increasingly dependent on help from fellow Christian rulers. Where there had been two empires, there were now also two Churches.

This split could not have come at a worse time, as the death of the 70-year-old Empress Theodora was followed by truly Byzantine intrigues, which finally brought to the throne Constantine X, a member of the oldest and richest noble family, the Dukas. On his death in 1067, the Empress-Regent married the commander-in-chief who, as Romanos IV Diogenes, sustained the second great Islamic onslaught.

If one had to be conquered by a Central Asian horde, the Seljuks were among the less disastrous. They were a branch of the T'u-Kin—a Chinese name that eventually resolved into Turk—reputed for their prowess. In the tenth century they had become sufficiently populous and powerful to follow their leader Seljuk into Persia, where they adopted Islam and were initiated in the art of government. Incursions by isolated groups, advancing along the great Asian trade routes in search of grazing grounds for their innumerable flocks, were followed by the conquest of Armenia and Persia. The Abbasid caliph of Baghdad, titular head of Islam, appointed the Seljuk Togrul Bey (1038–63) Sultan of East and West, and thus the real ruler of the eastern Moslem world. The disappearance of Armenia, which had served for a thousand years as a buffer against eastern aggression, forced Romanos IV into direct confrontation with the Seljuk Sultan Alp Arslan (1063–72). Betrayed by the envious and resentful Dukas clan, the Emperor was decisively defeated and captured at Manzikert (now Malazgirt) in 1071, one of the major catastrophes in Byzantine history and, like so many, self-inflicted.

To the Sultan's question of what would he have done if fate had reversed their roles, the Emperor reputedly admitted: "I would have run you through with a sword." Arslan replied: "I would not be guilty of an act so contrary to the teachings of your Lord Jesus Christ" and set Romanos free. On the Emperor's return to his capital, Michael VII, son of Theodora, had his stepfather's eyes put out, which not only prevented bickering but also caused Romanos' death.

Anatolia lay at the mercy of the invaders. Malik Shah (1072–92) appointed his nephew Süleyman governor of Rum (Anatolia). Michael VII as well as sundry Byzantine usurpers mortgaged the future for immediate Seljuk help in their sordid civil wars, till Süleyman took the lead, proclaimed himself sultan and made Nikaea his capital in 1078. Eight years later he declared his independence from the Great Seljuk of Persia. The Sultanate of Rum now stretched from the Sea of Marmara to Mount Ararat, but the swift Seljuk ascendancy had only been made possible by Byzantine disunity. This proved contagious to the victors, as no less than six deposed Seljuk sultans found refuge in Constantinople. Naturally, after the city's fall to the Latins, the exiled emperors in turn sought the assistance of their former foes.

The Crusades

This third disaster proved in the end more destructive to the age-old interaction between Occident and Orient than the previous calamities of Arab and Seljuk incursions. Shifting alliances between Byzantines, Crusaders, Arabs and Seljuks permanently weakened the great bulwark of Eastern Christendom, despite an auspicious beginning with the First Crusade 25 years after Manzikert.

After protracted vintage Byzantine intrigues with emperors being retired blinded or whole into monasteries, Alexios Komnenos was accepted as ruler by the warring factions in 1081. In the following year, surrounded by enemies and under the growing Norman threat in the Adriatic, the Emperor granted Venice free trade throughout his shrunken dominions. The foundation stone of the Serene Republic's prosperity turned finally into the Empire's tombstone, but in a reign of 37 years Alexios I proved the greatest statesman of his time, restoring Byzantine prestige and firmly establishing a powerful dynasty. He admirably dealt with the dangerous and intolerant lords of the First Crusade and persuaded them to hand over all conquests in Asia Minor, beginning with the Seljuk capital, Nikaea. After the victory at Dorylaion (Eskişehir) in 1097 all the western coastal lands were regained, but the underlying antagonism came to the surface when the Crusaders broke their solemn oaths and refused to restore Antiochia to the Emperor.

The fall of the Crusader County of Edessa (Urfa) inspired the Second Crusade, which was even less congenial to the Eastern Christians. But Konrad III of Germany was defeated at fateful Dorylaion, fell ill at Ephesos and returned humbled to Constantinople. Louis VII of France gave up at Attalia (Antalya) and took ship to the Holy Land.

In the Third Crusade Emperor Frederick I Barbarossa roughly followed the road taken by Alexander the Great, occupied the new Seljuk capital, Konya, in 1190, but was drowned while crossing the Kalykadnos (Göksu) above Silifke. The imperial army as well as the imperial corpse quickly disintegrated in the heat of the Cilician summer. Ineffectively preserved in vinegar, the Emperor's decaying remains were hastily buried in the cathedral of Antiochia. No further Christian army set foot in Anatolia till 1920.

John I (1118–43) and Manuel I (1143–80) successfully maintained the Empire against incessant attacks from East and West, despite the crushing defeat at the hand of Sultan Kılıç Arslan II at Myriokephalon near Lake Egridir in 1176. But—after the mob had torn to pieces the last of the Komnenos emperors, Andronikos I—Isaak II Angelos came to the throne, admittedly unwillingly, and with him a family dramatically guilty of its own and the Empire's downfall. After blinding, bribery, broken promises and murder had run their ignoble course in Venice and Constantinople, the lords of the Fourth Crusade elected Count Baldwin of Flanders as Latin Emperor. Two grandsons of Andronikos I escaped the massacre in Constantinople to become emperors in Trapezunt (Trabzon), but though it lasted for over 250 years this "Empire on the Black Sea" never extended far beyond the town itself. Of more consequence was the continuation of the Byzantine Empire in exile at Nikaea, where the Palaeologos family soon predominated.

Baldwin I's reign lasted barely a year before he was taken prisoner by the Bulgars in the Battle of Adrianople (Edirne). His Latin successors possessed a great title and no power, so that in 1261 Michael VIII Palaeologos could return from Nikaea and establish his dynasty in the rightful capital of an ever-diminishing Empire. In 1274 the Emperor tried to obtain western support by promising union of the two Christian Churches, but this, like several later attempts, proved unacceptable to the Constantinopolitans, embittered by the Latin occupation. To the religious strife was added the equally bitter commercial rivalry between Genoa and Venice, both ready to ally themselves to Moslem princes for a passing advantage. The Empire gradually shrank to the capital and its surroundings, plus the eastern part of the Peloponnese reconquered from Frankish princes.

Leadership in Anatolia passed back to the Sultanate of Rum, which reached its apogee under Alaeddin Keykubat (1219–36). He defeated the Kwarismian Turks at Erzincan in 1230 and annexed most of their extensive dominions in the East, but 13 years later his successor was in his turn decisively defeated by the Mongols of Genghis Khan near the same town. The Sultanate disintegrated into Mongolian and Turkish beyliks (principalities), among which the Osmanli Turks quickly achieved pre-eminence.

The Rise of Empire

Ertuğrul Bey led a last tribal invasion into southern Bithynia and established a beylik at Söğüt, near the Byzantine border. Like his Seljuk predecessor 200 years earlier, his son Osman Bey (1281–1326) gave his name to the tribe and a sultanate that was within another 200 years to extend over three continents. In the West the name based on Osman Bey which the sultanate was to carry—Osmanli—is often rendered as Ottoman, without any real justification. For the sake of accuracy, we have adopted the correct spelling throughout this book.

Osman increased his territories by constant warfare against the Byzantines and Seljuk beys. His sons, Orhan and Alaeddin, made Bursa (Prusa) the capital of a strong quadrilateral including Iznik (Nikaea), Izmit (Nikomedia) and Bergama (Pergamon). The brothers built up a standing army, well disciplined and regularly paid, far in advance of any fighting force in Europe. Murat I (1359–89) balanced the *sipahis* (cavalry) drawn from the feudal landowners and *piyade* (infantry) with the Janissaries

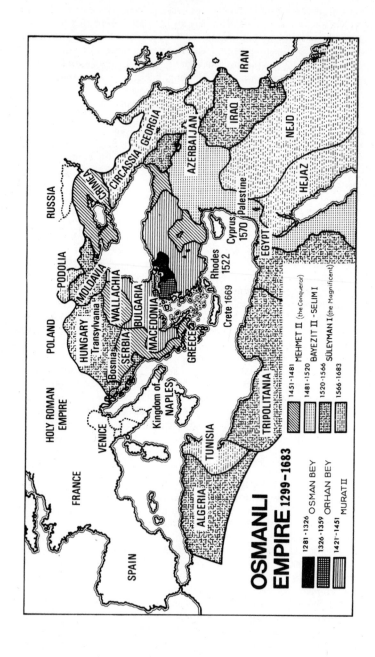

OSMANLI
EMPIRE 1299-1683

1281-1326 OSMAN BEY
1326-1359 ORHAN BEY
1421-1451 MURAT II

1451-1481 MEHMET II (the Conqueror)
1481-1520 BAYEZIT II - SELIMI
1520-1566 SÜLEYMAN I (the Magnificent)
1566-1683

(Yeni-Ceri, New Troops) composed for long of Christian boys taken as slaves. Converted to Islam, carefully educated and encouraged to enter the civil service, they remained nominally the slaves of the sultans, whose master they eventually became. Murat made good use of this formidable war machine in constant wars on two fronts. He first took Ankara, then turned against his most powerful Turkish rivals, the Karamanoğlu in the south, with whom hostilities were to drag on for over a century. He enlarged the Turkish foothold in Europe by capturing Adrianople (Edirne) in 1361, levied a tribute on the Empire, subjugated Bulgaria and carried the red Crescent Banner northward in the opening shots in the Turkish advance to Vienna. The Serbs, Bosnians and Albanians with their Hungarian and Polish allies were routed at Kossovo in 1389; before the victory was decided, a Serbian nobleman stabbed the Sultan, who had time to give a decisive order before dying.

His son Bayezit ordered his younger brother—who had fought at his side all day—to be killed in the tent where their father lay dead, the first in the liquidation of brothers that soon became routine at each accession. Fratricide was the only way to prevent civil war, as the sultanate passed from father to son, but without any law of primogeniture to determine *which* son. Bayezit I (1389–1403) quickly earned his sobriquet Yıldırım (the Thunderbolt) by a victory over the Karamanoğlu and by reducing the Empire to little more than the capital. Manuel II Palaeologos appealed to the Western Emperor Sigismund, who was also King of Hungary and thus was likewise threatened. A crusade was proclaimed and in 1396 the flower of Christian chivalry was hacked to pieces at Nikopolis in Bulgaria by Bayezit, who prepared to lay siege to Constantinople.

The answer to Byzantine prayers came in the unorthodox form of a cataract of destruction descending from Central Asia. In 1402 Tamerlane's Mongolian horde faced the Thunderbolt before Ankara; the Sultan was defeated and captured, the towns of Anatolia laid waste. Conqueror and conquered soon died, the Sultan's body was brought back to Bursa, and the Turkish impetus had merely suffered a temporary setback. The need to eliminate surplus brothers was dramatically illustrated by ten years of civil war, before Mehmet I reunified the dismembered Osmanli territories. He only blinded his surviving brother, who was consigned to a comfortable residence in Bursa. Assisted by Manuel II, the Sultan reduced at last the Karamanoğlu and died peacefully at the age of 47 in Edirne.

In 1430, Murat II conquered Thessaloniki from the Venetians, but was defeated at the Battle of Morava in 1443 by a coalition of Christian Balkan rulers, helped by the defection of an Albanian prince. Skander Beg had been enrolled among the Janissaries, but baulked at fighting his own people. Reconverting to Christianity, he led a heroic resistance before his tragic end. In an unprecedented move, Murat abdicated in 1444 in favor of his 12-year-old son, Mehmet II, but as was only to be expected, the Christian powers united against the unstable government of vizirs in Edirne. Murat was forced to return from retirement in Bursa to put a stop to these violent rivalries and to win a victory at Varna on the Black Sea over what rather grandiloquently claimed to be the last crusade. Murat resumed the throne in 1446 and Mehmet went back to his governorship in Manisa till his father's death five years later.

The Zenith of Empire—Suleiman the Magnificent

With the second accession of Mehmet II, Turkey assumed the role of a leading European power, confirmed by the conquest of Constantinople in 1453, quickly followed by the occupation of the last Frankish and Byzantine principalities in Greece. Mehmet imposed tribute on the Venetian possessions, incorporated Serbia and Bosnia, but was checked at Belgrade and Rhodes. Moldavia, Wallachia and the Crimea acknowledged his sovereignty, and in 1461 he put an end to the Empire of Trapezunt. Victory over the Turmen at Erzincan secured his domination in Anatolia and the Black Sea became a Turkish lake. Mehmet II was not only a brilliant military leader, but also an outstanding administrator, reorganizing the government and codifying the law. He resurrected the Eastern Empire, even calling himself Kayser-ı-Rum (Caesar of Rome), though Padishah (Emperor) became the official title. A Turkish raid on Otranto in 1480 was in preparation for the invasion of Italy, but the Sultan died the following year, perhaps poisoned.

The ensuing war between the brothers confirmed the need to liquidate inherent pretenders for reasons of state. The winner, Bayezit II, repulsed a Mameluk invasion, fought in Albania and defeated the Venetians, yet he was essentially a man of peace and, like his father, encouraged the arts. He particularly admired the works of the Moslem philosopher Averroes and was sufficiently broad minded to send Pope Innocent VII one of Christianity's most sacred relics, the lance that had pierced Christ's heart.

His son, Selim I, plotted with the Janissaries and deposed his father in 1512. In his eight years' reign, this most ruthless of the sultans put to death eight grand vizirs, yet wept over the elegy left by the brother he murdered and himself wrote elegant verse. Nicknamed Yavuz (the Grim) he made Moslem unity his priority and persecuted the Shi'as. He marched into the Persian capital and tripled the size of the Empire by adding Syria, Palestine, Arabia and Egypt. He massacred the Mameluks together with 50,000 inhabitants of Cairo, yet wept once again when praying after victory. Carrying the mantle, standard and swords of the Prophet to Istanbul, he assumed the title of Caliph (Successor of Mohammed), which was borne by the Osmanli dynasty for 407 years and disappeared with its fall.

In the tenth generation, Süleyman I (1520–66) had at 26 already been governor of Manisa and viceroy during the Persian war. He soon became Kanuni (the Lawgiver) in his states, Suleiman the Magnificent to the Europeans who admired him as the mightiest among a remarkable bevy of contemporary monarchs. The Sultan increased the power of the Empire to an extent unknown since the reign of that previous great legislator, Justinian I, exactly 1,000 years earlier. Belgrade was captured in 1521, Rhodes after an epic siege a year later. The "Destruction of Mohacs" eliminated the Hungarian king and his army in 1526, and within three years Süleyman was before the walls of Vienna, capital of the Western Emperor. The heroic resistance forced him to withdraw, but the truce of 1547 brought most of Hungary, Transylvania and 30,000 ducats.

Three campaigns against Persia extended the Empire eastwards and added Iraq. Khayr ad-Din (Hayrettin) and Oruc Barbarossa, Moslem convert brothers, annexed Algeria and made the Turkish navy supreme in the Mediterranean. The Empire stretched from the Atlas to the Caucasus, including most of the famous cities of the ancient world. To the core of the two vast central provinces, Anatolia and Rumeli, were added the semi-autonomous governments of Egypt, Tripoli, Tunisia, Algiers and Yemen, as well as the kingdom of Hungary, the principalities of Crimea, Moldavia, Wallachia, Transylvania and the emirate of Hejaz. Secure as the greatest power in Central Europe, the Near East and North Africa, local self-government was granted in religious, municipal and religious affairs. The army was doubled, its artillery and discipline unmatched in the West, and the number of Janissaries raised to 20,000, but they began to give trouble and Süleyman had to cut down two of the ringleaders with his own hands.

As the Osmanli tide of victory swept on, the numbers of Moslem converts increased; out of ten grand vizirs of that period eight were renegades, likewise twelve of the most renowned generals and almost all of the celebrated admirals. Trade, however, remained in the hands of Christians and Jews, as it was an occupation despised by the Turks. The Divan (Council of State) granted the first capitulations to France in 1535, followed by similar tax exemptions for foreign merchants and consular court jurisdiction to Austria in 1567, to England in 1592 and to Russia in 1711. These were acts of goodwill by a warrior nation contemptuous of trade, yet the results were disastrous; decline of revenues and loss of sovereignty sapped the Porte's sovereignty.

Despite dazzling successes, the old age of the great Sultan was clouded with sorrow. The intrigues of his Caucasian wife Roxelana caused the death of some elder heirs and brought her own incapable son to the throne. One year after his accession Süleyman had driven the Knights of St. John from Rhodes, but one year before his death the Knights repulsed the equally memorable siege of Malta. At the age of 72, Süleyman was borne in his litter to lead the army in Hungary, where he died during the siege of Szigetvar after a reign that had lasted 46 years and 46 days. The army of 150,000 men fought on for seven weeks as if their monarch was still alive.

The impetus of conquest continued under Selim II—officially called the Blond, the coloring inherited from his Caucasian mother, but less flatteringly the Sot (shades of Michael VIII the Drunkard). The capture of Cyprus aroused Christendom, and in 1571 under the command of the brilliant Don Juan d'Austria, Emperor Charles V's natural son, the fleets of the Catholic powers put an end at Lepanto to Turkish supremacy, but not to the Turkish presence in the Mediterranean. The Empire remained a valuable ally and Queen Elizabeth of England offered an alliance "against the idolaters," Catholic Spain.

The Decline of Empire

Murat III (1574–95) subjected the Caucasus and rekindled the war with Austria which dragged on under Mehmet III (1595–1603) to end in 1606 with the loss of Turkish superiority on land. The great sultans were dead, the limits of expansion had been reached, the Empire had become too far-flung and too heterogeneous. To avoid civil war, 19 brothers were strangled at the accession of Mehmet III, but there were extensive peasant revolts in Anatolia. Despite the unswerving bravery of the Turkish soldiers, the endless wars resulted in ever more disastrous treaties, attack gradually changed into defense during three centuries of regression.

Most ominous, the Janissaries were no longer Christian slave boys but freeborn Moslems, who soon became the arbiters of the Empire. They forced on Süleyman's grandson the deposition of three vizirs, and in 1622 strangled 19-year-old Osman II, the Caliph whose person had hitherto been held sacred. But Murat IV, who survived the terrors of his adolescence, mastered the Janissaries in a ruthless bloodbath and led the remainder to the conquest of Baghdad, the last sultan to head his army. Yet when he died at 28 in 1640, the Janissaries relapsed into indiscipline and revolt.

The next remission was initiated by a humble Balkan family who climbed the ladder up the imperial bureaucracy, which was neither as inefficient nor as corrupt as the prevailing harem influence would have suggested. Mehmet Köprülü served 25 years as kitchen boy and cook before becoming Master of the Horse and successively governor in Damascus, Tripoli and Jerusalem. On the recommendation of his mother, Mehmet IV (1648–87), who had succeeded at the age of six, appointed Mehmet Pasha as Grand Vizir. The 70-year-old brought order into the administrative chaos by executing some 36,000 people during the five years of his government. His son, Fazil Ahmet Pasha, ruled Turkey in all but name from 1661 to 1676; he won the long struggle for Crete, reformed the finances of the Empire, and ended his life with an advantageous peace that kept the Ukraine. But the armies he led were no longer the best-equipped and were increasingly out-generalled by the Austrians. His brother-in-law Kara Mustafa led the Crescent Banner for the last time into Central Europe to the mismanaged second siege of Vienna in 1683. Even though Mehmet IV had opposed his Grand Vizir's grandiose scheme and had him strangled after its spectacular failure, the Sultan was deposed but allowed to retire to Edirne.

Another turning point in the 1,000-year-old struggle between the Cross and the Crescent had been passed. Austria led a coalition with Poland and Venice to the reconquest of Croatia, Hungary, Transylvania and the Peloponnese, Russia claimed the Crimea, and Persia recaptured Azerbeijan. The stages of the Turkish retreat were marked by the treaties of Karlowitz in 1699, of Passarovitz in 1718, the humiliation of Küçük Kaynarca in 1774, and of Jassy in 1792. By a victory over Peter the Great in the marshes of the Pruth, Ahmet III (1703–30) retrieved some territories, but was unable to hold them and was deposed by the Janissaries. Austria dominated the Balkans to Belgrade, while Russia closed in on the Black Sea.

Mahmut I (1730–54), Mustafa III (1757–74) and Abdül Hamid I (1774–89) attempted civil and military reforms, always thwarted by the Janissaries, who clung fanatically to tradition. The Napoleonic wars occupied Turkey's main assailants and during this respite Selim III (1789–1807) trained a small body of troops in the western way, armed with muskets and bayonets. They earned Napoleon's attention at the siege of Acre, but medieval customs lost the Battle of Aboukir, when the already victorious Turks dispersed to cut off their enemies' heads. Nationalism was spreading in the Balkans and revolt had broken out in Serbia when the Janissaries overthrew Selim III, but from his confinement before assassination he impressed his cousin to carry on with reforms.

A patient realist, Mahmut II (1809–39) waited through 18 years of chaos until he was able to end the tyranny of the Janissaries. Free at last after annihilating those incurable fomenters of rebellion, Mahmut put into practice radical reforms in all spheres of government. Education became compulsory for all boys before they could take up any craft. European officers taught in a military academy and trained an army of 40,000. Administration and justice were brought up to a new standard. A few years of peace were needed, but not granted. No sooner had the rebellion of Ali Pasha in Albania and western Greece been put down by the Grand Vizir, than nationalist insurgencies started in Romania and Greece. The European powers wiped out the new navy at Navarino in 1826, the Russians marched to Edirne, and another bitter treaty was signed in 1829 giving autonomy to Moldavia and Wallachia as well as independence to southern Greece. The following year, Algeria, still nominally under Turkish sovereignty, was taken by the French, while in 1832 only Russian intervention kept the Egyptian Pasha's son from disembarking his troops on the Bosphorus. Seven years later, the Egyptian army advanced through Syria into Anatolia, once again only stopped by the great powers. Mehmet Ali was recognized as Khedive of Egypt, *de jure* viceroy, *de facto* independent, but Syria was handed back to Abdül Mecit I (1839–61) and more important, the Dardanelles were closed to foreign warships.

The Sick Man of Europe

Tsar Nicholas I remarked to the British ambassador: "We have on our hands a very sick man and he may suddenly die." But continuing attempts at reform and, above all, British-Russian rivalry prolonged the death agony for 80 years. The 16-year-old Sultan had been educated in Europe, was open to western ideas and, assisted by the Grand Vizir Mustafa Reshit, immediately decreed a revolutionary concept of equality among all Turkish subjects, regardless of race and creed. But the reorganization of the civil administration and the law codes were defeated by corruption and inertia.

As the sequel to a quarrel between the Catholics and the Orthodox Christians concerning the holy places in Palestine, Tsar Nicholas I demanded tutelage over his ten million co-religionists within the Turkish Empire. The Sultan naturally refused such interference and war broke out in 1853. The initial Russian successes drove the French and British into an alliance and intervention in the Crimea. After three years of bloody fighting, the Treaty of Paris upheld the status quo and guaranteed equal rights for the Eastern Christians. But the unpopular reform movement had to be slowed down and all attention was concentrated on avoiding bankruptcy.

Under Abdül Aziz (1861–76) the Balkan provinces sank into a perpetual state of insurrection. European-educated politicians and writers united as Young Turks, stressing the concept of one Turkish nation in a constitutional monarchy with a parliament representing all religious communities. They deposed Abdül Aziz; his nephew Murat V lasted three months; then Murat's brother Abdül Hamid II came to the throne. He managed to preserve the Empire for an unexpected 33 years. Midhat Pasha, leader of the Young Turks, appointed Grand Vizir, drafted a constitution, but the parliament, representing all nations and religions of the still vast Empire, quickly disintegrated under petty quarrels. The Bosnian and Bulgarian uprising, supported by Russia, seemed to spell the end of Turkey in Europe, but as the Western Powers refused to accept Russian domination of the eastern Mediterranean, the losses imposed by the Treaty of San Stefano were mitigated by the Treaty of Berlin in 1878. Still, Romania and Serbia gained independence, Bulgaria autonomy, Bosnia and Herzegovina became an Austrian protectorate, Cyprus a British one, and Russia kept Kars. Midhat Pasha was exiled to the Hejaz and eventually executed. This was the Sultan's usual treatment of opponents, hardly surprising considering the dynastic history, and the menace that the dethroned brother might be recalled.

So far all reforms had been imposed by enlightened sultans on the recalcitrant Moslem majority. Abdül Hamid attempted to restore unity through the prestige of the caliphate and developed modern communications and amenities, which were useful to a centralizing autocracy, but resisted western political systems. Constitutional rule had been tried and failed, the Young Turks' idealistic notions were unrealistic and unacceptable in a multiracial, multireligious and multilingual empire. The Sultan was a consummate diplomat in playing off Turkey's rival would-be protectors, bringing emerging Germany into the concert of powers by using Kaiser Wilhelm II's *Drang nach Osten* (Drive to the East) to build the Berlin-Baghdad railway. Education was extended to girls, universities were founded, and the army was trained by French and German officers. Greece was defeated in 1897, and only British intervention halted the victorious Turkish forces.

But those who benefited most by the material progress and reforms considered them too little, too late. In 1889, intellectuals, officers and students formed the Committee for Union and Progress in Thessaloniki, birthplace and garrison of a young officer, Mustafa Kemal, who quickly became an influential member. This conspiratorial core of the Young Turks eventually prevailed on the two army corps of Macedonia and Edirne to issue an ultimatum to the Sultan, who restored the constitution in 1908. General rejoicing was followed by the inevitable reaction; the army corps stationed in Istanbul rallied round Abdül Hamid, who abrogated the constitution. This time the Balkan armies marched on Istanbul, deposed the Sultan and sent him for safekeeping to Thessaloniki.

His brother, Mehmet V (1909–18) became the Empire's first constitutional monarch, but not for long. The brotherhood of nations and religions could be proclaimed, but not practised, and foreign response was worse than disheartening. Austria annexed Bosnia and Herzegovina, Bulgaria declared independence, Crete declared union with Greece. The Young Turks split and the Liberal Union came to power. Colonel Enver Bey, one of the prime movers of Abdül Hamid's deposition, was sent as military attaché to Berlin, but when Italy invaded Tripoli in 1911 he organized the resistance and was appointed pasha. Nationalism had spread to the Arab provinces, where the policy of "Turkification" was as violently resisted as in the Balkans. The First Balkan War united all Christian states and deprived Turkey of all its European possessions except Istanbul. The government had become so unpopular that Enver Pasha could lead a few soldiers to the Sublime Porte, where the Minister of War was shot in the archetypal coup d'état of January 1913. When the former allies fell on Bulgaria later in the year, Enver as Turkish chief-of-staff recaptured Edirne. The moderate generals of the original liberal movement were discarded and the triumvirate of Enver, Talaat and Cemal Pasha established a military dictatorship, more ruthless but hardly more efficient than the sultans and viziers in the past century.

An attack on Russian shipping by warships given to Turkey but still under German command precipitated the Empire into the First World War. Enver's grandiose Pan-Turkic schemes in Central Asia ended temporarily with the Russian occupation of Erzurum and Van. But the British Imperial Forces failed in 1916 to take Gallipoli, which was defended by General Mustafa Kemal and the German General Liman von Sanders. Yet other British forces were moving north from the Persian Gulf and east from Egypt; in 1917 they reached Baghdad, in the following year Jerusalem and Damascus.

A cousin came to the throne as Mehmet VI (1918–22), as clever as Abdül Hamid, but facing an impossible situation and finally sharing the same fate. He instituted a personal government and disbanded the Committee of Union and Progress, whose leaders fled abroad. An armistice was signed at Mudros, on board *H.M.S. Agamemnon.* 60 Allied ships anchored at Istanbul to safeguard the Straits, the British occupied Mosul, the French moved into Adana, Maraş and Urfa, the Italians into Antalya and Konya, and in 1919 Greek forces landed in Izmir under cover of Allied battleships, partly to forestall further Italian encroachment. In the chaos of these partitions secret patriotic societies were formed throughout Anatolia, rejecting not only the temporal authority of the Sultan, but gradually and much more agonizingly also the spiritual authority of the Caliph.

Mustafa Kemal Pasha, the hero of Gallipoli, persuaded the Sultan to send him as inspector general of the Ninth Army to the Black Sea coast. On May 19, 1919 he landed at Samsun and organized congresses at Erzurum and Sivas which confirmed the unity of Turkey. Under the threat of a provisional government, the Sultan called a parliament which accepted a National Pact based on the congresses' resolutions. Alarmed by this unexpected show of firmness, the Allies formally occupied Istanbul, parliament was closed, some of the nationalist deputies were exiled to Malta while others escaped to Ankara. The Grand National Assembly opened in Ankara in April 1920, and despite the attempts of Enver Pasha, who had escaped to Berlin and then gone to Moscow, to take over the Anatolian resistance, Kemal was elected president of the Assembly and head of the provisional government.

The Treaty of Sèvres in August 1920 corroborated the dismemberment of Turkey, but also strengthened her will to resist. The Greek armies had started moving in Thrace as well as towards Bursa and Uşak, while in eastern Anatolia the Armenians tried to establish an independent state. By December they had been defeated, Kars was retaken from the Russians, who likewise ceded Ardahan and Artvin the following year. Enver Pasha was rendering at last a real service to his country by leading a Moslem rebellion against the Soviet government in Central Asia, where he was killed in action in 1922 after providing a vital diversion beyond the eastern border. The tide had begun to turn. Exhausted by four years of war and privation, inadequately armed, but inspired by national pride and brilliantly led, the Turkish forces twice defeated the Greeks at Inönü, whence the victorious Ismet Pasha, Kemal's friend and successor, took his name. The French were driven from the southern towns they had occupied; in August 1921 Mustafa Kemal commanded the Turkish army at the Battle on the Sakarya which lasted for 22 days. On September 13th, a laconic communiqué announced that not a single Greek had been left alive east of the Sakarya River.

The National State

The Grand National Assembly awarded Kemal the title of Ghazi, the Victor, and confirmed him as commander-in-chief. In the final Battle of Dumlupınar in late August 1922, he routed the Greek forces, who struggled back to Izmir to re-embark together with the Christian inhabitants in British ships, while a catastrophic fire raged in the town. The Victor entered the smoking ruins on September 9th, but the British were still holding the Dardanelles till dislodged by a gigantic bluff. Four years after the humiliation of Mudros, the Mudanya Armistice recognized the inviolability of Anatolia, which was confirmed by the Treaty of Lausanne on July 24, 1923. The Evros River was again the border in Europe, the Straits would be demilitarized but controlled by Turkey, the Greek and Turkish minorities were exchanged, except in Istanbul. Enver's "Turkification," which had contributed to the fall of the Empire, had been achieved in a smaller but homogeneous state.

Kemal's real work could at last begin. So far, loyalty to Islam and the Osmanli dynasty had decided the course of empire, but the Empire was no more and its twin pillars had become an obstacle to the westernization the Ghazi was about to impose. The sultanate was abolished on November 1, 1922, Mehmet VI left on a British warship and the dynasty came to an end after 641 years, though his cousin Abdül Mecit was chosen Caliph. The time was not yet ripe for a definite break with religion, only with the imperial past. Ankara became the capital on October 13, 1923, on the 29th the Republic was proclaimed and the Ghazi was elected president. Ismet İnönü was appointed prime minister, no more Grand Vizir, and the headlong rush into a secularized 20th century was about to start.

In March 1924, the caliphate was abolished, all members of the Osmanli family were exiled, and a new Ministry of Public Education took over all schools and educational institutions, while medreses and religious foundations were closed. In the following year all religious orders were dissolved, the wearing of the fez, turban and other traditional headgear was forbidden, while women were encouraged to abandon the veil. 1926 was the year of legal reforms: the new civil code, based on Swiss law, prohibited polygamy and guaranteed the rights of women; the penal code was based on Italian, the commercial code on German law. A law school opened at Ankara University. The Islamic calendar of lunar years starting with the Hegira in A.D. 622 was replaced by the Gregorian calendar and the weekly day of rest was moved from Friday to Sunday. The metric system was adopted in 1934, and in the same year women acquired the right to vote.

Naturally these revolutionary changes in all aspects of the daily life had not gone unopposed, and it needed the charisma and tremendous popularity of the Ghazi to overcome the deeply rooted conservatism of the Anatolian peasants who formed the vast majority of the population. Antagonism found an outlet in religion, whose language was Arabic as Islam does not permit the Koran to be recited in another language. Kemal forbade its study, stopped the muezzins using it in their call to prayer, and even more radical, decided to eliminate its influence on Turkish. It would be useful at this point to have a short detour into an examination of the history of language in Turkey.

Language and Literature

The Turkish language is a branch of the Ural-Altaic group, and thus a distant relative of Finnish, Hungarian and Mongolian. The earliest writing is an epic poem carved in the eighth century on two stone tablets found in Northern Mongolia. Today, Turkish is spoken throughout Central Asia in a multitude of dialects by almost a hundred million Moslems in western China and eastern U.S.S.R.

When the Seljuks became in the 11th century the ruling elite throughout the Abbasid Caliphate of Baghdad, a large admixture of the much richer Arabic and Persian vocabulary inevitably occurred. The *Treatise and Dictionary of the Turkish Language* compiled by Mahmud Kashgari in 1074 remains the standard reference before the adulteration, but about the same time the first Turkish work in Arabic script, the *Science of Happiness*, a long didactic poem, appeared.

The great mystic Mevlana (1207–73) dictated his enormous poetic work in Persian, while the preacher and teacher Nasreddin Hoca (1208–84), the immortal personification of Turkish humor, wrote in the Seljuk of his native Akşehir. Though the traditional and popular modes of expression never ceased, poetry, the main literary form, developed in the Turko-Arabic-Persian language of the imperial court, which was incomprehensible to the vast majority of the population. In the classical period of Osmanli literature, which began at the conquest of Istanbul, poets achieved distinctly personal styles in an increasingly subtle and esoteric manner. All sultans appreciated this court poetry, in which the greatest rulers indulged quite creditably. The post-classical period of the 18th century was typified by the decadence of Achmed III's Tulip Reign, when refinement turned into preciousness, an artificial estheticism and symbolism.

When Abdül Mecit I introduced western ideas in the 1840s, poetry lost its predominance to a prose mainly concerned with expressing ardent patriotic sentiments. A language overburdened with foreign elements ill-suited the budding nationalism, which sought for a return to a purer Turkish. The first important Turkish play, *The Fatherland* by Namik Kemal, earned the playwright exile, but after the promulgation of the 1908 constitution modern theater asserted itself. Yet the linguistic problem was far from being solved.

Together with Islam, the Turks had adopted the Arabic script, which contains only three vowels while Turkish distinguishes between eight. This made for pronunciation changes from individual to individual, and was incompatible with the ideal of a uniform national language, which Mustafa Kemal considered an essential part of his reforms. In 1928 he banned the use of Arabic letters and introduced the Latin alphabet with minor additions to make spelling entirely phonetic. He likewise replaced the Arabic and Persian words with Turkish equivalents, wherever possible, or by new words in accordance with the morphology of the language. Added to this return to original racial sources was the adoption of a large number of European words, necessitated by westernization. Derived mainly from French, Kemal's foreign language, the Turkish form, spelled phonetically, is often somewhat bizarre (e.g. *koaför* for coiffeur). In 1932 Kemal founded the Turkish Linguistic Society to safeguard the development of the language on a scientific basis.

A law in 1934 required everyone to take a family name, and the National Assembly voted Mustafa Kemal the surname Atatürk, Father of the Turks. But old customs are difficult to change, and the usual form of addressing even comparative strangers is still the first name followed by Effendi or more politely Bey, and for ladies by Hanim. But then the names are usually charming, flowers are even more popular than in English, with Lâle (Tulip) a frontrunner, while Aslan (Lion) and Demir (Iron) seem fitting for the rough and tumble of politics.

Religion

Islam means Submission to God's Will as revealed by His Prophet, Mohammed. It recognizes the traditions of Judaism, and, to a lesser extent, Christianity; the Old Testament prophets and Jesus himself are viewed as moral leaders of mankind, but are looked on only as forerunners of Mohammed, the greatest of all.

The sacred book of the Moslems, the Koran, offers the faithful a set of moral rules whereby they may better the good that dwells in every man. All Moslem law, all social and political institutions of the Osmanli Empire were taken from the Koran. As in Christianity, heresies and schisms from the supreme power of the religious ruler, the Caliph, have split the Moslem religion into sects. In Islam, the oneness of God ("there is no God but God") is a sharp contrast to the Christian concept of the Holy Trinity.

Mohammed was born in Mecca around A.D. 570. Banished for his belief in one God, he went to Medina in the year 622, the year of the *Hegira,* the flight which marks the beginning of the Islamic calendar. He returned in 630 to conquer his native town, where he died two years later.

Atatürk created a secular national republic on the ruins of a multinational theocracy, where the sultan was also the caliph—that is to say the emperor was also the pope. Only the immense prestige of the Victor in the War of Liberation could carry through the separation of religion and state, despite the all-pervading influence of Islam. Though secularism was enshrined in the constitution, the reaction against reforms which had shattered immemorial beliefs came into the open in the 1950s. Some of the old ways have returned especially in the countryside, the *hocas* have regained some influence, *ulemas* may speak to their Moslem brothers before addressing them as brother Turks, the call to prayer can again be chanted by the *muezzin* in Arabic, the sacred language, women wear a kerchief though hardly ever a veil. The armed forces stopped this trend three times, a trend particularly pronounced when two small Islamic parties held the balance of power in the Grand National Assembly from 1973 to 1980. But the construction of large mosques, often financed by Saudi Arabia and the Gulf States, has provided the new quarters of all major towns with highly visible religious centers. A sign of more tolerant times, Turgut Özal is the son of a *hoca* at Malatya, was once a candidate of a religious party in parliamentary elections, and is the Republic's first prime minister to have made the pilgrimage to Mecca. Though the remaining Christians and Jews represent less than one percent of the population, they enjoy complete freedom of worship.

Modern Turkey

In 1931 the Republican People's Party, which under Ismet Inönü dominated the Grand National Assembly practically unopposed, defined the six principles of Kemalism—republicanism, nationalism, populism, etatism, laicism and reformism—which in 1937 were enshrined in the constitution. On November 10, 1938, Kemal Atatürk died and on the following day Ismet Inönü was elected the Republic's second President. He continued the policy of Kemalism and kept Turkey neutral during World War II till the merely symbolic declaration of war on Germany and Japan in February 1945.

In 1943 Inönü was re-elected and two years later additional political parties were authorized. The Democratic Party gained the majority in 1950, another sweeping victory four years later, but during its third term in power an increasingly conservative policy, supported by the deeply religious peasantry, led to the intervention of the army to safeguard Kemalism. The military coup of 1960 deposed the third President, hanged the prime minister, and dissolved the Democratic Party which, however, was resurrected as the Justice Party when the next elections took place under a new constitution approved by referendum the following year.

The Justice Party won the elections of 1965 and 1969, but had to face new social tensions in the shanty towns that had grown round all the larger cities, while the villages of Anatolia emptied. About two million villagers went as guest workers to Central and North Europe where they still constitute the biggest racial minority, especially in Germany—which accounts for German replacing English as the principal foreign language. The high birthrate drove many more millions in search for work to the industrializing regions. The Justice Party advocated a liberal economy and free enterprise, while the Republican People's Party sought a social democratic solution by state intervention. Rising discontent, student unrest and social violence led to a second army intervention in 1971, this time bloodless. After achieving order the army again restored democracy, but neither of the two main parties gained a majority in the elections of 1973 and 1977. Unstable coalition governments depended on the support of two small nationalist and religious formations, while the mounting economic crisis exacerbated political terrorism, with which the squabbling politicians were unable to deal.

When assassinations had reached an average of 30 a day, the armed forces once again intervened. Another bloodless coup in 1980 pulled the country back from the brink of civil war; the Chief of Staff, General Evren, headed the National Security Council, which entrusted Turgut Özal, a former executive of the World Bank, with the arduous task of restructuring the economy. The restoration of law and order after years of increasing political violence provided the necessary basis for the success of the stabilization program. And limiting their role as previously to overcoming the acute crisis, the armed forces turned Turkey over to democracy for a third time.

The immensely popular General Evren was elected President for seven years in 1982 by more than 90 percent of the voters who also, in the simultaneous plebiscite, approved the presidential system of the new constitution. Parliamentary elections in the following year gave Özal's center-right

Motherland Party 211 representatives in the 400-seat unicameral Grand National Assembly. Özal formed a government of technocrats who radically reorganized the civil service and resolutely opted for a free-enterprise system. Municipal elections in 1984 confirmed the preeminence of the Motherland Party, but byelections in 1986 favored the traditional Right.

Political stability has enabled Özal to concentrate on the daunting economic and social problems, all connected in one way or another with the population explosion. Though the annual growth rate of the population has declined to less than two and a half percent due to a comprehensive birth control program, it is still by far the highest in Europe and doubles the population in 34 years. Greatly improved public health services have increased the life expectancy to almost 60, but the over-65s represent barely five percent in the population of 53 millions, while the under-20s account for well over 50 percent.

Primary education is free and compulsory. Almost six million pupils are taught by more than 200,000 teachers in over 46,000 schools for five years. Some two million continue in some 7,000 secondary schools for three years in junior and another three in senior high school. Close to 320,000 students are inscribed at over 400 faculties in some 30 universities. Secondary and graduate education give priority to technical training, with the turning out of qualified specialists, scientists and technicians the main objective. Thus about half-a-million enter the labor force every year, adding to an unemployment rate of roughly 20 percent, not to talk about the under-employed. The safety valve of emigration to Europe has been closed, but about two million workers still remain in the E.E.C countries. Some have returned with Christian wives, thereby adding social difficulties, and even the Middle East has been slimming down on the 150,000 Turkish engineers and construction workers since the oil bubble burst. The university students come for the most part from the middle class, with an ever-increasing percentage of women, but the scarcity of appropriate jobs has created an inflammable situation.

There is no press censorship, but journalists and editors can be prosecuted if their publications present a threat to the state. There are several national newspapers, but the most popular mass medium is television with one set for every ten inhabitants. Using the purified language, some novelists have gained international recognition: Yasar Kemal, whose *Memed My Hawk,* a tale of banditry in the Taurus Mountains, has been translated into 28 languages and was made into a film; Yilmaz Güney's *Fields of Yureghir* portraying the infinite, pitiless highlands; and Mahmut Makal's *Bizim,* a vivid account of life in an Anatolian village.

The National Theater, presenting operas and plays, has won renown on foreign tours. Outside Ankara it performs at the various festivals in the antique theaters along the Mediterranean coast, as well as at the Istanbul Festival, where famous companies and orchestras participate in the unique settings of Topkapı and Rumeli Hisar. The movie industry is flourishing, with melodrama, pistol-packing easterns and song-and-dance stories. Quantity before quality, supplemented by foreign films.

Despite the recent revival of religious observances, there is no risk of fanaticism, but respect is demanded. As in every house of worship, silence and discretion should be observed at prayer time. Shoes must be removed at the entrance of mosques, not as a doctrinal but a practical ritual; like many of Mohammed's laws, it is merely a measure of cleanliness, as the praying Moslem touches the ground with his head. As an alternative to walking about in socks or stockings, huge slippers to pull over shoes are supplied at the entrance of all mosques likely to be visited by tourists.

The Economy

Agriculture still forms the basis of the national economy, employing about one half of the labor force, contributing one fifth to the G.N.P. and slightly more to export earnings, a very creditable performance after feeding the rapidly increasing population. Since the foundation of the Republic the cultivated area has increased fivefold, taking over not only pastures, but reclaiming the steppes.

The planted area has risen to almost 40 percent of the total surface, with wheat the main crop. The annual harvest of some 14 million metric tons has raised Turkey into the league of the top ten wheat-exporting countries. There is a sufficiency of other cereals, while the colorful abundance of fruits and vegetables can be seen in open markets throughout the country. Citrus exports have passed one quarter million tons, while Turkey is the world's largest supplier of figs, hazelnuts, raisins and Oriental tobacco. Beet sugar and olive oil more than cover domestic needs, cotton and lentils are important sources of foreign exchange. New crops like peanut and soya are planted after the spring cereal harvest.

Crossbreeding with European strains has improved the meat and milk yields from some 90 million head of cattle. Incentives are offered to prevent the early slaughtering of lambs and Turkey remains a major wool producer, but the number of goats has been reduced as their valuable mohair is grown at the expense of the precarious ecology of the Anatolian plateau. Donkeys, horses, buffaloes and a few camels make up the remaining livestock.

Until 1982 the *agas* still owned more than 800 villages in the eastern provinces, under a feudal system which was only broken when the military regime redistributed the land to half a million families on terms which prevented future fragmentation.

Industrialization and the development of mining resources began in earnest with the first Five Year Plan in 1933. The availability of cotton, wool and silk has fostered the expansion of the textile industry, besides maintaining the traditional rugmaking. Iron and coal deposits have sprouted large metallurgical complexes on the Black Sea coast, while the uranium reserves are sufficient for the nuclear plant under construction. About a quarter of the petrol needs are locally covered, but prospects for further discoveries are poor, except in disputed waters offshore. But Iraq's main pipeline terminates at a Turkish port, perhaps soon joined by an Iranian outlet. Copper and chromium are prominent among the minerals, whose share in exports has, however, been overtaken by cement and vegetables as Turkey has increasingly become the grocer and mechanic of the Middle East.

Attempts to extend industrialization to backward regions involved the state enterprises in heavy losses. But since the stabilization program of 1981 private enterprise has been encouraged, important structural changes have been made, and since 1984 the free-enterprise system has been increasingly adopted. The stock exchange, busy in the days of empire, has been reactivated, and an American bank has prepared a master plan for major privatizations. Industrial production is rising in accordance with the current Five Year Plan to 1990, but agriculture and the energy sector are given top priority. Due to the construction of huge dams and artificial lakes, hydroelectricity covers about one half of the country's needs, with irrigation a valuable by-product.

Though Turkey's per capita income is the lowest among the 24 O.E.C.D. countries, its increase in the G.N.P. has remained the highest bar one for a number of years. Due to the crisis in the Middle East, the unprecedented export boom of the early 1980s has slowed to a more sustainable rate, but still exceeds the percentage rise in imports, which come mainly from the U.S.A. and the E.E.C. Two-way trade with Iran is balanced and still on the increase. The trade deficit is partly covered by remittances from workers abroad, which are declining, and tourism, which is growing. Inflation had dropped from a peak of over 100 to 30 percent, but has recently been on the rise again, despite the government's endeavor to the contrary.

Turkey has been a faithful N.A.T.O. ally since 1952, and an associate member of the E.E.C. since 1963.

Turkey, with its eastern culture and religion, is trying to raise the standard of living by western reforms, which entails giving up age-old customs which were the source of her strength for centuries. This schism between an Asian and a European identity lies at the root of the bloody struggles that have recently plagued the nation. The symptoms have disappeared, but it will take exceptional acumen to reconcile the entrenched opposites.

ART AND ARCHITECTURE

Four Epochs of Vigor and Grace

The jutting peninsula that Asia throws out towards Europe has always been a meeting place for Orient and Occident. Peoples coming from the West or the East occupied it again and again. Some managed only to create an ephemeral sovereignty with no developed cultural tradition; others used it as a base for powerful empires or dominated it from outside. When these nations reached the height of their political supremacy and the full flowering of their art, they left an indelible imprint on Anatolia.

Anatolia's artistic past is marked by four great epochs: the Hittite period, the Greek and Roman colonization, the Byzantine Empire, and the reign of the Turks, whether Seljuk or Osmanli.

Hittite Art

The high Anatolian plateaus were the scene of a brilliant civilization which lasted for almost 1,000 years and whose influence spread as far as Upper Syria. From around 2000 until 1200 B.C. the Hittites built thick-walled palaces and temples and powerful fortifications. Their buildings were as massive as the surrounding scenery, but their metal workers were capable of creating delicate statuettes.

The burial ground of Alacahöyük to the east of Ankara has proved literally a gold mine. Turkish archeologists have uncovered a multitude of gold and copper vases, jewelry fashioned with cornaline and rock crystal, statuettes of bulls and stags, the latter with slender bodies and hooves and extraordinarily developed antlers, plus many decorative pierced metal plaques with geometric designs. Most of these objects held religious significance—the statuettes and plaques, for instance, were often equipped with sockets so they could be attached to staffs and held aloft during ceremonial processions. Unfortunately we know very little about these rites held 4,000 years ago. The best of these funerary objects—belonging to the proto-Hittite period—are on view in the Ankara Museum of Anatolian Civilization.

More Hittite art of this period has been discovered at Kültepe near Kayseri. Here the motifs were obviously influenced by Sumer and Babylon—there are highly stylized female idols, engraved cylindrical seals, goddesses with animals, the struggle of Gilgamesh and the bull, and lions and stags crossed like X's among the themes. The Ankara Museum also has some long-mouthed, large-handled vases made by the potters of Kültepe.

The principal Hittite period begins with the New Kingdom in around 1335 B.C.; its showcase is the capital city, Hattushash. The site has been only partially excavated, but it is evident to the most unpracticed eye that the Hittites here were preoccupied with defense and with power. Hattushash was built on a rocky spur in the heart of Anatolia, high above a ravine which has given its name to the present village of Boğazköy, or "village of the gorge." The floorplan of several buildings is visible on the ground, and one may make out angular corridors leading to the halls, and the paved courtyards of palaces and shrines. A double wall of irregular but well-fitted stone blocks protected the capital on the plateau side, and the ravine formed a natural rampart on the other. The vaulted gates are defended by porches surrounded by bastions, and on each side of these gates, Hittite artists carved animal or human guardians. Two panels with lions have been left on the site. They are not statues added as decoration after construction of the edifice as in Mesopotamia, but wrought directly from the mass of rock. The lions seem to leap out from the walls, but are imprisoned in the stone at their waists, and it is evident that the artist was less interested in imitating nature than in giving his creation the most terrifying appearance possible. The paws are thick, the mane suggested symbolically by short locks chiseled on the muscled body, the jaws are open and threatening.

Hittite sculpture is more forceful than graceful, with a few notable exceptions. One, at Alacahöyük, is a sphinx whose feminine face has a sort of Mona Lisa smile; some will prefer her to her sister from Hattushash, now in Istanbul, whose countenance, in spite of damage, gives a good idea of what ideal feminine beauty must have been for the Hittites.

The best example of relief sculpture is probably the "king" who guarded one of the gates of Hattushash and who now may be seen in Ankara's museum. He is actually the great god Teshub, but the confusion is understandable since he is dressed and armed like a royal Hittite. His head is sculptured in profile while the torso is seen from the front; and like most statues of men of the period, he wears a short tunic whose wide belt secures a curved dagger with a large grip. The left arm is folded back towards the body, its closed fist ready to strike; while the right hand grasps a hatchet of a type still frequently seen in Luristan (a present-day province of Iran). The god wears the up-turned pointed shoes typical of all personages in reliefs of this style, and looks as though he were ready to set off on a march. The head conveys the general impression of strength—a heavy jaw, thick lips, massive nose, and a far-from-pleasant look in the eye. Teshub wears a conical helmet with a lock of his hair hanging down from the top of it.

Hittite sculpture is much the same everywhere and it would be useless to look for an evolution in the style or for differences among "schools." However, the choice of locations and the ways of treating groups of figures vary and from this point of view, the Yazılıkaya friezes, near Boğazköy, are quite remarkable.

Here are relief sculptures alive with figures measuring anywhere up to 2.50 meters (seven feet) tall. They parade along the rocky walls of two galleries—in the great gallery is the whole roster of Hittite deities, men on one side, women on the other. The two ranks converge towards a central panel at the end; it depicts the mystical union between the god Teshub and the goddess Hepatu.

The members of this pantheon all have the same stiff hieratic attitude, and can only be distinguished by their size, costume, and particular godly attributes. The male divinities wear short tunics around their hips and pointed headdresses. The goddesses, like women everywhere, are more ornamental, with their long pleated skirts, cylindrical tiaras, earrings and bracelets. Some in the procession stand aloft on symbolic animals in the Assyrian style, while others stand beneath ideograms somewhat like Egyptian hieroglyphics. In spite of their static appearance and their rather stereotyped decoration, the friezes of the great gallery constitute without a doubt an original work of art both as to style and technique.

One of the bas-reliefs in the small gallery is more cosmopolitan and exemplifies a number of influences which Hittite art synthesized. It shows a sword whose handle is fashioned of a human head placed above two horizontal lions "resting" and two more lions lying head downwards along the edge of the blade. Is this a stone copy of some king's fabulous sword? Experts say it is more likely a god itself, and cite examples of "hoplolatry" (weapon-worship) ranging from Sumerian and Assyrian daggers through Syrian hatchets to a whole range of objects from Crete and the Aegean world. Recalling how much the Hittites admired force, one is hardly surprised at this example of the cult of arms.

Hittite sculptors chiseled busily for hundreds of years on any number of cliff faces in Anatolia. Another example of their work can be seen at Ivriz (or in Istanbul's Archeological Museum, where there is a cast of these reliefs).

The New Kingdom inaugurated grandeur in sculpture, but its official business also kept the gem cutters busy producing seals and signets, and several Turkish museums have fine collections of these. The Hittites at this point stopped copying their Mesopotamian counterparts, and began producing seals with original designs—usually a god or animal in the center, with braid and scrolls around the edges. The style reminds one generally of that of the reliefs.

About 3,000 years ago, the cultural and political influence of the Hattushash Hittite Kingdom began to wane, with a few die-hard outposts remaining here and there. The tablets from Karatepe in the Ankara Museum tell a tale of long-forgotten feasts and festivities at the palace of the Hittite kings of Cilicia (southern Turkey), who reigned until the eighth century B.C. In Upper Syria around Kargamish and Zincirli, the Hittite tradition persists until about the seventh century, but the sculpture deteriorates, and instead of conveying strength, begins to look merely heavy. The Mesopotamian influence, vanquished for a few centuries, returns to the fore. The Hittite tunic gives way to the Babylonian robe, the typical Assyrian beard seems to grow on every face and the turned-up toes of Hittite shoes are rarely seen. When Hittite politics could no longer improve a culture, they simply went out of style.

Greek and Roman Art in Anatolia

The Greeks who fled from the Dorian invasions around 1100 B.C. took refuge on friendlier shores of the Aegean in Anatolia. Here they set up confederations and leagues of cities which did much to keep the cultural and ethnic traditions of these immigrants alive. Aeolians settled north of the Gulf of Smyrna, Acheans colonized the valley of the Hermos, and Ionians founded a confederation of 12 cities around Ephesos and Miletus whose influence was to determine in large measure the art, literature and philosophy of the western world. The Dorians themselves crossed the Aegean a little later and settled in the south, above and below the Knidos peninsula. These cities in turn established colonies and trade centers on the shores of the Propontis (the Sea of Marmara) and the Pontus Euxinus (Black Sea). The sea lanes between all these centers were crowded with ships carrying not only wares and riches, but art and culture too.

The states of the interior of Anatolia welcomed Greek civilization, whose traditions blended easily with their own. One might say that nobody missed the Hittites, for a number of other peoples came to fill the role they had left vacant. Between the 12th and the eighth centuries, the Phrygians built up a powerful state; several archeological discoveries serve to acquaint us with their civilization. A sculpture of a temple façade carved on a rock at Midas Şehir ("City of Midas"—the one whose touch turned everything to gold) near Eskişehir gives a good idea of Phrygian sacred architecture. The French archeologist Albert Gabriel made an important find nearby—the remains of a foundry, which confirms legends that these people were not only accomplished metal workers, but metal worshippers as well. At the ancient site of Gordion, about 106 km. (66 miles) southwest of Ankara, an American team has uncovered a richly furnished tomb chamber, the supposed resting place of King Midas.

While the Phrygians were busy in the north, the Lydians in central Anatolia and the Karians round Hallikarnassos in the south were creating their own civilizations. Both peoples were in constant contact with the coastal Greeks and their art shows this influence. In the rough country of the southwest between Fethiye and Antalya, the Lykians developed four types of tombs: a high rectangular pillar supporting a massive sarcophagus, often with sculptural friezes; a rock-cut temple with columned façade carved out of a cliff; a stone replica of a wooden house; and a grave chamber on an elevated base.

Inside Anatolia, local tradition and Greek culture mingled to create original forms, but on the coast the works of art are indistinguishable from those of Greece itself. There are remnants from the archaic period onward, and if there is not too much evidence to go on, it can be blamed on Anatolia's particularly lively history and not on the lack of artists.

The Byzantines pillaged and destroyed the Temple of Athena at Assos, built in the sixth century B.C. There are still a few handsome Doric capitals on columns of the acropolis high above the entry of the Gulf of Edremit, but the delightful archaic friezes are now in the Louvre—the result of a princely gift from Sultan Mahmut II to France in the 19th century. Istanbul has, however, its share of the remains of the temple. In its Archeological Museum are numerous remains from Anatolia's archaic Greek art— red vases decorated in black, terra cotta sarcophagi, ancient coins, and memorial stones to the dead. They pre-date the Persian occupation, which considerably hindered the development of Greek art in Anatolia. One notable exception—it was here that the Ionian order (columns with scroll capitals) was first created; it soon replaced the more severe Dorian throughout the Greek world.

Alexander the Great and the Macedonian conquest changed not only the face of history, but the face of art. Artists and architects could now count not only on their own talent but on the enormous financial means placed at their disposal by ambitious oriental potentates who wanted buildings splendid enough to further their own prestige. Among the many kingdoms patched together out of the debris of the Macedonian Empire was that of the Attalids; its capital, Pergamon (Bergama), is the most typical representative of the Hellenistic style.

Roman domination supplied the material bases to continue what had developed so gracefully. Excavations under the direction of Dr. Erim on a *National Geographic Society* grant have unearthed an incredible number of archeological treasures at Aphrodisias, 153 km. (95 miles) southeast of Izmir. This is a Greco-Roman city which flourished for several hundred years from the first century B.C. and so rich in finds that marble heads literally fall out of old walls. Digging has been undertaken since 1961, and a theater, concert hall, agora, acropolis, and baths have been unearthed with probably much more to come. The Romans kept everything that the Greeks had built, and added the marks of their own genius.

The same principle holds true at Didyma, where the huge temple of Apollo, begun by Alexander, was finished by the Romans in much the same style. And, as everywhere in the empire, they improved general conditions in the country with roads, bridges and aqueducts, while adding baths to the amenities of the cities at municipal or private expense, plus temples built to the glory of their emperors. Augustus' temple at Ankara is embellished by his last will and testament, engraved on one of its walls.

There are of course some stylistic changes—Roman architects used the arch to a far greater degree, and certain types of edifices like the basilica and the triumphal arch make their appearance for the first time. Hadrian's Arch at Antalya is decorated with acanthus leaves, scrolls, carved ox-skulls and lion heads.

Wealth and power have their disadvantages. One of them in architecture is the desire for the colossal—and what was best in the Hellenistic style soon tended to exaggeration. Corinthian capitals, richer but less graceful than the Ionian, came to be used almost exclusively. Cities like Ephesus were graced with wide streets, bordered with colonnades. At Miletus, a 25,000-seat theater rose from the ground. The southern coast of Anatolia between Antalya and Mersin is literally covered with Roman buildings, and almost every hill is the site of some ruin or other. But quality does not always run with quantity, and most of these vestiges lack the subtlety and grace of Hellenistic art.

Byzantine Art

Christianity sowed its first seeds in Anatolia very early, and by the fourth century a rich harvest of churches and monasteries had grown throughout the land. Some were built in groups; the most remarkable of these is certainly the cluster of religious shrines at Bin Bir Kilise Deresı (The Valley of a Thousand and One Churches) near Karaman, which is largely intact. In this neighborhood, most of the churches date from about the tenth century. Some are built on the classic lines of a basilica with three parallel naves or a single one; others follow the plan of the cross. Near Ürgüp in Cappadocia there is a multitude of churches hollowed out of volcanic stone. But it was only natural that the handsomest shrines were built in Byzantium itself.

Rome had been the inventor of the basilica with parallel naves, but the Byzantine architects developed it in their own style, building on Roman tradition with oriental techniques and splendor. The dome came into common use, and some churches also had a narthex or vestibule preceding the sanctuary itself, as in Romanesque architecture in Europe later on. Saint Irene in Istanbul, built under Justinian in the sixth century, is a fine example of a basilica with three naves, a dome and a narthex.

Emperor Justinian's reign also witnessed the construction of one of the world's biggest religious edifices—the great Saint Sophia Basilica. A narthex 59.5 meters (195 feet) long by 12 meters (39 feet) wide precedes the long central nave, which is surmounted by a dome 30.5 meters (100 feet) in diameter. The dome is flanked by two half domes and supported by four gigantic pillars; the great arches of two half domes and four pendentives (or triangular vaults) serving as intermediaries between the circular dome and the square floor-plan outlined by the pillars. The side naves have galleries high above the floor which look out onto the central nave. The group of domes is supported outside by thick buttresses, giving Saint Sophia a heavy silhouette; inside, however, there is a feeling of lightness, space and freedom.

Justinian ordered the great church to be covered with mosaics on a background of gold, but the few still decorating the basilica belong to the 11th century. On the tympanum above the door in the vestibule is a fine Virgin and Child with Emperors Justinian and Constantine on either side. The arch of the narthex is covered with gold mosaic with geometric designs in color. The royal door leading from the narthex to the nave is guarded by a severe-looking Christ enthroned, while the walls of the nave are covered with beautifully-veined marble plaques.

There is no other example that matches the Byzantine grandeur of Saint Sophia, for shortly after its construction, tastes changed and architects came to prefer more intimate sanctuaries and less solemn decoration. A new and charming style came into being after the ninth century, of which the Church of the Holy Savior in Chora (Kariye Museum), with its mosaics and paintings, is an attractive specimen.

Byzantine art is inseperable from the Eastern Empire, a totally medieval form which preserved Greek and Roman elements changed by the stylistic influence of older oriental modes. It was, above all, a unique synthesis within the religious framework of the Empire. It is, therefore, only fitting that the greatest churches have survived, at least structurally, while of the fabulous Sacred Palace nothing remains but the imperial stables, now the Mosaic Museum. The walls of Constantine VII Porphyrogenitos' palace are still standing near the Kariye Museum, but of Alexios Komnenos' Blachernae Palace only the foundations are discernible.

Byzantine military architecture ranks far below that of medieval Europe for quality and inventiveness. The walls of Constantinople may be long, but they are poorly put together of inferior materials. The only monumental gateway worth looking at is the Golden Portal, which is now part of the castle of Yedikule. The rough ramparts of fortresses, like those of Miletus or Assos, were thrown together with stone stolen from fine classical monuments.

Turkish Art: Seljuk and Osmanli

Anatolia had already played host to more conquerors than was healthy, when in 1071, the Seljuk sultan, Alp Arslan, opened the gates of Asia Minor to the Turks, founding a "new Turkestan."

From the tenth to the 13th century, Turkey was very prosperous, thanks to its location on the caravan routes linking the Orient to the Occident. As usual, wealth fostered art, and the new ease in communications brought not only goods but artists from Persia and the Far East to the Seljuk capital at Konya. Here they met the artisans and architects who had come in on the first Turkish wave, and between them they created an entirely new style. The Turks did not abandon their traditions, but with the help of these new outside influences, they adapted them intelligently to local conditions. With the Seljuk dynasty, Turkey witnessed for the first time a number of architectural features commonly used in Asia—tall gateways with niches, triangular vaults decorated with stalactites and prisms, ogival archways, and ceramic tiling.

Most of these features, combined with Byzantine building techniques, were later taken over by the Osmanlis, who brought Turkish art to its zenith, but the Seljuks must be credited with making the transition from the art of nomadic tribesmen to the delicate and refined products of their Osmanli successors. There are few examples of Seljuk palace architecture extant (except for the insignificant ruins of the Beyşehir palace), but many public, religious and funerary monuments are still standing.

The mosque—which is in many Moslem countries an elegant and graceful affair—in Anatolia had to contend with the rigorous climate while respecting sacred tradition. Both help to explain the austerity of such mosques as the Alaeddin (built in 1220 at Konya), whose almost blank façade is pierced with narrow windows at the top. Inside however, the colonnaded prayer hall is reminiscent of its Syrian counterparts. At Erzurum, in the far northeast, the altitude is 1,900 meters (6,500 feet), and the high plateau almost reminds one of Tibet. Here the Ulu Cami (Great Mosque), with its thick walls and only occasional arched door or small square window, looks more like a fortress than a place of worship. Next door, the medrese (Koranic school) looks less formidable. Its grey stone gateway is flanked by two square bases, from which rise two fluted minarets covered with enameled brick. Carved bands of scrolls and stylized palm leaves adorn the gateway, while the vault is honeycombed and embellished with stalactites, as will also be the case with the Osmanli style. The interior is designed along traditional lines—the courtyard is bordered on two sides by short, thick columns supporting broken arches. Two large broken cylindrical arches cut the colonnade in half. The cells must have been uncomfortable with no light and low ceilings. A high nave, now in ruins, once prolonged the courtyard.

Part of the severity of Erzurum is due to its grey building stone. At Konya, the stone used is black and white marble, which gives a much more inviting aspect to monuments like the Karatay medrese. The two colors are alternated on its façade, which is further adorned with scrolls and intertwined bands, plus three chiseled cabochons on the upper part. We find some of the same motifs, including the cabochons, on the façade of Ince Minare Cami ("the mosque with the slim minaret"), not far away. This mosque is also decorated with wide stone ribbons, and if these carvings seem odd, it is because they are a sculptured transposition of the fancy work on saddles and bridles, of which Turkish nomadic horsemen were so fond.

The memories of tribal days on the steppes are still strong in Seljuk funerary architecture. Their mausoleums, called türbe or kümbet look exactly like yurts, or Turkish tents, which were fashioned of circular wooden slats, then covered with felt. Probably the most famous is the Döner Kümbet (Turning Vault) of Kayseri, which owes its name to a legend claiming that its conical roof will turn at the slightest touch; and looking at the graceful roof poised on the slender shaft of the tower, one can believe the tale.

The House of Osman, leader of one of the latest Turkish tribes to arrive in Anatolia, chose Bursa as capital from 1325 until 1413, and even today, Bursa boasts 188 mosques, many of which date back to the beginnings of the Osmanlis. The biggest of these is the Ulu Cami, which took 36 years to complete (1379–1415), and whose floor plan of four parallel naves is reminiscent of the first Seljuk mosques. The Ulu Cami is roofed by 25 little cupolas, with a shaft in the center for the light to pour through. The earlier Orhan Mosque is far more like a Byzantine church, but its decoration of scrolls and arabesques, its gateway and its mihrab (the niche that indicates the direction of Mecca) with stalactites and honeycombing are pure Turkish.

The Green Mosque (1415–24) exemplifies Osmanli art at the height of its glory. The plan is one often found in Bursa—an upside down T: two long halls, one after the other, and two smaller ones opening off the sides of the first. The walls are covered up to eye level with green ceramic tile accented in blue, and the motifs on the marble that outlines the windows are far more refined than comparable Seljuk work.

1453 is marked by the fall of Constantinople, the death in battle of the last of the Constantines, and the end of Byzantine civilization. What had been Byzantium, then Constantinople, became Istanbul—the new capital of the Osmanli Empire. Osmanli rulers lost no time in transforming the churches into mosques and in beginning construction of other shrines worthy of their captured prize. Saint Sophia with its majestic dome impressed the Turks, and in 1506 Beyazit II, the son of the conqueror, ordered that a mosque bearing his name be built along the same lines. This mosque, with its dome supported by four pillars and its side naves, not only adapts intelligently the style of the Byzantine basilica but also ushers in the golden age of Osmanli architecture. The 16th century witnessed the zenith of the empire's political power, the height of its religious fervor, and the full splendor of its art.

In 1328 Sultan Orhan had minted the first Osmanli silver coins in the tradition of earlier Moslem rulers, but now the *tughrah,* the elaborately calligraphed signature of the sultan, replaced the Koranic quotations. Mother-of-pearl was increasingly used in decoration, as in the ebony and silver throne shown together with illuminated books, gold-inlaid and jeweled weapons and helmets in "The Age of Sultan Süleyman the Magnificent" exhibition in the U.S. and London in 1987–8. The Sultan commissioned Sinan, the greatest of Turkish architects, to build his splendid mosque, one of the masterworks of Osmanli art. Here, Turkish architecture comes into its own, freed from restrictive Byzantine influence. The elegant ascent of the cupolas towards the great dome, and the soaring minarets give the mosque an outline which is both slender and majestic. This classic Osmanli art continued to flourish throughout the 17th century, the finest example being the mosque of Ahmet I, better known as the Blue Mosque because of its extraordinary ceramic interior decoration.

Did the Turks then lose confidence in themselves and in the uniqueness of their own style? Perhaps so, for the 18th century is stamped with increasingly foreign influences from Europe or Persia. For a while, under Ahmed III (1703–30), the tulip becomes almost an obsession with Turkish artists, this flower replacing all other decorative motifs. Later in the century, the Baroque movement, imported into Turkey by foreign craftsmen, was in vogue, as evidenced in the Nuru Osmaniye Mosque of 1757.

This decadence, once begun, became predominant in the 19th century. The Dolmabahçe Palace, begun in 1840, on the Bosphorus, is a strange hybrid—a cross between a Moorish castle, Italian Baroque palazzo, and a Hindu shrine. Built by the famous Balian family of architects, 14,000 kgs (about 30,000 lbs) of gold were used in the decoration and furnishing. The ostentatious opulence expressed the resolve of the sultans to sustain the rank and grandeur of their declining empire in the heydays of European imperialism. Slightly higher up the Bosphorus, Sultan Abdül Aziz constructed the Çiragan Palace in another Osmanli blend of Italianate and neo-Gothic. The enforced residence of the deposed Murat V burned down in 1911 and is being restored as a luxury hotel with full respect for the original design.

Across the road are the hills of the vast Yıldız Park where, in the last quarter of the 19th century, Abdül Hamid II returned to the tents in stone of his earliest ancestors in preference to the European-inspired huge palaces. The sultans loved gardens and the kiosks are scattered over a wider space than within the limitations of Topkapı, albeit in a minor key. But though the layout is traditional, the architecture is the bewildering hotchpotch of the late Empire. On the highest point, the Chalet Kiosk accommodated Kaiser Wilhelm II during several visits in a highly incongruous elongated Swiss villa. Some of the elaborate furniture was, however, carved by Abdül Hamid himself, the doors are inlaid with mother-of-pearl, while the porcelain stoves and bathrooms were manufactured in the factory below.

The most impressive architectural work of the contemporary republican period is without a doubt the Mausoleum of Kemal Atatürk in Ankara. Its severe and majestic lines happily blend ancient Anatolian and modern styles in a new era in Turkish art.

But the return to a somewhat fanciful Hittite style, that marked most of the new capital's public buildings, is on the wane. Osmanli tradition is coming again into its own, and that means Istanbul. The highest Islamic architectural distinction, the triennial Aga Khan Award, was in 1986 given to the Social Security Complex at Zeyrek for harmoniously fitting the terraced pavilions into the surrounding city fabric. The Historic Sites Development Scheme that has preserved and restored so many highlights of the Old Town received a richly deserved honorable mention.

FOOD AND DRINK

A Medley of Turkish Delights

As long as the Turks were nomads, their food was necessarily extremely limited, but when they settled they soon adopted the national dishes of the conquered, to whom the culinary gifts were eventually returned after centuries of refinement in the great palaces of Istanbul. This accounts for a certain uniformity of taste throughout the vast expanse of the former Turkish Empire. From the Balkans, the Crimea and the Russian coast of the Black Sea down to Egypt and Tunisia, you will come across Turkish dishes, and at once know them by the taste, if not always by the name.

The kebabs, other mutton dishes and smoked meats have a long history, deriving from the Turks' days on the Central Asian plateaus of their forefathers. Many vegetable dishes, especially those served stuffed with rice, onions, pinenuts and currants, are creations of Seljuk courts at Isfahan and Khorasan (in modern Iran). Vegetable dishes cooked in oil and served hot or cold are, however, an Osmanli inspiration.

Turkish cuisine is varied and delicious, though not necessarily in proportion to the price. The restaurants of the better hotels mostly serve so-called international fare, which, as elsewhere, can mean tasteless dishes served with a great deal of fuss by a crowd of waiters. Unless you prefer show to a good meal, it is often not worth the cost. The motels pride themselves on a mixture of European and Turkish fare, e.g., meat with rice as well as potatoes, to the neglect of vegetables. Far wiser to eat as the Turks do. The cooking is done occasionally with butter, but mostly with oil, for cold dishes. No need to worry—the oil has none of the strong taste and

off-putting smell often found elsewhere. Furthermore, spices are used here
with a masterly discrimination. Indeed, it would need an entire book to
sing the praises of the range of Turkish cooking. There are cookbooks in
English on sale in the larger cities which are well worth looking into.

The top hotels serve Continental breakfast in your room. Below the Es,
the first meal, served in the dining room, consists of tea without milk,
bread, butter—not a strong point—sweet jam, "sharp" cheese, and olives.
Coffee is most likely to be the Turkish kind, to which milk is added at
considerable risk.

In many Turkish restaurants the dishes are on display, behind glass in
the better ones, on a counter in the others. You may even be called into
the kitchen to lift the lid off the pots and pans, and have a look inside—a
pleasant and practical way of choosing for foreigners among strange food.
However, for those who have to deal with a bill of fare, here is a list of
the most common dishes—by no means in a pejorative sense.

Basic Requirements

Bread	Ekmek	Meat	Et
Water	Su	Mutton	Koyun eti
Ice	Buz	Lamb	Kuzu eti
Fish	Balık	Beef	Siğir eti
Chicken	Piliç	Veal	Dana eti

Menu

Mezeler	*Hors d'oeuvres*
Arnavut ciğeri	Spiced fried liver with onions
Çerkes tavuğlu	Boiled chicken in walnut puree with red pepper
Çig köfte	Spiced fried meatballs
Lakerda	Salted slices of fish
Midye dolması	Stuffed mussels
Pastırma	Meat cured with garlic and other spices
Tarama	Fishroe salad
Turşu	Vegetable pickle
Yaprak dolması	Stuffed vineleaves

Çorbalar	*Soups*
Yayla çorbası	Yogurt soup
Dügün çorbası	Meat broth, egg yolk and lemon juice
Işkembe çorbası	Tripe soup with eggs

Izgaralar	*Grills*
Bonfile	Fillet steak
Döner kebap	Lamb grilled on a revolving spit
Pirzola	Lamb chop
Şiş kebap	Skewered pieces of meat broiled over charcoal

Pilavlar	*Pilafs*
Sade pilav	Plain rice pilaf
Iç pilav	Rice with pine nuts, currants and onions
Bulgur pilavı	Cracked wheat pilaf

Zeytinyağlılar	*Vegetables in olive oil*
Imam bayıldı	Eggplant slices with layers of onion and tomato
Kabak kızartması	Fried marrow slices with yogurt
Patlıcan kızartması	Fried eggplant slices with yogurt
Zeytinyağlı fasulye	Green beans in tomato sauce
Börekler	*Savory pastries*
Sigara böregi	Fried filo pastry stuffed with cheese
Su böreği	Baked filo pastry with cheese or meat stuffing
Talaş böregi	Puff pastry stuffed with meat
Salatalar	*Salads*
Cacik	Chopped cucumber in garlic-flavored yogurt
Çoban salatası	Mixed cucumber, onion, pepper and tomato salad
Patlıcan salatası	Mashed eggplant with pepper and onion
Piyaz	Haricot bean salad
Tatlılar	*Desserts*
Baklava	Flaky pastry stuffed with nuts in syrup
Sütlaç	Creamy cold rice pudding
Tel kadayıf	Shredded wheat stuffed with nuts in syrup
Dondurma	Ice cream
Komposto	Cold stewed fruit

Vine leaves and Nightingale's Nests

A big meal starts usually with a glass of *raki,* a colorless distillation of grape mash flavored with aniseed. It is usual to add water, which turns it a cloudy white. Raki is always accompanied by *mezeler* (tidbits) and sometimes by *hors d'oeuvres*. This is followed by the main course. Meat is usually eaten alone, more often than not cut up into small pieces; grilled as kebab served on its own; cooked in tomato sauce topped with a liberal helping of yogurt. Salad is served apart. Last come the pastry and tea or coffee.

Here are two recommended meals:

1) Begin with a *dolma. Dolmak* means "to stuff," and the *yalancı dolma* is a vine-leaf stuffed with rice and herbs and cooked in oil. Then, *hünkar begend,* literally "His Majesty liked it," lamb stewed with chopped aubergine; followed by *bülbül yuvası* "nightingale's nest," flaky pastry stuffed with pistachios, shaped like a nest.

2) *Tarhana* is a vegetable soup with flour and yogurt. For the main dish try *kılıç şiş,* bits of swordfish broiled with bayleaves and onion on a spit. For dessert, a *zerde,* rice pudding with saffron, and a *kavun,* melon.

It will all be a great change from the dull meals served in the so-called international restaurant. If you wish to taste real Turkish cooking, go to one of the few restaurants recommended in this book or to any of the obscure cheaper places, the ordinary *lokanta*.

To drink, you have water in capped bottles, *maden suyu* (mineral water), and *meyva suyu* (fruit juice). Very popular and refreshing is *ayran* (yogurt thinned with water). *Bira* (beer) is *Efes* and *Tuborg* (light lager). Turkish wines, red (*kırmız şarap*) or white *(beyaz şarap)* whether from Tekirdağ, from around Izmir, or from Anatolia, are palatable. A few names: *Doluca, Kavak, Kulüp, Marmara, Trakya* (dry white); *Buzbağ, Dikmen, Yakut* (full red), *Lâl* (rosé). The *Kavaklidere* champagne is sickeningly sweet and not worth even its cheap price. Soft drinks include *Fruko,* a kind of bitter lemon, and the ubiquitous Coke and Pepsi. The traditional *şerbet,* a cooled sweet fruit drink which as sorbet became a water-ice in the West, has largely been relegated to street vendors, as also *simit,* rings of bread sprinkled with sesame seeds.

Fruit is best chosen from the market stalls, centrally situated in smaller towns and scattered throughout the bigger ones. Almonds, hazelnuts, chick-peas, peanuts, pistachios and roasted marrow seeds are all sold from carts or tiny stalls.

The famed Turkish coffee, *kahve,* finely powdered, boiled to a froth in a brass pot—with a lot of sugar, *şekerli;* medium, *orta şekerli;* little sugar, *az şekerli;* or without sugar, *sade*—is more expensive than tea. All other kinds of coffee are the preserve of the pricier establishments. To be on the safe side, take a can of instant coffee, which is also the most appreciated present for Turkish friends.

During the last war, tea bushes were planted on the Black Sea coast, where there is both hot sun and plenty of rain. Cay (tea) is everywhere served in glasses, with sugar and sometimes with lemon, never with milk.

Raki (87 proof) made from distilled grapes with aniseed, is the national alcoholic beverage; the State Monopoly, Tekel, also produces brandy *(konyak),* gin, *viski* and vodka. Schweppes or local brands of tonic water will go with your gin, sparkling Kızılay (Red Crescent) Karahisar mineral water with whiskey. Local liqueurs, all exceedingly sweet, include a pink concoction made from rose petals (about 50 proof) and *Mersin,* a clear liqueur made from oranges (about 70 proof).

EXPLORING
TURKEY

ISTANBUL

Capital of Empires

Once upon a time, this city was a rival of Rome: as the star of one city sank that of the other rose. Commanding the narrow straits between Europe and Asia, Byzantion was the key to the gateways between east and west. A melting pot of countless nationalities as capital of the Eastern Roman Empire, it was only after the Moslem conquest that the population became sharply divided on religious lines into Turks, Greeks, Armenians and Jews. Racial intermarriages, often with western Christians, produced the superficially Europeanized, cosmopolitan Levantines who dominated trade but were despised by the "pure" races.

Stripped of political power, Istanbul has remained a great port and the commercial capital, as well as becoming the main industrial center of Turkey. Factories have spread along the approaches on the European side right to the crumbling city walls, into which gaping holes have been torn to allow for the flow of traffic to the airport on wide but featureless avenues; industries are also encroaching on the Asiatic shore, contributing to the prosperity and pollution but hardly the beauty of the town, whose site the 19th-century traveler Alexander von Humbold ranked second only to that of Rio de Janeiro. Inevitably progress was achieved at the expense of the idyllic countryside where shepherds grazed their flocks below the ramparts a mere 50 years ago. Though the glory that was Constantinople is faded, the innumerable mosques, palaces, churches and fortifications still combine in an unique and unforgettable setting.

The City State

In about 660 B.C., surprisingly late in the Greek colonizing race, Byzas anchored his ship of Megarian emigrants in the haven of a deep inlet and founded the town which bears his name: Byzantion. Consulted about the site of the new colony, the Delphic oracle indicated "opposite the country of the blind," which Byzas rightly interpreted to mean the European entrance to the Bosphorus, opposite Chalcedon, whose earlier Megarian settlers had been blinded by the fertility of the Asian shore. The splendid natural harbor of the Golden Horn brought about a far greater commercial prosperity, with its inevitable outcome: the greed of neighbors. The Persian king Darius having taken it by force of arms, the Spartan regent, Pausanias, "liberated" it in 478 B.C., only to enter into treasonable negotiations with Darius' successor Xerxes till driven out by the Athenians. Independent once again, Byzantion held out against Philip of Macedonia—father of Alexander the Great—and against the Gauls.

The sign of the Crescent dates from these battles—it was the light of the moon that betrayed Philip's movements to the besieged townsmen.

As to the war with the wild Gallic hordes, it ended in a commercial agreement—tribute from Byzantion, to be levied by payment for each crossing of the straits, following the example set by Troy at the Dardanelles some thousand years earlier and revived 2,000 years later on the Bosphorus bridge.

Weakened by unceasing warfare against invaders, Byzantion fell at last to the Roman legions. Because of its unique but precarious position on a triangular promontory bounded on the south by the Sea of Marmara and on the north by the navigable Golden Horn, expanding Roman Byzantium prospered in the long centuries of the Pax Romana. But in the struggle for the empire between Priscennius Niger and Septimius Severus, having backed the former, Byzantium was taken after a long and bloody siege, to be severely chastized by Severus in 196. The first Roman emperor born outside Europe rebuilt Byzantium on a grander scale, but it was sacked again by Galienus in 208, though it successfully resisted a Gothic invasion two years later.

Imperial Capital I

After defeating the rival emperor Licinius at nearby Chrysopolis, Constantine (soon to become the Great) chose this incomparable base for operations on the Danube as well as the Euphrates for his Eastern capital in 324. Six years later, on May 11, 330, Nea Roma was officially inaugurated, after the imposing new palace and public buildings had been adorned with the architectural plunder from the Greek sanctuaries. To the prestigious geographical position the sole Emperor of the East and West added a new ingredient that bound together the heterogeneous population for over 11 centuries. Though only baptized just before his death in 337, Constantine made Christianity the state religion and planned Constantinople as a Christian capital, with the splendor of the first Church of St. Sophia (Holy Wisdom) overshadowing even the imperial Sacred Palace.

The transition from Neo-Platonic paganism to Christianity and from deified emperor to vicar of God upon earth was gradual and smoother than might have been expected. Constantine was firm in his theocratic attitude and insisted on being the regent of the Church. At the opening of the Hippodrome, a statue of Apollo, transformed into a likeness of Constantine, was carried by legionaries dressed neutrally in white, signifying Christian or pagan holiness. The emperor and his court continued to wear Roman fashions, although their dress became increasingly priestly. The scarlet boots embroidered with golden eagles which Diocletian had worn as a demi-god were of the same pattern as those by which the last of the Byzantine emperors was recognized under the walls of Theodosius among the heaps of corpses in 1453.

In the safety of these walls, able soldier emperors succeeded in withstanding the waves of barbarian onslaughts during the 5th and 6th centuries, while their western colleagues succumbed. Justinian I (527–63) briefly seemed to realize the never-abandoned dream of imperial reconquest. But within the walls rose an even greater danger when religious fanatics identified themselves with sports fans: the Orthodox and the Monophysites (believers in the single nature of Christ) with the Greens and the Blues, supporters of the main chariot racing clubs. In 532 the Nika Insurrection spread from the Hippodrome over the whole town, which was sacked and burnt to the gates of the Sacred Palace. The Empress Theodora (daughter of a bearkeeper in the Hippodrome, where she had herself performed as a girl) courageously declared that "who has borne the purple must be ready to die in the purple" and refused to flee. The mob was finally put down with ruthless slaughter, and the city was rebuilt more magnificently than before at ruinous cost to the imperial treasury.

However bloodstained, this was the golden age and the true beginning of the Byzantine Empire. Despite the temporary occupation of Italy, New Rome substituted Greek for Latin as the official language, and changed from the earlier Latin Codex Justinianus to the Greek Pandektae: Justinian is best remembered as a great legislator who had enormous influence on law in the Middle Ages. Even at the height of imperial power, however, Constantinople was attacked by yet another barbarian tribe, and from then on, it was harassed relentlessly by Asiatic hordes, and by the Persians and the Arabs, whose early raiding expeditions developed into regular sieges throughout the later 7th century. A new weapon, Greek fire, based on gasoline, saved the city, but its secret eventually became known to the enemy.

The Envy of the World

Hardly had the last Arab incursion been repulsed and the destruction wrought by the Ikonoklasts been healed, when for a change the Rus, a Viking tribe which gave its name to the Russians, attacked Constantinople in 860. Described by the Patriarch Photios as "a thick, sudden hailstorm of barbarians," they came again in 941 and 1043. Though they never succeeded in penetrating the defences, their martial bearing impressed the emperors sufficiently for them to have a bodyguard of Vikings, the Varangian Guard, who played a considerable part until the Frankish occupation. The Bulgars waited a hundred years after their first assault in 813, while in 1090 the Pechenegs, a particularly dreaded Turkish tribe, made their most unwelcome appearance from the Balkans.

Few towns ever faced a deadlier mix of would-be conquerors, but then the Queen of Cities was the most glittering prize of the Middle Ages, un-

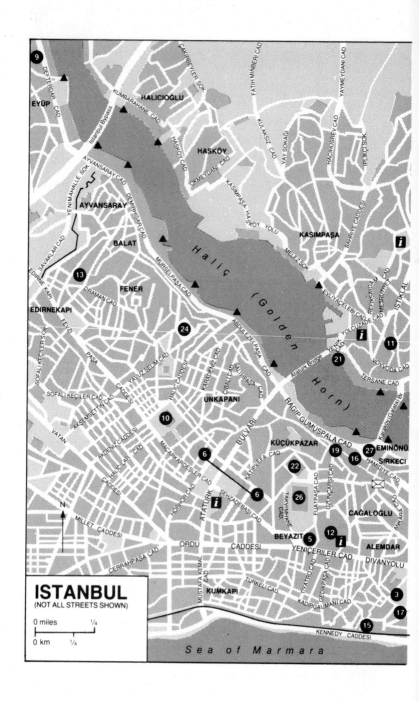

ISTANBUL
(NOT ALL STREETS SHOWN)

0 miles   ¼

0 km   ¼

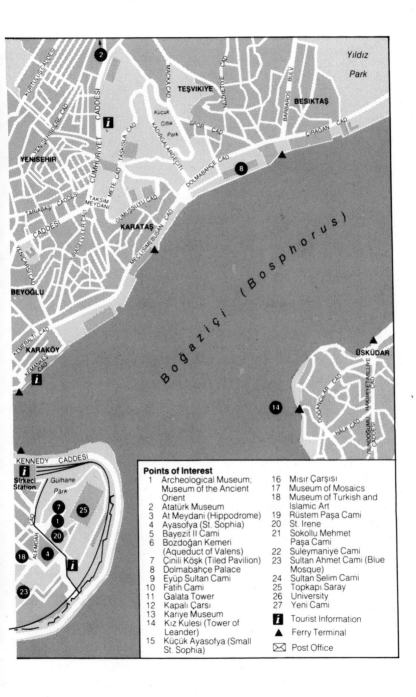

Points of Interest

1. Archeological Museum; Museum of the Ancient Orient
2. Atatürk Museum
3. At Meydani (Hippodrome)
4. Ayasofya (St. Sophia)
5. Bayezit II Cami
6. Bozdoğan Kemeri (Aqueduct of Valens)
7. Çinili Köşk (Tiled Pavilion)
8. Dolmabahçe Palace
9. Eyüp Sultan Cami
10. Fatih Cami
11. Galata Tower
12. Kapalı Çarsı
13. Kariye Museum
14. Kız Kulesi (Tower of Leander)
15. Küçük Ayasofya (Small St. Sophia)
16. Mısır Çarşısı
17. Museum of Mosaics
18. Museum of Turkish and Islamic Art
19. Rüstem Paşa Cami
20. St. Irene
21. Sokollu Mehmet Paşa Cami
22. Suleymaniye Cami
23. Sultan Ahmet Cami (Blue Mosque)
24. Sultan Selim Cami
25. Topkapı Saray
26. University
27. Yeni Cami

i Tourist Information
▲ Ferry Terminal
✉ Post Office

equalled in Christian lands and even more splendid than the Caliphs' Baghdad and Cordova. The ten percent levied on goods coming or going between the Bosphorus and the Dardanelles provided a good steady income, supplemented from the east-west routes of Asia. From the 6th century on, the Persians disrupted travel on the Silk Road from China to Constantinople, while the alternative sea route through the Persian Gulf or the Red Sea was cut off by the Arabs some hundred years later, but not before two monks had brought eggs and the secret of the silkworms in a hollow bamboo from China. Justinian's factory within the palace walls continued to be supplied with the most precious of all Byzantine raw materials for the government silk-weaving monopoly, whose brocades were the highest-prized materials known to the west, used by emperors and kings. A surviving example is Charlemagne's robes in Vienna. Another, increasing, revenue collected was the ten percent duty on slaves carried first in Byzantine and later in Italian ships from Russia and Bulgaria to Europe.

The revival under the Macedonian dynasty (867–1056) regilded the somewhat tarnished prestige of the Empire: the reign of Constantine VII Porphyrogenitos (913–59) was a second golden age. The most scholarly of emperors, he ascended the throne at the age of seven, but assumed the reins of government only a few years before his death. This gave him ample time to write *De Administrando Imperio,* which contained a wealth of information about the Avars, Bulgars and Persians, as well as *De Ceremoniis Aulae Byzantinae,* a detailed description of the elaborate ceremonies of the Byzantine court, where appearance increasingly replaced the substance of power. But the flowering of the arts of peace led eventually to a decline in the arts of war. The extraordinary beauty, pageantry and wealth of Constantinople excited the greed of every adventurer in the known world.

God was sumptuously served in magnificent churches, while Byzantine Orthodoxy decreed that His vicar was surrounded by appropriate pomp. Constantine's Sacred Palace was enlarged and embellished by successive emperors, till the imperial residence covered one tenth of the capital. Four battalions of the imperial guard were quartered in the Brazen House, named after its roof of brass tiles, to protect the throneroom, the state banqueting halls and the state prison. Government business was transacted in the Daphne Palace, connected by a colonnade with the imperial box in the Hippodrome that ran parallel with the palace grounds. The sovereign's sleeping quarters were in the Sigma Palace. These buildings, as well as the residence of the eunuchs occupied in the civil service, were of white, yellow, red or green marble, while a small square palace with a pyramidal roof was of purple-specked marble. Here the empress had to give birth, so that the children could be said to be "born in the purple." Mechanical gold toys, life-sized lions that roared, birds singing on golden trees, and peacocks displaying their tails awed western ambassadors no less than the superb oriental ceremonial.

Soldier-emperors tended to escape from the rigid confinement of this huge complex, with its churches, halls and gardens, which was not in keeping with the need for mobility required to defend the shrinking frontiers. Nor were the diminishing imperial revenues sufficient for the upkeep. Alexios I Komnenos (1081–1118) built the Palace of Blachernae, overlooking the Golden Horn and the city, close to the ramparts to communicate easily with the troops encamped beyond or to enjoy a day's hunting in the open country. One year after his accession, surrounded by enemies within and without, the Emperor allowed Venice to trade free of all customs' dues throughout his domains and conceded warehouses and three quays on the Golden Horn. An inevitable move to strengthen the Empire against the Sicilian Normans, the treaty led to a critical loss of much-needed revenues and an increasing reliance on foreign shipping.

But Alexios displayed brilliant diplomacy in dealing with the People's Crusade in 1096, inviting its leader, Peter the Hermit, to court, while ferrying the plundering rabble speedily across the Bosphorus. He followed the same tactic with the truculent lords of the First Crusade three years later. Similarly, his grandson Manuel I (1143–80) faced the rapacious Germans of Konrad III and the French of Louis VII the Pious out to plunder Constantinople during the Second Crusade in 1147. After the German king had lost his army and his health, he let himself be charmed by the Emperor into an alliance against the Normans. Yet whether the crusaders returned with tales of Byzantine treachery or wealth, they equally inflamed Latin hatred and greed.

At the death of Manuel I, his widow assumed the regency for her son, Alexios II, aged 11. But the Empress-Mother was a Latin from Antioch, disliked by the Konstantinopolitans, who massacred all the Latins in the capital two years later. Manuel's brilliant but unreliable cousin was recalled from exile in Pontus to become joint Emperor. Andronikos I forced the boy to sign the death warrant of his mother, only to be murdered himself two months later. Andronikos at the age of 62 married Alexios' widow, the 12-year-old Agnes of France. In an atmosphere of suspicion, danger and repression, nobles, merchants and simple artisans alike were blinded or sent to the scaffold. Revolt broke out when the Emperor's elderly and inoffensive cousin, Isaak Angelos, escaped from prison and appealed from the altar of St. Sophia for help. Andronikos, deserted by his bodyguard, was captured by the mob and paraded round the city on a mangy camel, then tortured and torn to death in the hippodrome. Isaak II was proclaimed Emperor, but he was utterly ineffectual and under the Angeli the Empire became a third-rate power.

Yet another respite came when Emperor Frederick I Barbarossa resisted suggestions that he attack the "City of the Wily Greeks" and instead crossed the Dardanelles with the German contingent of the Third Crusade in 1190, while Philip II of France and Richard the Lionheart of England sailed from Sicily to the Holy Land.

A Surfeit of Alexios

The Fourth Crusade chartered the Venetian fleet to transport 20,000 men and their horses to Egypt, but the enormous fee of 80,000 francs could never be found. The Doge of Venice, Byron's

Blind old Dandolo

Th'octogenerian chief, Byzantium's conquering foe,

was, therefore, able to divert the fleet to Constantinople, where Isaak II had been deposed, blinded and imprisoned by his brother, Alexios III. Isaak's son, another Alexios, rushed for help to Venice and promised not only to pay for the Crusade, but also to reunite the two Churches. A first attack in 1203 failed, but Alexios III fled, while Isaak and Alexios IV were proclaimed joint Emperors. But the father was senile, the son presumptuous, and Enrico Dandolo foretold his fate: "You stupid youth, we pulled you out of the dung and we'll soon put you back there." Strong words to an emperor, which contributed to the Protovestiarios (Grand Chamberlain), Alexios III's son-in-law, heading a nationalist counterrevolution of the Orthodox party. Isaak II died, perhaps even from natural causes, Alexios IV was strangled in his palace, the chamberlain was crowned Alexios V and given the epithet Murzuphlos (He of the Bushy Eyebrows) to distinguish him in those hectic days. He attempted to repair the walls, but the mob preferred to destroy Phidias' great statue of Athena which Constantine the Great had shipped from Athens and placed on the Forum; the goddess was facing west and seemed to be beckoning to the invaders. Incited by Dandolo, the Crusaders stormed Constantinople in Holy Week 1204, the defense collapsed, Alexios V fled to his father-in-law in Thrace, while his brother-in-law, Theodore Laskaris, escaped with the Orthodox Patriarch to Nikaea to continue the Byzantine Empire in exile.

For three days the Queen of Cities was subject to pillage and rape on a scale unparalleled in history. Only the Venetians looted systematically, but even the French booty was a staggering seven times the annual revenue of England. Dandolo declined the imperial throne, but obtained for Venice an island empire in the Aegean plus three-eighths of Constantinople, comprising St. Sophia where Baldwin of Flanders was crowned Latin Emperor by the Latin Patriarch—always a Venetian. From the despoilt Blachernae Palace, shadowy emperors tried in vain to impose their suzerainty on the barons who had shared out the empire into feudal principalities.

Having lost his Kingdom of Jerusalem to his son-in-law, Frederick II of Germany, John de Brienne became in 1228 regent for Baldwin II to whom he married his four-year-old daughter. In the declining Roman Empire one ruler had occasionally fathered the emperors of the East and West, but never before had there been one father-in-law of both. For good measure, John became joint Emperor till his death in 1237, well in his 90s. But not even bizarre marriage alliances could save Latin rule, though titular Latin emperors and heiresses haunted European courts for centuries.

In 1261, Michael VIII Palaeologos, the Byzantine Emperor of Nikaea, recaptured Constantinople without resistance, or at least what was left of it. To neutralize the Venetians, he signed a treaty, similar to the one concluded in 1082, with their Genoese rivals conceding freedom from customs and a commercial quarter at Galata. At the expense of further concessions, he played off the two maritime powers against one another. He gained time, but the Byzantine merchants were swept off their own seas and there could be no financial recovery in sight.

His dynasty valiantly defended the Empire against enemies on all sides. Some rebuilding of the capital was accomplished, but by the middle of the 14th century there was no more money, only decay, ruins and vacant grounds. After the annihilation of the last crusade at Nikopolis in 1396, Bayezit I was closing in on Constantinople, which was given yet another miraculous breathing-space by the Sultan's defeat at the hands of Tamerlane before Ankara. Provoked by the support given to an Osmanli pretender, Murat II laid siege in 1422, but once more the Sultan was called away by troubles in Anatolia.

In 1449 Constantine XI Dragases, who had governed the last Byzantine possessions in the Peloponnese, succeeded his father as emperor. In a desperate appeal to the Christian rulers, he proclaimed in 1452 the Union of the Eastern and Western Churches, but this raised such a storm of protest that one of the highest imperial officers openly declared that he preferred the green flag of the Prophet to the Latin Cross on St. Sophia. He did not have to wait for long. Mehmet II blockaded the Bosphorus, from which he hauled his fleet overland into the Golden Horn. The Turkish artillery, organized by Christian renegades, pounded the thinly-manned walls in preparation for the final assault on the gate of St. Romanus at dawn on May 29. Despite heroic resistance, in which the Emperor was killed, the Janissaries broke through the breaches. At noon the Sultan rode with his suite to St. Sophia and commanded the muezzin's call to prayer. The imperial double-headed eagle was replaced by the Crescent of old Byzantion, to which he added his star that had led him to glory. Mehmet had earned his title of Fatih (Conqueror) and Constantinople became officially Istanbul, though in the West it was referred to by its previous name till well into the present century.

Imperial Capital II

Once the town was taken, Islam showed more mercy in victory than Christianity, though cynics might say that poverty and depopulation had greatly reduced the temptation. The Greek Patriarch, who was moved from St. Sophia to the Church of the Pammakaristos Virgin, represented the Orthodox subjects, and the *rayas,* the conquered, Christians and Jews, were free to practise their religions. Moslems from Anatolia, Christians from the Balkans flocked to the great city, and to them were added Jews and Moors chased from Spain in 1492.

After the capital had been transferred from Edirne in 1457, Istanbul enjoyed its first prolonged period of peaceful growth since the Pax Romana, interrupted only by natural disasters, earthquakes, fires and pestilence. Spiritual and temporal power were reunited in 1518, when Sultan Selim I also became Caliph, Commander of the Faithful. The reign of his son, Süleyman the Magnificent (1520–66) saw the city's transformation into the Islamic capital of a world empire, with the building of mosques, palaces, charitable foundations and fountains. This imposing architecture fittingly expressed the victorious expansion to give way, once the zenith was passed, to the graceful elegance of the Tulip Reign of Ahmet III (1703–30), in turn followed by a strong Baroque influence.

By then the Janissaries, encamped before the Topkapı Palace, were making, unmaking and murdering the sultans, and looting and burning in the town. After the assassination of Selim III in the harem in 1808, the Tanzimat (Era of Internal Reform) was prepared by his cousin, Mahmut II (1809–39), but started only after the Sultan had ordered the massacre of these obstreperous pretorians in the same hippodrome that in 1,600 years had witnessed so many incidents that changed history. The first bridge over the Golden Horn was opened by Abdül Mecit in 1838; public utilities were introduced later in the century, the railroad was begun in 1870, and the tunnel from Galata to Pera opened three years later.

In 1908 the Young Turks led the army from Europe into the town, and the following year the last absolute sultan, Abdül Hamid II, was dethroned. In 1912, the Bulgars nearly captured Istanbul, which was blockaded throughout World War I.

Decline and Resurgence

The government of Mehmet VI underestimated the strength of the national resistance and the capital became divorced from the country. The Grand National Assembly in Ankara abolished the sultanate, and history once again neatly tied up the ends when the namesake of the Conqueror left the capital on a British warship in 1922. The last caliph lingered in the deserted Dolmabahçe Palace till the following year, but the Republican government moved to Ankara.

Atatürk's distrust of cosmopolitan Istanbul led to a temporary decline accentuated by the demolition of large sections of the old town to make way for broad, featureless avenues. But the unique position on the maritime and overland crossroads of East and West, North and South, guaranteed a quick revival that, if anything, has gone too far, too fast. Since the 1950s vast suburbs have sprung up especially along and across the Bosphorus, and form the least attractive addition to the pageant of styles and architectures.

EXPLORING ISTANBUL

Most of Greater Istanbul's six million inhabitants live in Europe: in the old town, roughly corresponding to medieval Constantinople and still hemmed in by mighty walls, partially restored, and in the new town, whose featureless suburbs spread ever wider towards and along the Bosphorus. Between them lies the Haliç (Canal), crossed by the bridges of Galata, of Atatürk and, higher up, near Eyüp, the bridge of the Istanbul bypass. The deep drowned valley has been known throughout history more poetically, as the Golden Horn as it is shaped like a deer's horn and certainly has earned vast amounts of gold from the safe anchorage. A massive regilding was furnished when two ships, reputedly full of gold, were sunk during the siege of 1453. But the refusal of Abdül Hamid II, not at all averse to gold whatever its provenance, to allow salvage operations, makes this a doubtful story. It should, however, be soon resolved by the clean-up of the Horn.

The Bosphorus winds between green banks from the Sea of Marmara 30 km. (19 miles) north to the Black Sea. The closest Asian suburbs are Üsküdar (the Scutari of the Crimean War, where Florence Nightingale revolutionized nursing in the notorious hospital which still serves as a barracks; the actual lamp that earned her the title of "Lady of the Lamp" is preserved in an alcove of her room open to the public) and Kadiköy, built on the site of Chalkedon (Chalcedon), which was sufficiently important in Roman times to host the Fourth Ecumenical Council in 451.

For a sweeping view over all Istanbul, cross the Bosphorus by Europe's largest suspension bridge, the only one to connect two continents. Opened in 1973 for the 50th anniversary of the Republic, the bridge was crossed by almost 34 million cars in the first 28 months, paying off the entire building in tolls. Privatized in 1984, it is insufficient for the constantly increasing traffic, and a second bridge from Rumeli Hisar to Anadolu Hisar was due to open in 1988. The view from the heights of Çamlıca ("Pines of the Hot Springs"), recently restored as a pleasure park, is unequaled. Above the huge square of Üsküdar rises the tall Iskele (Landing Stage) Cami, built by the great architect Sinan in 1547 for the daughter of Süleyman I. Early in the morning, a soft mist shrouds the Bosphorus, but the waterways are already crowded, and the big ferry-boats nose their way through the jostling *kayiks*. These are odd-looking craft: flat and wide, they taper inwards at both ends, the stern and stem turning sharply upwards; the gunwale almost forms a half-moon.

Adding to the noise and bustle, a crowd of fishermen throng around the harbor, picking up the flotsam thrown overboard to use as bait. The main catch in the Bosphorus is the striped tunny; gutted, boned, and left to soak in salt, it becomes the *lakerda*, a dish much appreciated by lovers of good food. There is also plenty of mullet. The roe, dried, pressed, and preserved in a thin skin of wax, is held by many to be better than caviar.

At sundown, all the day's catch is spread out for sale on the wharf below the Galata Bridge, sometimes on an old newspaper, more often on the very stones. The bargaining begins; prices go down with the sun, and the poorer buyers wait patiently until the fish is within their means.

The Pilgrimage to Eyüp

The outstanding sights are concentrated on the blunt promontory that juts out between the Sea of Marmara and the Golden Horn. For a splendid silhouetted view of these famous monuments visit the café on an eminence above the Golden Horn at Eyüp, where Pierre Loti—who captured the unique atmosphere of the declining imperial city in his novels—used to sit and gaze upon the wondrous city. Boats leave from Eminonu.

The Golden Horn was not only a safe port, but also the playground of emperors and caliphs, whose gilded pleasure craft conveyed the court to outings in the open country at the headwater. Industrialization transformed it into an open sewer, into which factories, shipyards and a slaughterhouse were spewing filth. In 1984, the newly elected mayor promised to make the black muck as blue as his eyes, and against tremendous odds and assisted by a loan from the World Bank he seems near success. On the cleared banks, parks and playgrounds have been laid out, several summer pavilions of the sultans and a 19th-century Bulgarian church have been renovated, and the Eyüp mosque complex can again be fully appreciated. Eventually, the foul slough will be pumped out to be replaced by fresh water from the Bosphorus. The stench that kept tourists away has lifted, and it is again possible to enjoy the splendid view over the tangle of streets, houses, and hills pierced by the sharp spires of countless minarets. Istanbul has about 450 mosques, each surmounted by from one to four minarets, only the Blue Mosque, unique in the world, has six: at least a thousand needles pricking the unruffled blue sky.

In the first Arab siege of Byzantium, in 669, the standard-bearer and friend of Mohammed fell in battle. His name was Eyüp-ul-Ensari Halit bin Zeyd, and he was buried on the battlefield. During the siege of the city in 1453, the location of his tomb was revealed to the Sultan in a dream. Mehmet at once gave orders to unearth it, and the dream was found true. The Conqueror then ordered a tomb and a mosque to be built over the burial-ground. It soon became a place of worship and pilgrimage for all Islam.

Built in 1458, enlarged by Murat III towards the end of the 15th century, the mosque, shaken loose and cracked open by earthquakes, was torn down and rebuilt in 1798. Up to the present day, it is still a focus of Moslem piety. Here, the caliph came in great pomp to gird the sword of Osman, founder of the Osmanli dynasty, a sword that was the symbol of the caliphate.

Only a few old wooden houses have resisted the encroaching featureless cement. At the door of the all-white mosque, you are offered water, held to be good for the health of body and soul. Inside is a vast paved courtyard, teeming with devout humanity. Inside the second courtyard there is a huge tree, surrounded by an enormous railing. The inner walls are covered all around with magnificent glazed tiles, with red and sometimes yellowish designs on a blue ground. There are storks and pigeons. But what most catches the visitor's eye is the long row of faithful come to beg a favor at Eyüp's tomb. One by one, they stop in front of the Window of Help where, strangely enough, the star of David stands out on the highly-worked brass lattice. Under the archways, merchants sell their wares, and crowds of people come and go. But at the door, where visitors take off their shoes, all is quiet. A heavy curtain falls between the mosque and the outside world. Inside it is all white, with the usual writings of Koranic prayer. The prayer-rug is blue, worked in blue. Along the walls runs a design, also in mingled blues. Everywhere, withdrawn and open to God alone, men and women pray in the rapt inwardness of the faithful. The mosque is surrounded by small graveyards and lonely türbes, marking an underground maze of the dead.

An Islamic Masterpiece

The Sultan Ahmet Cami, better known as the Blue Mosque, is the centerpiece of a concentrated sightseeing tour. To the northeast lies St. Sophia and, farther on, the Topkapı Palace, with the church of St. Irene between the two. To the southwest, Küçük Ayasofya (Small St. Sophia). To the west the hippodrome and, facing the obelisk is the Museum of Turkish and Islamic Art in the restored Ibrahim Paşa Palace; a little higher up is the cistern of Yerebatan, the Sunken Palace. To the southeast is the Museum of Mosaics. The main sights are, therefore, all at Eminönü in the old town, within walking distance.

Alone of all mosques, the Blue Mosque boasts six minarets. In spite of its immoderate size, its proportions are admirable. The architect was Mehmet Ağă, who built it by order of Sultan Ahmet I in seven years, beginning in 1609. The blue glazed tiles that cover the inside walls have given it its name. Many art critics place it higher than St. Sophia; it is certainly the masterpiece of Turkish architecture, together with the Süleymaniye Cami and the Sultan Selim Cami in Edirne.

The center dome—33 meters (109 ft.) wide, almost 5 meters (15 ft.) wider than that of St. Sophia—rests together with the smaller domes and half-domes on four massive pillars, 4½ meters (15 ft.) thick. The blue glazed tiles shine in the daylight, itself tinged with blue as it floods through the 260 stained-glass windows, unfortunately only copies as the originals were shattered in an earthquake. On the floor is a very fine carpet, on which are scattered beautiful old prayer-rugs. The vast courtyard is surrounded by columns. The nightly Sound and Light performances in summer are spectacular.

A Christian Masterpiece

The first St. Sophia was a basilica open to the Christian cult in 360. Destroyed by the conflagration which devastated the entire district in the Hippodrome riots of 532, St. Sophia was rebuilt within five years as Christendom's most magnificent church, adorned with gold mosaics and marbles from all parts of the Empire, under Justinian's personal supervision. On seeing the finished cathedral, the overjoyed Emperor cried out: "I am now greater than Solomon." However, the earthquakes of 553, 557 and 559 were so powerful that the dome caved in. The piers were reinforced by buttresses, the dome was raised and the second consecration took place in 562, still presided over by Justinian.

As if earthquakes were not enough, and they never ceased to cause damage, the Ikonoklasts destroyed all the splendid original mosaics, which were replaced, hardly less sumptuously, under the Macedonian dynasty. Looted by the Crusaders, who even removed the carved gilded bronze doors, the upkeep of the building strained resources in the Byzantine twilight. The church was in a bad condition and crammed with terrified worshippers when Mehmet the Conqueror entered and dismissed them home in safety. Repairs, but no structural changes, were speedily effected and even the name was only slightly Turkified. The brick minaret was added then, another more slender by Bayezit II and the two broader ones by Selim II. The mosaics were covered by Süleyman I who, not surprisingly, found them inappropriate. Most sultans contributed further embellishments, especially Mahmut I who renovated the gallery, built a beautiful library adorned with Iznik and Kütahya tiles as well as outstanding bronze lattice within, and a fountain, one of the masterpieces of Turkish 18th-century architecture, as well as a medrese and public kitchen outside. The last full-scale restoration was carried out between 1847 and 1849 by Abdül Mecit, whose monogram appears over the outer portal.

Atatürk demonstrated his secularism by turning St. Sophia into a museum. Murat IV's gilt calligraphic inscriptions bearing the titles of Allah, the names of the Prophet and the first four caliphs were taken down, leaving huge round marks. They were put back in the 1950s in recognition of Islamic sentiment, but St. Sophia remains a museum, visited by two popes, Paul VI and John Paul II. Only an annex, the Kasr-i-Humayun (Imperial Pavilion), became again a place of prayer in 1980, reserved for visiting Moslem dignitaries.

The big middle dome rests on two half-domes; the whole is an amazing feat of architecture. The church was dedicated to Agia Sophia (Holy Wisdom), and not to the saint who bore that name. The beautiful marblework round the entrance and the bronze doorframe (but not the panels) are original. The mosaics in the narthex are well preserved, depicting Constantine offering his new city and Justinian his new basilica to the Virgin.

Justinian beggared the Empire by lavishing the costliest materials: marble from Asia and Egypt, as well as columns from the ruins of Ephesus, on whose capitals the monogram of the Empress Theodora was engraved. The Weeping Column of porous stone draws water up from the cistern below. The water that oozes out is said to work miracles, especially in curing eye diseases; for wishes to come true you have to put your hand into a hole of the Sacred Column near the entrance.

The gold and silver throne, altar table, altar screens and wall panels, all studded with jewels, were looted by the Crusaders. All that is left is the description made by Paul of Silentium. The original mosaics were defaced by the Ikonoklasts in the 8th century, and the equally sumptuous mosaics of the Macedonian dynasty were plastered over by Mehmet the Conqueror; to top it all, an earthquake, in the 19th century, cracked open the walls, loosening the stonework. In 1932, a team of archeologists began uncovering the little that is left of the mosaics. Of the famous *Deisis* upstairs in the Women's Gallery (Gynecaeum), only the wonderfully expressive head of the Virgin, as well as parts of Christ and St. John the Baptist, remain. At the end of the gallery next to the great apsis, Christ stands between the Empress Zoe and Constantine Monomachos, the latter's likeness having been superimposed on Zoe's two previous husbands. The Virgin is surrounded by John II Komnenos, Irene and Alexios (12th century), while a rare portrait of the Macedonian Emperor Alexander (10th century) came to light on a pillar of the north gallery. On the south gallery a plain oblong slab indicates where the Doge Enrico Dandolo's sarcophagus stood in 1205, when he died in his 90s after making Venice an imperial power.

When the Moslems turned the church into a mosque, they of course replaced the furnishings of the Christian cult by their own. The *mihrab* (niche indicating direction of Mecca) is in the apse. The *mimber* (pulpit) and the platform for the choristers were put in later, by Murat III, who also brought from Pergamon the two great alabaster urns for ablutions. The baptistery became a türbe, and shelters the tomb of the sultans Mustafa I and Ibrahim. In the garden, among the fragments of columns, capitals, friezes and panels are the tombs of three more sultans—Murat III, Selim II and Mehmet III—as well as of several murdered princes.

Just behind St. Sophia, Mehmet III in 1478 constructed the Imperial Gate (Bab-ı-Humayun), which leads to St. Irene, one of Constantinople's earliest churches, built over a temple of Aphrodite. Enlarged by Constantine the Great, it housed the Second Ecumenical Council in 381. Burnt in the great fire of 532, St. Irene, too, was rebuilt by Justinian, second in size only to St. Sophia, to which it was joined by a group of buildings. The three-naved basilica surmounted by a dome suffered badly in the earthquake of 740. Restored by Leo the Isaurian, it was transformed into an arsenal after the Turkish conquest, as it stood close to the parade ground of the Janissaries. The degradation of Divine Peace (Irene means "peace" in Greek) for purposes of war was not yet over, as the arsenal later became the Artillery Museum. Old cannons still lie in front of the imposing brick building, restored for performances of the Istanbul Festival.

Restoration is proceeding apace in the historical Sultanahmet district, including the Sultan Hamam and the Sultan Mahmut I Library, with its mother-of-pearl encrusted tiles a fine example of Turkish decorative arts in 1736. At Meydani, the Hippodrome dating back to 203 holds a few monuments of more historical than artistic interest: a fountain offered by the German Kaiser Wilhelm II to Abdül-Hamid II; the obelisk of Thutmes III brought back from Egypt by Theodosius the Great—a monolith almost 20 meters (66 ft.) high, it was topped by a metal ball that rolled off in the earthquake of 865. The bronze Serpent Column originally commemorated the Greek victory over the Persians, at Apollo's shrine in Delphi. Brought some 800 years later to his new capital by Constantine the Great, the three serpent's heads disappeared in the 18th century and it has been somewhat battered by time, from 8 meters (26 ft.) down to less than 2 meters (6 ft.). A second obelisk, once 30 meters (over 97 ft.) high, is now broken into bits; the 10th-century gilt metal sheath was melted down by the Crusaders. The superb quadriga of golden horses once above the imperial box now adorns St. Mark's in Venice. The Museum of Turkish and Islamic Art in the Ibrahim Paşa Palace displays illuminated Korans, miniatures and prayer rugs beside the manuscripts and books from Mahmut I's library in St. Sophia.

Küçük Ayasofya (Small St. Sophia) is beyond the Blue Mosque, on the southern shore of Istanbul. This church, dedicated to the saints Sergius and Bacchus, was built in 550 by Justinian. It experienced the same fate as its neighbors, and was converted into a mosque.

The only remains of the Roman imperial palace, the stables, were sufficiently rebuilt to house the Museum of Mosaics, preserving in situ the most important nonreligious mosaics in town. The small colored stones from pictures from mythology, nymphs and griffins and hunting-scenes, embellished with birds and fruit. Scholars are at odds over the age of this workmanship; some date it back to Theodosius II, some to Justinian II, any time from the beginning of the 5th to the end of the 7th century.

Topkapı Saray

The triangle of land between the Bosphorus and the Sea of Marmara was the site of Constantine's Sacred Palace, which remained unparalleled in Christendom for 800 years. But with the decline of the empire's fortune, the Komneni became unable to maintain the splendor of earlier dynasties and withdrew to the much more modest Blachernae Palace, higher up the Golden Horn. Plundered by the Latins, the Sacred Palace and its no less magnificent dependencies were a sad ruin by the time of the Turkish conquest. Mehmet II chose for his first palace the site of the present university, but he soon moved his residence higher up, where once the Byzantine arsenal had stood and a battery still fired the imperial salute. Hence the name Topkapı ("Gate of the Cannon"). He began to build in 1462 with the construction of a double rampart and the first kiosks, to which subsequent sultans added ever-more-elaborate architectural fantasies, till a bewildering conglomeration of buildings extended over four vast courtyards. Turkish conservatism perpetuated the tents of the nomadic past in stone and resisted the imperial tradition of huge palaces till the middle of the 19th century, when Dolmabahçe rose across the Golden Horn. Only once thereafter did a sultan return to the blood-stained Topkapı—in 1876, Abdül Aziz was detained in one of the pavilions before committing suicide.

St. Irene stands in the vast outer courtyard, the Court of the Janissaries. Close by is the former Mint (Darphane); in the shade of the plane trees, the turbulent Janissaries prepared their meals and indicated their discontent by overturning the soup-kettles, a dreaded protest followed several times by the murder of the reigning sultan.

A lane to the left descends to the Archeological Museum, which houses one of the finest collections of Greek, Hellenistic and Roman antiquities, including finds from Ephesus, Miletus, Sidon, Troy and numerous other ancient sites. Outstanding in the remarkable collection of sarcophagi is a perfectly preserved masterpiece of white marble, that of the King of Sidon, a vassal of Alexander the Great, whose coffin it erroneously was supposed to be, as the relief depicts Alexander's hunt. The adjoining Museum of the Ancient Orient accommodates Sumerian, Babylonian, and especially Hittite treasures. Opposite is the Çinili Köşk (Tiled Pavilion), the Conqueror's summer kiosk, Istanbul's oldest secular Osmanli building, covered with superb green and blue tiles, and appropriately housing a collection of Seljuk and Osmanli ceramics.

The Gülhane Park extends below the encircling wall, which is topped by a small pavilion, now containing an uninspiring ethnographical collection, from which the sultans could without being seen watch ambassadors and dignitaries entering the Bab-ı-Âli (Sublime Gate), the name by which the Osmanli government was known for centuries. The rococo gate was until 1923 the entrance to the Grand Vizir's palace, which, though partly destroyed in 1911, houses the provincial administration.

Back among the Janissaries' plane trees, the road stops at the ticket office in the Bab-ı-Selam (Gate of Salutation), constructed by Süleyman the Magnificent in 1524 and which only the sultan was allowed to enter on horseback. From the towers on either side, state prisoners were led to execution beside the fountain outside in the first courtyard. The second or Divan Court, a vast rose garden shaded by lovely trees, is dominated by the Divan. This restful-sounding word means, in Turkish, a place of hard work—the Assembly Room of the Council of State, presided over by the Grand Vizir (Prime Minister). The sultan might choose to be present, but behind a latticed window, hidden by a curtain. Nobody ever knew when he was listening in on the debate, though he sometimes pulled the hangings aside to put in a word. Adjoining the Divan is an exhibition of Turkish porcelains and a fine show of arms.

The small gate, the tradesmen's entrance, opens into the harem, a bewildering maze of nearly 400 halls, terraces, rooms, wings and apartments grouped round the two large chambers of Süleyman the Magnificent and Murat III. Forty are open to the public after meticulous restoration. The eunuchs were lodged next to the entrance in tiny cubicles as cramped and uncomfortable as those of the lesser concubines, of whom there were up to 200. The compulsory guide explains that only when they were found gifted (one wonders in what, seeing the judgment was made by eunuchs) did they qualify for presentation to the sultan; even then, not all walked the Golden Way by which the favorite of the night entered the sultan's private quarters. Each of the four legitimate wives had her own private apartment giving onto the same small court, but only the Empire's first lady, Valide Sultan, the sultan's mother, was spaciously accommodated, on the entire first floor above. The great Sinan, excelling not only as architect but likewise as interior decorator, designed the reception and entertainment suite as well as the Hall of the Imperial Sons under a unique dome of painted linen descending to the lovely Iznik tiles. The bathroom was heated from below, but even in this most private place the sultans were protected by marble grills against the intrusion of assassins. The Gate of the Dead in the court's lowest corner leads to the sumptuous imperial coaches in the former stables.

In the kitchens, opposite, meals were prepared for some 5,000 people. Now they house a magnificent collection of 10th-century T'ang, Yuan celadon, Ming blue-and-white china, up to the 18th century, when the Chinese worked to order for the palace. Some exquisite Japanese porcelain is also displayed. European glassware is relegated to the old royal sweetmeat and pastry kitchen, lately restored. On the stone next to the Bab-ı-Saadet (Gate of Felicity) the Prophet's standard was raised whenever Holy War was declared, the last time being in 1914.

In the third court, the quarters of the black and white eunuchs inside the harem face Ahmet II's Audience Chamber (Arzodasi), where the sultans received foreign ambassadors. Just behind is the library of Ahmet III, containing priceless Arabic and Greek manuscripts. To the right, a portico of seven columns precedes the lodgings of the Seferlis, the corps of pages chosen for their beauty from among the boys of the Christian blood-tribute, who rivalled the occupants of the harem for the sultans' favor. In this wing are now shown the collection of miniatures and sultans' signatures from the first to the last ruler, masterpieces of the dying art of calligraphy, the foundation of Moslem decorative art. Imperial fashion (male of course) evolves slowly in the magnificent display of the sultan's robes, from the first to the last ruler, some bloodstained and torn from assassin's daggers, garments stiff with gold and silver thread, tooled leather, gold, silver, and jewels.

Yet even this splendor is but an introduction to the fabulous jewels of the Treasury, a true cave of Aladdin overspilling into four rooms. The breathtaking effect is enhanced by the beautiful display of turban crests, jewel-studded armor and helmets, every possible utensil and weapon encrusted with diamonds and pearls, no less than three thrones (including an Indian one, reputedly once belonging to Shah Ismail, and part of the spoil from Selim I's victorious Persian campaign), and the reliquary containing the arm and hand of St. John the Baptist. The famous emerald dagger, star of the film *Topkapi,* is outshone by the 84-carat Spoonmaker diamond.

There are trinkets, chalices, candelabra and medals, and jewels, jewels, jewels. Even so, it is but a trifling sample of the old Osmanli treasures. Gone is the gold paving on the floor of the royal reception room, gone are most of the painted panels and all of the silk hangings. But prominent in the showcases are the two uncut emeralds, weighing 3 and 1½ kilos (6 and 3 lb.), which once hung from the ceiling like green lights.

Yet firework displays of dragons and castles no longer light up the dark sky over the sultan's world-renowned tulip garden, where long-dead peacocks once flaunted their tails. (It is to the Turks that we owe the tulip *(Lâle),* brought back to Louis XIV by the French ambassador to the Osmanli court.) Here, too, roses have replaced tulips in the stunning setting for the operas and plays, once most fittingly Mozart's *Abduction from the Seraglio,* as part of the Istanbul Festival; there are also performances of ballets and music by the Janissary Mehter Band. In the small Ağalar Cami, manuscripts from the palace's 17 libraries have been gathered, and in the Hasoda Pavilion are displays of Turkish textiles.

In the fourth and last court, small, elegant summer houses, mosques, fountains and pools are scattered through gardens on different levels. The grey granite Column of the Goths—one of many still commemorating Roman victories, but minus the original statue on top—celebrates the triumph of Claudius II Gothicus over the barbarians.

The Pavilion of Circumcision faces the gilded bronze Baldachin of Sultan Ibrahim and the loveliest of the pavilions, the famed Baghdad Kiosk (covered with Iznik tiles), built by Murat IV after his conquest of Baghdad in 1638. The Erivan Kiosk was known as the Golden Cage, where the reigning sultan's closest relatives lived in strict confinement after the old custom of murdering all possible rivals at each accession had been softened in the 19th century. The greatest number of brothers—19—were strangled in 1595 by order of Mehmet III. House arrest effectively kept the internal peace, but deprived the heirs to the throne of any chance to prepare themselves for the formidable task of ruling a great empire.

The scant showing in the portrait gallery is due to the Prophet's ban of the representational arts; even Bellini's famous portrait of Mehmet II was painted on the sly. The few Turkish miniatures imitate the Persian style—the same lack of perspective but more brightly colored. Where the Persians painted love stories and legends in rose gardens, the Turks painted soldiers in battle; when they did paint holy legends, the sky was always gold. On the ground floor is a display of ceremonial keys from towns and fortresses throughout the Empire. All clocks in the clock museum are stopped at five past nine, the time of Atatürk's death.

In the middle of the paved forecourt, bright with colored tiles, is a magnificent fountain. A signboard asks visitors to speak in low voices and to show respect. But even Islam's most sacred relics can no longer be openly displayed in the two beautifully tiled chambers. As a safeguard against vandals and terrorists, the Prophet's mantle, in a chest from the *Thousand and One Nights* made for Murat III, the solid gold casket for the Prophet's standard, and Mohammed's two swords, weapons of Allah with which Islam was able to conquer a great part of the world, are all crowded into an alcove behind shatter-proof glass, where a *hoca* constantly recites the Koran. Also on view is the wooden Gate of Repentance of the Kaaba, brought complete with bolts and keys to Murat II from Mecca, and a bronze impression of the Prophet's footprint.

The marble-paved terrace gives on to one of the most beautiful views over the Golden Horn, Beyoğlu and the Galata Tower. Fishing-smacks, kayiks, islands, mosques, domes, crescents shining in the sun, fine houses and tumbledown shacks, boats and water: here is the Golden Horn, a wonderland as seen by a thousand romantic 19th-century travelers; the Constantinople, at last, of our dreams. Equally stunning is the panorama from the adjoining 19th-century rococo Mecidiye pavilion, the last addition to the vast imperial compound, now occupied by the Topkapı restaurant.

Cisterns and Mosques

Water had always been a problem in Constantinople and still is in summer, even in the modern hotels. Constantine the Great began the construction of an aqueduct, which was finished in 375 by Emperor Valens, whose name the impressive two stories of arches across Atatürk Boulevard still bears, though officially called Bozdoğan Kemeri. Next to it is the Belediye Müzesi (Municipal Museum), in a former medrese, displaying models of the town at all periods. Constantine also excavated the Sunken Palace Cistern (Yerebatan Saray), which was enlarged by Justinian and connected to Valens' Aqueduct to provision the imperial palaces. From two entrances steps descend 12 meters (39 ft.) into the spectacular vaults, upheld by 336 marble columns rising from the well-lit water.

The Cistern of a Thousand and One Columns *(Binbirdirek),* though actually possessing only 224 (in 12 rows), is south of the Divan Yolu Highway; it also dates from Justinian, and is equally impressive. The vast two-story catacombs near Aksaray Square, discovered in 1972, were at first believed to be a third Justinian cistern, but after being pumped dry were revealed as a sixth-century burial ground. In the prosperous days of the Macedonian dynasty the palaces of the great nobles, as well as the monasteries, had their own private cisterns, which fell into disrepair after the conquest. But the public fountains were always maintained and embellished. The most beautiful was reconstructed by Ahmet III in 1728 to the south of St. Sophia.

The Süleymaniye Cami was built between 1550 and 1557 by the most gifted architect of the Turkish world—Sinan, who also built the beautiful mosque of Edirne, as well as many wings of Topkapı and embellishments in St. Sophia. The Süleymaniye is to the city of the Moslems what St. Sophia was to that of the Christians. Built on the third of Istanbul's seven hills, it bears the name of Süleyman the Magnificent, whose octagonal türbe (as well as that of his Sultana, Roxelane) stands in the cemetery to the east. In spite of its wonderful glazed tiles, carpets, and stained glass, it has a striking look of bare austerity, the acme of artistic achievement. Under the rule of this sovereign, Turkey reached the heights of greatness and power, and this contrast of simplicity seems, therefore, all the more deliberate. The proportions are overwhelming—the middle dome is 55 meters (181 ft.) high and 25 meters (84 ft.) wide. The half-dome between the Mihrab and the Door of Mecca is 37 meters (122 ft.) high and 23 meters (76 ft.) wide. Four massive columns uphold the whole. One hundred and thirty-eight openings, covered in stained glass, let through an eerie light. The four minarets have twice three and twice two balconies to make the sum of ten: Süleyman, fourth sultan to reign over Istanbul, was the tenth ruler of the Osmanli Empire. A medrese, medical school, caravanserai, hospice and hamam form part of the huge complex.

On the banks of the Golden Horn, Sinan built the mosque of Rüstem Paşa, son-in-law of Süleyman, and Grand Vizir, in 1561. It has beautiful glazed tiles and remarkable designs of green, black, and brown marble. In 1571 Sinan built the mosque of Sokollu Mehmet Paşa, with its lone minaret and its undamaged glazed tiles; as well as that of Selim I, whose single dome above the austere prayer room rises from the portico of 18 columns which support 22 cupolas. Selim's türbe faces that of Abdül Mecit.

Outstanding among the innumerable mosques deserving a visit is that of Bayezit II, an important architectural link between the 15th-century Anatolian mosques, and those of Sinan. The Moorish gate opposite leads to the university, which replaced the Conqueror's first palace. In the garden stands the white marble Beyazıt Kulesi, topped by a curious roof, that in 1828 replaced a wooden firewatch tower.

Across the square is one of the numerous entrances to the Kapalı Çarşi (Covered Bazaar), partly rebuilt after the great fire of 1954 and the smaller one of 1975. It is a town in itself, made up of some 4,000 tiny shops covering over 186,000 square meters (2,000,000 sq. ft.).

Only the Royal Gate remains of the original Fatih Cami, built by the Conqueror on the site of the Church of the St. Apostles, burial ground of the Byzantine emperors on the fourth hill. Though Mehmet II was an excessively harsh ruler, he was also broadminded: he wrote a *divan,* a collection of poems in the traditional classical Osmanli style, and surrounded

his mosque with eight colleges where Italian humanists and Greek scholars taught alongside Moslem theologians, mathematicians and astrono-
mers. Levelled by the destructive earthquake of 1667, the present Italianate edifice, whose four half-cupolas support the vast central dome, was
finished a hundred years later by Mustafa III. Moslems cannot be buried
inside mosques, so the Conqueror's türbe and that of his mother are in
the garden.

The Monastery Church of Christ Pantokrator was built by the Empress
Irene in the early 12th century; the Church of the Virgin Panmakaristos,
near Atatürk Boulevard, dates from the same century; converted respectively into the Zeyrek Cami and the Fethiye Cami, both are now museums
with fine 14th-century mosaics.

The Yeni Cami (New Mosque), built between 1597 and 1663, with elaborate interior decorations and preceded by a large colonnaded courtyard,
separates the Karaköy Bridge from the Mısır Çarşısı, the Egyptian Spice
Bazaar, so-called because most spices came from Egypt when the mother
of Mehmet IV presented the Bazaar to the Yeni Cami in 1660. The Nuru-
osmaniye Mosque, at the entrance to the Covered Bazaar, is a pleasing
sample of Turkish 18th-century baroque.

The Galata Bridge

Millions of people throughout the world unwittingly mention every day
what was for a long time the only bridge across the Golden Horn. Two
English families living on opposite shores were in the habit of meeting
most evenings for a game of cards, a variation of whist. Neither much liked
crossing the bridge after nightfall, sometimes in the rain, always with the
risk of holdups. So they took turns, saying, "Tomorrow is your night to
bridge." And this became the name of a card game.

The original Galata pontoon bridge is now being replaced with a fixed-
pier crossing that will interfere less with the current. But the new Karaküy
Köprüsü will be just as crowded with pedestrians and cars. Innumerable
catamaran speed-boats going up the Golden Horn, and ferries to the Asiatic shore and the islands start from the piers on both banks. A second bridge
built by and named after Atatürk was supplemented in 1975 by that of
the Istanbul bypass higher up near Eyüp, relieving the town from much
heavy through-traffic.

Between the Galata Bridge and Gülhane Park is the lowlife district of
Sirkeci (Vinegarmakers) with the railway station of that name. Workmen
eat and drink in the company of "highly professional" women in big halls
rarely visited by tourists. On a wooden platform, in a deafening din height-
ened by microphones and loudspeakers, dancing-girls do sad turns, half
belly dance and half striptease, neither erotic nor genuine belly-dancing.
They add to the hubbub by rattling the *kasik,* metal spoons used like casta-
nets. Incurable romantics abstain: the houris of the Moslem paradise and
the odalisques of 19th-century novels have been replaced by stout middle-
aged females or even female impersonators. The show, what there is of
it, is among the spectators.

The Walls and Kariye Museum

Wide breaches for highways make a walk atop the 7 km. (4 miles) long
restored walls problematic, but it is possible to drive alongside their entire

length. Badly shaken by the earthquake of 1894, the inner rampart, 3½ meters (12 ft.) thick and 13 meters (43 ft.) high, with 90 towers and seven monumental gates, is still the most imposing secular Byzantine monument. Begun by Theodosius II in 413, complemented by an outer wall and a moat connecting the Castle of the Seven Towers (Yedikule)—used by the sultans as a state prison for high dignitaries and European ambassadors—at the Sea of Marmara with the Golden Horn, these walls, the strongest fortifications of the Middle Ages, were breached only twice—by the Latins in 1204 and the Turks in 1453.

On this itinerary, or any other, a must is the Kariye Museum near the Edirne gate. The church of the Monastery of Chora, dating back to the reign of Theodosius II (408–50), was rebuilt by Justinian after the earthquake of 558. In the 12th century, it was again restored by order of Maria Dukas, a niece of Alexios Komnenos. There are remnants of mosaics, belonging to that period, but the superb masterpieces whose fame has spread throughout the world date from the 14th century. Above the front door, you can still make out a kneeling Theodosius, offering Christ a model of the church. The whole story of the beginnings of Christianity is told on these walls, with a careful and even homely realism far removed from the formal Byzantine images of God in His glory, hieratic saints and emperors. The Turks only converted the church of the Holy Savior in Chora into the Kariye Cami in the reign of Bayezit II (1481–1512). Now a museum, the splendid mosaics and frescoes were restored with the help of the Byzantine Institute of America. The two-story Osmanli residential houses around the church square have been tastefully renovated and repainted in pastel colors, but continue to be inhabited by their former tenants. A ground-floor shop sells tea and pastry, which can be sampled in the shade of trees on the garden terrace in one of Istanbul's most authentic settings.

Higher up, backed against the ramparts are the romantic ruins of the Tekfur Saray (Imperial Palace), supposedly of Constantine Porphyrogenitos, a mere façade of two stories with rounded arches. Further along lie the sad remnants of the once magnificent Blachernae Palace, built by Alexios I Komnenos, to which his grandson Manuel II transferred the imperial court in 1150. The Latin emperors resided there in unwonted luxury, as well as the Palaeolog dynasty in ever greater poverty, abandoning wing after wing till the bitter end in 1453, when the palace fell a victim because of its proximity to the walls.

The New Town

On the other side of the bridge, Galata was once a Genoese settlement, a town apart from Constantinople, and powerful enough to remain neutral during the siege of its neighbor by the Turks. Galata derives from the Italian *calata,* meaning a slope. The name is now only used for the famous Tower of Galata, built in 1349, which houses a rooftop restaurant and nightclub with a sweeping view over the town. The populous, crowded quarters of Karaköy and Sishane have taken Galata's place, connected by Beyoglu's Istiklal (Independence) Caddesi with Taksim Square, the center of the new town. Together with Cumhuriyet Caddesi (Republic Street) it forms the modern shopping center. Between Istiklal Caddesi and the fish market is Çiçek Pasaji, the flower market, a large courtyard lined with bars, cafés and small restaurants, popular with locals and tourists.

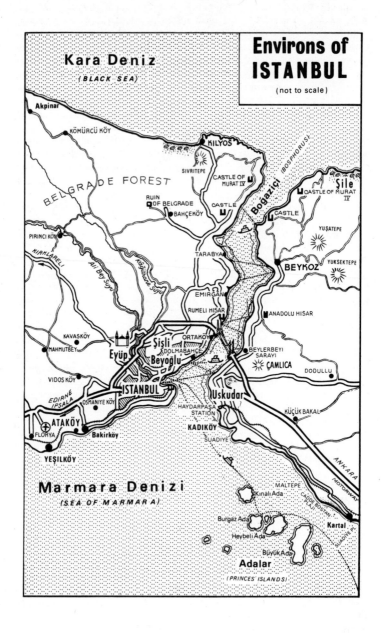

Environs of ISTANBUL

(not to scale)

In 1854, Sultan Abdül Mecit transferred his court and harem to the gleaming, white-marble Baroque Palace of Dolmabahçe (Filled-in Garden). Stretching 600 meters along the Bosphorus, the two long wings containing 365 rooms extend from the higher middle section of the enormous throne room—reputedly the largest in the world—in an extraordinary mixture of Hindu, Turkish and Italian styles. Occasional state balls and receptions are given in that lavish setting where the apartments of four sultans and the bedroom in which Atatürk died in 1938 are faithfully preserved. Queen Victoria presented a four-and-a-half-ton chandelier and the taste of her period permeates the entire accumulation of ornamental gimcracks, culminating in a verdantique bath and crystal railings on the staircases. Once the Prophet's ban on the representative arts was violated, there was no holding back, and the walls are overloaded with innumerable pictures (mainly Russian land- and sea-scapes) of dubious artistic value. Two floors have been adapted as a Culture-Science Promotion Center. The Quarters of the Crown Prince house the Painting and Sculpture Museum of the Sinan University, while the adjoining two Operation Kiosks, the men's and women's quarters, are alloted to exhibitions, of which the *Palaces, Kiosks* and *Mansions* are of outstanding interest. The palace mosque and ornamental gates add the finishing touch to an unforgettable sight, most effective when flood-lit and reflected in the water.

An avenue shaded by plane trees follows the Bosphorus past the Statue of Hayrettin Barbarossa and the Naval Museum to the large Beşiktaş High School for Girls, founded by Abdül Hamid II, opposite the extensive Yıldız Park. Here the haunted Sultan resided in a small replica of the Dolmabahçe Palace, the Yıldız Kiosk, now used for exhibitions and concerts, but occasionally the residence of visiting heads of state: Queen Elizabeth II has stayed here. Abdül Mecit's hunting kiosk is a small museum of 19th-century memorabilia; a larger kiosk has been converted into a cultural center with an auditorium and seminar rooms with facilities for simultaneous translation, the Sultan's small private theater is open again for performances, while the delightfully restored Malta Kiosk on an artificial lake is a pleasant restaurant commanding a superb view.

The former British, French and Russian embassies in Mesrutiyet Caddesi are now unusually sumptuous consulates; the first also houses the British Council. Other sites are:—the *tekke* of the Whirling Dervishes at Beyoğlu; the black lead domes of the Tophane Cami, and the fine fountain of the same name; and some old wooden houses along the Golden Horn.

The Tower of Leander (Kız Kulesi, Girl's Tower), on an islet at the entrance of the Bosphorus, was supposedly constructed by Constantine the Great in the 330s and still serves as a lighthouse, but its name derives from an ancient Greek romance. Though swimming was not a popular sport in antiquity, Leander daily braved the waters of the Bosphorus in a rigorous keep-fit campaign. One day the strong current carried him to the islet, where beautiful Hero was shut away by her suspicious father. The inevitable happened. Leander returned under cover of darkness and stayed till dawn. This pleasant routine was broken one stormy night, when Hero waited in vain. The body of her dead lover was eventually washed up on the beach—leaving Hero alone, to die of a broken heart.

The Bosphorus (Boğaziçi) owes its name to a still older legend. When the gods of Greece were young, Zeus fell in love with a maiden called Io. Hera, the wife of Zeus—endlessly jealous, and with good cause—turned her rival into a cow. Then, to add insult to injury, she sent a gadfly to sting the poor girl as she was placidly munching grass. Goaded beyond endurance, the metamorphosed maiden plunged into the sea, ever since known as the Ionian, and intrepidly crossed into Asia by the Bosphorus, the cow's ford.

Üsküdar is a vast Asian suburb, with a busy ferry pier next to the pretty Iskele (Landing Stage) Cami and Haidarpaşa Station, the grandiose terminus of Kaiser Wilhelm II's Baghdad railway. Now, as when it was known as Scutari, it is dominated by the massive, four-turreted, 18th-century Selimiye Barracks, where from 1853 to 1855 Florence Nightingale nursed and buried the British wounded of the Crimean War. The intrepid spinster established the first army hospital deserving that name and rightly achieved immortality. Her two rooms with the original furniture are preserved in what is now the HQ of the Turkish 1st Army. Her memorial towers above the nearby British cemetery.

The Princes' Islands

The nearest fresh air, trees and quiet are to be found on the nine Adalar, called the Princes' Islands because they were used for the pleasure as well as the exile of Byzantine princes. Ferries ply back and forth from the Galata Bridge all day long to the four inhabited islands, Kınalı, Burgaz, Heybeli and the largest, Büyük Ada. They are wonderfully peaceful; no cars are allowed and the only way to get around is by the horse-and-buggy, called a *fayton,* the Turkish version of phaeton.

Most of the wooden houses were built at the turn of the century. Much of the land on Büyük Ada is not for sale, a wise law to keep the island unspoilt. Time has been set back a hundred years, allowing you to slow down and rest.

Towards the Black Sea

The shores of the Bosphorus, between a third of a mile and two miles apart, are like the riverbanks of most large cities, lined with cafés, restaurants and outdoor taverns for almost the entire 30 km. (19 miles) from Istanbul to the Black Sea. The villages on the European shore have merged and been submerged along the all too narrow coastal road, thronged with cars and buses.

Yet in summer the comfortable hotels offer still the most agreeable accommodation close to the capital, in the easygoing atmosphere of resort suburbs. From Ortaköy, bordering on Yıldız park, a feeder road ascends to the Bosphorus bridge across to Beylerbey in Asia. The Beylerbeyi Saray, built in 1865, housed Napoleon III's Empress Eugenie on her way to open the Suez Canal built by her cousin Lesseps. Abdül Hamid II was confined here till his death in 1913. Sultan Abdül Aziz built this dream of Hollywood come true, with the ornamental fountain in the main drawing room, white marble painted in inexplicable blue in another, costly furniture of no recognizable style, innumerable Sèvres vases and gilded clocks. Only recently opened after extensive restoration, the first floor is used for exhibitions, the top floor for international congresses. Seen from the Bosphorus, the white marble façade has a definite grandeur.

A little higher up, the lovely marble Art Nouveau residence of Abbas Hilmi, the last Khedive of Egypt, dethroned by the British in 1914, has been converted into a restaurant with a few hotel rooms. The Turkish Touring and Automobile Association has likewise brought new life to the popular excursion park on Çamlıca Hill, where two restaurants and seven refreshment kiosks are connected by a path along which horse and bullock carts move at a leisurely pace. The marvelous view over the Bosphorus is enlivened by the ever-flowing varied traffic of freighters and tankers, fishing boats and pleasure craft, water-skiers and swimmers. Large flights of migratory birds, including storks, eagles and raptors, pass in April and September. But above all, there is Istanbul's unforgettable skyline: the domes and minarets shining through the morning mist, shimmering in the midday heat, etched black against the sunset as the water pales to whiteness beneath the dark town slowly lighting up as night falls, and at its most magical when floodlights illuminate the mosques and palaces.

On the European shore the coastal road passes the beach of Lido, pocket-sized like all along the Bosphorus; the ungainly docks at Kuruçeşme, Arnavutköy, and the seafood restaurants of Bebek to the well-restored fortress of Rumeli Hisar. It was built in 1452, one year before the fall of Constantinople, by Mehmet the Conqueror, together with other fortifications preparing the siege of the city. It has since served as a watchtower at the very place where the narrowing of the Bosphorus makes it almost impossible to force a way through the strait. Shakespeare's plays are expertly performed in the vast courtyard in summer as part of the Istanbul Festival.

Just opposite rise the few remaining towers of Anadolu Hisar, a stronghold built over 50 years earlier by Bayezit I. It was most probably here that Darius passed from Asia into Europe, in 512 B.C. Here too, in all likelihood, the Crusaders crossed into Asia at the end of the 11th century.

Other beautiful places: Emirgan, where the Şerifler Yalıse, an 18th-century wooden mansion, is open to visitors; Istinye around its small and pretty bay, unfortunately spoilt by a naval repairs dock; Yeniköy and the charming bay of Tarabya with its excellent hotel, fish restaurants and the large new conference center; pleasant Büyükdere; Sarıyer, where the road turns inland towards the long, sandy beach of Kilyos on the Black Sea.

Finally, two delightful place-names: the Sweet Waters of Europe, a charming spot formed by two small valleys at the head of the Golden Horn, after Eyüp; and the Sweet Waters of Asia, near Anadolu Hisar.

The Neighboring Beaches

Besides the tiny Bosphorus beaches, often mere bathing terraces, there are many more within easy reach from Istanbul in Europe and Asia, on the Black Sea and on the Sea of Marmara.

On the European shore of the Sea of Marmara, there are Ataköy, Yeşilköy and Florya. The Russian troops advanced up to here in 1878 to impose the ephemeral peace treaty of San Stefano which was superseded in the same year by the decisions of the Congress of Berlin, restoring Turkish rule in the Balkans. A little farther along the shore is Büyük Çekmece with an inland lake for fishing. Innumerable hotels, motels, restaurants and cafés line the coast for mile after overcrowded mile all the way to Silivri; no wonder the sea is badly polluted and an uninviting muddy grey.

Near the Asiatic shore the Princes' Islands offer more attractive scenery than Fenerbahçe, Caddebostan, Suadiye, Kartal and Pendik on the mainland.

There remains the Black Sea, which means a day's outing at Kilyos. From Sarıyer the road cuts across the forest of Belgrade, which took its name from Süleyman the Magnificent's Serbian prisoners, past the dam and aqueduct built by Mahmut I and the Valide dam, built at the end of the 18th century by order of Sultan Selim III's mother.

PRACTICAL INFORMATION FOR ISTANBUL

TOURIST OFFICES. There are tourist offices at: Meşrutiyet Cad. 57 (tel. 145 65 93); Hilton Hotel (tel. 133 05 92); Karaköy Maritime Station (tel. 149 57 76); Sultan Ahmet Square (tel. 522 49 03) and at Atatürk Airport (tel. 573 73 99).

WHEN TO COME. Spring or the beginning of summer. In April and May, when the weather is warm without being hot, the former capital is at its best, though the beaches open in June at the earliest. Some may prefer the mellow mildness of October and early November. The country's main cultural event, the Istanbul Festival, lasts from mid-June for one month at the peak of the tourist season. Every day towards sundown a breeze from the Black Sea cools the city. It is fairly cold in winter but often sunny in spite of rainy spells.

HOTELS. Reservations are essential June through September. The first two categories are air-conditioned, the first three, and all motels, have restaurants. All rooms with bath or shower, though water flows only sporadically in the lesser establishments in summer. The top hotels are located in the new town, with several under construction, but old mansions have been converted into expensive hotels complementing the new moderate and inexpensive hotels near the main sites in the old town. Reductions of 10 to 30% are usual in winter.

NEW TOWN

Deluxe

Etap Marmara, Taksim Sq. (tel. 151 46 96). 424 rooms, 8 suites. Choice of restaurants, bars, cafés; nightclub; pool and sauna; panoramic view.

Hilton, Cumhuriyet Cad. (tel. 131 46 46). 410 rooms, 13 suites. The usual luxury town-within-a-town with a Turkish touch; casino, large swimming pool, restaurants. Connected to Convention and Exhibition Center.

Sheraton, in Taksim Park (tel. 131 21 21). 437 rooms. Turkey's largest, with beautiful view over the Bosphorus, pool, nightclub, 2 restaurants.

Expensive

Divan, Cumhuriyet Cad. (tel. 131 41 00). 98 rooms. Excellent restaurant and pub.

Etap Istanbul, Meşrutiyet Cad. (tel. 151 46 46). 200 rooms. Pool, disco.

Maçka, Eytem Cad. 35 (tel. 140 10 53). 184 rooms. Not central, close to Bosphorus.

Pera Palas, Meşrutiyet Cad. 98 (tel. 151 45 60). 120 modernized rooms, but preserving the opulent 1892 decor demanded by Orient Express travelers for whom it was constructed; good restaurant and historical bar; splendid view over the old town. Next to U.S. Consulate.

Moderate

Büyük Londra, Meşrutiyet Cad. 117 (tel. 149 10 25). 42 rooms.
Dilson, Sıraselviler Cad. 49, Taksim (tel. 143 20 32). 90 rooms.
Keban, Sıraselviler Cad. 51, Taksim (tel. 143 33 10). 87 rooms.
T.M.T., Büyükdere Cad. 84, Gayrettepe (tel. 167 33 34). 103 rooms. Sauna.

Inexpensive

Bale, Refik Saydam Cad. 62 (tel. 153 07 00). 63 rooms. Near British Consulate.
Çırağan, Müvezzi Cad. 3, Beşiktaş (tel. 160 02 30). 66 rooms. With rooftop restaurant; near Dolmabahçe.
Inka, Meşrutiyet Cad. 225 (tel. 143 17 28). 42 rooms.
Kavak, Meşrutiyet Cad. 201 (tel. 144 58 44). 42 rooms.
Opera, İnönü Cad. 38, Taksim (tel. 143 55 27). 50 rooms. Restaurant.
Santral, Billurcu Sok. 26, Taksim (tel. 145 41 20). 112 rooms, Garage, restaurant.
Yenişehir Palas, Balyoz Sok. 113, Meşrutiyet Cad. (tel. 149 88 10). 48 rooms.

OLD TOWN

Expensive

Green Mansion (Yeşil Ev), Sultanahmet (tel. 528 67 64). 20 rooms. 19th-century wooden mansion between St. Sophia and the Blue Mosque; period furnishing; attractive dining room and garden restaurant round marble fountain.
Kalyon, Sahil Yolu, Sultanahmet (tel. 511 44 00). 38 rooms. Garage; faces Sea of Marmara.
Ramada Hotel, Ordu Caddesi 226, Lalelil (tel. 519 40 50). Opened in 1987—the first international chain to open a hotel in the old town—after being converted from four apartment buildings. 275 rooms. Casino and swimming pool. The Blue Mosque is a 25-minute walk away.
Two mansions in Soğukçeşme Cad. along the outer wall of Topkapı have been converted into boarding houses; **Ayasofia Pansiyons** (tel. 512 57 32/513 36 60) has 60 rooms furnished in late Osmanli style; the other houses the 50,000-volume Istanbul Library, while a Byzantine cistern operates as the restaurant **Sarnic.**

Moderate

Akgün, Haznedar Sok., Ordu Cad. (tel. 512 02 60). 87 rooms.
Anka, Molla Gürani Cad., Fındıkzade (tel. 525 60 02). 65 air-conditioned rooms. Garage.
Büyük Keban, Gençtürk Cad. 47, Aksaray (tel. 512 00 20). 132 rooms. Garage.
Cidde, Aksaray Cad. 10 (tel. 522 42 11). 84 rooms.
Hali, Klodfarer Cad. 20 (tel. 513 62 17).
Kent, Haznedar Sok. 12, Beyazıt (tel. 512 01 35). 78 rooms.
Olcay, Millet Cad. 187 (tel. 585 32 20). 134 rooms. Pool, garage, on road to airport.

Sözmen, Millet Cad. 104 (tel. 524 52 94). 74 rooms. Garage.

Topkapı Oğuzhan Cad., Fındıkzade. (tel. 525 42 40). 40 rooms. Restaurant.

Toro, Koska Cad., Laleli (tel. 528 02 73/4). 54 air-conditioned rooms.

Inexpensive

Astor, Laleli Cad. (tel. 522 44 23). 42 rooms.

Barut's Guesthouse, Ishakpasa Cad. 8, Sultanahmet (tel. 520 12 27). 22 rooms.

Berk Guesthouse, Kutlugun Sok. 27, Sultanahmet (tel. 511 07 37). 7 rooms.

Bern, Muratpaşa Sok. (tel. 523 24 62). 46 rooms.

Burç Gençtürk Cad. 18, Laleli. (tel. 520 76 67). 32 rooms.

Ebru, Gazi Mustafa Kemal Bul. (tel. 586 75 57). 35 rooms.

Florida, Fefziye Cad., Laleli. (tel. 528 10 21). 28 rooms.

Geçit, Aksaray Cad. (tel. 527 88 39). 25 rooms.

Hakan, Gençtürk Cad. (tel. 512 23 70). 40 rooms.

Hislon, Mollagürani Cad., Fındıkzade. (tel. 525 58 17). 30 rooms.

Kilim, Millet Cad., Fındıkzade. (tel. 586 08 80). 72 rooms. Restaurant.

Pamukkale, Ordu Cad. (tel. 527 67 93). 24 rooms.

Side, Koska Cad., Laleli. (tel. 526 71 78). 42 rooms.

Sözer, Topkapı Şehremini Cad. (tel. 523 97 53). 39 rooms. Turkish bath.

Tura, Valide Camii Sok., Aksaray. (tel. 586 75 48). 35 rooms.

Ulubat, Kalburcu Mehmet Çeşme Sok. (tel. 585 17 88). 34 rooms.

Yaşmak, Ebussuut Cad., Sirkeci. (tel. 526 31 55). 65 rooms. Garage.

Yılmaz, Valide Camii Sok., Aksaray. (tel. 586 74 00). 33 rooms.

BOSPHORUS

European Coast

Probably the most enjoyable stay for the motorist is along this famous waterway, where bathing can be ideally combined with sightseeing, while a wide choice of restaurants and nightspots is in walking distance.

Büyük Tarabya (L), Kefeliköy Cad. (tel. 162 10 00). 262 rooms. On private beach in lovely bay of same name.

Carlton (E), Köybaşi Cad. 119, Yeniköy (tel. 162 10 20). 88 rooms in hotel directly on Bosphorus; 34 rooms in motel round pool; excellent restaurant.

Bebek (M), Cevdetpaşa Cad. (tel. 163 30 00). 38 rooms. Well-situated in village of the same name; sporting facilities.

Asian Coast

Hıdıv Kasrı (E), Çubuklu (tel. 331 26 51). 25 rooms. Former residence of Egyptian Khedive in large park. Elegant restaurant and tea room.

Harem (M), (tel. 333 20 25). 100 rooms. Near car ferry at Selimiye in Üsküdar. Pool.

Engin (I), (tel. 336 03 79). 17 rooms. In Kadiköy.

Idealtepe Motel (I). 31 rooms. Private beach; at bottom of (I) category; in Kadiköy.

Mini-Harem (I), (tel. 333 51 76). 14 rooms. Even closer to car ferry at Selimiye in Üsküdar.

BLACK SEA

European Coast

Turban Kilyos Motel (M), (tel. 142 24 64). 24 rooms. On lovely sandy beach 35 km. (22 miles) north of Istanbul, invigorating even at height of summer.
Gurup (I), Kale Cad. 21 (tel. 194). 31 rooms. Restaurant, beach.
Kilyos Kale (I), Kale Cad. 78 (tel. 54). 27 rooms. Restaurant.

Asian Coast

Değirmen (I), (tel. 1048/1148). 73 rooms. At Şile.
Kumbaba Oberj (I), (tel. 1038). 40 rooms. Also at Şile.

SEA OF MARMARA

European Coast

Çinar (L), (tel. 573 29 10). 201 rooms. Many amenities include fine beach and pool, nightclub and restaurant. Conveniently situated at Yeşilköy, near the airport.
Ataköy C Motel (M), Sahil Yolu (tel. 572 08 02). 206 rooms. Sauna, pool, beach.
Baler (M), Avcilar Anbarli (tel. 591 95 29). 62 rooms. Comfortable, at Küçükçekmece on the beach.
Demirköy (M), (tel. 572 95 80). 290 rooms. Pool; on same beach as *Ataköy C Motel.*
Istanbul (I). 82 rooms. At Güzelceköy, on highway west of Istanbul.
Sultan (I). 24 rooms. Very close to Istanbul.
Yeşilköy (I), Havan Sok. 4 (tel. 573 29 95). 30 rooms. Near beach.

Asian Coast

Dragos (E), (tel. 352 05 03). 63 rooms. Pool, beach; at Maltepe.
Suadiye (M), (tel. 358 11 20). 109 rooms. At Suadiye.
Çamlı (I), Ayazma Şifasuyu Yani Yakacik (tel. 353 36 09). 32 rooms. At Kartal.
Çınardibi (I), (tel. 358 11 50). 22 rooms. At Suadiye.
Erdim Motel (I), Ankara Cad. 156 (tel. 353 78 87). 52 rooms. Private beach; at Kartal.
Motel 212 (I), Eskibağdat Cad. Kaynarca Mah. (tel. 354 00 60). 30 rooms. At Pendik.
Petek Pansiyon (I), Alptekin Sok. 4 (tel. 336 22 59). 46 rooms. At Fenerbahçe.
Villa Marmara (I), Sümerevleri Cevizli (tel. 352 24 16). 14 rooms. At Kartal.

PRINCES' ISLANDS

There are small boarding houses on all the inhabited islands, but the only hotels are all on the largest, Büyükada.
Splendid (M), 23 Nisan Cad. 71 (tel. 351 64 51). 70 rooms, 22 with showers. Not all that splendid, but pleasantly away from it all.
Villa Rıfat (I), Yilmaztürk Cad. 80 (tel. 351 60 68). 12 rooms, 6 with shower. Small beach.

STUDENT HOSTELS. *Kadırga Student Hostel,* Cömertler Sok. 6, Kumkapı. *Ortaköy Student Hostel,* Palango Cad. 20, Ortaköy; for girls. *Topkapı Atatürk Student Center,* Londra Asfalti, Cevizlibağ Durağı.

CAMPING. All the camp sites listed below are on the E5 near Atatürk airport and all are open April through October. *Ataköy Mokamp* (capacity 1,500), on the beach. *Mocamp Kartaltepe* (capacity 600), near Atatürk Airport on E5, 11 km. (7 miles) from Istanbul, pool, 6 km. (4 miles) from beach. *Yeşilyurt,* Feneryolu Cad. 25 (capacity 100), on the beach.

RESTAURANTS. Most hotels down to the moderate category have restaurants. In the big hotels, the food is for the most part insipidly international. It's far more rewarding to eat out, especially at night and in places where local people go.

Many restaurants have a grill for the *kebap,* broiled on a spit within sight of the diner. Order Turkish dishes without misgivings: the cooking is tasty and full of surprises, as for instance yogurt with meat; fish is excellent. The restaurants in the new town are more expensive and touristy than in the old. The cost of a meal in Istanbul is based more on the setting and the service than on the quality of the food. Try a *lokanta* (tavern) around Sirkeci, if you're feeling adventurous.

NEW TOWN

Expensive

The luxury hotels provide American and French food, though they also serve good and authentic local dishes. The restaurant of the *Divan* is outstanding, while the grand period setting of the *Pera Palas* dining room greatly enhances the very adequate meals. Other restaurants are:

Dört Mevsim (Four Seasons), Istiklal Caddesi 509, Beyoğlu (tel. 145 89 41). Turkish dishes as well as an international menu. Comments range from enthusiastic to highly critical.

Galata Tower, Şişhane (tel. 145 11 60). The setting and the spectacular view of the floodlit old town compensate for the food and price of the dinner dances.

Liman, Rıhtım Cad, Karaköy (tel. 144 93 49). Lunch only. Rendezvous for Istanbul's business and finance community overlooking waterfront. Excellent seafood.

Ziya, Mim Kemal, M. Kemal, Öke Cad. 21, Nişantaşı (tel. 140 75 23). Excellent local food.

Moderate

Bonjur Café, Halaskargazi Cad., Şişli (tel. 147 09 82).

Flora, Vali Konağı Cad. 9, Harbiye (tel. 148 76 94). In walking distance of main hotels.

Hacıbaba, Istiklal Cad. 49, Taksim (tel. 144 18 86). Excellent Turkish food.

Hanedan Restoran, Cigdem Sok. 27, Barbaros Meydani, Besiktas (tel. 160 48 54).

Ilyas, Halaskargazi Cad. 306, Şişli (tel. 175 47 63). For succulent *döner kebap.*

Malta Köşkü, Yildiz Park (tel. 160 04 54). Stunning view over the Bosphorus enhances the food.

Motorest Lokantası, Dolmabahçe Cad. 1, Beşiktaş (tel. 161 01 31). Convenient after sightseeing in the neighborhood.

Pizza Prima, Halaskargazi Cad. 40, Şişli (tel. 147 38 61).

Rejans, Olivo Gecidi 15, off Istiklal Cad., Galatasaray (tel. 144 16 10).

Şamdan, Harbiye Eytam Cad. 12, Şişli. Unlike nos. 1 and 2, stays put.

Şamdan 2, Nisbetiye Cad. 30, Etiler (tel. 163 48 98). Winter quarters of *Samdan 1*.

Swiss Pub, Cumhuriyet Cad. 14 (tel. 148 80 49). Valiantly living up to its name.

Inexpensive

Bab Kafeterya, Yeşilcam Sok. 24, off Istiklal Cad.

Haci Salih, Anadolu Han 201, Alyon Sok., off Istiklal Cad. (tel. 143 45 28).

Kafe Bulvar, Cumhuriyet Cad. 5, Taksim.

OLD TOWN

Moderate

Borsa Lokantasi, Yalikosku Cad., Yalikosku Han 60–62, Eminonu (tel. 522 41 73).

Hanuzlu, next to post office in Covered Bazaar. Light and airy. Lunch only; closed Sunday.

Pandeli, (tel. 522 55 34), at the entrance to the Spice Market. Lunch only, traditional Turkish cuisine, with sea bass in parchment a specialty.

Topkapı Saray Lokantası, (tel. 513 96 96), in the Mecidiye Kiosk in the Topkapı Palace grounds. Provides adequate lunches after strenuous sightseeing. Good view over the city.

BOSPHORUS

European Coast

You will find innumerable elegant, medium range and modest eating places strung all along the European shore of the Bosphorus.

Abdullah (E), Koru Cad. 11, Emirgan (tel. 163 64 06). A famous restaurant that occasionally fails to live up to its reputation. Try the "shrimps diplomat" or the *midye dolmasi* (stuffed mussels).

Balıkçıl (E), Kefeliköy Cad. 7, Tarabya (tel. 162 08 93). Overlooks pretty bay; good seafood.

Façyo (E), Kireçburnu Cad. 13, Tarabya (tel. 162 00 24). More delicious seafood.

Fondü (E), Emirgan Cad. 92, Istinye (tel. 165 55 77). The name indicates more than seafood.

Kaptan (E), Birinci Cad. 53, Arnavutkoy (tel. 165 84 87).

Köşem Bistro (E), Kefeliköy Cad. 72, Tarabya (tel. 162 18 66). Lovely view of the bay.

Palet 2 (E), Yeniköy Cad. 80, Tarabya (tel. 162 00 20). Good seafood and a Janissary band and dancing in the evening. More "with it" than *Palet 1*.

Pembe Köşk (E) and Sarıköşk (E) in Emirgan are both so grand that they give neither address nor phone number, on the assumption that everyone knows. Most taxi drivers do.

Şamdan 1 (E), Piyasa Cad. 101, Büyükdere (tel. 142 03 79). Laid out on several levels in an attractive garden.

Sürreya (E), Bebek Cad., Arnavutköy (tel. 163 55 76). Very fashionable.

Zarifler (E), Kefeliköy Cad. 116, Tarabya (tel. 162 08 57).

Ziya (E), Muallim Naci Cad. 109, Ortaköy (tel. 161 60 05). Moves in winter to the New Town, where it is listed.

Palet 1 (M), Kefeliköy Cad. 110, Tarabya (tel. 161 01 18). Less fashionable than *Palet 2.*

Asian Coast

Çamlıca Excursion Park. Revolving Tower Restaurant (M). Seven refreshment kiosks.

Sea of Marmara

Oleyis Havalimanı (M), (tel. 573 29 20). The efficient Atatürk Airport restaurant.

Ömür (M), Yeni Londra Asfalti, Bakırköy (tel. 571 68 18).

NIGHTCLUBS. If you expect a Thousand and One Nights come true in Istanbul, you will be sorely disappointed. The *Hilton* houses a rare casino, open from 8 P.M. to early morning; winners paid in the currency in which they play; roulette, baccarat, black jack, slot machines. The *Etap Marmara* and the *Sheraton* present floor shows in a fancy Turkish decor, as does the slightly cheaper *Etap.* No need to be impressed by names including Gazino or Kulüp, strictly no gambling or membership requirements. As for what the leaflets grandly call "Turkish-style cabarets," promising bellydancers and stripteasers, the bait is bigger than the fish. Unless you enjoy sitting in a noisy crowd, deafened by the blare of a band, spearing tidbits on a toothpick while looking at a rather repetitious display, better stay away. Turkish gin, *konyak, viski* and vodka are all relatively inexpensive.

Balim (E), Hamalbaşı Cad. 8, Beyoğlu. At least fairly central.

Çinar (E), Hotel Çinar, Yeşilköy. Dinner-dancing, bellydancing; not necessarily combined.

Club 29 (E), Iskele Cad. Frit Tek Sok. 1; Moda.

Disco 2000 (E) (Sultan), Sheraton Hotel, Taksim.

Galata Tower (E), Şişane. Nightclub part is preferable to the restaurant. Fine view.

Kervansaray (E), Cumhuriyet Cad. 30. Good floor show.

Pariziyen (E), Cumhuriyet Cad. 18, Harbiye. Some might detect the Parisian touch.

Pembe Köşk (E), Kennedy Cad. 11, Sultanahmet. The best in the Old Town.

Regine (E), Cumhuriyet Cad. 16, Elmdağ.

Hydromel (M), Cumhuriyet Cad. 12, Elmdag.

Kulüp 33 (M), Cumhuriyet Cad. Fairly good floor show.

Şenzelize (M), Istiklal Cad. 220, Galatsaray.

Yeni Hydromel (M), Cumhuriyet Cad.

Elize (I), Meşrutiyet Cad. 123, Tepebaşı. No more French than *Şenzelize* above.

Olimpia (I), Acar Sok., Tomtom Mah., Beyoglu.

GETTING AROUND. By Train. There are several electric lines from Sirkeci Station to Ataköy and Florya beaches on the Sea of Marmara, while the suburban line for the Asian shore of the Marmara leaves from Haydarpaşa.

By Car. Avoid the steep narrow streets of the old town, and the chaos of Eminönü between Galata Bridge, the rail station and Topkapı Palace. Keep to the wide boulevards opened up through the old town and, whenever possible, use the Istanbul bypass, from Atatürk Airport to the Bosphorus bridge, and its feeder roads. What seems a detour will actually save time. *Never* leave the car at an unattended lot overnight. There are few filling stations in town; best fill up in the suburbs.

Parking lots. *Hilton Otopark,* at the hotel; *Ilhan Otopark,* opposite Divan Hotel; *Kabataş Otopark,* next to car-ferry jetties and convenient for Dolmabahçe; *Kat Otopark,* covered, opposite Maritime Station, Karaköy; *Opera Garaj,* Taksim, next to Atatürk Cultural Palace; *Şişli Otopark,* next to Post Office; *Tepebası Otopark,* Meşrutiyet Cad., Tepebasi. In the Old Town: *Akin Garaj,* Harikzedeler Sok. 2, Laleli. *Eminönü Otopark,* next to Galata Bridge, opposite Egyptian Bazaar. All are open 24 hours a day.

Car hire. *Avis* and *Hertz* have rental facilities at the airport and in luxury hotels; Hertz also have an outlet at Cumhuriyet Cad. 295. *Europcar* and *Kontur* are based at Cumhuriyet Cad. 47 and 283, respectively. Mainly Turkish-made Fiats and Renaults are available for hire.

By Taxi. Taxis are available at hotel and station entrances, or you can flag one down. *Dolmuş,* shared taxis, leave from the red, black, and white signs; reasonable rates according to meter.

By Minibus. Private but very economical minibuses run along fixed routes with frequent stops. At the Sirkeci rail station and Taksim Square termini are signposts indicating the various destinations; elsewhere it's difficult for the foreigner to make out where they're going. You do not tip the driver nor talk to the other passengers, any more than on a town bus. If you want to get off along the way just say *dour* (stop) and pay the driver your fare.

Minibuses start from Taksim Square for Sirkeci rail station, and the European shore of the Bosphorus; at Sirkeci rail station for the European shore of the Marmara; at Eminönü Meydani (the square opposite the Galata Bridge) for Eyüp, the ancient ramparts at Edirnekapı and Topkapı; at the landing wharf of Kadiköy for the Asian shore of the Marmara; at the landing wharf in Üsküdar for the Asian shore of the Bosphorus.

By Bus. The city trolley-bus service is good, what there is. From Topkapı Bus Terminal take No. 83 for Taksim, No. 84 for Eminönü. Buses for the European shore of the Marmara set out from Taksim Square: No. 94 for Florya, No. 96 for Yeşilköy. For the European shore of the Bosphorus up to Sarıyer take No. 40 from Taksim Square.

For the Asian shore of the Marmara buses set out from the landing wharf in Kadiköy (Üsküdar); for the Asian shore of the Bosphorus up to Beykoz, from Üsküdar. These buses are not numbered.

Buses for Ankara and the provinces mostly set out from Edirnekapı and Topkapı, outside the ramparts.

By Boat. This is a practical, enjoyable and cheap means of transport. Landing-wharfs for both shores of the Bosphorus (there are three runs: European shore, Asian shore, and a to-and-fro ferry): for Üsküdar–Haydarpaşa–Salacak, to the right of the Galata Bridge at Eminönü (on the Sirkeci side). For the Princes' Islands (Adalar) and Yalova, the slow run starts at the beginning of the bridge, the express run a little farther along the bridge. The landing-wharf for Kadiköy and Haydarpaşa is to the right of the bridge (towards the Bosphorus) on the Karaköy side. The car ferry Kabataş–Üsküdar comes in at the mouth of the Bosphorus, to the south of the Dolmabahçe Palace. The Sirkeci–Üsküdar car ferry docks to the right of the Galata Bridge, beyond the wharves first mentioned above. Avoid morning and afternoon rush hours when the boats are unpleasantly overloaded. The landing wharf for all stops on the Golden Horn (Haliç) is to the left (on the Golden Horn side) at the new town end.

EXCURSIONS. By Air. Day trips by plane to Bursa, capital of the Osmanli Empire in the 15th century, are operated by *Sönmez Holding Hava Yollari,* Atatürk Airport (tel. 573 72 40). The 20-minute flight allows a full day in Bursa, but departures are from Atatürk Airport, 16 km. (10 miles) from the center of Istanbul.

Sancak Air, Londra Asfaltı (tel. 579 07 24), have a variety of helicopter trips on offer, three of which cover Istanbul and vicinity. It's an expensive way of taking fabulous snaps.

By Car. You can drive to Bursa, cutting 150 km. (93 miles) off the journey by taking the ferry at Kartal. But at the height of the tourist season make sure to arrive well ahead of ferry departure times; boats leave every hour and the crossing takes about 1½ hours.

By Bus. Trolley buses (only so far), buses and motor coaches will take you along the all-too-narrow road running along the European shore of the Bosphorus, passing through docks as well as residential quarters. If you are a group, take a minibus. On the Asian side of the Bosphorus, the road follows the shore as far as Beykoz.

The big beach at Kilyos on the Black Sea (European side) can be reached by buses, which stop at the small beaches all along the Bosphorus. Şile, on the Asian side of the Black Sea, is served by buses setting out from Üsküdar.

By Boat. A boat trip on the Bosphorus, one of the most beautiful waterways of the world, is something no traveler should miss. From Eminönü three boats depart on weekdays and five on Sundays from April through September, and once every day during the winter, going the 30 km. (19 miles) up to the boom that closes the Bosphorus at the northeastern outlet, leaving a fairly narrow passage for shipping. You can glimpse the Black Sea at a distance.

The nine wooded Adalar, the Princes' Islands, are grouped in the Sea of Marmara 16–32 km. (10–20 miles) southeast. There are frequent ferries from the Eminönü side of the Galata Bridge, taking an hour to the last and largest, Büyük Ada (Big Island). Phaetons drive through the pine woods to the small beaches, and there are a number of pleasant restaurants near the wharf.

Another half-day outing is a trip across the Bosphorus to the pleasure park on Camlıca Hill, with breathtaking views.

PLACES TO VISIT. One rule of the Islamic religion, strictly observed until recently, forbids the representation of the human body. Some Osmanli rulers got around this law by inviting foreign artists who were supposed to paint them by stealth, "without their knowledge." There are, however, some Turkish miniatures. Statuary is entirely pre-Islamic, mostly Hellenistic or Roman. The Topkapı Palace is closed on Tuesdays, most museums on Mondays, some palaces also on Tuesdays, but check the opening hours to be on the safe side.

Museum of the Ancient Orient and **Archeological Museum.** The first displays finds from Mesopotamia and the Hittites, the second Greek, Roman, and Byzantine archeology. Many fine statues. Renowned collection of old coins. Open 9.30–5.

Atatürk Museum. Kemal Atatürk's house, Halaskargazi Cad., Şişli. Unchanged, together with a display of souvenirs and documents dating from the birth of the Turkish Republic. Open daily 9–5.30; closed 15th of every month.

Museum of Ayasofya (St. Sophia). The fourth-century church was destroyed by fire and rebuilt almost entirely as it stands today by Justinian. Turned into a mosque by Mehmet II, it became a museum in the thirties. Remarkable Byzantine interior. Open 9.30–4.30, Tues. to Sun.

Beylerbey. Palace on the Asiatic coast of the Bosphorus, built in 1865; magnificent interior, terraced gardens. It houses a cultural center since extensive restorations. Open 9–12.30, 1.30–5; closed Mon. and Sat.

Çinili Köşk (Tiled Kiosk), opposite the Archeological Museum. Summer residence of Mehmet II, now the **Museum of Tiles.** Open 10–5.

Dolmabahçe. Palace built on land claimed from the Bosphorus (as the name indicates) in 1854 in storybook Turkish-Indian Baroque style. Floodlit at night. Open daily except Mon. and Thurs., 9–11.30, 1.30–4.30.

Ihlamur Quasr. At Beşiktaş inland from contemporary Dolmabahçe. The two remaining ornate pavilions of the sultans' recreation complex have been restored as a palace museum. Open daily except Mon. and Thurs. 9.30–4.30.

Kariye Museum (Church of the Holy Savior in Chora), near the Edirne Gate. Byzantine era. Fine mosaics and frescoes. Open daily except Tues., 9.30–5.

Military Museum, opposite the Sports and Exhibition Hall at Harbiye, near the Hilton. Afternoon performances by the Mehter Band. Open daily except Mon. and Tues., 9–5.30.

Municipal Museum in an old medrese below the aqueduct of Valens. Plaster models of Istanbul throughout its history, projecting into the year 2,000. Open 9–5; closed 5th of every month.

Museum of Mosaics. The only remains of the Roman imperial palace, with mosaics in their original setting, mosaic pictures and architectural designs. Open 10–5.

Museum of Turkish and Islamic Art, in the restored Ibrahim Paşa Palace facing the Hippodrome. Turkish religious art, miniatures, illuminated copies of the Koran, exquisite prayer rugs. Open 10–5.

Naval Museum, beyond Domabahçe Palace. Contains the Sultans' barges and other maritime exhibits. Open daily except Mon. and Tues., 9–12, 12.30–5.

Serifler Yalise, at Emirgan on the Bosphorus. Characteristic 18th-century mansion.

Topkapı Palace Museum. Dazzling display of the treasure of the Sultans, together with fine collections of glazed earthenware, china, old weapons and armor, enamels, miniatures, and Islamic relics; the *harem* requires a separate ticket; conducted visit only, every half hour. Open 9.30–5.30, except Tues.

Yerebatan Saray (Sunken Palace), the largest and most accessible of several cisterns. Open daily 9–5.

Yıldız. A series of late 19th-century kiosks of varied architecture and use, even including a Swiss chalet. All recently restored and open to the public in a vast park with lovely old trees; splendid view over the Bosphorus. The main kiosk, where Abdül Hamid II led his haunted life until his dethronement and subsequent confinement in Beylerbey, is now used as a cultural center. A smaller kiosk is an excellent restaurant, and another houses a **Museum of Abdül Hamid's Reign.**

Ceramic Factory, closed after the Sultan's deposition, produces again fine traditional porcelain. Open Wed. to Sun. 9–11, 1.30–4.

ENTERTAINMENT. Theater: the season lasts from October to the beginning of June. More interesting than the plays, in Turkish, are the opera and ballet in the 1,300-seat opera house, the Atatürk Cultural Palace on Taksim Square.

Concerts: the Musical Academy of Istanbul gives concerts of classical music, eastern and western, in the Atatürk Cultural Palace.

Cinemas: there are a great many movie houses in Istanbul, some of which show films in the original version.

SHOPPING. There are three district shopping centers, the first decidedly Oriental, the last determinedly European, and one peculiarly Istanbul. The best bargains are to be found in the Old Town at Sultanahmet. The Türk Taş Medresesi, an 18th-century masonry school, opened in 1986 as a Turkish Handicraft Market, where artisans are at work at the traditional crafts. The 4,000 minute shops of the Covered Bazaar (Kapalı Çarşı) in a fascinating maze of crowded streets and alleys are a contemporary approximation of an oriental market. Silver, brass and copper ware, embroideries, junk and, of course, Turkish rugs of all kinds, from hand-woven 18th-century masterpieces down to modern machine-made imitations. There are wares for all tastes and all purses, and bargaining is the order of the day. The shops, to make things easier, are grouped together in kind. If you need information, the shopkeepers all speak a smattering of several languages. The big bargain in Turkey is leather, very soft and beautifully worked, in all shapes and sizes. There is an endless choice of jackets, coats, and suits for both men and women. In the heart of the Bazaar, the Bedesten, are the most precious objects, meerschaum and fine onyx jewelry, but beware of antiques, whose provenance is not even doubtful in most cases, while the rare genuine article is not allowed to be exported. The Covered Bazaar is open Mon.–Sat., 8.30 A.M. to 6.30 P.M. Sections of the Egyptian Bazaar (Mısır Çarşısı) smell deliciously of spice which gave it the alternative name of Spice Bazaar.

The shops along Istiklal Cad. have preserved a nostalgic pre-war atmosphere, but except for a few, like the sweetshop *Haci Bekir,* renowned for Turkish Delight *(Lokum),* are gently declining.

The smart boutiques have opened on Cumhuriyet Cad., with the most expensive fashion shops and jewelers in the shopping arcades of the three luxury hotels. Other fashionable streets are Rumeli, Halaskargazi, and Valikonagi Caddessi.

SPORTS. Visitors are welcome at the various clubs. **Golf:** *Golf Kulüp,* Büyükdere Caddesi, Ayazağa (tel. 164 07 42). **Tennis:** *Taşlik Tenis Kulüp,* Macka; and at the *Hilton.* **Water Sports:** *Marmara Yacht Club,* Cami Sok., Erenköy.

BEACHES. None to be recommended on the muddy European shore of the Sea of Marmara, though the closer and particularly overcrowded can easily be reached by electric train from the Sirkeci rail station. On the Bosphorus, the beaches are cleaner but small. Keep to the places listed below because of the dangerously strong currents that cross the Bosphorus. On the European shore: Lido, Yeniköy, Tarabya, Bebek, near the castle of Rumeli Hisar, and Beyaz Park in Büyükdere. There are a few small beaches on the Asian shore, but only three of interest to foreigners— Moda, in Kadiköy, southeast of Istanbul, with yachting, Salacak and Küçüksu.

TURKISH BATHS. The baths in Istanbul are disappointing, really no more than utilitarian washing establishments with no steam rooms, dry heat only (and not very hot at that) and an exceedingly rough massage on marble slabs. Of some interest are the historical *Galatasaray Hamami,* Istiklal Cad., and the 300-year-old *Cagaloglu Hamami,* Hilaliahmer Cad., near the Blue Mosque, open daily until midnight to men and women— separately of course.

CHURCHES. *Protestant:* Anglican chapel of St. Helena, in the grounds of the British Consulate, Meşrutiyet Cad.; Dutch Protestant Chapel, Istiklal Cad. *Catholic:* Cathedral of the Holy Ghost, Cumhuriyet Cad. and several other churches in the New Town. *Jewish:* Synagogue Beth Israel in Şişli; Neve Shalom, near Galata Tower.

USEFUL ADDRESSES. Consulates. *U.S.A.:* Meşrutiyet Cad. 106, Tepebası (tel. 151 36 02). *Great Britain:* Meşrutiyet Cad. 34, Tepebası (tel. 144 75 40).

Travel Agencies. *American Express and Türk Express,* at the entrance to the Hilton Hotel. Other main agencies on Cumhuriyet Cad.: *Vip* at No. 12, *Van Der Zee* 16; *Visitur,* 129; *Setur,* 131; *Miltur,* 135.

Airlines. Virtually all of them have offices on Cumhuriyet Caddesi: *British Airways* at No. 10; *Pan American* in the Hilton arcade. *Turkish Airlines* (THY) at No. 131 and terminal on Şişane Square.

Shipping Lines. *Denizyollari* (Turkish Maritime Lines), Denizcilik Bankas, Rihtim Cad., Karaköy (tel. 144 02 07).

Rail Stations. For Europe: *Sirkeci* (tel. 527 59 84) in the old town, just past Galata Bridge. For Asia: *Haydarpaşa* (tel. 337 87 24) on Asian side of the Bosphorus.

Auto Information. The *Turkish Automobile Club (Turing ve Otomobil Kurumu),* Halaskargazi Cad. 364, Şişli; there is also an office on the E5 at the Topkapı entrance to Istanbul.

Tourist Police (Turizm Polisi). Alemdar Karakolu, Sultan Ahmet, tel. 528 53 69.

Post Office. Head Office, Yeni Postahane Cad., Eminönü, Old Town; branch offices in Meşrutiyet Cad., near British Consulate-General, and in Cumhuriyet Cad., near Taksim Square.

Hospitals. *American,* Güzelbahçe Sok., Nisantası (tel. 131 40 50), *French (Pasteur),* behind Divan Hotel, Taksim (tel. 148 47 56) and *La Paix,* Büyükdere Cad., Şişli (tel. 148 18 32). *German,* Sıraselviler Cad., Taksim (tel. 143 81 00). *Beyoğlu Hospital,* Kuledibi, Karaköy (tel. 151 59 00) has English-speaking doctors. Dial 011 to get the names and numbers of all-night pharmacies.

THRACE

Gateway to Europe

Thrace, Europe's easternmost promontory, is washed by the Mediterranean, the Sea of Marmara and the Black Sea, connected by the Straits of the Dardanelles and the Bosphorus. But the three seas fail to temper the harsh dry climate of freezing winters and sizzling summers. This might explain why the endless stream of conquerors rarely stayed long or made it the center of their dominions.

Greek city states began founding colonies on the more hospitable south and east shores in the 7th century B.C., constantly fighting back the savage native tribes. Athens became dominant in the 5th century, but even after annexation by Philip II of Macedonia in 350 B.C., the Thracians retained their unenviable reputation for wildness and drunkenness. Mythology starts Dionysos' drunken progress in Thrace and poetically explains the struggle between the traditional beerdrinkers and the devotees of grapejuice, newly introduced from the East.

By the War of the Successors following Alexander the Great's death, the Sea of Marmara was surrounded by the dominions of Lysimachos who, true to the custom of the Hellenistic kingdoms, built his capital Lysimachia on the Chersonese (Gelibolu Peninsula). In 279 B.C., two years after his death in the battle of Korupedion, the even wilder Gauls occupied Thrace. Most left for the richer plunder of Asia Minor, but the remainder lorded it till a bloody Thracian rebellion in 216 B.C. Petty chiefs continued their infights under the Macedonian kings till the imposition of the Pax Romana in 168 B.C.

In the decline and fall of the Roman empire, Thrace resumed its role as springboard and bridgehead for European-Asian relations—military more often than cultural. The first Turkish foothold in Europe was established at Gelibolu (Gallipolis) in 1357, and Sultan Murat I captured Adrianople four years later. Having temporarily defeated the Karamanoğlu emirs in the south, he chose red for the background of the Turkish crescent banner, and carried it northward in a long series of Balkan wars. His son, Bayezit I, annihilated the last crusade making for Anatolia at Nikopolis, on Thrace's northern confines, in 1396.

In 1413 Mehmet I transferred the capital from Bursa to Edirne. With the sultans in residence when not campaigning, Thrace occupied for almost 50 years the center of the world stage until the Turkish conquest of Constantinople. It then reverted to its more natural function as a base for military enterprises, until well into the 19th century: northwest against Austria, northeast against Poland and Russia, until the withering Russian attack that led to the cession of all Turkish possessions in the Balkans by the treaty of San Stefano of 1878. Though this treaty was voided in the same year by the Congress of Berlin, Turkey had become the Sick Man of Europe and the First Balkan War brought the frontier again to the suburbs of Constantinople in 1912. But the allies fell out among themselves and in the following year Turkey recovered Eastern Thrace up to the Meriç (Evros) river, and this has remained the border except for a brief Greek occupation after World War I. History has come full circle, and Turkey's first foothold in Europe is now its last, but so thoroughly Turkified that the three *vilayets* (provinces) are an integral part of an ethnically united nation.

Since 1945 East and West have been paradoxically reversed. The huge red star, lit at night, on top of the Bulgarian border station, is the Eastern Bloc's challenge to travelers coming by train or along the E5 from the west, while Turkey, a faithful member of the Western Alliance, is geographically to the east. And Edirne's splendid domes and minarets rising 13 km. (8 miles) southeast of the border station of Kapikule, are, moreover, Turkey's most oriental skyline. The Greek border at Pazarkule is even closer, just across the Meriç.

EXPLORING THRACE

Edirne was founded in the 2nd century as Hadrianopolis by Emperor Hadrian. It was the site of the battle in which Constantine the Great defeated the rival Emperor Licinius in 323, was plundered by the Avars, besieged by the Bulgars and the Crusaders, gloried as the first Turkish capital in Europe, and was occupied by the Russians in 1829. Today it is the gateway to the east, of a unique, undiluted turn-of-the-century Balkan variety. Having yielded its western and southern hinterlands in 1913 to Bulgaria and Greece, which lost no time eradicating all the reminders of the Turkish past, it has hardly grown since then and thus escaped the asphyxiating encroachment of featureless concrete blocks of other Turkish towns. The splendid edifices of Edirne's imperial past deserve a much more prominent place on tourist itineraries than they normally get.

Strolling through the narrow, cobbled lanes, below the overhanging balconies of wooden houses, you notice tiny shops, whose occupants, tailors, shoemakers, blacksmiths, artisans and craftsmen of all kinds work in the open air, at least when the weather permits. The local bazaar provides a lively and diverting spectacle. The minarets and domes of the mosques largely account for the sensation of having been transferred into a different world, an impression further enhanced by seeing some dilapidated horse carriages.

Above the huge, central Cumhuriyet Square rises the masterpiece of the architect Sinan, Sultan Selim's mosque, the Selimiye Cami, built between 1568 and 1574 in the reign of Selim II. The central dome, more than 30 meters (100 ft.) in diameter, rests on eight pillars supported by buttresses above the muezzin's loft. The beautiful *mimber,* or pulpit, stands to the right of the main entrance, and slightly to the left is the *mihrab,* the niche that points toward Mecca. The sultan's private loge is also on the left. The mosque's interior lighting, a masterpiece of effect in its own right, further enhances the impression of airiness and weightlessness. Legend has it that the architect wanted to put in a thousand windows, but Sultan Selim objected: "One thousand," he said, "is not an interesting number. Let's have 999 windows—there's a figure that people will remember." The mosque is preceded by a large courtyard surrounded by three colonnades covered by 18 domes (the summer mosque), with a fountain for the faithful to perform their ablutions.

The complex includes a library and medrese, now a Museum of Islamic Art, whose prize exhibits are, however, yellowed photographs of past generations of wrestlers. Opposite is the Archeological and Ethnographical Museum, displaying some Roman statuary, coins and Turkish costumes.

In the center of the square stands the monument to Edirne's great passion: two enormous wrestlers, stealing the limelight from Atatürk's obligatory statue. The backdrop is provided by the Eski Cami, built by Mehmet I in 1413, and as its name states the earliest Ottoman monument in the city.

Adjoining is the Caravanserai of Rustem Pasha, grand vizir of Süleyman the Magnificent, expertly restored according to the designs of Sinan, a successful model of similar restorations planned in Anatolia. The Bedestan (Covered Bazaar), under 19 cupolas across the road, provided the income for the Eski Cami. The Ali Pasha Bazaar next to it is another of Sinan's works.

Higher up on the square, Murat II built between 1437 and 1447 the Üc Serefeli Cami, the mosque with the three galleries which encircle the tallest of the four minarets, remarkable for their lovely brick inlay. The two medrese at the back are badly neglected, but the 15th-century Sokurlu Hamam opposite still functions, like several other baths of the same period throughout the city.

Murat II's earlier (1435–6) and smaller mosque, the Muradiye, decorated with lovely tiles, belonged to the Whirling Dervishes. Beyond the Tunca is the Bayezit Mosque (1484–8), remarkable for the absence of pillars and arches to support the large dome which rests on the four walls; the marble fretwork of the mihrab is impressive. This religious foundation included two schools, a lunatic asylum, a poorhouse, kitchens and a pharmacy, all fairly well preserved.

The original lead on the roof of the Ekmekcioğlu Ahmet Paşa Kervansaray has been replaced by tiles, and the whole of the building has been repaired. Beyond repair, alas, are the sad remains of the palace pavilions constructed by successive sultans between the 15th and 17th centuries on the Sarayici island in the Tunca, site of Edirne's great annual event, the Greased Wrestling Tournament. This is reached by Süleyman's Kanuni Bridge, one of several graceful old bridges over the Tunca and Meriç, of which that of Ghazi Mihal, on the road from Bulgaria, is partly Byzantine. Of Hadrian's mighty fortifications only one tower remains.

Beyond Edirne

A short way out of Edirne, Route 020 branches off E5 east (left) for 56 km. (35 miles) to Kırklareli below the Yıldız Mountains, which form the border with Bulgaria. Most of Turkish Thrace gives a foretaste of what to expect on the high plateau of Anatolia, by contrast with the bosky wooded copses in neighboring Greece and the fertile Bulgarian hills. Long before the Christian era, Asian tribes were in Thrace, not so intent on set-tling down as on assuring themselves of a passageway to more temperate climes. Still later, the Turks, who were laying siege to Byzantium, estab-lished themselves in the area. Kırklareli's monuments include the Hizir Bey Cami (1407), Kadi Cami and the Huseyin Ağa Hamam. Route 020 traverses the whole of northern Thrace to Istanbul, with several branches to the Black Sea fishing villages of Limanköy, Kıyıköy, Karacaköy, Duru-su and Terkoz.

E5, the main highway to Istanbul, passes through Babaeski, graced by Sinan's Çedid Ali Paş Cami. After a lovely 17th-century bridge topped by a tower, larger Lüleburgaz, ancient Arkadiopolis, features the Söküllü Mehmet Paşa Cami, complete with a hamam and a poorhouse, a mausole-um and a caravanserai. Beyond Çorlu, with two interesting mosques, are the ruins of a Roman bridge, part of the Via Egnatia which connected the Adriatic with the Bosphorus. 156 km. (97 miles) southeast of Edirne is the junction with the E25, 171 km. (106 miles) from Greece.

The E25 crosses the Meriç delta by the long Ipsala bridge, with the fron-tier right in the middle. 29 km. (18 miles) east is Keşan, an important crossroads with Route 550 north to Edirne, south to the beach of Erikli on the Saroz Gulf, whence it continues as E24 to the ferryboat crossings of the Dardanelles to Asia, from Gelibolu (Gallipoli) to Lapeski, or from Eceabat to Çanakkale. From these two ports boats ply to the two islands, Gökçe Ada (Imroz) and Bozcaada, guarding the western entrance to the straits.

The whole drive along the Gelibolu promontory, but especially beyond Eceabat to Abide, ancient Abydos, is scenically most rewarding, affording lovely views over two seas, the Saroz Gulf west and the Dardanelles east. During the Crimean War (1854–6), when British and French troops were stationed in the region, a cholera epidemic broke out. This was the occa-sion for Florence Nightingale to perform her prodigious feat of nursing. On March 18, 1915, during World War I, British and French warships vainly strove to break through the Dardanelles Straits at the Eceabat bot-tleneck; and so the abortive Gallipoli campaign began. Many Franco-British monuments and cemeteries lie near the village of Seddulbahir, at the tip of the peninsula.

No need to return to Keşan, as a lovelier coastal road passes through vineyards belonging to the fishing villages of Şarköy and Murefte to the junction with E25, which proceeds from Keşan, 84 km. (52 miles) east through uninteresting, flattish country at Tekirdağ, ancient Rodestos. The remaining journey along the shore of the Sea of Marmara starts auspiciously on a wide thoroughfare planted with flower beds, where the local inhabitants enjoy their evening strolls. Sinan also built a mosque here, the Rustem Paşa Cami (Rustem Paşa was the son-in-law of Süleyman the Magnificent).

Tekirdağ was at one time the refuge of the famous Hungarian patriot Rakoczy, who found a haven here after a series of harrowing adventures. Acting as an ally of Louis XIV and the Turks, Rakoczy had mustered an army of peasants to fight against Emperor Joseph I. When the court of Versailles offered him the crown of Poland, Prince Francis II Rakoczy refused. Deserted by all, he went into exile in Turkey. In Tekirdağ, you can visit the house, now a museum, in which he lived until his death in 1735. The *Rakoczy March* which Berlioz inserted into his score for the *Damnation of Faust* is none other than the battle hymn Rakoczy's troops used to sing before going forth into battle.

The 58 km. (36 miles) stretch to the junction with the E5 closely hugs the seashore, past the good beach of Marmara Ereğlisi. For the last 76 km. (47 miles) to Istanbul the concentration of houses, motels and camp sites increases along an unattractive piece of coast. Overdevelopment has polluted the sea and jammed the road till it widens at Florya into four lanes, eventually becoming a six-lane highway. From Istanbul's Atatürk Airport a bypass over the Haliç (Golden Horn) Bridge provides easy access to the hotels in the new town or to the Bosphorus Bridge; branches enter the old Byzantine ramparts of the city stretched out ahead.

PRACTICAL INFORMATION FOR THRACE

TOURIST OFFICES. There are tourist offices in the following towns: **Edirne,** Talat Paşa Asfaltı 76, (tel. 152 60/214 90), **Ipsala,** Ipsala Hudut Kapisi (tel. 8); **Iskele** (Port), (tel. 20 83); **Kapıkule,** Customs House (tel. 110 19); **Tekirdağ,** Müze Müdürlüğü Binasi, Vali Konaği Cad. 1 (tel. 20 83).

WHEN TO COME. Thrace is mainly visited in transit, so the most likely time is the hot but dry summer, on the way to the beaches of the Mediterranean. Late spring and early fall are more pleasant.

SPECIAL EVENT. July. *Greased Wrestling Tournament* at Edirne, six days in early July: fierce colossi anointed with olive oil throw each other till exhausted on an island in the Tunca, where the ruins of the sultans' 15th-century palace provide an unusual background to this popular fair.

HOTELS AND RESTAURANTS

Abide. *Abide* (M). 20 rooms. Comfortable motel on the Dardanelles.

Çorlu. *Marmara Tour* (M). 40 rooms. On beach. *Alp Motel* (I). 13 rooms. Also on beach. *Balkan I* (I), Omurtak Cad. 59 (tel. 130 41). 20 rooms. (Beware adjoining *Balkan II:* no private showers.)

Eceabat. *Dardanel* (I). 19 rooms. 2 km. (1 mile) west at Kilitbahir. *ECE* (I). 20 rooms. At the ferry terminal.

Edirne. *Kervan* (M), Talat Paşa Cad. (tel. 11382). 48 rooms. *Onar* (M), Kaleici Maarif Cad. (tel. 4610). 34 rooms. *Sultan* (M), Talat Paşa Cad. (tel. 1372). 83 rooms, most with showers. *Kervansaray* (I), Eski Istanbul Cad. 100 rooms with showers. Rustem Pasha's 16th-century foundation beautifully restored and modernized; despite the language difficulty, recommended as a genuine introduction to the east.

Restaurants. There are several *lokanta*-type (M–I) restaurants, where the food is better than the communication. *Cinar,* Daraclar Cad. *Kırkpinar,* on the island of the same name. *Meriç Lokantasi,* in Karagac; open summer only. *Şehir Kulüb,* Hurrivet Meydani Square.

Erikli. *Erikli Oberj* (I), (tel. 48). 43 rooms. *Işçimen* (I), (tel. 22). 30 rooms. Both are on beach.

Gelibolu. *Boncuk* (M), Sütlüce Köyü (tel. 296). 48 rooms. Pool; on beach; the best on the European shore of the Dardanelles.

Ipsala. *Motel Ipsala* (I). 20 rooms. 2 km. (1 mile) from the border bridge.

Kapıkule. *Bosfor Motel* (I). 30 rooms. *Kapıkule Motel* (I). 32 rooms.

Keşan. *Yener* (M), Demirciler Cad. 20 (tel. 3660).

Kumbağ Köyü. *Miltur Turistik* (M), (tel. 2101). 83 rooms. *Arzum Motel* (I) Kumbag Köyü (tel. 8). 20 rooms. Both on beach east of Tekirdağ.

Kumburgaz. *Motel Marin* (M), (tel. 146 85 44). 150 rooms. At Silivri Yolu, 6 km. (4 miles) away. *Motel 49* (I). 44 rooms. Both on beach.

Lüleburgaz. *Işık Motel* (I), Yenibedir Köyü (tel. 1754). 11 rooms.

Şarköy. *Durak Motel* (I). 24 rooms. On beach.

Silivri. *Motel Solu* (M), Semiz Kumlar Mevki (tel. 1430). 20 rooms. On beach.

Tekirdağ. *Yat* (I), Yali Cad. 8 (tel. 11054). 51 rooms.

CAMPING. Edirne, *Kervansaray Mokamp* (tel. 11290) (capacity 600), half a mile along the Istanbul road; *Kapıkule Mokamp* (capacity 500), administered by the Touring and Automobile Club of Turkey, half a mile from the Bulgarian border. **Ipsala,** *Kervansaray Mokamp* (capacity 300), near the Greek border. **Marmara Ereğlisi,** three camping grounds, all below par, 82 km. (51 miles) from Istanbul. **Silivri,** *Camping Topkapı,* 73 km. (45 miles) from Istanbul. **Tekirdağ,** *Camping Marmara Tur,* 105 km. (65 miles) from Istanbul.

GETTING AROUND. By Train. The different versions of what used to be the *Orient Express* enter Turkey from Bulgaria at Kapıkule. The track meanders about for no apparent reason: the company entrusted with the construction was allegedly paid by the kilometer, which might explain why the train journey takes five hours.

By Car. The main access from Europe, E5, has a rough surface well adapted to the winter snows on the way southeast to Istanbul. Despite the enlargement into a six-lane highway for the last 20 km. (12 miles), the heavy traffic slows down progress. The E25 from Greece has relatively little traffic on its four lanes till the junction with E5.

The principal north-south axis, Route 550 and E24, from Edirne via Keşan to the ferries, continues from Çanakkale along the Aegean coast to Izmir and beyond.

By Bus. There are frequent bus and minibus connections between all towns.

By Boat. Boats ply to the four islands, Marmara and Avşa in the Sea of Marmara, and to Gökçe Ada and Bozcaada at the entrance to the Dardanelles. On the last two there is as yet no accommodation worth the name, but there is a yacht supply station on Gökçe Ada.

Car ferries operate between Gelibolu and Lapseki, Eceabat and Çanakkale hourly, from 7 A.M. to 10 P.M.

FROM THE BOSPHORUS
TO THE DARDANELLES

Around the Sea of Marmara

The Straits of the Bosphorus and the Dardanelles divide Europe from Asia so perfunctorily that they have acted as bridges rather than barriers between conflicting surges of religions, cultures and imperial powers. They have never prevented an invader worth that name from crossing, but connecting the Three Seas of antiquity—the Black Sea via the Sea of Marmara with the Mediterranean—the Straits are the world's oldest maritime trade route, along which great cities were bound to rise. Troy is the most fabulous, Istanbul the most glamorous, but Nikaea (Iznik), Nikomedia (Izmit) and Prusa (Bursa) each had their considerable hours of glory.

The northwest corner of Asia Minor was occupied by Thracian tribes late in the 2nd millennium B.C. From the 8th century B.C. Greek colonies flourished along the coasts, but the Thracians were never completely subdued by the Persians. One of their chiefs, Zipoetes (328–280 B.C.), avoided submission to Alexander the Great, successfully resisted Lysimachos, and assumed the title of King of Bithynia in 297. He repelled the Seleukids, but in a dynastic struggle his son, Nikomedes I (280–255) made the mistake of calling in the barbaric Gauls, who plundered friend and foe alike before being at last confined to Galatia further east. Bithynia prospered under Prusias I Cholos (the Lame, 230–182), who narrowly avoided a breach with Rome by offering to extradite Hannibal, a refugee at his court after the battle of Magnesia. Rather than being handed over to his lifelong enemies, the great Carthaginian committed suicide in 182. The Bithynian monarchs became increasingly dependent on Rome, and the last ruler, Nikomedes IV Philopator (the Fatherloving, 94–74) bequeathed her his kingdom, in the fashion of Hellenistic Asia Minor.

In the Roman province of Bithynia, Antinous, the favorite of Emperor Hadrian, was born in the 2nd century A.D. His sensuous beauty gave antique sculpture a last inspiration, but his deification after his suicide on discovering a first wrinkle strained the credulity of tolerant paganism. One of its last defenders, Emperor Diocletian, realizing the shift of power to the East, demoted Rome in favor of Nikomedia, from which he instituted the most systematic persecution of the Christians. Ironically, the Creed of triumphant Christianity was formulated only some 30 years later in neighboring Nicaea, which in turn became the first Seljuk capital in Anatolia, capital of the exiled Byzantine emperors, to fall between 1326 and 1330 with the whole of Bithynia to Akçakoca, general of Sultan Orhan. The Christians, after exactly 1,000 years, became again a persecuted minority in Asia Minor.

EXPLORING THE MARMARA AREA

The dreary 93 km. (58 miles) of E5 from the Bosphorus Bridge to Izmit are lined with factories and badly polluted, and—though unavoidable when heading directly for Ankara—a trip round the Marmara or to Bursa would better start with a ferry crossing from Kartal 16 km. (10 miles) to Yalova. (Hovercraft from Istanbul might have materialized at last.) The first town on the highway skirting the Gulf of Izmit is Gebze, where Hannibal committed suicide and was buried in a tomb which can still be seen.

Izmit, now an industrial town, was called Olbia at the time of its founding in the 8th century B.C., and was completely destroyed by Lysimachos. Rebuilt and renamed Nikomedia by Nikomedes I, the capital of the Hellenized Bithynian kingdom flourished, despite the misadventures of Nikomedes III at the hands of Mithridates VI of Pontus. Nikomedes III died without an heir in 74 B.C., bequeathing the city to Rome. Rebuilt by Diocletian after the Gothic raid of 259, Nikomedia became rapidly the fourth city of the Roman Empire and for a short, glorious moment was capital of the eastern half. Accusing the Christians of having set fire to his palace, Diocletian instituted their most violent persecution till he abdicated in 305 near Nikomedia.

It was here that the Seljuks first reached the shores of the Marmara. Not long after, in 1086, Emperor Alexios I recaptured Nikomedia, which remained Byzantine until the Osmanli conquest in the 14th century, when it was renamed Izmit.

The Hellenistic walls were restored by the Romans and the Byzantines. The Roman aqueduct is fairly well preserved. Ruins of a second-century *nymphaion* (fountain) must have been quite lovely before the dust from the cement factories polluted a large stretch of the coast.

A pleasant change from industry at its ugliest is to be found 12 km. (7 miles) east by Lake Sapanca, along the north shore, where Abant offers swimming, boating and fishing in a sunny mountain setting. The scenery is more impressive than the local historical relics, the most important of which is a 425-meter- (466 yards)-long stone bridge built by Emperor Justinian. The return trip via Sapanca, beside the south shore of Lake Sapanca, is a pleasant alternative. Lovelier still is the drive south through the Sakarya valley and across the mountains to Iznik, where the circular road round the much larger lake is highly recommended. Thence to Bursa, to return via Yalova, thus making a complete round trip.

Iznik (Nicaea)

Though there are numerous prehistoric sites round the 30 km. (20 miles) long Lake Iznik, the city was only founded in 316 B.C. Six years later it was conquered by Lysimachos and renamed Nikaea in honor of his wife. Bithynia's rival capital was the birthplace of Parthenios, a popular elegist, whose *Metamorphoses* passed elegy into Latin literature. As Roman Nicaea it hosted in 325 the First Ecumenical Council, which defined the Creed and rejected Arianism—the most widely disseminated heresy when Christianity became the state religion. In Byzantine Nikaea the Seventh Ecumenical Council—the second to be held in this town and the last uniting the whole Church—denounced iconoclasm, the prohibition of religious pictures and statuary, in 787.

Süleyman, the Seljuk governor of Rum—after three times assisting pretenders to the Byzantine throne as far as the Sea of Marmara—proclaimed himself sultan and settled his capital in Nikaea in 1078. His son and successor, Kılıç Arslan I (the Lion of the Sword), married the daughter of the Turkish Emir of Izmir, but then murdered his father-in-law at a banquet at Nikaea.

The People's Crusade, an enthusiastic rabble led by Peter the Hermit, cut a bloody swath through Europe in 1096. Conveyed by Emperor Alexios I across the Bosphorus, the 20,000 men pillaged and murdered along the Sea of Marmara until they were massacred by Kılıç Arslan's army at Drakon, near Civetot, on the road to Nikaea.

But the following year, the First Crusade of the Barons reconquered Nikaea with the help of the imperial fleet, transported on rollers from the Sea of Marmara across the mountains to the Lake of Nikaea. Handed back to the Byzantines, it became their capital during the occupation of Constantinople by the Latins. After a long siege, the Osmanli Turks returned under Sultan Orhan in 1331, and though plundered by Tamerlane's Mongols in 1402, Iznik became in the 16th century the center for the manufacture of the lovely tiles which decorate so many mosques and palaces throughout Turkey. Decline set in with the transfer of that thriving industry to the Tekfur Saray in Istanbul in the 18th century.

A good part of the Roman and Byzantine ramparts is still standing, complete with half-moon-shaped turrets. Four successive stages in their construction are clearly discernible, each one marking the advent of a new defender. Until fairly recently it was common practice to use building materials, principally marble, from ancient ruins. The conquerors' cause was abetted no end by a series of convenient earthquakes at the end of the fourth century, three of them occurring during one ten-year period alone. Men went on rebuilding unceasingly, and towers that had once been semicircular occasionally were turned into square ones.

The Roman relics include, first, the so-called Istanbul Gate, incorporating a triumphal arch of Vespasian. Nearby is a second-century tomb in the form of a pyramid. The Lefke Gate on the east was built in honor of

Hadrian's visit in A.D. 120. Perhaps the handsomest of all is the Yenişehir Gate on the south, built under Claudius II. Since invading attacks came mainly from the south, this last gate has had to undergo frequent restorations. The ruined Göl Kapısı (Lake Gate) leads to the blue waters of the large lake, on whose shores a solitary tree and a few stones mark the site of Constantine's palace, now mostly submerged. Here the emperor convoked the stormy First Ecumenical Council in 325. Pliny the Younger, who was a governor of the region and also left his stamp on Bursa, built the gymnasium and theater in the southwestern part of the city. A large, remarkably well-preserved 5th-century tomb, with glowing murals depicting peacocks, flowers and abstract designs, was discovered under a hill in 1967.

The Seventh Ecumenical Council was held in Nicaea's main monument, the St. Sophia Basilica. This building subsequently became identified with the third, or Seljuk, epoch, and later on with the fourth epoch—the Osmanli—when it was restored by the famous Turkish architect Sinan. Excavations in the city have unearthed traces of mosaics and frescoes.

Two other churches date from this same period, the Koimesis (Dormition of the Virgin, 11th century) and Aghios Triphon. The aqueducts were the work of Justinian, repaired by Orhan; they are still in use today.

The only outstanding souvenir of the Seljuk interlude is the Ismail Bey Hamam near the First Gate. The Osmanli period displayed greater activity. A Jewish community was probably established at Nikaea, renamed Iznik, from the evidence of the re-used stones in the well of the Bocek Ayazmasi (this underground room can be visited only with the permission of the archeological museum). A Hebrew inscription is recognizable on the well-curb, along with a design of the *menorah,* the seven-pronged candelabrum that is the emblem of Judaism.

Although Osmanli architecture has conserved a blend of characteristics from all four periods, in the 14th century it had not yet become completely crystallized and was still groping toward a definitive form of expression. This is apparent in the türbes of Haci Camaşas and of Yakup Çelebi, as well as in the Yeşil Cami (Green Mosque) built near the Lefke Gate in 1378 which, with its green-tiled minarets, foreshadows "Bursa the Green."

There are numerous fascinating monuments of this "golden age," during which the artists' and architects' preoccupations with new form prevented them from giving in to conformism. Examples are the Süleyman Paşa Medrese, the mosques of Mahmud Çelebi, Haci Hamza, and Haci Özbek. In memory of his mother Sultan Murat I established in 1388 the Nilüfer Hatun Imaret (Hospice) which now houses the local museum.

The shortest route to Bursa (77 km., 48 miles) is southeast via Yenişehir, which features a fine mosque. Certainly worth the few extra miles is the more northerly alternative, with the choice of either lakeshore, to the Gulf of Gemlik and the city of the same name, once a pirates' hideout, now a minor beach resort and spa.

A four-lane highway turns inland for 30 km. (19 miles) through gentle hills to one of Turkey's loveliest towns.

Bursa (Prusa)

Phrygians, Lydians and Mysians occupied the region, but Prusias I is credited with founding the town to which he gave his name, though the

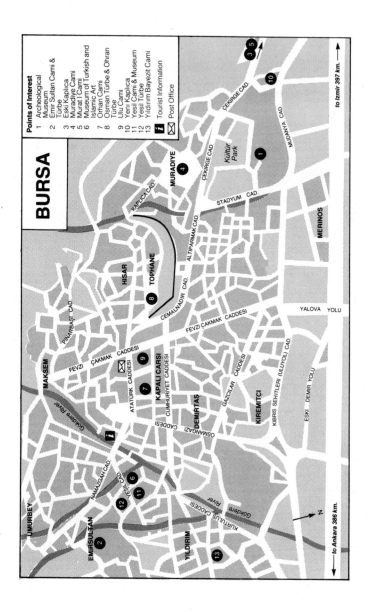

BURSA

Points of Interest

1 Archeological
   Museum
2 Emir Sultan Cami &
   Türbe
3 Eski Kaplica
4 Muradiye Cami
5 Murat I Cami
6 Museum of Turkish and
   Islamic Art
7 Orhan Cami
8 Osman Türbe & Ohran
   Türbe
9 Ulu Cami
10 Yeni Kaplica
11 Yesil Cami & Museum
12 Yesil Türbe
13 Yildirim Bayezit Cami

🛈 Tourist Information
✉ Post Office

distinguished geographer Pliny the Younger, who was Roman governor of Bithynia in the 1st century A.D., ascribes it to Prusias II Kynegos (the Hunter, 182–149 B.C.). Despite repeated Seljuk attacks, the Byzantines retained possession till the siege by Sultan Osman in 1325. The founder of Osmanli greatness died before the town fell to his son Orhan, who made it his capital until imperial expansion in Europe necessitated the transfer to Edirne in 1413. Bursa benefited from the first flowering of Osmanli architecture, only temporarily interrupted when Tamerlane's Mongol hordes stormed the town in 1402. Further damage was inflicted during wars between rival imperial claimants, but even the diminished political significance in no way interfered with Bursa's importance as a trading-post on the east-west caravan route, which lasted almost to the brief occupation by Greek forces in 1920. After the Turkish victory in 1922, Bursa's Greek residents were exchanged with Turks from Greece. Industrialization has created vast new suburbs containing a population of about a million and a half. Beside becoming Turkey's Detroit with large car factories, Bursa produces pretty towels and has remained the center of a flourishing silk industry.

The last two may assist tourism, but the main attractions are, of course, the position at the foot of Uludağ (2,543 meters, 8,340 ft.) overlooking a marvelously fertile plain, and the monuments of Yeşil Bursa, the lovely turquoise green characteristic of the Osmanli town. The landmark is the Ulu Cami (Great Mosque), at the eastern gate of the fortifications, begun by Murat I in 1379, completed in the reign of Mehmet I in 1421, and extensively restored in 1967 after an earthquake. The distinctive thrust of its silhouette, topped by a cluster of 20 domes, provides a magnificent spectacle. In the interior the domes are supported (in groups of four) by five naves, the latter in turn separated by 12 pillars. The central dome has a window covered by a grillwork through which the daylight filters. Directly beneath is the *sadirvan,* or fountain for ablutions, in the middle of the prayer room. Masterpieces of Koranic calligraphy decorate the walls; among the manuscripts in showcases is a Koran ornamented with gold thread work and dated in the year 770 of the Hegira. The tiled mihrab has unfortunately been daubed over with paint, but the cedarwood mimber has been preserved intact.

In 1339 Bursa's conqueror built the Orhan Cami, which is preceded by a portico of antique pillars. Higher up, across the Gökdere River, are Bursa's main sights—the Yeşil Cami (Green Mosque) and the Yeşil Türbe (Green Mausoleum), both completed in 1421 by Mehmet I Çelebi (the Gentleman). They face each other across Yeşil Caddesi, a block away from the Museum of Turkish and Islamic Art in the former medrese, the theological school, which contains precious rugs, tiles and lovely handwritten Korans.

The superb blue and green tiles seem as intriguingly iridescent as ever, though an earthquake at the end of the 19th century wrought considerable havoc, and the mosque's minarets suffered particular damage; the Turkish architect Asim Bey did a remarkable job of repairing and restoring the wrecked parts. The loggias superimposed above the main entrance are the *divan* (lecture hall) and the *mahfil* (prayer room) of Mehmet I. The mihrab stands over 15 meters (50 ft.) high. Before dying at the age of 47, the Sultan sent two infant sons for safety to the Byzantine emperor. Mehmet I was buried in a lavishly decorated sepulchre, surrounded by the simpler graves of his family, in the turquoise-blue and green tiled octagonal Yeşil Türbe crowned by a cone-shaped roof. The mihrab here is as handsome as the one in the mosque.

Further up the hill, surrounded by cypresses, is the Mosque and Mausoleum of Emir Sultan, Bayezit I's son-in-law, which was damaged by an earthquake at the end of the 18th century. It was restored by Selim III, suffered further damage from another quake in 1855 and had to be even more extensively rebuilt. Two km. (one mile) higher, a cable car starts up to Uludağ, but the view over the town and plain from Emir Sultan can hardly be bettered. Beyond a section of old pink and yellow houses is the Yıldırım Bayezit Cami, completed with its outbuildings in 1403, an outstanding example of early Osmanli architecture.

The crumbling walls of the Roman/Byzantine Citadel (Hisar) rise in the center of Bursa. Beyond, Murat II built a mosque and medrese in the 15th century. The mosque's distinguishing features, beside the use of ribbed arches, are a handsome sardivan and fine turquoise tiles.

The Muradiye Cami is surrounded by türbes. The Sultan's tomb is notable for its open dome above antique columns with Corinthian capitals. In addition, there are the türbes of Hevletsah Hatun (the wife of Bayezit I); of the latter's son Musa, distinguished by a blend of green tiles; of Prince Cem, the son of Süleyman the Magnificent; and of Sehzade Mahmut, where the coffins of four imperial princes are surrounded by a uniquely beautiful pattern of light and dark blue tiles. The 11 tombs grouped round a fountain are surely some of the world's most serene resting places. Equally peaceful is the atmosphere in the restored 18th-century house opposite, which preserves the dignity but also the discomfort of upper-class domesticity of the period.

Though Osman Ghazi failed to capture Bursa, he wished to be buried there. In pious fulfilment of this desire, his son Orhan erected a türbe for his father between the citadel and Tophane, on the site of the ancient basilica of St. Elijah, which had been converted into a mosque. Orhan himself reposes nearby, in the mausoleum of Orhan Ghazi, its square dome resting on four pillars. The tombs of both father and son were made of silver.

Below the Ulu Cami is the Emir Han, the two-storied caravanserai, admirably restored within the completely reconstructed covered bazaar.

During the Bursa Fair in July the *kılıç kalkan* (sword and shield dance) presents an admirable display of martial costumes, agile dancing and impeccable rhythm-keeping to the clashing of swords, without any musical instruments.

The Çekirge suburb begins at the Kültürpark, where the Archeological Museum contains a fine collection of ancient coins as well as Hellenistic, Roman and Byzantine finds. Further out, past the Süleyman Çelebi Türbe, is the Mosque of Murat I, remarkable for its Gothic arches; the architect is supposed to have been a 14th-century Italian prisoner. The sultan's tomb, opposite, is a restoration—another earthquake centered here.

Since Roman times Bursa has been a renowned spa, with thermal baths built on the Çekirge slopes. The Eski Kaplıca (Old Spring), probably the oldest bath in continuous use, dates from the 14th century and incorporates vestiges of Justinian's imperial baths. The Empress Theodora came here for her rheumatism, in style with a retinue of 4,000. The Kara Mustafa Kaplıca was built in the 15th century and restored in the 18th. The Yeni

Kaplıca (New Spring) was built by the Grand Vizir of Süleyman the Magnificent, paved with marble and blue tiles.

Mysia's Mount Olympos, Uludağ, is only 35 km. (21 miles) by road southwest of Bursa, or ten minutes by cable car. Turkey's main ski resort from December to April, the National Park is popular in all seasons for the invigorating air of the pinewoods. The Romans and Byzantines enjoyed it as a summer retreat, besides letting it supply the snow which cooled wine and fruit in the palaces of Constantinople. Yet another name of Uludağ (Great Mountain) was Kesisdagi, Monk's Mountain: this was in the 8th century when a monastery served as a refuge for persecuted priests under the ikonoklastic emperors.

Inegöl, 44 km. (27 miles) east, contains rock tombs and a 15th-century mosque, the Işak Cami. Nearby lie the ruins of the Ortaköy caravanserai.

On and Off the Coast

The only road along the southern shore of the Sea of Marmara is the 75 km. (47 miles) of Route 130 on the Izmit Körfez (Gulf) from Izmit to the ferry terminal at Yalova. 8 km. (5 miles) inland is Yalova Termal, a popular spa in extensive woods. A very secondary road circles the pretty peninsula via Çınarcık, a small spa and beach resort, but quicker and easier is the 30 km. (19 mile) inland stretch of Route 575 to Gemlik. Then go along the Gemlik Körfez to Bursa's port, Mudanya (ancient Myrlea), where the armistice ending Turkey's War of Independence was signed in 1922.

Like most archeological sites, ports and seaside resorts on this coast, Mudanya is reached by a branch road going north from the main east-west axis further inland. It is 29 km. (18 miles) back to Bursa and then west on Route 200, hugging the northern shore of Lake Ulubat. The ruins of a theater and stadium indicate ancient Apollonia on Ryndakos, but nothing remains of the great temple of Apollo. Further west, on the sea, is Bandırma (109 km., 74 miles), deriving from ancient Panormos, meaning "harbor of confidence." The Sea of Marmara can be pretty rough around these parts, and sailors are grateful for shelter. 20 km. (12 miles) south, Kuş Cenneti (Bird Paradise) National Park on Lake Kuş protects some 200 specimens in a bird sanctuary.

The province of Balıkesir provides a foretaste of the country's fantastic storehouse of archeological treasures. Moreover, this is one of the loveliest parts of Anatolia, combining scenery, sites and beaches. Balıkesir town, in the center, was built over Emperor Hadrian's 2nd-century A.D. foundations. Of interest are the 14th-century Yıldırım Cami and the 15th-century Paşa Cami. Erdek, north of Bandırma, and one of the most attractive ports on the Sea of Marmara, is blessed with only the gentlest southern breezes. Vineyards, olive groves, and fruit orchards surround it, and there's plenty of historical sightseeing to be done in the vicinity. Kyzikos, where Alcibiades won his great victory over the Spartans in the Peloponnesian War, is on the coast; farther inland are Demir-Kapı and Kocakilise (temple of Hadrian, the agora, and a fortress). For archeology fans there are also Balya, Edremit, Burhaniye, and Dursunbey. Inland are several spas: Gönen (for rheumatism), Susurluk (for skin afflictions), and Kazdağ (ancient Mount Ida)—its hot sulphur springs bubble forth at a temperature of 70°C (158°F)! For hunters, the game in the forests of this mythological peak (north of Edremit) includes boars.

Route 200 more or less follows the sea coast, with a branch to the spa of Gönen, then via Biga and Lapseki to Çanakkale, where it joins Route 550 (E24). Beaches are numerous and varied; accommodations are adequate.

Çanakkale Bogazi (The Dardanelles)

The Dardanelles, the Hellespont of antiquity—61 km. (38 miles) long and from 1.25 km. (¾ mile) to 7.5 km. (4½ miles) wide—separate the European Gelibolu (Gallipolis) promontory from the westernmost Asian cape, the ancient Troad. Such a geopolitical position attracted enterprising settlers as early as the 3rd millennium B.C. in the attempt to control the shipping. Troy was the earliest and most famous town, and the straits were named after its legendary King Dardanos. Crossed westwards by the Persians, fought over by the Athenians and Spartans in the Peloponnesian War, which was decided by the crushing defeat of the former at Aegospotami (Goat River, the present Cumalı), crossed eastwards by Alexander the Great and changing hands among his successors, the Dardanelles were fortified by the Byzantines, but in 668 and 672 the fleet of the Ommiad caliph forced a way through to the siege of Constantinople.

The region was devastated by unpaid Catalan mercenaries in the 14th century, and Turkish forces crossed into Europe for the first time in 1354. About 200 years later, Mehmet II the Conqueror built a strong castle at the mouth of the Koca Çay. Because earthenware (çanak) was produced at Sultaniye Hisar, the town that sprang up round the castle became known as Çanakkale. In World War I, in 1915, according to Churchill's plan, the Allied Powers tried to breach the Dardanelles defences in a series of bloody battles, but were foiled by Mustafa Kemal, the Turkish general who was to become Atatürk. His victory is commemorated by a great monument, 41 meters (135 ft.) tall, rising on the opposite shore at Gelibolu (Gallipoli). The French and British cemeteries are at the tip of the peninsula.

Again in 1922, Mustafa Kemal played the boldest hand in the whole poker game of his extraordinary career. Izmir had been recaptured, but the Greeks were mustering a new army in Thrace. These troops had to be defeated before they could advance on Constantinople. Kemal had no fleet and a British contingent blocked the way at Çanakkale. Though firmly entrenched, the British Commander-in-Chief had no clear orders as the situation was politically confused. By forcing his way through, Kemal was running the risk of thrusting Great Britain—plus France and Italy—over into the opposite camp. The substantial gains already won in his War of Independence would be wiped out overnight. It was imperative for him to get through and equally important for British neutrality to be preserved.

The Turks proceeded. When the British summoned them to halt, they kept on advancing, but without firing a shot. It was a colossal bluff by both sides. If a single nervewracked soldier had let fly a bullet in the unbearably tense atmosphere, the powder-barrel would have blown up. The British officer ordered his men to take aim, but the Turks just kept marching with their rifles slung over their shoulders. No fighting took place that day at Çanakkale.

The town has greatly improved since then. The castle is still the principal sight, but there is also an interesting Archeological Museum displaying

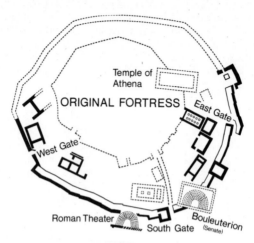

PLAN OF TROY VII TO IX

finds from several ancient towns. The main ferry crossing from Europe, Çanakkale is a convenient overnight stop before visiting Truva (Troy) 27 km. (17 miles) southwest through rolling hills.

The Trojan War

The story began with a beauty contest. The prize was a golden apple, cleverly supplied by the Goddess of Discord and inscribed "For the most beautiful of all." There were three contenders, Aphrodite, Hera and Athena (goddesses of love, marital fidelity and virginity—symbolically the three most prized female virtues). They chose as judge a shepherd named Paris, who was actually a prince of Troy who as a baby had been abandoned on the slopes of Mount Ida after a prophecy had said he would bring doom to his native land. He had grown up not knowing his true parents were the King and Queen of Troy, Priam and Hekuba. Each of the goddesses tried to bribe the young man: Hera with greatness, Athena with wisdom and Aphrodite with the promise of the most beautiful woman.

Paris gave the prize to Aphrodite, thus ensuring that the other two Olympians would be fixedly anti-Trojan in the forthcoming conflict. Under the protection of the Goddess of Love, Paris visited Sparta during the absence of King Menelaos, captivated his wife Helen and fled with her to Troy. Menelaos swore vengeance and enlisted the aid of his brother, King Agamemnon, and between them they raised a massive army, which included everyone who was anyone in Greece. The fleet set sail only after Agamemnon had sacrificed one of his daughters to ensure a fair wind—an act which he would live to regret. On arrival at Troy, they laid siege to the city.

The fortunes of battle varied depending on which goddess's day it happened to be. When Achilles refused to fight and sulked in his tent, the besiegers suffered a setback for lack of a leader. But the day came when Hektor, brother of Paris and leader of the Trojans, slew Patroklos, Achilles' boy friend. Achilles' vengeance was as swift as his grief was boundless. He killed Hektor in an unfair fight—at his birth, Achilles' mother, Thetis, had dipped him into the waters of the Styx, thereby rendering him invulnerable, except for the heel by which his mother had held him.

Now it was Paris's turn to avenge his brother. Poised on the ramparts, he shot an arrow that found its mark straight to Achilles' heel. The hero was dead and Troy's walls were intact. The war dragged on for ten years, until the crafty King of Ithaka, Odysseus, had an idea. There was a big show of getting the ships ready to leave, and sailing off with not a soul left on the shore—only a huge wooden horse that had been left behind as a last offering to the gods. The Trojans proceeded to haul the horse into the city, with singing and laughter, and celebrated their victory all through the night. Came the dawn's cold light, and all of Troy's warriors were out equally cold, dead drunk, some of them in their own beds or their neighbors', others sprawled where they had fallen. The time was ripe for the Trojan horse's belly to spring open and release Greece's ace swordsmen. While a few of them stole out to unlock the city gates for their secretly returned comrades, the rest launched the massacre. Not a brick was left standing in Troy.

The only record we have is the epic masterpiece written by the blind poet Homer, some 500 years later. The *Iliad* is the poetic equivalent of the retrospective covering of a battle by the world's first war correspondent.

The Troy in which these events took place was the seventh of nine layers that have been excavated: and that story is also a fascinating one.

Troy Times Nine

Until the middle of the 19th century Troy was commonly held to be a figment of a poet's imagination, a myth. But the son of a Protestant minister from Mecklenburg in Germany clung steadfastly to the conviction that enshrined in this ancient legend was an account of actual historical events. His name was Heinrich Schliemann, a grocery clerk, who took advantage of a long illness to study six foreign languages. In 1863, having amassed a fortune in the California goldrush, he gave up everything to devote himself to his consuming passion, which was to prove that a blind bard had sung of a true story, not a myth.

The few courageous scholars who admitted that Troy (Ilion) might actually have existed believed it to have been located near the village of Bunarbasi, because of the two nearby springs that corresponded with those in the Twelfth Canto of the *Iliad*. But this site was three hours' march from the sea where the Greeks were encamped, a somewhat tiring preliminary for the daily skirmish. Schliemann found that the Hisarlık hill, a rocky outcrop overlooking the Troad plain, fitted in much better with the circumstances. He began digging in the spring of 1870. For years, Schliemann paid about one hundred laborers and helpers out of his own pocket, while the scientific world, with few exceptions, looked disdainfully down on the efforts of this self-taught archeologist. And finally he discovered nine successive settlements, one on top of the other, dating back some 5,000 years and yielding a richer haul than he had dared to imagine.

The branch road ends before a huge wooden horse which, inexplicably, is saddled with a large hut. If the Trojans were taken in by anything like that, they deserve little sympathy. In the garden, dotted with broken Roman columns and capitals, a modern Helen of Troy acts as hostess, dressed in fetching ancient costumes, during the annual August Festival. Beyond the small museum, where more Roman finds are displayed, comes the inevitable shock: the size of the town that was besieged for ten years and not just by any odd army, but by legendary heroes. They must have been singularly neglectful to fail to prevent supplies passing so small a perimeter. And where were all those horses drawing the chariots stabled? These are only some of the questions to which an insignificant hole in the rock gives scant answer. Troy I (3000–2600 B.C.) was a small fortress in which a megaron-type house, a rectangular chamber with a central hearth, can be traced. Troy II (2600–2300) developed into a city enclosed by walls where Schliemann discovered a hoard of jewels that he wrongly attributed to Priam. This treasure in turn aroused lively arguments, and was spirited by Schliemann out of Turkey and worn by his Greek wife on festive occasions in Athens. After keeping the museums of the world in suspense for 20 years, German patriotism proved stronger than the justice of the Turkish claim and the emotional Greek appeal; the treasure was bequeathed to Berlin, where it stayed until 1945. After the war it inexplicably disappeared, and may today be in the U.S.S.R.

Schliemann concluded that Troy II was the city described in the *Iliad*. The existence of wide gates equipped with ramps for chariots seemed to bear out his theory. Despite careful excavation of the third, fourth, and fifth levels, ranging from 2300 to 1900 B.C., it is barely possible to make out where one ends and the other begins.

Troy VI (1900–1300) shows Hittite influence and it might be conceded that the walls are recognizable. Troy VII has been divided into two parts: A (1300–1220) and B (1200–900). Identification was possible through pottery from the Mycenean period. Troy VII A was rebuilt after an earthquake. The Greeks seized and sacked it around 1220 B.C.; after they had left, the Trojans and their allies began rebuilding. The result was Troy VII B, largely occupied by a new group of people.

Troy VIII (900–350) shows increasing Greek ascendancy, especially after the Aeolian invasion in around 700 B.C. and despite the centuries of Persian sovereignty. Troy IX (350 B.C.–400 A.D.) became a Hellenistic/Roman town, sponsored by Alexander the Great as well as Julius Caesar. The former saw himself and his beloved Hephaestion as another Achilles and Patroklos, in whose honor he instituted games which he opened by running naked three times round New Ilion. On a visit during a campaign, Caesar reasserted his claim to descend from Aeneas, the Trojan prince who led a few survivors to the vicinity of future Rome. The prestige of past glory continued into the Christian era, and Constantine the Great considered Ilion as a possible imperial capital before settling on Byzantion. Why only 70 years later, in about A.D. 400 Troy/Ilion disappeared from the map has remained a mystery.

A Brief Tour

To the right of the entrance, a small museum displays a few specimens of Greek pottery of the classical period. Just follow the arrows: first to the ancient ramparts and a bit of the enclosure wall of Troy VII, with the foundations of one square tower still visible. This was a redoubtable wall not unlike that of Mycenae, forming an oval some 600 meters (666 yards) in circumference. A wall almost 5 meters (16 ft.) high, made of rough-hewn stones and unbaked brick formed the top part, which was built up over a base 7.6 meters (25 ft.) high and nearly 5 meters (16 ft.) thick. It contained at least three entrance gates and a postern.

The tour leads through the east gate of Troy V, the only remains of which are a few unprepossessing fragments of a jumble of residential buildings. Turn around and walk back to an esplanade, from which there is a view over the coastal plains and the sea, and the distant foothills of Mount Ida. Proceed north to the ruins of the Temple of Athena, begun by Lysimachos and rebuilt by the Romans.

Along the northern ramparts lie scattered bits bequeathed by divers epochs. The 3rd millennium B.C. paved ramp up to the city affords one of the most vivid reminders of what Troy must at one time have looked like. Continue on to a trench containing a partially restored shrine from Troy VIII, including a sacrificial altar near two wells. On the southern side are the ruins of the Roman theater and fragments of a mosaic paving.

A gate of Troy VI opens onto the central acropolis where the public buildings were concentrated. To the right stands the *bouleuterion* (assembly building), designed along the same lines as the theater.

Other Sites

The aqueduct and amphitheater of Troas (Alexandria), needless to say, founded by Alexander the Great, rise 75 km. (46 miles) south of Çanakkale, off the E24. Further south, near Ezine, are the ruins of Neandria's 6th-century B.C. temple. And 20 km. (12 miles) southwest from Ayvacık, on a fortified escarpment overlooking the sea at Behramkale on the Edremit Körfez (Gulf) are the still impressive remains of Assos. This was considered one of the loveliest towns of antiquity, and Aristotle probably spent three years there.

Lapseki, 32 km. (20 miles) northwest from Çanakkale, is ancient Lampsakos, birthplace of the philosopher Anaxagoras, whose revolutionary theories about the universe scandalized the 5th century B.C. The shores of the straits are guarded by medieval and modern fortifications, flanked by memorials from the Crimean War and World War I.

PRACTICAL INFORMATION FOR
THE MARMARA AREA

TOURIST OFFICES. There are tourist offices in the following towns: **Balıkesir,** Gazi Bul. 27 (tel. 118 20); **Bursa,** Atatürk Cad. 82 (tel. 212 359); **Çanakkale,** Iskele Meydanı 67 (tel. 1187); **Izmit,** Ankara Asfaltı 2 (tel. 156 63); **Iznik,** Kılıçarslan Cad. 168 (tel. 1933); **Yalova,** Iskele Meydanı 5 (tel. 2108).

WHEN TO COME. The proximity of the sea prevents extremes of temperature, so that sightseeing continues throughout the year. Beaches are less visited than the more attractive resorts further south.

SPECIAL EVENTS. March. Uludağ Skiing Competition, late March.
July. Bursa Folklore Festival—highlight is the Sword and Shield Dance
performed in striking early Osmanli costumes—in the Kültür Park, last
three weeks of July. **August.** Troy Festival, with election of a Helen of
Troy, one week mid-month.

HOTELS AND RESTAURANTS

Abant. *Turban Abant* (M), (tel. 5573). 94 rooms, also detached cot-
tages. Halfboard; indoor pool; on lakeshore in pine forests.

Balikesir. *Imanoğlu* (M), Örücüler Cad. (tel. 171 44). 36 rooms. *Büyük
Çömlek* (I), Oto Terminal Karsisi (tel. 127 47). 21 rooms. *Kervansaray*
(I), Istasyon Mey. (tel. 116 35). 57 rooms. Good restaurant. *Molam* (I),
Yeşil Cad. (tel. 180 75). 24 rooms. *Yilmaz* (I), Mili Kuvvetler Cad. (tel.
174 93). 41 rooms. Good value.

Bayramoğlu (Darica). *Motel Bekir* (M). 17 rooms. Beach.

Bursa. *Çelik Palas* (E), Çekirge Cad. (tel. 361 900). 131 rooms. Part
of the Emek chain, with tennis and good restaurant.
   Akdoğan (M), Murat Cad. (tel. 360 610). 119 rooms. *Artıç* (M), Fevzi
Çakmak Cad. (tel. 219 500). 63 rooms. No restaurant; central. *Büyük Yıldız* (M), Uludağ Yolu (tel. 366 605). 58 rooms. Sauna. *Dilmen* (M), Hamamlar Cad. (tel. 366 115). 88 rooms. Near thermal springs, with own
thermal pool and Turkish bath. *Hünkar* (M), Acemler Cad. (tel. 317 084).
44 rooms. Also near thermal springs, with own thermal pool and Turkish
bath. *Gönlüferah* (M), Murat Cad. (tel. 362 700). 62 rooms.
   Acar (I), Çekirge Cad. 47 rooms. In pleasant Çekirge suburb, near thermal springs but without own thermal facilities. *Akçam* (I), Uludağ Yolu
(tel. 368 303). 22 rooms. *Dikmen* (I), Maksem Cad. (tel. 214 995). 50
rooms. *Diyar* (I), Çekirge Cad. (tel. 365 130). 45 rooms. In pleasant Çekirge suburb; no thermal facilities, however. *Yat* (I), Hamamlar Cad. (tel.
363 112). 47 rooms. Thermal pool and Turkish bath; near thermal springs.
   Restaurants. Best among the numerous establishments (all M–I) serving
the local specialty, *döner kebap* are: *Özkent,* Kültür Park; *Papağan,* Murat
Cad.; and *Sömez,* 9 km. (6 miles) along Yeni Yalova Yolu.

Çannakale. All on seafront with fine view over the Dardanelles. *Truva*
(M), (tel. 1024). 66 rooms. Good restaurant. *Anafartalar* (I), (tel. 4451).
42 rooms. *Bakır* (I), (tel. 4088). 35 rooms.
   Mola Motel (I), (tel. 22). 32 rooms. 12 km. (8 miles) along the road to
Troy.

Cinarcik. *Motel Üç Reis* (I). 27 rooms.

Denizkent. *Motel Denizkent* (I). 78 rooms.

Erdek. All on beach. *Pınar* (M), Mangirci Mev. (tel. 1123). 78 rooms.
Gül Plaj (I), Kumluyali Cad. (tel. 1053). 41 rooms. *Yücel* (I), Çuğra Mev.
(tel. 1307). 60 rooms.

Gebze. *Doğuş* (I), Eskihisar Köyü (tel. 2877). 13 rooms. On beach.

Gemlik. *Atamar,* (E), Kumlu Yolu, Hasanağa Mev. (tel. 4594). *Terme Ilıca* (I). 30 rooms. *Tibel* (I), Kumsal Sok. 18 (tel. 2146). 30 rooms. On beach.

Gönen. Both hotels have a full range of thermal installations. *Park* (M), (tel. 1840). 54 rooms. *Yıldız* (M), Banyolar Cad. (tel. 18403). 150 rooms.

Hereke. On the Istanbul-Izmit motorway. *Totaş* (M). 26 rooms. On beach.

Inegöl. *Oylat Motel* (I). 24 rooms.

Intepe. 11 km. (6 miles) north of Troy. *Tusan-Truva Motel* (M), (tel. 1461). 64 rooms. Often booked up; good restaurant; beach.

Izmit. *Altınnal* (M), Alemdar Cad. 7 (tel. 1154 70). 103 rooms. *Asya* (M), Ankara Cad. 3 (tel. 1132 25). 64 rooms. *Kozluca* (I), Ankara Cad. 152 (tel. 1152 75). 39 rooms.

Iznik. *Iznik Motel* (I). 18 rooms. On lake. Taverns on the waterfront serve lake fish.

Marmara Ada (Island). *Mermer* (I). 23 rooms.

Mudanya. *Köksal* (M), (tel. 2400). 51 rooms. Beach, pool.

Sapanca. *Vakif* (M), Rüstempaşa Mah. Kumbaz Sok. 10 (tel. 1168). 34 rooms. On lake, with swimming, riding, tennis.

Türkeli Ada (Avşa Islands). *Çınar* (M), (tel. 360). 52 rooms. Beach.

Uludağ. Skiing and summer resort in the mountains above Bursa. Mountain hotels built Chalet-style are usually called oberj (auberge). *Beceren Oberj* (E), (tel. 1111). 67 rooms. Sauna. *Yazıcı Oberj* (E), (tel. 1040). 39 rooms. *Clup Datça Dağ Oberj* (M), (tel. 1020). 44 rooms. *Fahri Oberj* (M), (tel. 1010). 66 rooms. Sauna. *Panorama Oberj* (M), (tel. 1237). 98 rooms. *Turistik Uludağ* (M), (tel. 1187). 127 rooms. *Uludağ Turistik Pansiyon* (M), (tel. 1001). 100 rooms. *Alkoçlar* (I), (tel. 1130). 56 rooms. Restaurant.

Restaurants. *Panorama* (I), at the cable car terminal. Several open-air establishments sell meat and provide *mangals* (charcoal braziers) for a cook-it-yourself.

Yalova Termal. *Turban Thermal* (M), (tel. 4905). 107 rooms in three buildings. Thermal bath from Roman period, outdoor pool.

Yarimca. *Gülistan* (I), Yeniyali Mah. 88 Tütünçifitlik (tel. 1343). 31 rooms. Restaurants.

CAMPING. Balıkesir, *Altin Kamp* (capacity 175). **Bursa,** *Kumluk Kervansaray Mokamp* (capacity 600), 7 km. (4 miles) north on the Yalova road; with pool. **Çanakkale,** *Sen Mokamp* (capacity 500), 5 km. (3 miles) south on the Izmir road, beach; *Truva Mokamp* (capacity 400), 14 km.

(9 miles) south, near beach; *Intepe Camping* (capacity 300), 21 km. (13 miles) south, near beach.

GETTING AROUND. By Air. There are daily flights—which we have already mentioned under *Excursions* in the *Practical Information* for Istanbul—between Istanbul and Bursa, taking about 20 minutes. Timetables vary, so ask your travel agent.

By Train. The Marmara Express makes three runs weekly from Izmir to Bandırma, connecting with the Bandırma–Istanbul ferry.

By Car. The six-lane European and Asian sections of the E5 (Route 100) are connected by the Istanbul bypass, which runs from Atatürk Airport over the Golden Horn and the Bosphorus Bridge (toll payable crossing from the European side). Beware of the pedestrian crossings on the 93 km. (58 miles) toll motorway from the Bridge to Izmit. After 16 km. (10 miles) the branch right leads to Kartal and the ferry for Yalova which lops 140 km. (88 miles) off the distance to Bursa.

Since Bursa merits a full day's trip, the best way is to catch the 8.10 A.M. ferry at Kartal and return from Yalova with the 6.20 P.M. ferry (this means leaving Bursa by 4.45 P.M. at the latest to allow at least a half-hour's wait for the ferry). Weekends or holidays it might be quicker to drive via Izmit on the highway.

The Eceabat–Çanakkale and Gelibolu–Lapseki car ferries across the Dardanelles sail hourly from 7 A.M. to 10 P.M.

By Bus. There are frequent connections between all towns by bus and minibus, and organized sightseeing tours to Bursa and Troy.

By Boat. There are Hovercraft and hydrofoil services from Istanbul to Yalova and Mudanya. The following places are connected by ferries or boats: Istanbul–Marmara and Türkeli Ada (Avşa Islands); Istanbul–Mudanya, Istanbul–Bandırma, Istanbul–Çanakkale and Gelibolu; Çanakkale–Bozcaada and Gökçe Ada (Islands).

SPORTS. Uludağ, 33 km. (21 miles) southwest of Bursa, reached by cable car or by road from Bursa, is Turkey's largest **winter sports** resort. The season runs from November to April with **skiing** competitions in the last week in March. There are five chair lifts. Accommodations are rather thin on the ground, so book well in advance.

SHOPPING in Bursa's bazaar, which is vast and attractive, is much cheaper for all items than in Istanbul, with the sole exception of leather clothing.

IZMIR

N.A.T.O. and the Velvet Fortress

At the long inlet east from the head of a vast bay, the busy port of Izmir is backed by Mount Pagos, closest of the mountains half-enclosing the town. From the palm-lined seafront, modern blocks of flats climb the foothills. Karşiyaka, a garden suburb with a large stadium, is across the inlet, 15 minutes by ferry, but hardly any longer in time along the E24 hugging the north coast or by electric train.

Legend attributes the first settlement at Tepekule near Bayraklı to the northeast of the bay to Smyrna, a queen of the Amazons, or to the Leleges, a roving piratical tribe. Aeolians took over in the 11th century B.C., to be replaced by the Ionians some 400 years later. Around 600 B.C., Alyattes III, King of Lydia, put the town to fire and sword. It was to be rebuilt 200 years later by Alexander the Great near a sanctuary of Nemesis on the slopes of Mount Pagos, according to the advice of the goddess in a dream.

At his death, the town fell to the lot of Lysimachos. For a time, Smyrna belonged to the kingdom of Pergamon, until it passed to the Romans. Rebuilt by the Emperor Aurelius after the earthquake of 178 (Smyrna is exceptionally vulnerable to quakes), the prosperous town became the site of one of the Seven Churches of the Apocalypse in Anatolia. The Arabs made several attempts to capture it, but the town held out, to fall at last, in the 11th century, before the onslaught of the Seljuk Turks.

From 1097 on, Smyrna became a battlefield in the Crusades, passing back and forth between the forces of Islam and Christendom. Destroyed and restored successively by Byzantines and Seljuks, Smyrna was held by the Knights of Rhodes when Tamerlane sacked the town and slaughtered its inhabitants in 1402. 13 years later Sultan Mehmet I Çelebi incorporated it in the Osmanli Empire.

Towards the end of the 15th century, Jews driven from Spain settled in Smyrna, forming a lasting Sephardic community. But the Greeks still were in the majority, though from the 16th century on, English traders as well as Dutch and French had formed an important foreign colony, mostly engaged in the lucrative tobacco trade. Despite repeated destructive earthquakes, especially in 1688 and 1778, Smyrna remained prosperous, the most important trading port of West Anatolia.

At the end of World War I the Greeks occupied the town. The Treaty of Sèvres in 1920 provided for Greek administration of the entire Aegean coast, but the Turkish revival under Mustafa Kemal led to a bloody struggle, ending in his victory at Dumlupınar. After appalling losses the remnants of the Greek forces fell back on Smyrna and were evacuated across the Aegean together with the Christian townspeople.

On September 9, 1922, he whom his people called the Gazi made a widely-cheered entry into the liberated port. The joy of the crowds was shortlived; the outbreak of a fire caught everybody, civilians and soldiers, friend and foe alike, in the blaze. The wind, benign Aeolus of the ancient Greeks, made a last stand for its routed countrymen by blowing on the flames. The wooden houses burned like matches, while hidden stores of munitions exploded. It was, in Mustafa Kemal's own words, "the end of an era." The liberation of Smyrna—from now on known by its Turkish name, Izmir—marked the end of the War of Independence.

EXPLORING IZMIR

The great fire made possible the lay-out of a new town. Izmir compares favorably with most Mediterranean ports, as the large new apartment houses are well constructed (a necessary precaution against the recurrent earthquakes), painted shining white or pleasing pastel shades. There is a Kültürpark, a large oasis of green round an artificial lake, accommodating recreation centers, restaurants, and a yearly international fair.

Turkey's third-largest town, with over 2,000,000 inhabitants, has kept its old renown; it is still known as Güzel Izmir, "beautiful Smyrna." Nowadays, however, the beauty lies more in the sea and hills than in the houses on the side of Mount Pagos; it lies in the curving bay, in the moving greens and blues of the water, and in the *imbat,* the soft breeze that cools the harsh summer heat. Every afternoon, it ruffles the waves that beat more strongly against the stones of the wharf, dying down again towards evening.

Izmir is the N.A.T.O. headquarters for the southeast sector, and the large number of foreign military personnel adds to the modern international atmosphere. The solid frontage of tall apartment blocks is only broken at Cumhuriyet Square with its statue of Atatürk and in the very center by Konak Square, called after the large administrative building in the background. A Moorish clock tower—all the rage in the reign of Sultan Abdül Hamid II—faces the delicate Konak Cami, dating from the 18th century. Behind stretches the bazaar, a maze of narrow alleys not particularly interesting but the liveliest quarter.

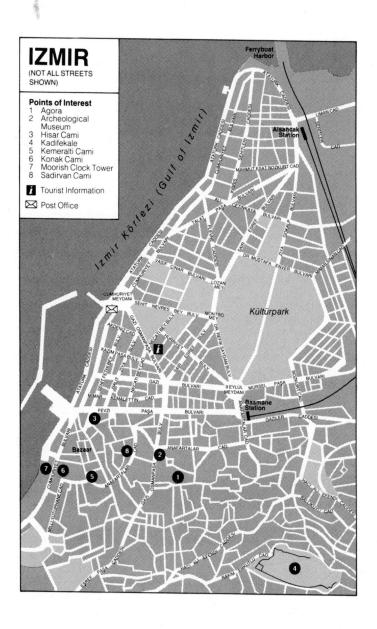

IZMIR
(NOT ALL STREETS SHOWN)

Points of Interest
1 Agora
2 Archeological Museum
3 Hisar Cami
4 Kadifekale
5 Kemeralti Cami
6 Konak Cami
7 Moorish Clock Tower
8 Sadirvan Cami

i Tourist Information

✉ Post Office

Izmir is, after Istanbul, Turkey's second port and industrial center, ranking first in export trade. The annual Fair from August 20 to September 20 is the most important in the eastern Mediterranean. If Istanbul is a main stopover for passengers on cruise ships, most cargo boats go to Izmir. Large warehouses are part of the well-equipped deep-water port at Alsancak.

What with earthquakes and fires, however, there is little left of historical interest outside of the agora and Kadifekale. To the ancient Greeks, the agora was both a public square and a marketplace. That of Izmir has the imposing remains of what was once a two-storied marble basilica, 160 meters (525 ft.) long, the flagstones surrounded by a colonnade upholding the upper stories which fell in when the colonnade itself slowly crumbled in the rain and wind of centuries. The reconstruction undertaken by the Romans in the time of Marcus Aurelius was necessitated by a devastating earthquake in the year 178.

Today, the word basilica calls to mind a church. In antiquity, it meant an indoor meeting place for merchants and bankers, politicians and statesmen, who gathered there to talk business and discuss policy. It was a sort of town hall and stock exchange, and, being the center of city life, had its market and temple, sometimes several.

At the far end of the alley, a glass frame protects the valuable remains of three carefully restored statues: Poseidon, one of whose arms and a bit of whose left foot is missing; Demeter, recognizable as such, and Artemis, less recognizable.

Kadifekale, the Velvet Fortress, overlooks the town from the top of Mount Pagos. It was originally part of the fortified wall of Smyrna, and a Roman road connected it to the agora. One of the reasons for the somewhat mysterious "velvet," discounted by scholars but pleasing to the romantic-minded traveler, might have been the appearance of these walls that have blended their red stone with the grey rock to assume the changing sheen of rubbed velvet. The imposing fortifications, enlarged and strengthened by successive conquerors, have been sufficiently restored to allow a walk along the parapet. The ramparts enclose a tea-garden and a Byzantine cistern. The round towers show Byzantine workmanship on Hellenistic foundations. It is a windy place, with a panoramic view over the town, the harbor, the rounding bay, the sea, and the mountain belt that protected Smyrna from the inland. Cable cars ascend a wooded hill to restaurants and cafés.

Noteworthy among the numerous mosques are the 16th-century Hisar and Kemeraltı, as well as the 18th-century Sadirvan, all heavily restored in the 19th century. Near the first is the Mirkelam Han, now a covered bazaar, and like the other caravanserais, Kızlaragası and Cakaloglu, models of Osmanli architecture. There are still a few traces of the original acropolis at Tepekule, where continuing excavations have brought to light nine layers of settlements dating from 1050 to 300 B.C. At the foot of the steep hill is a round edifice, supposedly the tomb of the tyrant Tantalos, who ruled in Smyrna's golden age from 620 to 580 B.C. Three Roman aqueducts, restored by Byzantines and Turks, span the Melez stream; the Baths of Artemis are at Halkapınar, and those of Agamemnon near Inciraltı.

In the town center, at Bahribaba, is the Archeological Museum, which houses finds from the whole Aegean coast, including rare mushroom-shaped capitals from the 7th century B.C., as Smyrna contained one of Anatolia's oldest Greek sanctuaries, and an equally rare 2nd-century A.D. statue of Hadrian's lover Antinous as Androklos, beside beautifully displayed jewelry and coins. On Konak Square below, the Art Gallery exhibits modern Turkish art.

Excursions from Izmir

Atatürk Caddesı, Izmir's fine palm-lined seafront promenade, continues southwest of Konak Square as a coastal corniche to the beaches and spas along Route 300 for the 81 km. (50 miles) west to Çeşme, where the land juts out to sea opposite the Greek island of Chios. Leaving Izmir through the suburb of Güzelyalı, at a mere 12 km. (7 miles), the cafés and restaurants on the fine sand of Inciraltı tend to be overcrowded. Slightly inland, the very name Agamemnon indicates that this spa has been used since antiquity for the treatment of rheumatic diseases. 22 km. (14 miles) beyond Inciraltı, between the thermal springs of Güzelbahçe and Urla, a road branches south (left) via Seferihisar to Sigacık, a small picturesque port below a Genoese fortress. Near the former are the ruins of the ancient Ionian city of Teos, where Croesus left some artefacts and Anakreon sang the praises of wine some 400 years before the erection of the famous Hellenistic temple of Dionysos, the Greek god of wine. There is also an Odeon (concerthall) at Teos. Beyond stretches the lovely white sand of Akkum.

The next branch, in the opposite direction to Çeşmealtı on the western tip of a promontory, passes near Urla Iskele (Port), the ruins of the Aeolian port of Klazomenai, home of Perikles' tutor the philosopher Anaxagoras, condemned to death in Athens for maintaining that the sun was a ball of fire. Next, Route 505 branches likewise right along the western shore of the vast bay of Izmir, round the northern tip of the Çeşme peninsula between Karaburun and Küçükbahçe, an outstanding scenic drive. The main branch cuts across the widest part of the peninsula to Çeşme, where a 15th-century Genoese fortress, now a museum, dominates the port, while some pretty fountains and a large derelict church add interest to the town. The town beach is poor, but hotels line the beach below the sulphur springs at Ilıca spa, 4 km. (2 miles) west, from which the road continues past Şifne beach along the Ildır Körfezi (Gulf) to the ruins of Erythrai, built by Greek survivors of the Trojan War. Other nearby beaches are round Tursite and Alaçatı on the peninsula's south coast, and at Dalayanköy in the north.

Izmir's numerous hotels make it a natural center for excursions along the Aegean coast, especially to the three great archeological sites of Pergamon, Ephesus and Sardis.

PRACTICAL INFORMATION FOR IZMIR

TOURIST OFFICES. There are tourist offices at: Gazi Osman Paşa Bul. 10 (tel. 142 147), outstandingly helpful; and Atatürk Cad. 418 (tel. 216 841).

SPECIAL EVENTS. July. Çeşme Sea Festival, a week of art and sports events early in the month. **August.** Annual Industrial Fair, one of the biggest in the Near East, August 20 to September 20. **September.** Anniversary of the liberation of Izmir, September 9.

HOTELS

Deluxe

Büyük Efes, Cumhuriyet Meydani (tel. 144 300). 270 rooms and 24 suites. Rooms have balconies facing hillside or sea. Pool, bars, with tea-dancing Oct. to June, nightclub (suppers and dancing), roof and terrace restaurants; in garden on central square facing the sea; at lower end of deluxe.

Expensive

Izmir Palas, Vasif Çinar Bul. 2 (tel. 215 583). 148 rooms. Facing the sea.

Pullman Izmir, Cumhuriyet Bul. 138 (tel. 144 290). 128 rooms.

Moderate

Anba, Cumhuriyet Bul. (tel. 144 380). 53 air-conditioned rooms. Good value.

Karaca, 1379 Sok. (tel. 144 445). 68 rooms. Near Kültür Park.

Kilim, Atatürk Cad. (tel. 145 340). 89 rooms. Faces sea; air-conditioned restaurant.

Kismet, 1377 Sok. (tel. 217 050). 68 rooms. Air-conditioned restaurant; near *Büyük Efes.*

Inexpensive

Babadan, Gazi Osman Paşa Bul. (tel. 139 640). 37 rooms. Air-conditioned restaurant.

Billur, Basmane Meydani (tel. 136 250). 60 rooms. Just makes the grade.

Kaya, Gazi Osman Paşa Bul. (tel. 139 771). 50 rooms.

CAMPING. *Inciraltı Kervansaray Mokamp,* 4 km. (3 miles) west of Izmir on the Çeşme road.

RESTAURANTS

Expensive

Bergama, Atatürk Cad. Excellent seafood, on the seafront.

Büyük Efes, Cumhuriyet Meydani (tel. 144 300). Roof restaurant serves international cuisine.

Café Plaza, Mustafa Bey Cad. (tel. 255 587). International cuisine.

Deniz, Erolum Yeri. Excellent seafood.

Golf Club, Kültürpark (tel. 131 777). In pleasant setting.

Imbat, Atatürk Cad. More good seafood on the seafront.

Park, Kültürpark (tel. 141 311).

Moderate

Golden Restaurant, Atatürk Cad. (tel. 214 914).

Kervansaray, Kültürpark.

Mangal, Atatürk Cad.

Yenisedir, Sehit Nevres Bul.

Out of Town. At **Bornova,** 5 km. (3 miles) on the Manisa road, near the Aegean University campus, *Izikler* (M) justifies the drive. At **Karsiyaka,** across the bay, *Palet* (M), (tel. 118 436), for enjoyable meals.

HOTELS AND RESTAURANTS IN THE AREA

Çeşme. *Kanuni Kervansaray* (E), (tel. 264 90). *Turban Çeşme* (E), (tel. 312 40). 214 rooms. Rooms in two hotel buildings and bungalows, on beach halfway to Ilıca; large pool, watersports, disco. *Ertan* (M), (tel. 267 95). 60 rooms. On seafront, in walking distance of beach. *Otel A* (M), (tel. 368 81). 15 rooms. Sun terrace with good views; no restaurant; excellently managed.

At **Ilıca,** 5 km. (3 miles) west. *Altınyunus Tatil Köyü (Golden Dolphin Holiday Village),* (E), (tel. 312 50). 515 rooms in four blocks and bungalows. A self-contained resort on beach with thermal baths, large pool, gaming arcade and 5 restaurants. *Turban Ilıca* (M), (tel. 321 28). 60 rooms. Pool and beach.

Restaurants. Good fish at *Imren* and *Körfez* (M) on Çeşme seafront.

Urla Iskele (Port). *Gen* (M), Yüce Sahil 71 (tel. 437). 38 rooms. Beach. *Nebioğlu Holiday Village* (M), (tel. 7/36). 60 bungalows. Beach, pool, tennis.

GETTING AROUND. By Plane. Frequent direct flights from several European capitals to Izmir's new Adnan Menderes Airport. There are six flights daily between Istanbul and Izmir (55 min.) and two flights daily between Ankara and Izmir (1 hour 10 min.).

By Train. A daily train from Bandırma connects with the boat from Istanbul, altogether 22 hours. There is a daily service between Ankara and Izmir, and a night express three times weekly.

By Boat. There are frequent services from Marseille and Genoa. The Turkish Maritime Lines' car ferry *Istanbul* sails from Ancona (Italy) to Izmir once a week. There is a weekly Greek ferry from Athens, and a daily ferry from Chios (Greece) to Çeşme (40 min.); summer only. Overnight car ferries leave from Istanbul on Friday year round, and on Monday and Wednesday during the summer.

For coastal cruises see *Practical Information* for the Aegean Coast, p. 165.

NIGHTLIFE. Oriental dances at the nightclub of the *Büyük Efes* hotel; dinner dancing at the *Izmir Palas, Kismet* and *Taner* hotels. Also at *Bonjour* (M), Cumhuriyet Bul., *Santana* (I), Kazim Dirik, and *Dalyan* (M), at the Alsancak boat station. *Ada, Gol* (M), *Kubana* and *Mogambo* (E), open-air nightclub restaurants in the Kültürpark, summer only.

USEFUL ADDRESSES. Consulates. *United States,* Atatürk Cad. 92 (tel. 131 369); *United Kingdom,* 1442 Sok. 49 (tel. 211 795).

Airlines. *THY,* in Büyük Efes hotel.

Turkish Maritime Lines. Atatürk Cad. 128.

Car Hire. *Avis,* at the airport and Sehit Nevres Bul. 19 (tel. 211 226); *Hertz,* at the airport and Cumhuriyet Bul. 123 (tel. 217 002).

Post Office. On Atatürk Cad.

THE AEGEAN COAST

A Showcase of Antiquity

Driven from European Greece by the Dorian invaders of the 12th century B.C., Aeolians and Ionians found a refuge on the hospitable islands and
eastern shores of the Aegean. It was here that the slow awakening of the
human spirit was transformed by the epic and lyric poets of genius some
300 years later. Inspired by Homer, Sappho, Anakreon and Simonides,
to name but the best known, philosophers, mathematicians, architects and
sculptors in the glorious 6th century B.C. laid the foundation of Western
thought and art. Withdrawing temporarily before the alien Persian conqueror across the sea, Greek civilization returned triumphantly with Alexander the Great 200 years later, not only to the coastal towns where it
originated, but spreading all over western Asia. And thanks to the wealth
and liberality of art-loving Hellenistic kings, temples, palaces and monuments of astonishing beauty and size multiplied in town and country alike.
Greek temples and theaters, Hellenistic and Roman palaces and public
buildings abound along the coastline of the Aegean Sea, through the ancient kingdoms of Mysia and Pergamon, the 12 towns of the Ionian
League, and down to Fethiye in Lykia.

EXPLORING THE AEGEAN COAST

The first lords of Pergamon (now Bergama) claimed descent from the
nymph Kallisto, whom Zeus lifted to heaven in the shape of the Great
Bear. In 401 B.C. the city gave lodging to Xenophon and his Ten Thousand,

as is recorded in his history. But it was left to Philetaeros, a eunuch officer of Antigonos I Monophthalmos to exploit the strategic potentialities of the great rock 18 km. (11 miles) from the sea. After the Battle of the Kings at Ipsos in 301 B.C., he was appointed military governor of Pergamon by Lysimachos, whom he deserted for Seleukos I in 282, bringing along the enormous treasure under his guard. For 19 years he ruled under Seleukid overlordship and successfully resisted the Gauls, who were obliged to move further east to their eventual home in Galatia.

His nephew and adopted son Eumenes I (263–241) threw off the Seleukid sovereignty, aided by Ptolemaeos (Ptolemy) III of Egypt. This led to constant wars, until Attalos I (241–197) won a spectacular victory over the Galatians, assumed the royal title and was honored with the epithet Soter (Savior) by his grateful subjects. His close alliance with Rome was continued by his son Eumenes II (197–159), likewise Soter, thus securing the most advanced part of Asia Minor, including Lydia and Phrygia, from the defeated Seleukid Antiochos III by the Treaty of Apamea in 188.

Though favored later by several Roman emperors, it was to the Attalid dynasty (214–133 B.C.) that Pergamon owed its glory. As the richest ruler of the East, Eumenes II made Pergamon one of the world's most magnificent architectural and artistic centers, and asserted like all Attalids the claim to be protectors of Hellenism. His brother Attalos II Philadelphos (Brotherloving) assisted Rome in local wars, an alliance which brought spectacular benefits. At the age of 82 he was poisoned by his nephew Attalos III Philometor (Motherloving) who, his brief outburst over, retired from public life to pursue gardening and alchemy. He left his royal estates and treasure to Rome when he died in 133, and by a liberal interpretation of his ambiguous bequest the Kingdom became the Province of Asia and transformed Rome's economy by its wealth.

The Asklepieion

Pergamon was not only the homeland of the renowned doctor and surgeon Galen, but was also the center of the cult of Asklepios (Aesculapius), god of medicine, to whom a temple was dedicated, with a medical library and a theater holding 3,500 spectators. This is the Asklepieion, which is the first site after branching off E24, 2 km. (1 mile) to the left, just before the Tourist Information Office. Extensively restored, it is once more an impressive complex. Asklepios was the son of Apollo and the nymph Koronis. On learning that his love was faithless, Apollo killed her with an arrow and took from her body his unborn child, giving him into the care of the centaur Chiron. Taught the arts of healing by Chiron, the young Asklepios, elated by his own powers, went too far and annoyed Zeus by bringing humans back to life, thus cheating Hades of the dead. Zeus killed him with a thunderbolt; then, to show that he bore no grudge, put him in the sky among the immortals, his physician's staff etched in stars.

The words carved over the doorway of the Asklepieion still bear witness to the boundless pride of the healer: "In the name of the gods, Death may not enter here." In Roman times, both Marcus Aurelius and Caracalla came to the health resort, where the treatment comprised suggestions, dream interpretation and theatrical entertainment as well as bathing in the springs that are still flowing.

It is thought that the building of the Asklepieion was undertaken by a prince, Archias, who had gone to heal his wounds in Greece, at the currently most famous temple of Asklepios in Epidavros. Grateful for his recovery, he brought home with him a few doctor-priests, and built a temple in his own town. Like churches throughout the Middle Ages, the Asklepieion offered sanctuary.

The theater and the library were added by the Romans under Antoninus Pius (A.D. 138–161) and the Consul Lucius Rufinus. An earthquake in 175 destroyed most of the buildings, but they were at once rebuilt. The earthquake merely shook three Greek temples, safely built on lower ground—the circular shrine of Telesphoros, son of Asklepios and himself a great physician; that of his eldest daughter, Hygiea, patroness of health (his younger daughter, Panakeia/Panacea was patroness of medicines); and that of Asklepios himself, circular in construction like the first.

A Tour of Bergama

At the Asklepieion you cross a small courtyard once lined on three sides by Corinthian porticos; in the middle stands a marble altar engraved with a serpent, symbol of Asklepios. Beyond the propylaea (entrance halls) 12 steps descend to the big inner courtyard. To the right are the remains of the 2nd-century library, with its mosaic pavements, broken marble shelves, and a few remaining facings of colored marble. To the north of the courtyard a partly restored portico leads into the wide sweep of the theater, which seats around 3,500 people, and which is still in use during the Bergama Festival, in May. To the west, another portico led to the toilets. To the south, a two-storied portico makes up for a drop in the land. In the courtyard itself are traces of the sacred basins and the sacred spring of healing waters. Near the spring, a stairway goes downwards to a sacred tunnel, which the supplicants ran through after visiting the spring, while priests shouted words of encouragement from holes in the tunnel's roof. As they ran, they were told that the healing powers of the temple were taking effect, and that by the time they arrived at the round temple of Telesphoros, the god of cure-revealing dreams, they would be well again. To the north of the latter temple stands the round temple of Asklepios, built in the 2nd century; entered from the courtyard up a stairway and through a monumental hall, it was covered by a dome, and stood on a base 22 meters (75 ft.) wide.

The Asklepieion was connected to the town by a sacred way, partly excavated, which ended in a gate today in ruins, the Viran Kapı. To the left, across the fields, are the remains of a Roman theater, with a fine view over modern Bergama. Further to the north is an amphitheater astride the Tellidoros, a stream feeding the Üç Kemer Cayı arena, part of which rested on archways, could be flooded with river water to make a lake for the combats involving crocodiles and hippopotami. It seated 50,000 spectators.

Heading back to Bergama's main street, the Archeological Museum past the Tourist Office contains work from every period of Pergamon's history, but mainly of the tempestuous style of the Hellenistic kingdom. That Athena was the patron deity of Pergamon as well as Athens provided not only a religious but also an artistic and cultural link. Attalos I, one of the earliest art collectors, bought 5th-century B.C. Athenian masterpieces, whose simplifying classicism combined with the novel directness and emotional impact of Baroque Hellenistic realism. Only Roman copies are left of the bronze groups of statuary dedicated by Attalos I in about

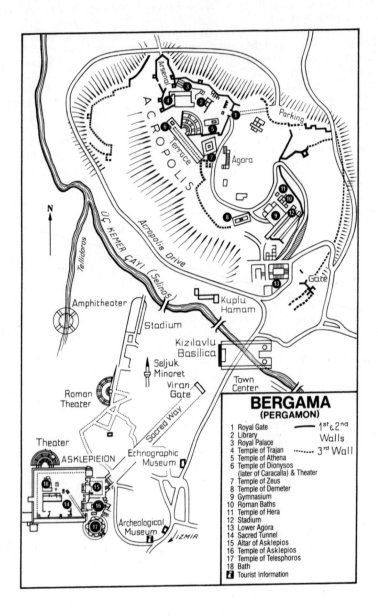

BERGAMA
(PERGAMON)

1 Royal Gate
2 Library
3 Royal Palace
4 Temple of Trajan
5 Temple of Athena
6 Temple of Dionysos
  (later of Caracalla) & Theater
7 Temple of Zeus
8 Temple of Demeter
9 Gymnasium
10 Roman Baths
11 Temple of Hera
12 Stadium
13 Lower Agora
14 Sacred Tunnel
15 Altar of Asklepios
16 Temple of Asklepios
17 Temple of Telesphoros
18 Bath
🛈 Tourist Information

——— 1ˢᵗ & 2ⁿᵈ Walls

········ 3ʳᵈ Wall

200 B.C. to celebrate his victory over the Galatians. The famous *Dying Gaul* at the Capitoline Museum in Rome was part of a circle of half-recumbent figures; in the central piece, the *Ludovisi Group*, a defeated Gaul plunges a dagger into his neck. Only the vanquished are represented in what must have been one of the most ambitious sculptural complexes ever attempted, judging from the marble copies in the Roman museums. The *Barberini Faun* at Munich was probably made for the royal palace, as also *Laokoön and His Two Sons* struggling in the deadly embrace of snakes, the climax of dynamic art, now in the Vatican Museum. What is on display at Bergama is interesting on a much diminished scale.

The lane left, after the Ethnographic Museum with the usual miscellany, leads to a 14th-century Seljuk minaret, in brick and emblazoned with glazed tiles. A maze of cobbled alleys extends to the river, on whose further bank stands the Ulu Cami built by Bayezit I. A gale toppled the original minaret, which was replaced in the 19th century. The surrounding walls belong to pagan times and a few of the stones, which still bear the sign of Demeter, show that the building materials were brought from the nearby ruins. The Kuplu Hamam, baths built in 1427, are still in use; they are named after a marble jar, once by the biggest pool, which rests today in the Paris Louvre.

Downstream, screened from the main street by old houses, rises a huge basilica, whose red brick has given it the name of Kızıl Avlu (Red Hall). The Hellenistic temple of the 2nd century B.C. was enlarged by the inveterate builder, the Emperor Hadrian, and rededicated to the rival Egyptian god of medicine, Serapis, whose cult had spread throughout Greece and Rome. Serapis was a Greek merger of the god Osiris and the sacred ox Apix, shortened from Osiriapis into Serapis. His cult, established in Egypt in the 3rd century B.C. under Ptolemaios I, later spread to Asia Minor, Greece, and Italy. Transformed into a basilica by the Byzantines, it was then divided into three naves by two rows of columns. The building was 57 meters (188 ft.) by 25 meters (84 ft.) high. The curve of the naves stands to its full height, though parts of the wall fell in the 8th century after a fire started by the Arabs back from the siege of Constantinople. To the east lies a vast courtyard, once surrounded by porticos under which the Üç Kemer Çayı (Selinos) flows through two tunnels, the two aqueducts of the Turkish name. To the north and to the south stand two squat round towers, maybe old chapels. The north tower is restored, and is today a mosque. A fine Roman bridge with three arches spans the stream.

On Pergamon's lower agora the city laws were proclaimed. The growth of the town, both on the hillside and in the plain, was such that two public gathering-places were needed, both constructed from trachyte (a light-colored feldspar, rougher to the touch) instead of the marble usual to the Greek and Roman periods.

The Acropolis

Cars can drive up the 6 km. (4 miles) to the parking place at the entrance of the Acropolis. Broken but still mighty triple ramparts enclose the Upper Town with its temples, palaces, private houses and gymnasia. In later Roman times, the town spread outwards and downwards to the plain, where the Byzantines subsequently settled for good, after a short-term stay on the mountain side.

The Royal Gate opens on to the famous library, which a team of German archeologists dug up towards the end of the last century, to the north of the Temple of Athena, where a statue of the goddess, clearly a copy of Phidias' masterpiece, was found. This proximity was natural, as Athena's patronage assisted in establishing a connection between the Platonic Academy as well as the Aristotelian Lyceum in Athens and the Lyceum founded by Attalos I. This was the nucleus of the great library, the earliest traced by archeologists in the Greek-speaking world, but quickly imitated and rivalled in Alexandria. Hoping to cripple his competitors' book acquisitions, Ptolemaios V imposed an export embargo on papyrus from Egypt. Eumenes II retaliated by producing a new writing material made of sheepskin, parchment, named after the city where it was invented. The *charta pergamena* was more expensive, but could be used on both sides. The high prices both libraries were prepared to pay for imported books encouraged the use of forgeries.

The foundations of the four rooms, the biggest measuring 16 by 14 meters (54 by 47 ft.), can be traced. Inscriptions on pedestals indicate the statues of Homer and Sappho, as well as of Herodikos, the supposed inventor of parchment. The number of manuscripts in the old library was staggering. Plutarch writes that after the fire set by the troops of Julius Caesar to the library of Alexandria, Mark Antony "took 200,000 books from the library in Pergamon as a gift to Cleopatra," to make up for her loss. It was a handsome but unlucky gesture, for the library of Alexandria was to go up in flames again 400 years later in the wars between Arabs and Christians, and every last book was lost forever. Among the known scholars of Pergamon were the Greek philosophers Parmenides and Zenon.

Following the traces of the first wall, of which only the foundation stones persist, a pillar and a cistern indicate the threshold of the royal palace built by Eumenes II, today a broken stone skeleton under the timeless sun. To the north juts out a vast embankment used by the Romans as a storehouse for arms and food. There is a fine view and, on the slope below, the awesome remains of ramparts, which ascend to the top of the Acropolis and the temple of Trajan. Facing south, it was built on a terrace over archways upheld by a strong wall. To the southeast, the temple of Athena, dating from the 4th century B.C., was in the 6th A.D. converted into a church by Justinian. Nothing is left but a flagged courtyard, bright with weeds, and a few broken porticos. The water in the cistern, if no longer held sacred, is still pure.

Steps descend from the temple of Athena towards the 2nd-century B.C. theater, backed by the steep westward slope of the hillside. The royal box is placed in the lower middle of the stone steps. The acoustics are as good as ever. The most remarkable monument on the Acropolis, its 80 rows of seats held 15,000 spectators. The wooden stage marked the transition from the classic Greek to the Roman theater. The steep slope of the seats gave every spectator an unhampered view of the stage.

Level with the stage, a 206-meter (677 ft.) terrace leads to the partly restored Temple of Dionysos, rededicated to Caracalla (A.D. 211–217). It was this Roman emperor who declared Pergamon to be *Neocorus* or guardian of the Imperial cult. It was preceded by an impressive Ionian portico and a stairway of 25 steps between the altar and the temple.

The Altar of Zeus

On the east side of the terrace, where most columns have been re-erected, the ruins of a vast altar to Zeus on top of a slope, are separated by the first wall from the temple of Athena on its own ledge, 23 meters (76 ft.) higher up. The altar stood on an embankment of 167 square meters (1,800 sq. ft.), in the middle of the second terrace, at a height of almost 12 meters (39 ft.). Its base is still standing, 2.5 meters (over 8 ft.) above the remains of the five stone steps. The altar was formed by a large portico, 35.5 by 33.5 meters (117 by 100 ft.), open to the west on top of a monumental stairway, and by two smaller porticos placed at right angles to the north and to the south. Both inner and outer walls were embellished with friezes; the votive altar itself was in an inner courtyard, behind the west portico. There is nothing left but a few broken stones half-hidden by the blown grass, an empty place long forsaken by the god.

Sparing nothing but the foundations, the German archeologists sent every unearthed stone to the Pergamon Museum in what is now East Berlin. There, the altar was put together, complete with the splendid frieze commissioned by Eumenes II, glorifying Pergamon's victory over the Galatians by depicting the Gigantomachy, the Battle of the Gods against the Giants. More than 1,200 divinities and part-human, part-animal giants figure in this enormous series of reliefs that runs in a single continuous band, over 2 meters (7 ft.) high, more than 130 meters (400 ft.) long round the outer wall. The extraordinary turmoil of the writhing figures, the triumph of the gods over chaos and evil, represented the Attalids' achievement. This culmination of the contemporary drive towards realism is the largest ancient Greek work still in existence. An entirely different mode, inspired by the Parthenon frieze in Athens, prevails in the story of Pergamon's legendary founder, Telephos, in the frieze round the altar's interior wall; it is divided into episodic scenes, precursors of the narrative reliefs on the Roman imperial columns.

To the south of where the Zeus altar stood are vestiges of another small temple of Dionysos. On the other side of the ancient road that once led down from the Royal Gate, now barely traceable by a few slabs of worn stone, is the empty site of the upper agora, the oldest marketplace in Pergamon. A right turn in the street leads to the temple of Demeter; the south portico was once 88.6 meters (291 ft.) long, and was upheld by strong foundations walls. The people sat on the north steps to watch the religious rites. To the east of the temple of Demeter are vestiges of the temple of Hera, with an altar. Nearby to the south stand the ruins of the three-storied Gymnasium, an establishment for both the training of the body and the schooling of the mind. The upper story, for boys between 16 and 18, had a *palaestra* or courtyard for wrestling and other sports, surrounded by porticos; beyond that lay the classrooms and a chapel for the cult of the emperor. To the northeast are the remains of a small theater. At the east end, parts of the walls of a bathing establishment are still standing; both they and the gymnasium are bounded to the south by a stadium 208 meters (684 ft.) long. The middle story was the gymnasium for the boys from 10 to 15. A long corridor below the stadium, the middle terrace was bounded to the south by the city's second wall and the old road, reached, together with the children's gymnasium, by a vaulted stairway to the left of a Byzantine tower. Farther down the length of the old road, are ruins of Roman houses and the lower agora, once surrounded by porticoes and shops. The heap of stone balls comes from the storehouse of the Acropolis, and served to arm the catapults. Below the gate of the third wall, the road descends to the lower car park.

At the end of May is Bergama's yearly festival or *Kermes* with many displays of Turkish folklore: songs and dances, riding and hunting, and the time-honored shadow plays or Karagöz.

The Aeolian Coast

The Bakır Çayı (Kaikos) flows west through rich agricultural land to the junction with E24, which turns north before the fishing port of Dikili to skirt the gulfs of Ayvalık and Edremit, always in view of the outline of the Greek island of Lesbos across the blue water. The Place of Quinces, which abound indeed but whose blossoms are more attractive than their fruit, Ayvalık is perhaps the prettiest village on the coast. Behind Sarmısaklı beach rises the Şeytan Sofrası (Devil's Table), which offers a marvelous view over the gulf and Alibey island to Mount Ida towering on the way to Troy. Short branch roads lead to beach resorts, from Burhaniye to Ören, from Edremit to Akçay, a thermal center with many springs. Altınoluk is another pleasant resort on the Gulf's north coast.

The first branch south of the junction is to Çandarlı, dominated by one of the best-preserved Genoese castles on the coast. The ruins of Kyme, the center of the Aeolian confederacy, were used for the construction of Aliağa, now a budding beach resort. The next branch is to Yenice (Yenifoça) with another Genoese fortress, and through lovely orchards to Foça, ancient Phokaea. This northernmost Ionian settlement, from which Marseille was colonized in 546 B.C., has experienced a modern colonization-in-reverse with the establishment of the Club Méditerranée holiday village. Route 250 returns to E24 along which the ruins of pre-Hellenic Larisa lie near Menemen, connected by Route 250 with Manisa and the main roads east.

The last branch right (west) is to the airport of Izmir, followed by the ringroad through and round Turkey's largest Mediterranean town.

The Gulf of Kuşadası

After emerging from Izmir's sprawling suburbs, the first branch right (west) off E24 leads to the beach of Gümüldür near the vestiges of ancient Lebedos, and further south to three scattered ruins: the still conspicuous acropolis of Kolophon; the Doric temple of its dependency Klaros, a renowned oracle of Apollo which was felled by an earthquake; and the better preserved port of Notion, which took the place of the mother-town after Lysimachos forcibly populated rebuilt Ephesos with the inhabitants of Kolophon. It was in Kolophon in the 6th century B.C. that the poet philosopher Xenophanes voiced the first doubts concerning man's ability to attain knowledge. The Hellenistic painter Apelles was born here: he was the first to use mixed instead of pure colors and exploit foreshortening and *trompe l'oeil* effects. The 3rd-century B.C. writings of Hermeseniax of Kolophon about the masochistic cult of Cybele and Attis have survived in Latin adaptations by the Roman poet Catullus.

E24 continues south through gently undulating fertile hills to the plain of Selçuk, once an arm of the sea that carried shipping to Ephesos, but was silted up by the Kaystros. Though there is a small motel near the ruins and accommodation at Selçuk, it is preferable to continue another 18 km. (12 miles) to Kuşadası, an ideal center for exploring these parts.

The superb sweep of the gulf of Kuşadası—whose southern headland, ancient Mykale, extends within 2 km. (1 mile) of the Greek island of Samos—is broken up by small rocky promontories into several bays fringed by long sandy beaches. The first accessible by road, not yet paved and rather bumpy, is the finest, but so far only enjoyed by campers, as the ground turns marshy in winter.

The Tusan hotel stands in a cove of its own, divided by the rock of the Kismet hotel from the village bay, which is followed by an inlet below the Imbat hotel; then the promontory of the Club Méditerranée holiday village, more camps and a yet unexploited wide expanse of golden sand beyond Davutlar village, continuing far out below Cape Mykale. In all there are some 25 km. (15 miles) of lovely coast, the central sector touristically developed, with a good choice of hotels, holiday villages—answer to a vacationist's prayers, or eyesores, according to taste—organized camps, Turkey's largest yacht marina, a port and a road hugging the sea, not just leading up to isolated beaches.

Tiny Bird Island, Kuşadası, has given its name to the village to which it is now linked by a causeway. The seafront is lined with the hotels, restaurants and gaudy souvenir shops of a popular beach resort. The splendid Mehmet Öküz Paşa Caravanserai has been successfully converted into a hotel, while the equally expertly restored island fortress accommodates a good restaurant.

But in the 16th century the impressive vaulted keep was the retreat of the formidable brothers Barbarossa, Oruc and Hayrettin, Greek converts to Islam, the most notorious pirates in the Mediterranean, who ruthlessly pillaged the coasts of Spain and Italy, attacked the ships of all Christian nations, and sold passengers and crews into slavery in Algiers or Constantinople. Shipping in the Mediterranean had become so fraught with danger that the Emperor Charles V was forced personally to lead a punitive expedition against Tunis in 1530, where he liberated thousands of Christian slaves and killed the pirate leader.

Brother Hayrettin Barbarossa was even redder of hair and braver of heart. Appointed Grand Admiral by Süleyman the Magnificent, this legalized pirate conquered the Barbary States and made the Mediterranean a Turkish lake. Late though the season was, Charles V hurriedly launched a new expedition against Algiers, ignoring the warnings of his admiral, the Genoese Doge, Doria. The storms of the equinox as good as destroyed the fleet, and though Algiers was taken by a brilliant feat of arms, it soon had to be evacuated, and Hayrettin became governor.

Utterly ruthless, the pirate admiral plundered Italy's coast towns, defeated Andrea Doria's Christian fleet in the Gulf of Arta (off the west coast of Greece), won the naval battle of Candia in 1540, made war with the French against Charles V (bringing 7,000 captives back to Constantinople), and died at the age of 70, heaped with honors and riches, in 1546.

Ephesos, Ephesus, Selçuk

Throughout its long history, the town has been rebuilt so often and has changed so much that it has lost its very name. The blue and white sign-post indicates Selçuk, the yellow and black Greek Ephesos or Roman Ephesus.

Mounts Pion and Koressos, Greco-Roman remains, a Byzantine basilica, and a Seljuk mosque constitute a hodgepodge of history. In the village, on the road to the ruins, is the well-laid-out museum, whose pride are the two splendidly preserved marble statues, once gilded, of Artemis in the likeness of Cybele, patroness of Ephesos, Greek in name but unmistakably Anatolian in appearance. The triple row of breasts lack nipples and have, therefore, often been held to represent eggs, the universal fertility symbol. Only the archaic smile is Greek, while the headgear, the signs of the zodiac and a strange assortment of monsters on the garments are purely eastern. There is also the famous Boy on the Dolphin and a beautiful Greek mask made familiar throughout the world through photography and travel posters.

For ancient paganism as for the beginnings of Christianity, Ephesos was an important center, second only to Athens, and later, to Jerusalem. The cult of Artemis changed into the cult of the Virgin Mary, as St. Paul and St. John both preached in the town. Up to the Middle Ages, Ephesos kept its standing, owing in part to its being a well-placed port. The world's first bank, run on the lines of today's banks, opened here.

Ephesos was founded in pre-Ionian times in the 13th century B.C. by the Leleges or the Karians who, according to Strabo, the ancient Greek geographer, settled in the plain around the temple of Kybele, the goddess-mother. Further on in his writings, he also mentions tribes of Mycenaean origin. The first author of a guide book, Pausanias, writing in the 2nd century A.D., thought that the original settlers were Lydians.

In the 11th century B.C. the Ionians founded settlements without disturbing the people in place, that is to say, not by force of arms but by peaceful immigration. Under the leadership of their ruler Androkles, the Ionian colony settled on an island, today called Kurutepe, across from the town; over the years, silt from the river Kaystros (today the Küçük Menderes) bridged the gap of water. When the settlement grew too big for the island, Androkles consulted the famous oracle of Delphi, who as usual gave an ambiguous answer: "The site of the new town will be shown you by a fish; follow the wild boar." And it came to pass one day, while fishermen were cooking a meal, that the fish leapt off the hot stones into the burning embers and then landed in the brushwood, which caught fire; and a fleeing boar was hunted down and killed. This happened at the foot of Mount Koressos, called by the Turks Bülbül Dağı (Mount of the Nightingale). Androkles evicted the natives and settled in the new Ephesos. Time and the river merged the two settlements into one, which slowly grew into a big city.

Riches awake greed: Croesus, king of Lydia, captured Ephesos, and was himself defeated by Cyrus, the town thereby falling under Persian rule. The conquered Ionian cities made a secret alliance, and a widespread revolt broke out in 499 B.C. After initial successes which brought the Greeks to Sardis, a decisive battle near Ephesos heralded the collapse of the rising. Cyrus' successor Darius laid waste the rebel towns, sparing only Ephesos.

From that time on, Ephesos stayed carefully on the fringe of the wars between the Persians and the Greeks, the latter weakened by growing internal strife between Athens and Sparta. Keeping out of a war being no mean feat, then as now, the wily Ephesians even managed to keep on good terms with both sides, wisely giving the goddess Artemis full credit and thanks for keeping the town out of trouble. But she failed to protect her temple from an arsonist the night Alexander was born, and he was under a moral obligation to assist in the rebuilding, once he had become the Great.

When after Alexander's death Ephesos fell to Lysimachos, the port was half choked by sand from the Kaystros River. To maintain its political and commercial eminence, Lysimachos again shifted the site of the town, surrounding it with ramparts 10 meters (30 ft.) high and 9 km. (6 miles) long.

Roman Ephesus

In 133 B.C. Ephesos was part of Attalos III's doubtful legacy to Rome, but joined Mithridates VI of Pontus in 88 B.C. in killing thousands of Romans. With its usual flair the town changed sides at the right time, thus not only escaping punishment but becoming the capital of the Roman provinces of Asia. Destroyed by an earthquake in A.D. 17, Ephesus was quickly rebuilt into a Roman town of 300,000 inhabitants. A crossroads of trade, it fast became a center of culture, attracting the preachers of Christianity, who founded there the first of the Seven Churches of the Apocalypse. In the *Acts of the Apostles* St. Luke, a physician from Antioch (Antakya), writes at length of the cult of Artemis, under her Latin name, Diana. It was the city's silversmiths who drove St. Paul out of Ephesus, for fear that his preaching would lessen the sale of the "silver shrines for Diana," for "by this craft we have our wealth." When Paul addressed the entire town in the amphitheater, urging them to accept his doctrines, "they were full of wrath, and cried out, saying, "Great is Diana of the Ephesians" (Acts XIX. 24–40). St. John also came to the town, perhaps the first time with the Mother of Jesus between 37 and 48, then again in 95 when he is supposed to have died.

In the 4th century, the balance of power of the known world swung the other way. The pagan temples were plundered for the building of St. Sophia and other Christian churches. In 431, Theodosius II held the Third Ecumenical Council in Ephesus. The Patriarch of Constantinople, Nestorius, who claimed that Jesus was God in man but not God, and who denied the virgin birth, was charged with heresy and cast out of the Church.

About a hundred years later the port was once more choked up with silt. The Ephesians at last abandoned the pursuit of the retreating sea, resettling around the church built by Justinian on a hilltop, over St. John's tomb. The new city was surrounded by ramparts, and a citadel was built. In the year 1000, the Crusaders came from the west, the Turks from the east. Ephesus became known as Hagios Theologos, the "holy word of God," then by the Turkish twist to that name, Ayasoluk. The first Seljuk invaders were fought off in 1090, and the Byzantines held out until 1304. In 1348, Ayasoluk became the capital of the Aydinogullari emirate.

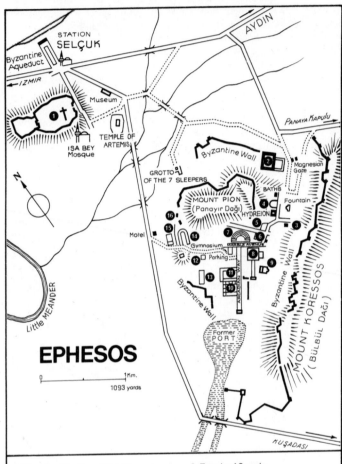

EPHESOS

0   1 Km.

1093 yards

1 Citadel and Basilica of St John	9 Temple of Serapis
2 East Gymnasium	10 Baths of the Port
3 Excavation Depot	11 Forum of Verulanus
4 Odeon	12 Byzantine Baths
5 Fountain of Trajan	13 Double Church
6 Temple of Hadrian and Baths of Scholastica	14 Stadium
7 Theater	15 Gymnasium of Vedius
8 Agora and Library of Celsus	16 Gate of Koressos and of the Acropolis

In the beginning of the 15th century, the town fell under the rule of the Osmanli Empire. The greatness of Ephesus was over. Without a port, it lost its trade to Izmir and to Kuşadası. All that 19th-century travelers have to say of the small town of Ayasoluk is that "it has a few classical ruins which lead one to think that it was built on the site of the ancient city of Ephesus, renowned for its famous Temple of Diana." In 1914 it was given the name of Selçuk.

The Cult of Artemis

Ephesus is inextricably tied up with Artemis, the daughter of Zeus and sister of Apollo, the goddess of the hunt and of chastity. So chaste, indeed, that overseen bathing in a stream by Aktaeon, she changed the young hunter into a stag to be torn to pieces by his own hounds. On their farflung travels the tolerant Greeks were prone to identifying their Twelve Olympians with local gods and goddesses in the most incongruous amalgamations. In Anatolia they came across the worship of Kybele (Cybele), daughter-in-law of Heaven and Earth, and wife of Time, Kronos. She was also known as Ops, the wife of Saturn, god of Nature; as Rhea, mother of Zeus; as Vesta, the Roman goddess of the hearth; and as the Earth Mother, symbol of fertility. There are many reasons for this strange-seeming shift to chastity. One, of course, is that on her travels Cybele, like all gods, was made over in the image of her worshippers. Another is that her very relationship to time and to nature made her, following the earth's rhythm, both fruitful and barren according to season. In Ephesus, the goddess of chastity becomes mother nature, Artemis Polymastros, with three rows of breasts.

The worship of Artemis-Cybele, in its Anatolian form, might derive from the Amazons, dedicated warriors—archetypal women's libbers—having sex with men once a year so that the race might not die out; the male children were left to die at birth. This seems a reasonable origin for the chastity cult of the goddess of the hunt, Artemis, always shown as an Amazon, one breast bare, the peplum draped over the right shoulder to hide the scar where the other breast had been cut off to allow full freedom for the bow arm. It also seems to be the origin of the yearly orgies on the feast day of Artemis in Ephesus.

The temple and the statue being, said the priests, a gift of the gods, the Artemision had the right of sanctuary. By Artemision was meant both the temple and the month of the year dedicated to the cult of the goddess. The Ephesians, like the rest of mankind, traded on their faith to make money, and the month of religious rites gave rise to many kinds of entertainment and feasts, not all of them spiritual.

A Visit to Ephesus

It takes a day to see Ephesus, one of the largest archeological sites in the world. In Selçuk, see the 14th-century Seljuk mosque and the remains of the Byzantine aqueduct near the fruit market. Signboards clearly indicate the main sights (tickets required), well-provided with parking space. The fortified town is entered through the Door of Persecution, so called because an 18th-century traveler, Choiseul Gouffier, mistook scenes from the Trojan War, engraved on marble slabs (at that time still on the door) for Christian imagery. Beyond it are the ruins of the basilica, built in the

6th century by Emperor Justinian over the remains of a small church, itself built over the tomb of the Apostle John. The tomb is under the altar, whose base is still visible. The basilica, 36.5 meters (420 ft.) long, was once topped by 11 domes upheld by columns, of which the least broken have been set upright. A marble tablet commemorates the recent visits of the Popes Paul VI and John Paul II. Behind is the Byzantine citadel, built on the site of the 11th-century B.C. town.

Below the basilica, whose retaining walls rise from beds of lovely flowers, stands the vast shell of the Isa Bey Cami, ruined by an earthquake. A superb stalactite portal and three rows of sculptured windows pierce the unusually high walls, partly built of marble taken from the Greek temples. The mosque was built in 1375 by the architect Ali Damessene. Its outer form differs from the conventional Islamic place of prayer, though the greater part of the square building is reserved, as usual, to the open inner courtyard around the fountain for ritual washing. Only one minaret remains out of three; and the missing stones were taken to embellish the mosques of Izmir. On the other hand, the columns of black granite upholding the two domes of the Isa Bey Cami were taken from the ancient baths in the port of Ephesus, together with fallen capitals from the rubble of the Artemision. Parts have been reconstructed and are again used as a mosque.

Waterlogged foundations and a few blocks of marble in a field to the right of the Kuşadası road are all that remain of the temple of Artemis, one of the Seven Wonders of the Ancient World. The first temple was burnt by the Cimmerians in the early 7th century B.C., rebuilt in about 600 B.C., succeeded by the first marble temple begun with the assistance of King Croesus of Lydia in the middle of the 6th century and finished 120 years later. Its glory did not last that long, because a certain Herostratos, wishing to make a name in history, set fire to the temple on the night Alexander the Great was born, in 356 B.C., the goddess being in Macedonia on obstetrical duties. He got his wish; for in spite of a town decree forbidding the use of his name, it became a byword for meaningless destruction. Rebuilt by Alexander, the Hellenistic Artemision was one of the Seven Wonders of the World until it was plundered by the Goths in A.D. 263. Rebuilt on a smaller scale, it was stripped of its marble for the building of St. Sophia in Constantinople, and St. John's basilica in Ephesus itself. But one of Artemis' statues was buried by a last worshipper in the *bouleuterion* (senate or town hall) to save it from destruction by Christian fanatics; and another colossal figure from the 1st century A.D. has also been unearthed.

Higher up the Kuşadası road a branch turns left at the Tusan motel straight into the midst of Greek and Roman ruins. Skirting the western slope of Mount Pion (Panayır Dağı), it ends in a parking lot near the large theater which has been restored to house the annual Ephesus Festival in early May.

The Stadium and Theater

Shortly after turning onto this branch, to the left, is a gymnasium given to the town in the 2nd century by a wealthy citizen, Vedius. Dedicated to Artemis and the Emperor Antoninus Pius, it was a luxurious establishment with hot, cold, and tepid baths (the heating system is still visible), toilets or *lavatoria* in good repair, and a wealth of statues and mosaics.

A little farther along, to the left of the road, is the monumental vaulted doorway of the 1st-century Stadium, where chariot and horse races were held on a track 217 meters (712 ft.) long, and where gladiators and wild beasts met in combat before 70,000 spectators. In front of the stadium, a marble-paved avenue led northeast to the Koressos Gate, now in ruins, and later to the Artemision, when Lysimachos rebuilt the town between Mounts Pion and Loressos in the 4th century B.C. The former was once crowned by the Acropolis of Ionian Ephesos. Across the road lie the remains of the Byzantine baths or "drunkards' baths," and beyond, the ruins of the Double Church. In this basilica, dedicated to the Virgin, and built on the site of the Roman Exchange, the Third Ecumenical Council was held in 431. The basin in the baptistery is so large because baptism was by total immersion. A second church was later built nearby, but it is difficult to tell the ruins apart.

To the south of the Double Church still stand the huge remains of the walls of the 4th-century Baths of Constantine, above the old port now silted up with sand. The Arcadian Way, 521 meters (1,710 ft.) long, led from the port to the big theater. Repaired in grand style by Emperor Arcadius around the year 400, it was lined by pavements under covered archways with shops, and lit up at night. Here, Cleopatra entered Ephesus in triumph. Past the Roman agora and the portico of Verulanus, a signboard points along a shopping street to the 2nd-century Serapis temple, whose eight massive Corinthian columns are of the finest white marble.

Backed by the western slope of Mount Pion, the theater, at the north end of the Arcadiana, begun by Lysimachos, was finished by the Emperors Claudius and Trajan in the 2nd century A.D. Its 66 tiers held 25,000 spectators, whether for plays or for the feasts of Artemis. There is a fine view from the top of the steps. Still higher up, near the top of Mount Pion, are vestiges of the Byzantine walls.

Along the Marble Avenue

At the top of the Marble Avenue stands the beautifully restored 2nd-century library of Celsus, a remarkable two-story building with a finely-worked frontage. Across the courtyard wide steps ascend to the reading room, where you can still see the rolls of papyrus. Also in the wall is a round recess, once an altar for offerings, over a cellar containing the carved marble sarcophagus of Julius Celsus, governor of the Roman province of Asia.

The Library adjoined the Hellenistic agora, a vast 106-meter (350-foot) square where porticos and shops were grouped round a water clock. A brothel stood in the strategic position at the corner of Marble Avenue and the Street of the Kuretes, named after the college of priests housed in it.

To the right are two monuments to the dead—the first, a block of marble on a rectangular base, was transformed into a fountain; the second shelters, in the hollow of its base, a mortuary chamber which held a sarcophagus. On the slopes beyond, the multi-storied houses, illustrating the architecture subsequent to the first century, were opened up on the 90th anniversary of the excavations. On the opposite side of the street is the charming façade of the temple of Hadrian, partly restored. The steps at the back of the temple lead to the Baths of Scholastica, a 2nd-century lady of Ephesus. Just after the baths a road has been cleared to the left, leading to a round funeral monument once two stories high, of which only the base remains. On the Avenue, the basin of the partly restored Trajan Fountain was surrounded by two levels of pillars and statutes and the sculptured remains of an archway. After a right turn in the street is a square which once held the Prytaneion, the town hall and civic center as well as the Nymphaion, a small temple decked with fountains, where a statue of the goddess of Fortune was found. To the south of the square is the Museum of Inscriptions installed in the basement of the Temple of Domitian, the only remains of what was once a vast sanctuary with a colossal statue of the Emperor whose head was found in the vaulted cellars. In the Odeon, over 2,000 spectators could listen to poetry readings and to music. Nearby, to the east, are more baths in ruins. Facing the Odeon, on the other side of the street, are vestiges of a fountain and, 196 meters (644 ft.) southeast, the so-called tomb of St. Luke, in fact a Greek temple turned into a church.

The street ends at last at the 1st-century Manisa (Magnesia) Gate, a starting place for the caravan trail and a colonnaded road to the Artemision. This road, following the boundary walls of Lysimachos, skirted, 98 meters (322 ft.) to the north, the great Roman Gymnasium of the East, with its still awesome remains. A branch to the left ends at a farmhouse, whence it is a short climb to the grotto of the Seven Sleepers, where seven legendary young Christians who were walled up during the persecutions of Emperor Decius (249–51) fell into a miraculous sleep to awake in the safety of Teodosius I's Christian reign some 150 years later. After their death, the Emperor had them buried in the same grotto and a church built at its entrance. A Byzantine necropolis rose round their graves.

If possible, have a car waiting at the Manisa Gate, to avoid the long walk back through the ruins to the main entrance, and drive right (east) up Bülbül Dağı. Its top is crowned by the walls built by Lysimachos around the new Ephesos in the 4th century B.C.; they are still in good repair, now about 4 km. (2 miles) long, marked by towers, steps and doorways, and end in the sand-choked port, where a big round tower is said to have been St. Paul's prison.

The road winds 7 km. (4 miles) across the mountain, affording splendid views over the plain of Selçuk to Meryemana, the reputed house of the Virgin Mary.

The House of Mary

It all began with a vision. Catherine Emmerich, a stigmatized nun, had never left Dulmen in Germany when she wrote the *Life of the Blessed Virgin Mary*. Two Lazarists, Father Jung and Father Poulain, who knew Ephesus well, were struck by her description of the house where the mother of Jesus is said to have died. In 1891, diggings were undertaken, though only partly (if at all) because of the sick woman's writings. The Basilica of Ephesus had been dedicated to the Virgin Mary, and in those days canon law only allowed a church to be dedicated to saints having lived or died in the place itself. And why else should the Third Ecumenical Council, proclaiming the dogma of "Mary, mother of God," have been held in Ephesus? A few families dating back to the early Christian settlement in Ephesus came down once a year from their mountain village of Kirkince to make a pilgrimage to the Panaya Kapula or Doorway of the

Virgin, on the Bülbül Dağı. To be sure, Islam honors Mary as the mother of a prophet, but why her name there? It can only mean that the Turks also held it to be her dwelling place. Finally, Pope Benedict XIV (1740–58) decreed that Mary died in Ephesus, which Pope Paul VI visited in 1967 and Pope John Paul II in 1983.

Catherine Emmerich, of course, had read the Gospels according to which Jesus, on the cross, had entrusted his mother to St. John's care; and it is known that St. John went to Ephesus. And it is a startling fact that the ruins unearthed bear out, in detail, Catherine Emmerich's plan of Mary's house.

Another version claims that it is in Jerusalem, on Mount Zion, in a place called the Church of the Dormition, where Mary closed her eyes for her last sleep. The faithful who uphold Catherine Emmerich point out that this belief only dates from the 7th century, whereas the tradition of Ephesus goes back to the beginnings of Christianity. The notice at the door of the house says, among other things: " . . . to escape the persecutions, he (St. John) probably brought her here."

Cars are left in the wide parking area on top. From the simple restaurant a treelined path leads to the indubitably ancient house, tastefully restored in 1951. Inside, there are ex votos (mostly crutches), a small and very simple altar, with the Room of Sleep to its right, and flowers. Outside, a plane tree seems rooted in the wall. You can still make out the foundations of the ancient chapel, marked by a line on the present walls. Behind the house is another beautiful plane tree. Under the leafy sun-dappled shadows, the house takes on a touching look.

Below the house is the fountain of Our Lady. The sacred spring gushes out of the rock above the densely wooded slopes falling away to the distant sea. Regardless of your beliefs, this truly serene setting leaves an unforgettable impression.

Priene

The second excursion from Kuşadası leads south into the heartland of the Ionian League, to two of the most important members of the alliance of 12 cities, and to its oracle at Didyma. The road winds through an idyllic, hilly landscape, often in view of the sea and the island of Samos, before reaching the lower Büyük Menderes (Great Meander or Maeandros) valley. The river is bridged at the pleasant market town of Söke, founded by the Seljuks in the 14th century to take the place of Magnesia on Meander, whose ruins are scattered at Ortaklar on both sides of the Aydın road 19 km. (12 miles) northeast.

After 5 km. (3 miles) to the south of Söke, a right (west) branch follows for 10 km. (6 miles) the southeastern slope of the Mykale promontory to Güllübahce, a shady village from which the road ascends steeply to the parking space below the gate.

A visit to Priene still necessitates some very steep climbing through the remains of the city laid out by town planners sent by King Mausolos in about 350 B.C. The reservoir was designed by Phile, the first woman architect, in around 100 B.C. The original Ionian seaport, birthplace of Bias, one of the Seven Sages of Greece, had been razed by the Persians after the suppression of the revolt in 494 B.C. The new Priene regained a certain commercial importance which lasted throughout the Byzantine era, despite the silting up of its two harbors, to succumb finally when its last port Naulochos, some miles distant, was in turn engulfed by alluvial soil which now extends for some 16 km. (10 miles) between the ruins and the sea.

Marble flagstones, where the gutters for the drainage are still discernible, ascend from the east gate to the theater, which seated some 6,000 spectators, probably the entire free population. The five seats of honor, inserted in the front row in the course of a Roman renovation in the 2nd century, are intact, but the many statutes that decked the theater were sent to Germany, before a law was passed forbidding the exportation of Turkey's archeological treasures. Incredible as it may seem now, up to the beginning of the century, foreign archeological teams crated and shipped home the best part of their finds.

Remains of a Byzantine church flank an earlier sanctuary, the Temple of Athena, designed by King Mausolos' architect Pytheos in the Ionian style, dedicated by Alexander the Great according to an inscription now in the British Museum and endowed with a colossal statue by the Romans. Five columns have been re-erected.

The pine-clad spur of Mount Mykale is crowned by a Hellenistic fortress—as it stands some 400 meters (1,200 ft.) high you might well dispense with a visit. Halfway up perched the temple of Demeter, goddess of harvest, as always mysteriously remote.

To the west is the Temple of Athena, goddess of wisdom, science, and art, who shared with Ares the godship of war. She was delivered, fully armed, by Hephaistos with a blow of his axe on the head of her father Zeus; so painful is the birth of wisdom and knowledge and the arts of peace and war, even for the greatest of gods. So we are told by Hesiod in his *Theogony:* "Then Zeus from his head gave birth to Athena of the gray eyes, weariless waker of battle noise, who delights in war, onslaughts and battles."

Her temple, once very beautiful, was the model of the Ionic style in Asia. Earthquakes have overthrown most of the columns; five have been set upright again with care.

As a backdrop, towering and majestic, is the acropolis on the mountaintop. Below it is the sanctuary of Demeter, goddess of the harvest, and of her daughter by Zeus, Persephone, goddess of spring. One day, when Persephone was in the fields picking flowers, she was kidnapped by her uncle Hades who took her down to his underworld kingdom and made her his queen. When Demeter, having looked everywhere in her despair, forbade all trees to bear fruit and all grain to grow, life was threatened with extinction. A compromise was hastily patched up whereby Persephone returned for nine months every year to her mother and descended for the winter to Hades, thus symbolizing the annual death and reawakening of nature. Today, the temple is a pile of rubble, except for the ditch dug long ago to drain the blood of animal sacrifices.

The Agora was in the middle of town. The western wall was engraved with 1,400 lines of writing; near the eastern wall was the Temple of Zeus, encroached upon by the Byzantine citadel. Beneath it was the lower Gymnasium, while the upper backed on the Prytaneion and well-preserved Bouleuterion, a rectangular amphitheater once roofed over, wrongly called the Council Chamber as it accommodated the 600 members of the Popular Assembly. Between the Bouleuterion and the Agora the Romans built a splendid Sacred Portico, from which a colonnaded street descended to the western gate opening on the port. Just inside this gate are the insignificant remains of Cybele's Temple, while the Stadium is to the south on a lower level.

Miletos (Miletus)

The direct road from Priene 26 km. (16 miles) southwest via Atburgazı to Milet, ancient Miletos, keeps close to the coast, while Route 525 continues south from the Söke junction for 29 km. (18 miles) through the rice paddies of the alluvial plain, which was in antiquity an arm of the sea extending inland as far as present Lake Bafa. Shortly after crossing the Büyük Menderes and leaving the lake to the left you turn right to the village of Akköy and back north again to Miletus, visible from afar on a hill in the river bend. But these ruins, somewhat disappointing except for the theater, are not those of the original city which witnessed the birth of Greek philosophy and science in the 6th century B.C. Vestiges of that famous town, going back to Mycenaean origins, crown a cliff some miles to the southwest.

After the arrival of the Ionians in the 11th century B.C., the settlement on the easily defensible promontory gradually assumed preponderance, based as much on sheep breeding, which supplied the raw material for the famous woolen fabrics, as on commerce, which led to the establishment of no less than 75 trading stations from Egypt to the Black Sea.

Economic prosperity, which made Miletos the first Greek city to coin money, reoriented the adventurous spirit from the exploration of the physical environment to the investigation of the mind. Thales, Anaximander and Anaximenes laid the foundations of western philosophy, Kadmos of history, and Hekataeos, by drawing the first map, of geography. Aristides wrote the *Miletica,* a collection of bawdy tales which inspired Boccaccio's *Decameron* some 2,000 years later.

Having retained its independence from the Lydians, Miletos came to an advantageous arrangement with the Persians who contented themselves with the appointment of a friendly chief magistrate. But in 499 B.C., contrary to the advice of the Didyma oracle, Miletos headed an Ionian revolt against the Persians. After initial successes which brought the Greeks to Sardes, the revolt was crushed at a decisive sea battle off the nearby islet of Lades. Miletos was razed to the ground, the male population massacred, women and children sold as slaves.

But a position so favored by nature could not remain unoccupied for long, and the town was rebuilt when the Persians withdrew from the coast after 478 B.C. Hippodamos, the first city planner, who had been born just before the outbreak of the revolt, was charged with the rebuilding. He applied his ideas of rectangular layout with such success that Pericles entrusted him with the planning of the port of Piraeus in Athens and the colony of Thurii in Italy. His model of straight streets cut across at right angles to form a chessboard pattern was followed some 100 years later on the much more difficult hillside of Priene.

Only under the Romans did the new Miletus regain prosperity, but here too, the encroaching sandbanks of the Meander River, winding around three sides of the town in a slowly narrowing bottleneck, choked off the port, and with it the livelihood of its people. It declined under the Byzantines, who called it Castro Palation after the fortress they erected atop the theater; the Turks contracted this to Balat, the name of the present tiny hamlet.

Miletus had two ports still in use in the 11th century when the newly-arrived Seljuks traded with Venice and the west, until sandbanks shoaled up the harbors and put a stop to shipping. Founded on water, the town was to founder on sand; its sudden downfall gave rise to the old saying: "like Miletus, once so great." Of its past greatness, the splendid 2nd-century Roman theater gives ample proof. It seated 25,000 spectators and might well do so again, as the festival habit is spreading in Turkey. The lower 22 tiers are in excellent condition, the solid arched corridors and entrances still usable, only the broken sculpture and reliefs from the ruined stage have been deposited before the immense frontage. A few hillocks in the surrounding plain were once islets rising from the waters.

The fields are full of forgotten beauty: stones of an old wall, the broken archway of an aqueduct, are scattered over the countryside; you stumble over priceless capitals as over rocks. This historic rubble is indeed such that, unlike at Priene, nothing is left of the city plan. A Byzantine archway, partly made of stones from the Greek ruins, leads to the Seljuk caravans-erai. Next to the remains of a gymnasium is the magnificent dome of the mosque of Ilyas Bey, built in 1404 by Isa Bey of the Menteşe Emirate, restored and still in use; only the minaret is incomplete. Across the road is the Museum, which displays what has not been taken to Izmir.

The central north-south street ended at the Bay of Lions, where fragments of vast stone lions still guard what used to be the harbor entrance. The town had two agoras, with the bouleuterion between. There was a Temple of Athena, a sanctuary of Apollo, and baths (all in a fairly good state of repair) dedicated to the Empress Faustina who, in spite of an unedifying life, was deified according to custom after her death. Fragments of the lavish decorations of the huge cold pool, into which water poured from an earthenware pipe ending in a lion's mouth, the hot baths, dressing rooms and courtyards bear eloquent witness to the opulent life in Asia Minor in the first centuries of the imperial era.

But no matter how sumptuous the profane buildings of antiquity might have been, they never equalled the sacred in nobility of detail and majestic dignity. An outstanding example is to be seen 18 km. (11 miles) south via Akköy.

Didim (Didyma)

The sanctuary of Didyma (Greek for twin) was dedicated to Apollo, twin brother of Artemis. The grandeur and beauty of the temple alone justifies the visit to this region. A Sacred Way led from the bay to the temple, whose oracles were as revered as those of Delphi, and it still is an awe-inspiring site. The earliest Hellenistic edifice was some 600 years under construction, from the time Alexander the Great decreed the building of a new sanctuary to replace the archaic temple which had perished at the end of the Ionian Revolt in 49 B.C.

An old Persian lion in marble marks the entrance. The colossal scale of the whole seems made to dwarf man into nothingness. A monumental stairway leads up to a forest of 124 mostly well-preserved Ionian columns, some still supporting their architraves. The proportions are overwhelming: 190 by 51 meters (623 by 167 ft.).

The columns were made of round blocks of marble set one over the other; the finished shaft was then fluted. The few unfluted columns show that the temple itself was never finished. The entrance portico, or *pronaos,* at the top of the stairway, consisted of 12 columns in three ranks of four. A huge slab of marble, weighing 60 tons, barred the entrance to the chamber where the oracle announced the will of the gods to the people. This tremendous entrance slab slid along shafts of well-soaped stone, like the wooden logs used today by fishermen to roll boats into the sea.

On both sides of the temple, passages hollowed in the stone sloped down into the great hall or *atrium,* from where another flight of stairs led to the sanctuary. The marble walls are still standing, thanks to ancient Greek workmanship and the pouring of lead between the stone slabs. The fountain in the middle, dry for centuries, flowed again on Alexander's birth, but has long since dried up.

Under the courtyard is a network of corridors whose walls, throwing back sound, made of the oracle's voice a deep and ghostly echo which filled the people with religious dread. The oracle or *naiskos* stood in a small marble chamber at the far end, and spoke out of a hole giving onto the maze of echos. The most impressive bas reliefs are a gigantic head of Medusa, and a small Poseidon and his wife Amphitrite.

The Byzantine church opposite the entrance has been converted into a mosque. The sanctuary of Artemisia was unearthed in 1983 and excavations continue. There is a small restaurant in the shade of a palm tree, but it is more pleasant to drive the 4 km. (3 miles) to Altınkum Plajı, Golden Sand Beach.

Lake Bafa and Milas

Route 525 hugs the wooded south shore of Lake Bafa, which maintains the illusion of still being an inlet of the sea as it was until Roman times. The ruins of a walled Byzantine monastery, whose church, tower and water gate rise above the encroaching vegetation, cover most of the nearest islet. Others are scattered to the foot of rugged Beşparmak Dağ (Five Finger Mountain, ancient Mount Latmos). According to legend, it was the birthplace of a handsome young man, Hermaphroditos, son of Hermes and Aphrodite. A nymph, Samakis, having fallen in love with him, he dived into the lake to shake her off; she swam in after him, but he swam faster. Despairing, Samakis cried out to Zeus, who, touched by her tears, merged her body with that of her lover.

From Çamiçi village a dirt road leads along part of the north shore to Heraklea by Latmos, whose impressive Hellenistic ramparts rise from the lake round a small village up the precipitous rocks. The theater is better preserved than the Temple of Athena, the foundation stones of the Agora and the ancient Town Hall. The castle on the hilltop dates back to the Middle Ages. The ruins can also be reached by boat from the fish taverns on the south shore.

Much easier to get to and easy to spot, thanks to its closeness to the main road 3 km. (2 miles) past Selimye, stands a delightfully romantic ruin. The slender Corinthian columns of an almost intact Roman temple soar above the olive grove which covers most of ancient Euromos. A more important Karian town was Labranda, the first capital and chief sanctuary, well worth the 13 km. (8 miles) left (northwest) into the fastness of the Batı Menteşe Dagları.

In the 7th century B.C. the Dorian Greeks invaded the lands of the Karians, with whom they eventually merged into a kingdom that kept its autonomy under the Persians and Alexander the Great. Antigonos I and Lysimachos fought over the towns. Then came the Romans, who entrusted the government of the province as far inland as Mylasa to Rhodes, but had to send out their legions to quell an uprising against the new rulers. The Byzantines were followed in the 11th century by the Seljuk Menteşe dynasty, dethroned by Bayezit I, restored by Tamerlane and in power until the final incorporation of what had become Milas into the Osmanli Empire.

The new town, like the old one before, rises from the river, lined by some attractive 18th-century mansions, to a spur of the mountains encircling a fertile plain. The 2nd-century A.D. Roman mausoleum atop the spur owes its Turkish name Gümüskeşen, the Silver Purse, to the pyramidical roof held by pillars and Corinthian columns above the large stone plinth of the burial chamber. Nearby are remains of a Roman temple, in the lower town those of an older sanctuary of Zeus and antique walls.

Of the three 14th-century mosques, Ulu Cami, Haci Ilias and Firuz Bey, the last is the most interesting, being partly built of marble from the Greek temples. There are a few ruins, among which is an aqueduct, on the outskirts.

The Byzantine fortress of Pecin Kalesi, 4 km. (2 miles) south of Milas, guards the crossroads to Bodrum southwest, the small port of Ören—not to be confounded with the beach of Ören near Burhaniye—near ancient Keramos southeast, and Muğla in the east. The road to the first, with a branch-off to the fine beach of Güllük, traverses the Milas plain, before winding through pineclad hills which suddenly open up to allow a breathtaking view of Bodrum (66 km., 41 miles).

Bodrum (Halikarnassos)

Herodotos (Herodotus), known as the Father of History—more precisely of Journalism because of his indiscriminate reporting and love of tall tales—was born in this hellenized Karian town in 484 B.C. After winning fame in Athens he returned to take part in a revolt and was exiled. His last journey led him to Thurii in Italy, perhaps accompanying its planner, Hippodamos of Miletos.

Just as the northern cities of the Aegean had formed the Ionian League, so the southern cities round Halikarnassos united in the Dorian League. Though the town had been expelled from the latter, it took part in the revolt of the Confederation of Ionian and Dorian Leagues against the Persians. The uprising was put down in 493 B.C., and 13 years later Queen Artemisia led five ships from Halikarnassos to Xerxes. "Although she was a woman," writes Herodotus, "she came to war against Greece; for, her husband being dead, she held the chief power and notwithstanding she had a son that was grown up, she came to the war herself, albeit there was no need, because of her spirit and courage." The Athenians offered a prize of 10,000 drachmae for anyone who took her alive, for "shame that a woman should make war on Athens." Xerxes entrusted his young sons to her, to take them back to Ephesos.

In 377 B.C. Mausolos became king and following an expansionist policy moved his capital from Mylasa to Halikarnassos on the coast. He had married his sister Artemisia, who reigned after his death in 353, defeated the Rhodian fleet and annexed some islands off the coast. The queen was an ardent botanist and medical researcher, but her greatest claim to glory is the completion of Mausolos' grandiose tomb, the famous Mausoleum, one of the Seven Wonders of the World. The outstanding sculptors of the age, Bryaxis, Leochares, Skopas and Timotheos, used the fashionable dramatic diagonals and twisted poses, deliberately indicating a distinctive foreignness.

Rome placed Karia temporarily under the rule of its old foe and rival, Rhodes, before incorporating both into the province of Asia. Serious trouble started again in the late 11th century, when the Seljuks and the Byzantines fought over it as it passed back and forth between them. The Knights of Rhodes landed here in 1402, rebuilding the ancient fortress already restored by the Seljuks, both times with the stones of the famous mausoleum.

Based on the descriptions in Pliny's *Natural History* and by the 15th-century Italian traveler Cepio, an English archeological team excavated the site in the middle of the 19th century. The meager finds, statues of Artemisia and Mausolos—or perhaps of his father by Lysippos, the creator of sculptural portraiture—as well as part of the frieze, are in the British Museum. The results of recent diggings, together with a model of antiquity's greatest tomb, are displayed in a small open-air exhibition in situ. On the hill above is the 10,000-seat theater built below much older rock-tombs in the 2nd century A.D.

The Petronion or Castle of St. Peter may not be to fortresses what Mausolos' tomb is to mausoleums, yet it is one of the great showpieces of late medieval military architecture. The Knights of Rhodes, founded during the Crusades as the military order of St. John of Jerusalem—the style still applied to the Anglican chapter, while the Catholic order is known as the Knights of Malta—used every known device to strengthen their foothold on the mainland, even installing the latest weapon, the cannon. Thus they victoriously resisted repeated Turkish onslaughts till Rhodes itself fell to Süleyman the Magnificent in 1523.

In the former church below the keep holding the center of the immense triple ramparts which are surrounded by a moat connected with the sea, is the small Museum of Underwater Archeology containing statues and amphorae recovered from the sea; the greatest find, however, the superb bronze Demeter, graces the Izmir museum.

Petronion became in Turkish Bodrum, an attractive village that developed too quickly into a popular holiday resort, bursting its seams. There is simply not enough room between the sea and the surrounding hills, whose slopes are crammed with white houses and hotels, up to the windmills on the ridge. The narrow lanes are crowded and the small town beaches are inadequate.

There are better beaches round Yalıkavak, a new resort 18 km. (11 miles) north and, equidistant west through lemon and orange orchards, at Karatoprak, also called Turgut Reis after the renowned 16th-century admiral. The road ends at Gümüşlük, where the ruins of the ancient port of Mindos are visible under the clear water.

The mountainous shores of the Gökova Gulf necessitate a wide detour inland to reach the southern promontory.

The easiest and pleasantest way to see this stretch of coast is by boat, either taking a Turkish Maritime Line trip or, ideally, exploring the numerous coves of the deep inlet on a yacht: sail from Bodrum at Kara Ada (Black Island), where warm mineral springs flow from the rocks in a grotto, then further east into the gulf, at the head of which between Akbuk and Gökova forested Mount Kiran rises vertically to 1,000 meters (3,000 ft.). After rounding the Knidos promontory, the Datça Gulf is entered past Sombeki Ada, partly hiding Bozborun on a peninsula rapidly developing into a priority tourist area. Beyond Kara Burun (Black Cape) the shores retreat until the spectacular gap in the cliffs screening the circular bay of Marmaris, the most sheltered harbor on the Aegean coastline.

But sailing means missing the inland sites and the infinitely varied drive through pine-clad hills, luxuriant plains and above magnificent bays. Nobody could regret doubling back the 66 km. (41 miles) through pine forests from Bodrum to Pecin Kalesi outside Milas. Less scenic are the 61 km. (38 miles) east to Muğla via Yatağan which gave its name to the short Turkish saber that slashed its way to the gates of Vienna, but is now an unprepossessing industrial center. Muğla, former capital of the emirate of Menteşe, has several mosques, among which is that of the Three Sages, Üç Erenler Cami.

Following Route 400 south, the descent to the Gökova Gulf affords superb views. A magnificent eucalyptus tree alley marks the 30-km. (19-mile) branch to Marmaris. Nothing remains of ancient Physkos, a flourishing port on the Anatolia–Rhodes–Egypt trade route, but the restored 16th-century citadel, a bridge and caravanserai enhance the most enchanting bay on this lovely coast. Even the spread of modernity along both headlands could not spoil the magnificent site below densely wooded mountains. Many enjoyable excursions can be made to lovely beaches and interesting archeological remains awaiting excavation. The 72-km. (45-mile) drive west over a densely wooded mountain affords splendid views over the Gökova and Datça Gulfs, then descends to the south coast before the 4-km. (3-mile) branch to the up-and-coming beach resort of Datça. The remaining 34 km. (21 miles) to Knidos are hard going.

Knidos was a famous center of art, birthplace of the architect Sostratos, who built one of the Seven Wonders of Antiquity, the lighthouse of Alexandria, and of the mathematician Eudoxos, the first to measure the earth's circumference. Aphrodite and Demeter, in a somewhat startling association of the voluptuous goddess of love with the stern matronly mother goddess, were equally venerated. Praxiteles' statue of the former, modelled on his mistress, the famous hetaera Phryne, so shocked the great sculptor's patrons at Kos across the sea that the Knidians were able to purchase the priceless masterpiece as a tourist attraction. Ships put in to admire the goddess, especially after a back entrance allowed a rear view. Only rather dull copies survive of what was considered the finest classical statue because of its unusual realism. The marble Demeter was no less perfect and would grace a cathedral better than the British Museum. The ruins of Aphrodite's circular temple, a theater and an odeon, lie surrounded by walls on a steep promontory. On the opposite headland, 47 km. (29 miles) lead to Bozburun.

Returning from Marmaris through idyllic wooded hills to the road junction, Route 400 turns southeast for the 112 km. (70 miles) to Fethiye. Near Köyceğiz hot springs flow into a lake joined to the sea by a natural channel. At its mouth, near the village of Dalyan, 8 km. (5 miles) off the main road, lie the ruins of the ancient Karian city of Kaunos, a 15,000-seat theater, ramparts and rock tombs cut into the cliff above the river.

But for the most dazzling display of that particular architectural fantasy you have first to pass Dalaman Airport and to skirt the magnificent Gulf of Fethiye. The setting between the rugged peaks of the western Taurus (Toros) and the wide sweep of the bay greatly enhances the attractions of the ruins of the Temple of Kabasbos, a Lykian god identified with Herakles, the sarcophagi carved out of the rocks, and the rock tombs of Telmessos above the castle built by the Knights of St. John. Finds from 19 antique cities in the vicinity are in the Archeological Museum, supplemented by medieval and Osmanli exhibits.

To the northeast, the most impressive tomb façades were undercut from the protective cliffs. The 4th-century B.C. Tomb of Amyntas, two Ionic columns supporting a pedestal topped by a sun disk above a false door, is typical of these funerary monuments of ancient Lykia all along the coast to Antalya.

Beware of the shortest but partly unpaved inland Route 350 to Antalya, 222 km. (138 miles) via Korkuteli. The scenically much lovelier 331 km. (206 miles) of Route 400, mostly along the coast of the Gelidonya peninsula, pass numerous delightful wooded coves, some already provided with accommodations of sorts. The first 25 km. (16 miles) head inland to the road junction at Uğurlu, then Route 400 turns sharp south, more or less along the Eşen Cayı, the border river between Karia and Lykia, at whose mouth the Aegean merges into the Mediterranean.

This short survey of the Aegean coast gives only an outline of the extraordinary archeological riches every step of the way. The entire coastline between Istanbul and Antakya (Antiochia) far southeast, is a veritable panorama of history and mythology.

PRACTICAL INFORMATION FOR
THE AEGEAN COAST

TOURIST OFFICES. There are local tourist offices in the following towns: **Akçay,** Barbaros Meydanı 1 (tel. 113); **Ayvalık,** Yat Limanı Karşısı (tel. 2122); **Bergama,** Izmir Cad. 54 (tel. 1862); **Bodrum,** Eylül Meydanı 12 (tel. 1091); **Datça,** Belediye Binası, Iskele (tel. 1163); **Fethiye,** Iskele Meydanı 1 (tel. 1527); **Foça,** Foça Girişi (tel. 1222); **Köyceğiz,** Kordon Gölpark 1 (tel. 1703); **Kuşadası,** Iskele Meydanı (tel. 1103); **Marmaris,** Iskele Meydanı 39 (tel. 1035); **Muğla,** Belediye Atapark Sitesi (tel. 3127); **Selçuk,** Efes Müzesi Karşısı 23 (tel. 1328).

WHEN TO COME. The mild weather of April and May is the best time. It is fairly pleasant in June and September, but July and August are hot months, in spite of the sea breezes.

SPECIAL EVENTS. May. Ephesus Festival, one week early May. Bergama *Kermes* (Folklore Festival), four days at end of month. **June.** Marmaris Art and Tourism Festival, early June. Foça Music and Water Sports Festival, mid-June. **September.** Bodrum Arts and Culture Festival, early September.

HOTELS AND RESTAURANTS

Akçay. *Turban Akçay Vacation Village* (M), Edremit (tel. 1205). 48 rooms in motel, 64 beach houses, 8 suites and 4 bungalows. Good beach, pool, tennis. *Aşiyan* (I), (tel. 1033). 45 rooms. Pool, restaurant. Motel on beach. *Beyazsaray* (I), (tel. 1245). 26 rooms. Motel on beach, with restaurant. *Doğan* (I), (tel. 1034). 37 rooms. The simplest of the 4 motels on the beach. *Öge* (I), (tel. 1004). 66 rooms. The most comfortable of the 4 motels on the beach, with restaurant. *Tüzün* (I), Oruçreis Cad. 2 (tel. 1554). Also on beach.

Aliaga. *Afacan* (M), (tel. 30). 15 rooms. Motel with restaurant.

Altinoluk. All on beach. *Çavusoğlu* (M). 76 rooms. Pool, tennis. *Akçam Motel* (I). 36 rooms. Restaurant. *Altınoluk Motel* (I). 31 rooms. Tennis, restaurant.

Ayvalik. *Ankara* (M), (tel. 1195). 57 rooms. Modest for category. *Büyük Berk* (M), on beach at Sarımsaklı (tel. 1045). 97 rooms. At top of (M) category; pool, nautical sports. *Murat Reis* (M), on beach at Küçük-köy (tel. 1456). 87 rooms. With pool and full range of sports facilities; top of (M) range. *Berk* (I), Orta Çamlik (tel. 1501). 50 rooms. In the village. On **Alibey Ada,** *Ortunç* (M), (tel. 2872). 22 rooms.

Balçova. *Balçova Kaplıcaları* (M), (tel. 159 442). 198 rooms. Thermal bath.

Bergama. *Tusan Motel* (M), (tel. 1173). 42 rooms. 3 km. (2 miles) west. **Restaurant.** *Kardeşler* (I). Recommended.

Bodrum. The hotels in the town are all small, booked out before the summer season starts, and rather expensive for what is offered. The accommodation on neighboring beaches is less claustrophobic. *T.M.T. Motel* (E), (tel. 1440). 171 rooms. Pool, sauna, sports facilities; on neighboring beach. *Baraz* (M), (tel. 1857). 24 rooms. *Gözen* (M), (tel. 1602). 20 rooms. *Halikarnas Motel* (M), (tel. 1073). 28 rooms. *Pansiyon Artemis* (M), all on Cumhuriyet Cad. 117 (tel. 2530). 22 air-conditioned rooms. *Regal* (M), Bitez Yalisi Kabakum (tel. 1058). 16 rooms. On nearby beach. *Seçkin Konaklar* (M), Neyzen Tevfik Cad. 228 (tel. 1351). 38 rooms. No restaurant. *Gala* (I), (tel. 2216). 11 rooms. In the yacht harbor. *Kaktüs* (I). 16 rooms. On neighboring beach.
Restaurants. There are numerous fish taverns on the seafront. *Ağıl* (M). *Han* (M). *Neşe* (M).

Burhaniye. *Urut* (M), Hürriyet Mey. 14 (tel. 1105). 37 rooms. Restaurant. *Keskin* (I), Oğretmen Evleri (tel. 11310). 86 rooms. Pool, beach.

Dalyan. *Kaunos* (M), Topel Cad. 37 (tel. 1057). *Turtle* (I), Sultaniye Köyü (tel. 1487). 10 rooms. Set in bay of orchards reached by boat. Excellent home cooking.

Datça. *Club Datça Tatil Köyü* (M), (tel. 1170). 92 rooms in bungalows. Pool, beach, nautical sports. *Dorya* (M), (tel. 3536). 32 rooms. Beach, pool.

Didim. *Didim Motel* (I). 33 rooms. On its own beach before the temple ruins.
At **Altınkum Plaj,** 3 km. (2 miles) beyond, are numerous hotels and pensions. *Göksu* (I). *Öner* (I). *Tuntaş* (I). *Üç Mevsim* (I).
Restaurants. *Aşiklar* (I). Near ruins. There are seafood taverns (I) on sea front.

Dikili. *Perla* (M), Badenli Cad. 97 (tel. 1145). 50 rooms. *Antur Motel* (I), (tel. 1103). 44 rooms. Restaurant, beach.

Fethiye. *Dedeoğlu* (M), Iskele Mey. (tel. 4010). 30 rooms. In port. *Likya* (I), Karagözler Mah. (tel. 1169). 16 rooms. On small beach of town fringe. *Seketur Motel* (I), Çaliş Gullükbaşi (tel. 1705). 35 rooms. Restaurant; on nearby beach.
Restaurants. Both on waterfront. *Pasaoğlu* (I). *Rafet* (I).

Foça. *Club Méditerranée* (E). French-run holiday village: for further information see p. 13. *Hanedan* (I), Büyükdeniz Sahil Cad. 1 (tel. 1515). 27 rooms.

Gökova. *Kerme-Tur* (M). Large complex on lovely, lonely beach.

Güllük. *Gül-Tur Holiday Village* (I).

Gümüldür. *Sultan* (M), Ozdere Köyü (tel. 140). 110 rooms. Fine beach, sports facilities. *Denizatı Motel* (I), Büyükalan Mev. (tel. 366). 24 rooms. Beach, restaurant.

Kara Ada. The first units of a 3,870-bed tourist complex opened on this island in late 1988.

Köycegiz. *Özay* (M), Kordon Boyu 11 (tel. 1300). On lakeside. Swimming pool.

Küçükkuyu. *Motel Ida-Tur* (M), (tel. 56). 62 rooms. Beach, pool.

Kuşadası. *Kervansaray* (E), (tel. 4115). 38 rooms. In the expertly restored Öküz Mehmet Paşa Caravanserai in village. *Tusan* (E), (tel. 4495). 63 rooms. On private beach; pool, sports facilities; the farthest out on the Selçuk road.
Even farther, but in the opposite direction, *Imbat* (E), (tel. 2000). 140 rooms. Pool, sports facilities; on private beach near village. *Akdeniz Hotel Club* (M), Karaova Mev., (tel. 1521). 191 rooms in several blocks. Large pool; mainly for package tours. *Akman* (M), Istiklal Cad. 13 (tel. 1501). 46 rooms. *Efe* (M), Güvercin Ada Cad. (tel. 3660). 44 rooms. On seafront. *Kismet* (M), (tel. 2005). 68 rooms. Also on private beach at Kadinlar Denizi. *Kuş-Tur Holiday Village* (M), (tel. 4110). 400 rooms in tiny bungalows. Large pool. *Martı* (M), (tel. 3650). 59 rooms. Across the coastal road, noisy. *Minik* (M), Cephane Sok. 8 (tel. 2359). 28 rooms. *Ömer* (M),

Yavansu Mev. (tel. 3700). 110 bungalows in pine grove; private beach. *Stella* (M), Bezirgan Sok. 44 (tel. 1632). 15 rooms. No restaurant.

Aran (I), Kaya Aldoğan (tel. 1325). 22 rooms. *Bektas Han* (I). 12 rooms; near bus station.

Restaurants. Among the large number along the seafront, *Alp* (M) is recommended for seafood. *Sultan Han* (M), Bahar Sok. 8 (tel. 3849).

Marmaris. *Martı Holiday Village* (E), (tel. 1440). 213 rooms. On good beach along bay; nautical sports. *Atlantik* (M), (tel. 1218). 40 rooms. On noisy seafront. *Lidya* (M), (tel. 2940). 220 rooms. Good beach along the bay. *Karadeniz* (M), Atatürk Cad. 46 (tel. 2837). 38 rooms. On noisy seafront. *Marmaris* (M), (tel. 1308). 63 rooms. Also on noisy Atatürk Cad. *Orkide* (M), (tel. 2580). 27 rooms. Near small crowded beach. *Otel* 47 (M), (tel. 4747). 50 rooms. On noisy seafront. *Poseidon* (M), (tel. 1840). 56 rooms. On small, crowded beach further out. *Turban Marmaris Holiday Village* (M), (tel. 1843). 234 bungalows, 12 suites. With disco; on good beach along the enchanting bay.

Restaurants. Among the chain along the seafront are *Bamboo* (M), *Huzur* (M), *Liman* (M) and *Tilla* (M).

Muğla. *Petur* (M), Marmaris Bul. (tel. 3135). 60 rooms, 4 suites. *Özalp* (I), Recai Gürel Cad. 5 (tel. 4629). 24 rooms.

Ölu Deniz. *Bayaş Yünus* (E). Beautiful setting. *Meri Oteli* (M), (tel. 4388) 1). 75 bungalows. *Han Camping* has room for tents and also has bungalows. On beach.

Ören. *Efem* (M), (tel. 1299). 84 rooms. Motel; beach, pool, sauna. *Turban Ören Holiday Village* (M), (tel. 1217). 115 rooms in several blocks. Two pools, beach, disco. *Ada* (I), (tel. 1225). 20 rooms. Beach, restaurant. *Erkal* (I). 32 rooms.

Selçuk. *Tusan Efes Motel* (I), (tel. 1060). 12 rooms. Small pool; at the entrance to the ruins. *Kale Han* (I), Atatürk Cad. (tel. 1154). 18 rooms. **Restaurants.** *Efes* (M). *Yeni Hitit* (M).

CAMPING. Of the large number along the coast, we list the best equipped. **Bodrum-Gümbet,** *Ayaz Kamp.* **Didim,** *Altınkum Plaji,* 5 km. (3 miles) south. **Fethiye,** *Deniz Kamping,* at Ölü Deniz, 14 km. (9 miles) away. **Gümüldür,** *Denizati Kamp.* **Kuşadasi,** *Kervansaray Mokamp,* 6 km. (4 miles) along the Selçuk road. **Ören,** *Altın Kamp,* 4 km. (2 miles) away.

GETTING AROUND. By Plane and Train. Most plane and train connections are to Izmir (see *Practical Information* for Izmir). There are bus and/or train connections from Izmir to Bergama, Selçuk and Salihli. The Dalaman airport, 56 km. (35 miles) west of Fethiye, provides easy access to the southern coastal region.

By Car. The coastal road, mainly E24 and Route 400, from Thrace across the Dardanelles to Bodrum, Marmaris and detouring inland via Muğla to Fethiye, as well as roads between main towns and places of interest, are paved, though often winding and narrow. The tracks to some archeological sites, such as Heraklea by Latmos and Xanthos are not easy going.

Drivers should note that ferry boats between Piraeus, the Greek islands and Turkish Aegean ports lop some 800 km. (500 miles) off the drive both to and from Europe. There are daily ferries in summer between Mytiline-Dikili, Chios-Çeşme, Samos-Kuşadası; less frequently, Kos-Bodrum and Rhodes-Marmaris.

Car Hire. *Avis* operates at: Bodrum, Neyzen Tevfik Cad. 80 (tel. 2333); Kuşadası, Atatürk Bul. Liman (tel. 1475); Marmaris, Kordon Cad. Sayar Apt. 16 (tel. 2771). *Hertz:* Dalaman Airport (tel. 1979); Kuşadası, Atatürk Bul. 62 (tel. 1319); Marmaris, Iskele Meydanı (tel. 125 52).

By Boat. *Turkish Maritime Lines* leave Istanbul every Wednesday in summer for a 10-day cruise to Alanya, with frequent stops along the coast. For a more leisurely trip, the *Blue Voyage* is a special yacht tour exploring the bays between Çeşme and Antalya.

The Kuşadası Marina is Turkey's largest with 600 berths, followed by Bodrum with 125 berths. Yachts and sailboats can also be chartered at Marmaris, for about $400 to $2,000 a day for 4 to 18 passengers. Inclusive tours are also available: return flight from London to Rhodes (Greece) and 12 days on a *gektirme,* a converted fishing vessel with one large cabin of up to 16 bunks, can cost as little as $500.

THE SEVEN CHURCHES OF ASIA MINOR. (Biblical reference Revelations II through VIII.) The sites of the seven Asian churches where St. Paul preached are of special interest to Christians and students of history. Any travel agent can arrange a tour of the seven, taking about 3 days and using Izmir as a base.

1) Pergamon (Bergama). Like the other cities, visited by Paul during his third journey (Acts XVIII:23 to XX:3), when he lived in Ephesus for two years. The place where, wrote St. John to the Church of Pergamon, "Satan's throne is sited."

2) Thyatira (Akhisar). Least important of the seven cities.

3) Smyrna (Izmir). Recipient of a letter from Paul praising the early believers for their faithfulness, and warning of future persecution.

4) Sardis (Salihli). The Lydian capital, where Croesus minted the first coins.

5) Philadelphia (Alaşehir). The youngest of the seven churches. Part of the city wall and some remains of an early church still standing.

6) Laodikea (Denizli). A crossroads of the ancient world, with recently-excavated theater and church. 19 km. (11 miles) from Hierapolis, home of Philip the Evangelist, and 23 km. (14 miles) from Kolossae, to whose citizens Paul wrote the Epistles emphasizing the union of Christians in the mystical body of Christ. See Colossians I:24–29, II:12–15 and II:20 to III:4, the best-known passages.

7) Ephesos (Selçuk). Visited briefly by Paul on his second journey, and then his home for two years on his third, Ephesos was also visited by St. John and Paul's disciple, Timothy. In the great amphitheater, when Paul preached that "there are no gods made with hands," the local silversmiths, led by Demetrius, one of their number, rioted against him for two hours, shouting "Great is Diana of the Ephesians" until the town clerk prevailed upon them to go home. Capital of the Roman Province of Asia, Ephesus was the site of the Temple of Diana, one of the Seven Wonders of the Ancient World. To the Christians of Ephesos, around A.D. 60, Paul is said to have written his Epistle to the Ephesians from captivity in Rome. This chapter of the New Testament is concerned with the doctrine of the mystical body of Christ and is famous for its metaphor of the Christian as a pure soldier.

Paul is thought to have written some of his Epistles here, and John may have written his Gospel here in A.D. 95. From Ephesos, indeed, where St. John brought Mary in fulfillment of his pledge to Jesus to protect her, she is believed to have been taken into heaven.

A pilgrim objective for longer than any other site in Christendom, Ephesos built the first basilica, and was the scene of the Third Ecumenical Council in 431, during which Mary was proclaimed the Mother of God.

THE TURQUOISE COAST

The Connoisseur's Choice

This is one Mediterranean shore that deserves its fancy colored name. The luxuriant coastal plain widens and narrows, obliterated where mountains tumble straight into the turquoise waters of the *Akdeniz* (the White Sea in contrast to the Black Sea in the north). Swimming is a pleasure from May through November, and possible all the year round, especially in the wide open bays of Antalya and Mersin.

The hot, dry summers and mild, wet winters produce the whole gamut of Mediterranean plants, with citrus groves, banana plantations and ornamental palms along the coast, and bay trees, broom, myrtle and pines in the foothills up to the cedars of the heights. Mighty mountain ranges, above all the Taurus, not only provide a formidable backdrop but thrust their spurs into the sea, thus breaking up what no one could dare to call monotonous. This protection from Central Anatolia's biting winds was appreciated by paleolithic man, who left remains in caves, but the first known settlers were the Lykians, of the *Iliad,* a fiercely independent people who might have chosen the wooded hills for their inaccessibility. Their federation of 23 towns was conquered by the Persians despite desperate resistance. The first Greek settlers came after the Trojan War, more in the 8th and 7th centuries B.C. Alexander the Great marched through Lykia and Pamphylia, which fell to the Seleukids till the Peace of Apamea in 188 B.C. when Pergamon became the dominant power. Imperial Rome brought unprecedented prosperity, which was rudely shattered by Arab incursions till the Isaurian dynasty of Byzantium restored the border at the Taurus Mountains. Byzantines, pirates, Seljuks, Crusaders and petty Turkish beys disputed the fertile region until it was incorporated into the Osmanli empire by Bayezit I in the late 14th century. Today this lovely stretch of coast has regained its ancient prosperity, partly through agriculture, more through tourism.

EXPLORING THE TURQUOISE COAST

Route 400 will take you 63 km. (39 miles) southeast from Fethiye through cedar and pine forests, to a branch descending on the right 3 km. (2 miles) to the once splendid now partly flooded Letoon. After giving birth to Artemis and Apollo on the island of Delos, the nymph Leto, abandoned by her seducer Zeus to the jealousy of his savage wife, fled to this coast to wash her children in the spring, round which a sanctuary was built.

Back on Route 400 to the village of Kınık from which an atrocious mile ascends to the ruins of Xanthos, the main Lykian city. Herodotos describes how the Xanthians burnt their women, children, slaves and treasures before making a final sortie against the Persians. This was confirmed by the thick layer of ashes discovered in the excavations. The capital of the Lykian Federation was destroyed by Brutus in 42 B.C., rebuilt by Mark Antony and favored by Emperor Vespasian. The city became the seat of a bishop before subsiding under the Arabs, piracy and malaria.

In 1838 the ruins were discovered by Fellows, who shipped the reliefs and sculptures in a frigate to London where they are now displayed in the Lycian rooms of the British Museum. Opposite the parking lot are the Hellenistic gate and the portal of Vespasian. Behind the remains of the walls are a stele with inscriptions in Lykian and Greek scripts, commemorating the struggle against Athens in the Peloponnesian War; and the 400 B.C. Monument of the Nereids, a temple on a high podium with reliefs below an architrave supported by four columns between which stood the statues of the Nereids. These charming mermaids were the daughters of Nereus, the original Old Man of the Sea. The well-preserved Roman theater stands on the site of the Lykian acropolis, which is flanked by a Lykian and a Roman columned tomb. Here is also the Monument of the Harpies—creatures with female faces, the bodies of vultures, claws and bears' ears—with plaster casts of the reliefs depicting a dynast and his wife receiving the homage of these monstrous daughters of Poseidon and his grandmother Earth.

The terrace on the furthest point overlooks the valley sloping down to the Eşen (Xanthos) River. To the rear is the Roman agora, facing a Byzantine basilica. As the Lykians placed their tombs right in the middle of the towns, there are monuments of the four architectural types scattered about.

At the fishing village of Kalkan, ancient Patara with more rock tombs, Route 400 joins the sea, which it follows for a lovely 20 km. (12 miles) to Kaş. Below an amphitheater of mountains at the head of a narrow bay dotted with islands, ancient Antiphellos, port of Lykian Phellos further inland, is becoming a popular resort, helped by the obligatory Lykian rock tombs in the harbor and a small Hellenistic theater on a hill commanding a superb view over the bay to the natural breakwater of Meis island, ancient Megiste, now Greek Kastellorizo.

A secondary road hugs the shore southeast to the Great Cape, Ulu Burun, where a ship that sank 3,400 years ago is the oldest excavated by archeologists. Part of the cargo of amphoras, Mycenaean vases, gold and ivory jewelry as well as the first examples of manufactured glass, two dozen cobalt-blue ingots, is in the Museum of Underwater Archeology in Bodrum (see p. 159).

Route 400 rises again into the mountains, offering stupendous views over the bay. The branch left (north) is lined for several miles with more rock tombs to Kasala, but then comes a bad stretch of 20 km. (12 miles) before Akçay and the Black Lake on the shorter inland road via Korkuteli to Antalya.

More interesting is the branch right to Üçağiz, ancient Simena, complete with rock tombs, a Lykian Senate building, a Roman bath and a Byzantine fortress from which the entire Kekova region with its bays and islets can be viewed. Across a narrow channel, Kekova island was shaken so often by earthquakes that the larger part of ancient Apollonia is now submerged. It is highly original, though not without danger to one's shins, to swim among the halls, columns and mosaics of buildings dating from the last four centuries B.C. The island's northwestern part is predominantly Byzantine, with churches, mansions and military installations. On the south a bay opens to the Mediterranean. The best way is to come on the daily motorboat tour from Kaş, or from Dalyan Ağzi (Andiake) near Demre. These bays and islets are ideal for yachting, with a wealth of ancient ruins scattered along the coast.

Santa Claus

Route 400 passes through featureless shrub country to a large tomb with Corinthian pillars in the middle of nowhere. It then goes down to a fertile alluvial plain formed by the Demre Çay, so that Demre, antique Myra, is now far back from the long beach of fine sand that extends east between the sea and a lagoon—a strange fate for the see of St. Nicholas, patron of sailors, who was born at Patara, educated at Xanthos and became bishop of Myra where he was martyred in the 4th century. For some complicated reasons he also became Santa Claus, and no less complicated is the plan of the Byzantine basilica, sufficiently restored to allow for a service over his tomb, on his feast on December 6, and also—for climatic and touristic reasons—in May. A further complication is the empty tomb, as the remains of Santa Claus were taken to Bari in Italy in 1087 and the few bones left behind are in a reliquary in the Antalya museum. The basilica is in Demre's mainstreet, but most of Myra has been washed away by the river, up to the Roman theater below a steep cliff honeycombed with Lykian tombs.

Route 400 skirts the lagoon and rounds a rocky headland to the next, even larger alluvial plain, this one formed by the Alakır Çay. But Finike spreads from a rocky spur and is thus still a port, blessed with so mild a climate that its ancient name, Phoinikos (Palmtree) seems fully justified, though orange groves now predominate. Here swimming is a pleasure almost the whole year round.

Alexander's Failure

Demre is normally visited from Antalya, best in a delightful round trip that comprises remarkable antiquities in superb seascapes and in fine mountain scenery. Finike is the roadfork from which Route 635 climbs north over the Karambeyli Geçidi (1,290 meters, 4,230 feet), to Elmalı. On its outskirts, the Karagöl (Black Lake) spills its waters into a yawning chasm, a gigantic slit in the rocky wall upholding the highland. At Semahöyük some rock tombs date back to 6,000 B.C.; frescoes in the most recent—c. 5,000 B.C.—have been restored. The village of Tekke has evolved from a dervish settlement, as its name indicates. Korkuteli, the Lykian mountains' main road junction, is graced by the Ömer Pasa Cami.

Route 635 continues north to Burdur, while Route 350 curves east over the northern spur of the Bey Dağları (Bey Mountains) to a 6 km. (4 miles) branch right (south) zigzagging up a tremendous gorge in the Düzler Çamı National Park. A watchtower and some tombs beside the road herald the ancient city. On this rocky site, the most modest attempt at urban expansion required enormous effort, as the town rises steeply for almost a thousand feet from the necropolis with its hundreds of sculptured sarcophagi just outside the first rampart, where the car must be left. The guard acts as guide, and though his English is likely to be rudimentary, he is indispensable among the precipitous ruins, which, except for the widely scattered main sites, are still largely buried beneath the forest.

The tour begins at the graceful little temple, dedicated by the most ubiquitous of all emperors, Hadrian. A stiff climb leads to the agora and the 600-seat odeon, next to the 4,000-seat theater which looks towards the distant sea. Most of the town, however, faces the narrow valley it dominates. Of particular interest are five huge cisterns, 11 meters (36 ft.) in diameter and 7 meters (24 ft.) deep, fed by a conduit still discernible at a dizzy height on the sheer rock face, an astounding technical achievement. This unfailing water supply in an impregnable position, strengthened by widely spaced triple walls, explains why Termessos was the only town Alexander the Great ever failed to take.

The Romans enhanced the city with many temples, public buildings, and statues. Because of the scarcity of Christian relics historians are inclined to set the date of the abandonment of the site at about the 5th century. What furnished the basis for Termessos' obvious prosperity remains a mystery, but if its inhabitants had any of the characteristics of the surrounding landscape, they must have been of a harsh and uncompromising nature, well able to put up a good fight against Alexander. However, judging from the magnificent remains of the ideally situated theater, it is also logical to conclude that the citizens of Termessos were blessed with extremely good taste. Despite the climbing and the tricky access to the ruins—all these stones were upheaved by earthquakes and the archeologists' work is far from done—this is an excursion not to be missed.

Shortly after the Evdir Han, a caravanserai built by the Seljuk Sultan Izettin Keykavus in 1219, Route 350 joins the four-lane Route 650 at 8 km. (5 miles) north of Antalya. Paleolithic fans might turn north on this main north-south axis and take the first branch left (northwest) to the Karain Caves, where vestiges of human occupation some 50,000 years ago have been found.

The Gelidonya Peninsula

This is the touristic jargon for what is geographically the eastern shore of the huge Lykian headland. The most accessible parts of this outstandingly beautiful coast have been transformed with the assistance of the World Bank into one of the Mediterranean's most attractive playgrounds.

Past Finike, Route 400 winds 111 km. (69 miles) through the pine-covered red cliffs at the foot of the Bey Mountains to Antalya. This splendidly serrated range rises to awesome peaks up to 2,375 meters (7,790 ft.) over a distance of 10 km. (6 miles), allowing a five-month skiing season. Yet the signpost to this Olympos is not for a divine mountain but the ruins of an ancient port.

Near Cıralı is the home of the Chimera, a rather unlovable mutant with a goat's body, a dragon's tail and a lion's head from whose jaws fire spewed forth. Legend has it that, as a boy, Bellerophon had inadvertently caused the death of one of his friends, Belleros, whence his surname, meaning "slayer of Belleros." He found refuge at the court of Proetos, King of Argos, and must have been a handsome lad, since Queen Stheneboe tried to seduce him, in the best Potiphar tradition. Proetos, reluctant to complicate his private life, rid himself of Bellerophon by turning him over to Iobates, King of Lycia. The latter, whose explicit instructions were to do away with the youth, couldn't quite bring himself to kill him. Instead, he assigned Bellerophon a mission from which it was believed no one could return alive—the slaying of the Chimera.

Bellerophon figured that the successful accomplishment of his assignment would require some sort of airborne operation. At that period, the only available air transportation happened to be the winged steed, Pegasos. And the only way to borrow Pegasos was through a petition to the goddess Athena. The latter, touched by Bellerophon's plight, handed over to him the golden reins, the only ones capable of controlling the divine horse. With the aerial problem solved, there still remained the bombing strategy to be worked out. Bellerophon placed a leaden sheathing over his lance blade, which he plunged into the Chimera's maw. The flames belching out of the creature's gullet melted the lead, thereby choking and suffocating the monster. But the flaming tongue, natural gas escaping from a hole in the rocks, is still burning high up on the mountain.

For romantic ruins, it would be hard to equal Phaselis. Founded by Dorian settlers in the 7th century B.C., the ruins of this major port with three harbors are mainly Roman. The agora, large theater, aqueduct and a necropolis with fine sarcophagi are scattered through the pinewoods that surround the Temple of Athena. Overgrown streets descend to the translucent water that invites for a swim.

Kemer, 15 km. (9 miles) further north, is the center of intensive touristic development, with hotels, holiday villages and a well-equipped large marina. The remaining 35 km. (26 miles) are increasingly occupied by villas, motels and restaurants to the smooth pebbles of Konyaaltı Beach stretching for miles to the outskirts of the region's capital.

Antalya

In the 2nd century B.C. Attalos II of Pergamon established a naval base in the small natural harbor at the northwestern head of this vast bay. In the happy days of imperial Rome, Attalia spread up and over the protect-ing cliffs that form a headland between the beaches of Konyaaltı and Lara. Horseshoe-shaped ramparts encircled the port as well as the upper town. The seawalls are still impressive, but the outer defense has been reduced to a few sections and towers on Kalekapisi (Tower Gate) Meydani, the main square. The only remaining gate is the triple marble arches, whose architrave is supported by Corinthian columns, commemorating Emperor Hadrian's visit in A.D. 130.

Palm-lined Atatürk Caddesi descends from Hadrian's Gate to the Inönü Park east of the port, the favorite stroll on balmy evenings and lively with music from cafés and cabarets below the Hıdırlık Kulesi, the round Roman tower built on a square Pergamese base that once served as a light-house.

The Seljuks came in the late 12th century and started the architectural transformation of what became after several other names Antalya. Just below Kalekapisi, the greatest of the Seljuk Sultans, Alaeddin Keykubat, converted in 1230 a Byzantine church into a mosque and added the 38-meter (125 ft.) high Yivli (Fluted) Minaret which gave the Cami its name. From the square base decorated with turquoise and dark blue tiles rise eight half-cylindrical sections in brick where, alas, little is left of the tile inset of Antalya's landmark. In the same complex are a medrese, hamam and two tombs. A Roman temple near the Inönü Park became a triple-naved basilica dedicated to the Panagia (the Virgin) and then a mosque, called since 1851 the Kesik (Truncated) Minare Cami. Decapitated like many others by lightning before the universal installation of lightning rods, the minaret resembles a candlestick with the candle three-fourths consumed.

Outside the walls are the 15th-century Bali Bey Cami and the 16th-century Murat Paşa Cami with three cupolas, the latter opposite the *otogar* (inter-city bus terminal). Above the harbor is the Karatay Medrese, dating from 1250. The pleasing Iskele (Port) Cami standing on four pillars is reached by a wooden staircase over the waters of the yacht harbor. The old town—the citadel—has been so successfully restored that it was awarded the *Golden Apple,* the Oscar of the Travel Writers, in 1985. Right-ly, because the area has preserved the architectural features even as a touristic leisure center with an excellent hotel and a string of restaurants on the seafront.

Through the ring of modern apartment blocks housing most of Antal-ya's 200,000 inhabitants, Kenan Evren Bulvari runs westwards to the Mu-seum. The wealth of exhibits starts with the finds from the Karain Caves and the Bronze Age remains from Karataş Semahöyük. There are classical Greek vases and delightful Hellenistic Tanagra figurines in the distinctive style of Myrina, slightly sentimental or mildly satirical. The larger statu-ary is mainly Roman, mostly from Perge; mosaics from Xanthos depict the infant Achilles dangling by one heel while his mother dips him into the River Styx; the sarcophagi overflow into the courtyard and garden. But the spacious 13 galleries also display interesting Byzantine ikons and the meager relics of St. Nicholas.

From the Museum Akdeniz Bulvari descends to Konyaaltı Plaj, rather crowded at the town end. More select is the fine sand of Lara Plaj, 11 km. (7 miles) east along the cliff edge, past the Düden waterfall plunging 50 meters (165 ft.) into the sea. The equally formidable Upper Düden falls are just outside the town.

Antalya's greatest attraction remains its site, with the spectacular views over the Bey Mountains.

To the East: Perge

The 137 km. (85 miles) to Alanya lead first through a fertile coastal plain, then close to the sea to three compulsory stopping points and two optional ones.

Perge lies only 19 km. (11 miles) from Antalya; take the left turn off Route 400 at Aksu. The useful plan at the entrance greatly facilitates a visit to the ruins. There is, however, no mistaking the Hellenistic exterior wall, strengthened by numerous turrets, which still encircles the vast ruins. Two round towers guard the gate and portico at the head of the monumental way which traversed the city. The ruins are so vast that it is advisable to drive to the second fortified enclosure. An impressive remnant and one corner of this enclosure are still visible through the entrance arch, as is the Victory Portal framed by two round towers. On the left is the Roman basilica that was converted into a church. Equally well preserved are the thermal baths on the right, facing the agora. The inside of the handsome Victory Portal was decorated with statues on two levels of niches. A few are in the Antalya Museum, more have been shattered and their fragments litter the grounds.

The main artery started at the entrance to the theater outside the first wall and led through the portal to the palaestra at the base of the acropolis. This original settlement on higher ground was soon outgrown and Roman Perge spilt southward into the plain. A drainage canal ran down the middle of this vast thoroughfare lined with vast porticos, two rows of columns with square shafts; the sidewalks were paved with mosaics and lined with shops.

Closer to the acropolis, a second avenue intersects the first one. The paving stones still bear the marks of chariot wheels. In the 13th century, a violent earthquake knocked down all the columns. They have now been placed back in an upright position, and some of them conserve their original capitals. The last four are adorned with figures representing, in the following order from the Victory Portal: Demeter, Zeus, Artemis, and Apollo. And here the centuries have spared a precious bit of mosaic that once served as a shop sign. Two other virtually intact columns stand opposite, topped with capitals and their connecting crosspiece. The three remaining letters—B E P—are undoubtedly part of a longer inscription, probably "Republic of Perge." In A.D. 45 St. Paul and St. Barnabus arrived in Perge from Cyprus.

The stadium, that lies outside the walls, could hold 22,000 people and is one of the biggest (over 240 meters, nearly 800 ft., long) and best-preserved stadiums of Roman times. Except for the stage, whose marble statuary is still half-buried among the debris, the restoration of the theater has been completed. The archeologists carefully numbered the stones of the tiered seats that have been put back into place after a bit of cleaning up. A fountain faces the restored arch of the crumbled entrance gate. For the time being, the theater stage is not quite ready for a performance, but should the festival habit spread it could soon be made usable. The theater seated 15,000, culture being as important as games and sports.

The ruins of Sillyon lie 29 km. (18 miles) along Route 400 and 5 km. (3 miles) left along the secondary road left (north). Because of the steepness of the hill—it is 250 meters (820 ft.) high—the city is not included even among the optional stops. Parts of the high flat rock were split off by an earthquake and a deep chasm cuts through the theater, dividing the stage from the auditorium. Hellenistic, Roman and Byzantine buildings as well as a Seljuk mosque are precariously perched on the remaining southern platform.

Aspendos

The next turn north leads to the best-preserved antique theater, at Aspendos (Belkıs), 44 km. (27 miles) from Antalya, on the banks of the Köprü Çay where, when the river was called Eurymedon, in 468 B.C. Kimon won the greatest of all Athenian naval victories over the Persians. Its excellent state of conservation may be partly due to the quality of the materials used or to the architect Zenon's skill, but above all to its conversion—of all the unlikely possibilities—into the palace of a Seljuk sultan.

Under the Romans, Aspendos prospered sufficiently to build an enormous theater which has kept a grandiose air. The acoustics are so fine that performances are put on here without amplifiers or microphones. Turkey's most outstanding acting groups perform ancient Greek plays (in Turkish) during the drama festival in early October. They also perform classical plays appropriate to the setting, such as *Julius Caesar* and *Britannicus.*

In the 13th century the north wing was threatening to collapse, and the Seljuks reinforced it with bricks, which accounts for the typically Islamic broken arch in the center. A few rows of seats have also been restored. But the theater as a whole has conserved its integrity, an impressive fact when one realizes that the diameter of the amphitheater is some 91 meters (300 ft.) It reportedly sat 20,000 people, but if you allow only one and a half feet per spectator, it's more likely that its total capacity was 15,000. The arches along the upper gallery are also mostly intact; they enabled members of the "promenade" audience to watch the performance while remaining comfortable in the shade. Of course, the wall niches that used to hold the ornamental statuary are now empty, but the raised box seats for guests of honor, on either side of the stage, and the decoratively-carved superstructures over the stage have survived. There are even traces of paint still visible on the south wall. The aisles on both sides of the orchestra are crowned with triple-arched vaulted ceilings, each arch higher than the one that precedes it, the tallest reaching a height of 24 meters (80 ft.)! The columns fell prey to the 13th-century quake, but the stone projecting pieces held firm. Various inscriptions are there to remind posterity that the building was financed by two worthy patrons of the arts, the brothers Curtius Crispinus and Curtius Auspicatus in the reign of Antoninus Pius, between the years A.D. 138 and 161.

Aspendos lies several miles inland today, but even in ancient times it had no actual seaport. Ships reached it via the Eurymedon River, which in those days was navigable. The river was spanned by a bridge "high enough for a ship to pass under," whence the Turkish name for it (*köprü*, bridge and *çay*, river). The first bridge gave up the ghost some seven centuries ago. It was replaced by a graceful Seljuk hogback bridge, only high enough to allow the passage of small boats, since the river port in the meantime had become sanded over.

The city at one time enjoyed a thriving commerce, its reputation resting mainly on cattle-breeding. Alexander the Great agreed to spare it in exchange for a ransom of 4,000 horses. The rest of the local industry was centered around silks, rugs and miscellaneous luxury items, with particular emphasis on tiny figurines carved out of lemon wood and decorated with ivory, a specialty that might be described as the "high class" souvenir of the times.

Aspendos was built up against two hills, the tallest of them being, of course, the acropolis, an easy climb, but the ruins are in a jumble and difficult to make out. They include the basic layout of the agora, with vestiges of the basilica and curia, a wall that was part of the fountain (or nympheum), and a semicircular altar in the odeum, or concert hall. North of the city, extensive segments of the aqueducts that channeled in water on brick arches 15 meters (49 ft.) high over a distance of 32 km. (20 miles) are still visible.

Side

Side (pronounced *See-day*), 76 km. (47 miles) from Antalya, lies at the end of a 3-km. (2-mile) branch to the right (south). Banana plantations vie with orange groves along the roadside, and the vegetation becomes more profuse as you travel east.

Byzantine ruins herald the proximity of the ancient city, spread over a rocky promontory between two beaches, long before the ramparts loom into view. Side means pomegranate in an Anatolian language, but according to the 6th-century B.C. geographer Hekataios it was founded by the Minotaur's sister Molos, which would indicate relations with Minoan Crete. Verifiable development came in the 7th century B.C. under the impetus of Greek colonists from Aeolia. Side was Pamphylia's main port and commercial center, bustling with piracy and a thriving slave trade. As everywhere along this coast, imperial Rome erected most of the monuments in the 2nd and 3rd centuries A.D. There is a curious symmetry in dates and derivations, as Side was deserted in the 7th century A.D. under the Arab onslaught, to be reborn only in 1923 as a haven for Moslem refugees from Crete. The commercial spirit has also been revived in major tourist developments, solidly based on a combination of spectacular ruins and good bathing.

The landward sections of the enclosure wall are more or less intact; various layers of Greek foundations and Roman and Byzantine additions are clearly discernible. The entrance portal is still flanked by two towers, but the statues that once embellished it are now in the museum. Opposite the entrance, outside the walls, stands an exquisite fountain which has a semicircular façade with three carved niches. Still more fountains are scattered throughout the city itself.

Just inside the entrance, two streets branch off. One is a main thoroughfare leading straight ahead toward the ruins. The other, forming an acute angle with the first one, veers off to the left, and along it stands a Byzantine basilica. Corinthian columns upheld the porticos of these streets, with two houses still standing, separated by a narrow passage, with marble-paved courtyards and a cistern in each courtyard.

Further on, to the left, the agora was enclosed on all sides by porticos, with shops on three sides. The remnants of a circular structure in the center are those of the temple of the goddess Tyche (Fortune). It has a central room surrounded by a gallery with 12 Corinthian columns, and a pyramidal twelve-sided dome. In one corner of the square, a marble-walled building, looking like a luxury shop, housed the public toilets. Another short street running southeast gives out onto a second agora, with a statue of Nemesis, the goddess of vengeance. The other statues have been removed to the local museum.

The theater backs on to the first agora and was built not, as customary, set against a hillside, but freestanding as in the West. Despite the claim of the tourist handouts that it held 25,000 spectators, 15,000 is more likely. With the help of U.N.E.S.C.O., 30 tiers of seats have been restored and the stage has been cleared of rubble: all is ready for performances. In the basement are singularly solid latrines with the antique lack of privacy.

At the end of this street, on the furthest point of the promontory, are what used to be Side's port facilities. A Roman temple casts its shade on a Byzantine fountain; two other temples, on the right, are dedicated to Athena and Apollo; and there's a Byzantine basilica. Still more Byzantine relics along the way include private houses, and public baths, on both sides of the street. Preceding and mixed with the Corinthian style are Ionian and Doric columns, and all these landmarks left by successive civilizations have become further and inextricably tangled up by the centuries.

Now retrace your steps back toward the agora—the museum rises up straight ahead, housed in the old Roman baths. Outstanding is the Hermes from the fountain, but most of the statues lost their heads through the fervor of Side's neophytes after conversion by St. Paul. The capacious hall on the right of the *tepidarium,* or lounge, features a large collection of detached heads, plus some handsomely-carved sarcophagi, more statues, and capitals. The arch has been restored, but the walls have withstood earthquakes and time.

The adjoining room used to be the *caldarium* (hot bath); it is now arrayed with showcases and statues. Nike, the goddess of victory, seems reassuringly confident; Herakles sports a splendid curly beard, but has only a single leg, impressively muscular. See also the Twelve Labors of Herakles in bas-relief, and the Torment of Ixion, who was changed into a hermaphrodite for having dared to gaze upon Hera.

First of the optional stops is at the Manavgat Falls, the drop of only a few meters makes them little more than rapids. Footbridges span several tributary streams to an island with a rustic restaurant and café. A mere 4 km. (2 miles) off Route 400, Şelale (Waterfall) offers a cool rest even on the hottest days. The second optional is another short turn left (north), to Alarahan, a 13th-century fortified caravanserai by the side of the Alara stream below a castle approached through a tunnelled entrance, in a wild landscape.

Alanya

Visible from the last few of the 137 km. (85 miles) from Antalya, is the almost 300-meter (985-ft.) high rock that was a pirate stronghold until the Romans put a stop to that. Called Korakesion in ancient times, it was conquered in 1220 by the great Alaeddin Keykubat who renamed it Alaiye and made it his winter residence. With the decline of the Seljuks, it became part of the Karamanoğullar dominions, fell to the Osmanlis in 1472, became Alanya in 1923, and Turkey's largest beach resort in the 1980s.

A road affording splendid views winds from the seaside up to the citadel. The outer wall is 8 km. (5 miles) long and required 12 years to build. The existence of some 400 cisterns made it possible to keep enough water on hand to withstand almost any length of siege. Arrows could be rained down on attackers through battlement crenels and 150 towers. When the defenders were finally submerged by the invaders, they withdrew to the ramparts of the second enclosure, and made their last stand in the confines of the third enclosure.

The Seljuk city was established inside the first wall, and the Seljuk shield is emblazoned on the postern gate of the second wall. Inside, there's a high-ceilinged room topped by a vast dome, pierced with loopholes on all sides. The entrance arch is probably of Roman design. A Seljuk-style broken arch adorns the outer façade. The fortress's rather small mosque, Kale Cami, is located between the second and third walls. Its foundations date back to Theodosius, and the restored dome is from the time of Süleyman the Magnificent (1530).

Toward the interior are the remains of the Bedesten, which boasted 26 rooms and vast storage spaces. It was probably a Seljuk caravanserai that housed a storeroom for the castle. Farther on, beyond the reservoirs, stands the small, attractive Akşabe Sultan Tekke (Dervish Lodge); the exterior is stone, the inside is red brick. The dome and the minaret—alas, truncated—are also of red brick. Behind the third wall, at the top of the promontory, are the foundations of Keykubat's palace and, less ruined, a Byzantine church with part of its frescoes still visible. Steps ascend to the partly restored battlement on the summit of the rock, and from it, with a stiff wind blowing, the view can quite literally take your breath away.

The tiniest detail of the reddish outline of the promontory is sharply etched against the technicolor blue-green of the Mediterranean. Beyond the two beaches a seemingly unending succession of cliffs juts into the sea from the foothills of the Taurus, whose highest peaks glitter most of the year with snow.

Kızıl Kule (Red Tower), which reinforces the low wall at the junction of the curtain—and sea—walls, served as a watchtower for the yards in which Keykubat's sailing vessels were built and kept shipshape. A small museum displays the enormous key to the tiny nail-studded door in the 3-meter (10-ft.) thick wall of the octagonal tower, built in 1225 by Abu Ali of Alepo after the model of the Crusader's castles and skillfully restored. The first two stories are made of the familiar reddish stone blocks, and the two upper ones are built from great red bricks.

The tremendous hollow central column inside was the cistern. Bricks are again used inside, with loopholes conveniently located just about everywhere for the archers to take aim, not to mention the troughs designed to hold the boiling tar and melted lead, which were the special treats in store for the besiegers below. The ceiling, which gives directly onto the lookout gallery, is pierced with holes through which alerts were sounded. A terrace leads to the sentry's path, which wound around the wall and continued all the way to the palace.

Another strong tower rises above the 13th-century shipyard, better approached by boat than along the seawall's catwalk. The entrance is flanked by a guardroom on the left, and a mosque to the right. The shipyard proper, which still shelters some fishing vessels, consisted of five compartments, each one 43 by 8 meters (140 by 25 ft.).

The small Damlataş (Weeping) Cave at the rock's eastern base owes its name to the multi-hued stalactites and stalagmites. The very high humidity, up to 98 percent at a constant temperature of around 22°C (72–74°F) benefits sufferers from asthma and respiratory illnesses for whom the grotto is reserved from 6 to 10 A.M., before being opened to some 100,000 visitors annually. Tea gardens and a small park connect with the Archeological and Ethnographical Museum.

Boat rides are a pleasure along the coves and inlets. Fosforlu Mağara (Blue Grotto) lives up to its Turkish name as the rocks really are phosphorescent. Aşiklar (Lovers') Mağara is a few meters above the landing stage on the Dilvarda Peninsula. At the Kızlar (Maidens') Mağara the pirates kept their fairer captives. The beaches east and west of the town are lined with hotels and motels.

Prime Coastline

The 55 km. (34 miles) to Gazipaşa skirt the sea in the ever narrowing coastal plain. After that small town, 4 km. (2 miles) from a fine beach, you enter some of the Mediterranean's most beautiful scenery, reminiscent of the famed Amalfi drive or parts of the Riviera. For most of the 267 km. (165 miles) to Mersin, forests of fragrant umbrella pines—in winter over a carpet of daffodils and anemones—cover the precipitous slopes to the red cliffs or long stretches of fine white sand which fringe the turquoise sea. The few coastal plains contrast with the luxuriant greens of banana plantations and orange groves, often below mighty medieval castles, Byzantine, Armenian, Crusader and Seljuk, while Hellenistic and Roman ruins fit harmoniously into the breathtaking panoramic views.

Just before the small inland town of Anamur in the first of the lush plains walled in by the Taurus Mountains, a branch right ends after 3 km. (2 miles) at the double ramparts, theater, odeon and necropolis of ancient Anemorion. 4 km. (2 miles) after the town's gardens, Route 400 joins the sea at Mamure Kalesi (Anamur Castle) on the promontory closest to Cyprus. This proximity induced the island's Lusignan kings to transform the Roman fortress on the beach further on into their main foothold in Cilicia in the 13th century. Protected by the sea and a moat, the 36 towers project from tremendously strong ramparts which extend to the 14-sided keep. The emirs of Karaman added a mosque, bath and fountain.

The pirate castle of Softa rises from the sea 20 km. (12 miles) further on. There is marvelous scenery along Route 400 all the way to Taşucu, 11 km. (7 miles) before Silifke, a small resort despite a nearby factory. Just south of Silifke, are the basilica and tomb of St. Thecla (Ayatekla), St. Paul's first convert and the very first female Christian martyr. Having resolved to keep her virginity, Thecla broke off her engagement, whereupon her outraged fiancé denounced her as a Christian. This pure maiden was exhibited naked in the amphitheater but, in the words of the ancient scribes, "since she was clothed in her innocence, the ignominy that was designed to strike her became instead an occasion of glory and triumph." The lions who were unleashed to devour her merely crouched docilely at Thecla's feet, and the flames—the third ordeal—failed to touch her. She finally ended her days peacefully in her retreat at Isauria.

Silifke (Seleukia on Kalykadnos) is 138 km. (86 miles) east of Anamur. It was founded in the 3rd century B.C. by Seleukos I. It has a Hittite Museum containing finds from the numerous archeological sites in the vicinity. Remarkable is a treasure of 5,215 Hellenistic silver coins, unearthed at Gülnar in the Taurus foothills. The Byzantine castle on the hill was transformed by the Knights of Rhodes into a formidable fortress with 23 towers and bastions. The cellars house a cistern whose waters "will never dry up." Bayezit built a mosque within the walls. A Roman bridge spans the Göksu (Kalykadnos); 8 km. (5 miles) upstream along Route 715 is the most dramatic site of the lovely valley where Emperor Frederick Barbarossa drowned in 1190, thereby bringing the Third Crusade to a sudden halt.

The ruins of Uzuncaburç (Olba-Diocaesarea), 30 km. (19 miles) north, are noteworthy for the temple of Zeus, the city walls and gates. But it hardly seems worthwhile to make a side trip if the same distance along the coastal road leads to miles upon miles of Hellenistic and Roman ruins. At Narlıkuyu is a Roman mosaic depicting the Three Graces that embellished the Roman baths. The water from the fountain was reputed to endow its users with intelligence, beauty, and long life—at least that's what the inscription on the mosaic says.

Cicero resided in Korykos when he was governor of Cilicia from 52 to 50 B.C. The fallen temples, palace, theater, aqueduct and vast necropolis are overshadowed by the imposing Armenian twin castles dating from the 13th century. Antique columns are built into the unusually high walls of the huge Land Castle; the Sea Castle on an offshore islet is called the Kız Kalesi, or Maiden's Tower. Legend claims that the local suzerain caused his beloved daughter to be confined in the island castle because of a dire prediction, according to which she was to die of snakebite. When one of her admirers sent her a gift of a basket of grapes, a serpent had concealed itself amid the fruit, and thus was the prediction fulfilled. The entire beach is taken up by a tent town in summer. 2 km. (1 mile) inland, the two Pits of Heaven and Hell—Cennet ve Cehennem Obrugu—afford the expected contrast; the former a serene orchard in front of a ruined Byzantine church at a spring issuing from a grotto, and on the lip of the 120-meter (394-ft.) chasm, the high-walled basilica of Roman Paperon, the latter a frightening narrow hole, accessible with a guide, to which condemned sinners were consigned.

Further along the coast, the ruins of Elaeussa include a temple, theater, aqueducts and basilicas. Near Kanlıdivane is the vast necropolis of Kanytelis with temple-tombs and Roman sarcophagi.

On the outskirts of Mersin, a branch right leads to Viranşehir on the sea. As a Rhodian and later Athenian colony it was called Soli, whence the word solecism, immortalizing its inhabitants' flagrant offenses against the rules of grammar. Destroyed by the Armenian King Tigran II in 91 B.C., it was rebuilt by Pompey in 63 B.C. and populated with the surviving pirates whose 1,300 ships and hideouts along the coast he had reduced in a brilliant campaign. From this Pompeiopolis date the long row of Corinthian columns which line the Sacred Way to the elliptical mote in the port.

In winter, an unusual sight is added to the local scene: the campsites of the yuruk, who are nomads of Turkoman origin. Each year, on schedule, they forsake the icy climes of their back-country mountainous pasturelands and come to pitch their goat skin tents casually among the antique relics hereabouts.

Mersin is growing even more rapidly than most Turkish towns, and there is some ungainly ribbon development through the surrounding or-

ange and lemon groves. But the fine palm-lined avenue along the modern
seafront is centered on a pleasant park. With almost 250,000 inhabitants
Mersin is the largest Turkish Mediterranean port and industry has raised
its ugly head. A choice of good hotels makes, however, for a comfortable
stopover, especially during the mild winters.

The oldest monument, the Ulu Cami, dates only from the late 19th century, yet this is one of the oldest continuously inhabited places in the
world. The history of the Yümüktepe settlement, 3 km. (2 miles) west,
can be traced through the Stone Age, the Bronze Age, and the Hittite
era—its 32 separate levels are distributed over 12 successive civilizations,
and among the sights to see there are the chalcolithic fortifications and
pottery from the 3rd millennium B.C.

PRACTICAL INFORMATION FOR
THE TURQUOISE COAST

TOURIST OFFICES. There are local tourist offices in the following
towns: **Alanya,** Çarşi Mah., Kalearkasi Cad. **Anamur,** Atatürk Bul. 24 (tel.
1677); **Antalya,** Selçuk Mah. Ahi Yusif Cami Yani, Mermerli Kaleiçi (tel.
152 71); **Kaş,** Cumhuriyet Meydani 6 (tel. 1238); **Kemer,** Belediye Binasi
(tel. 1466); **Manavgat,** Antalya Cad. 27 (tel. 3211); **Mersin,** İnönü Bul.
Liman (tel. 112 65); **Silifke,** Atatürk Cad. 1 (tel. 1151); **Taşucu,** Atatürk
Cad. 18 (tel. 234).

WHEN TO COME. The Turquoise Coast is pleasant the whole year
round; the mild winters are especially good for sightseeing, but hardly for
swimming.

SPECIAL EVENTS. May. Silifke Folklore Festival, late May. **June.**
Alanya Tourism Festival, late June. **July.** Anamur-Girne Festival, mid-
July. **September.** Fashion and Textile Festival, Mersin, continuing into
Oct. **October.** Antalya International Arts Festival, with performances in
the antique theater of Aspendos, one week. **December.** St. Nicholas cele-
bration at Demre, 4th to 8th.

HOTELS AND RESTAURANTS

Alanya. We list some of the numerous hotels and motels along the
coastal road east, on the less popular western beach; and on the fine beaches further west. *Alantur* (E), Çamyolu Köyü (tel. 1224). 267 rooms. 5 km.
(3 miles) out, the only one entirely on the beach on the coastal road east;
pool.

Alaadin (M), Atatürk Cad. (tel. 2624). 108 rooms. In town. *Alanya
Büyük* (M), Güllerpinar Mah. (tel. 1138). 66 rooms. Also in town, *Banana*
(M), Cikçikli Koyu (tel. 1568). 142 rooms. East. *Çimen* (M), (tel. 2283).
36 rooms. Likewise on eastern coastal road. *Kaptan* (M), Iskele Cad. (tel.
4900). 45 rooms. Best of those in town, above port; pool. *Merhaba* (M),
(tel. 1251). 62 rooms. On coastal road east. *Mesut* (M) (tel. 1339). 45
rooms. Also east. *Panorama* (M), (tel. 1181). 138 rooms. Another along

eastern coastal road. *Riviera* (M), (tel. 2918). 48 rooms; pool. Western beach. *Turtaş* (M) (tel. 1001). 47 rooms. Closest of the motels on the fine beaches west.
Park (I), Hürriyet Mey. (tel. 1675). 22 rooms. In town.
At **Incekum,** 20 km. (14 miles) west. *Incekum* (E), (tel. 149). 82 rooms. *Aspendos* (M), (tel. 1091). 83 rooms; pool. *Yalıhan* (M), (tel. 1010). 48 rooms. All on Avsaller Köyü.
Restaurants. There is a good choice of seafood restaurants—variously priced—along the seafront.

Anamur. *Karan* (I), Bozdoğan Köyü (tel. 3564). 16 rooms. On the beach. *Cephe* and *Saray,* in the small town, are adequate but not classified.

Antalya. *Talya* (E), (tel. 156 00). 150 rooms. Heated pool; on cliff top. *Büyük* (M), Cumhuriyet Cad. 57 (tel. 11499). 42 rooms. *Turban Adalya* (M), (tel. 180 66). 28 rooms. Converted old mansion above the yacht harbor; outstanding. *Altun Pansiyon* (I), Kaleici Cad. 7 (tel. 166 24). *Yalcın* (I). 23 rooms.
11 km. (7 miles) east on **Lara Beach,** *Club Sera* (E). 150 rooms; pool, disco. *Lara* (M). (tel. 152 99). 60 rooms. Pool.
Restaurants. All in the yacht harbor. *Hisar Turistik* (E). *Liman* (M). *Orkinos* (M). *Yat* (M).

Demre. *Myra Pansiyon* (I), Müze Cad. 4 (tel. 1026). 7 rooms.

Erdemli. *Yaka* (I), Kizkalesi (tel. 1041). 15 rooms. Beach.

Kalkan. *Kalkan Han* (M), Koyici Mev. (tel. 151). 16 rooms. *Balıkçıhan* (I), (tel. 1075). 7 rooms. *Pasha's Inn* (I), (tel. 1177). 60 rooms.

Kaş. *Kaş Oteli* (M), Hastane Cad. 15 (tel. 1271). *Mimosa* (M), Elmali Cad. (tel. 1272). 20 rooms.

Kemer. There are four self-contained holiday villages with a wide range of sports facilities, discos, shopping arcades and restaurants. *Beldibi* (E), 11 km (7 miles) north. 450 rooms in 18 units. 90 apartments. *Palmiye* (E) (tel. 2890). 3 km (2 miles) north. Hotel with 256 rooms, bungalows with 505 rooms. *Robinson Club* (E). 333 rooms. German; at Çamyuva.
Motel Akman (M). 40 duplex bungalows. *Olimpos* (M) Kemer Nahiyesi (tel. 1280). 56 rooms.

Kızıltepe. *Phaselis Holiday Village* (M), close to the ruins. 182 rooms, disco, sauna.

Kizkalesi. *Kizkalesi Motel* (I). 20 rooms.

Mersin. *Altıhan* (E), Istiklal Cad. 168 (tel. 241 53). 93 rooms. Central. *Mersin* (E), Gümrük Mey. (tel. 216 40). 120 rooms. The best, on the seafront with fine view over port. *Toros* (M), Atatürk Cad. 33 (tel. 122 01). 60 rooms. *Türkmen* (M), Inönü Mah. (tel. 110 04). 54 rooms. *Hosta* (I), Fasih Kayabalı Cad. (tel. 202 01). 52 rooms.
Restaurants. *Babil* (E), Mezitli Köyü (tel. 75). A few miles out of town. *Fuar Lokanta* (M), Yeni Sahil Yolu.

Saklikent. The coast's biggest skiing center, 42 km. (26 miles) from Antalya: some hotels and chalets have been opened.

Side. All on beach. *Asteria* (L) (tel. 1830). 154 rooms; 2 pools, gymnasium. Just opened. *Defne* (E), (tel. 1880). 90 rooms. Sports facilities. *Cennet* (M), (tel. 1167). 55 rooms. *Turtel* (M), (tel. 22 25). 46 rooms. Further out. On nearby beaches. At **Conakh**, *Jan-Al-Eka Turistpark,* the first 190-room unit (M) has just opened. At **Titreyengöl**, *Club Aldiana* (M), 300-room holiday village.

Taşucu. 11 km. (7 miles) west of Silifke (where no hotel can be recommended). *Lades Motel* (M). 28 rooms. *Taştur Motel* (M), (tel. 1090). 54 rooms. At top of category; rooms face sea; pool but no beach; beware of rooms above the orchestra, which plays enthusiastically till late.

Viranşehir. *Viranşehir Motel* (I). 24 rooms.

CAMPING. Among the many sites along the coast, the most reliable are: **Alanya,** *Kervansaray Mokamp,* 21 km. (13 miles) west; **Antalya,** *Turban Kızıltepe Kamping,* 37 km. (23 miles) southwest, in pine forest; **Erdemli,** *Kervansaray Kızkalesi Mokamp.*

GETTING AROUND. By Plane. *THY* has twice daily flights between Istanbul and Antalya (1 hour), and there are also once daily flights between Ankara and Antalya (1 hour).

By Car. Route 400 keeps closely to the sea so that most of the Mediterranean coast is easily accessible: particularly the spectacular stretch from Fethiye to Mersin with the mountains rising straight from the shore, or leaving only a narrow coastal strip (where, interestingly, bananas are one of the principal crops). Recommended roads from the coast inland are Route 635 from Finike via Korkuteli and Kızılkaya—where it joins the wider Route 650 to Burdur and Isparta—and Route 715 from Silifke, rising north to Mut, Karaman and Konya.

Car Hire. *Avis:* Alanya, Hükümet Cad. 135 (tel. 3513); Antalya, Talya Hotel (tel. 166 93); Mersin, Sahilyolu 75 (tel. 234 50). *Hertz:* Antalya, Anafartalar Cad. 91 (tel. 129 929).

By Bus. There are bus and minibus services between all towns.

By Boat. Besides the regular services and cruises, *Turkish Maritime Lines* sail twice monthly in summer from Istanbul and Izmir, stopping at Fethiye, Kaş, Finike, Antalya, Alanya and Mersin. There are regular ferries between Mersin and the Turkish ports of Cyprus, and a hovercraft service between Cyprus and Taşucu.

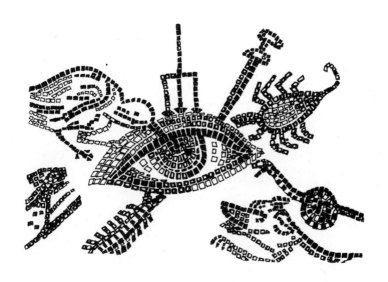

THE DEEP SOUTH

Seleukids and Crusaders

Officially, the Turquoise Coast continues east of Mersin round the Gulf of Iskenderun and south to the Syrian frontier. But it lacks the spectacular beauty of the western and central sections, and there is no coastal road to enjoy what is going, except for stretches before and after Iskenderun, much polluted by heavy industry. Beach life is very restricted and the real interest lies inland in the historic towns of Antakya (Antiochia) and Sanli-urfa (also known as Urfa, and in ancient times as Edessa).

The main range of the Taurus, a natural border for centuries both in antiquity and the Middle Ages, barred the way to invaders, except to Alexander the Great who passed through the Cilician Gates in 333 B.C. Hellenistic Kilikia, Roman Cilicia, extended on both sides, but despite the historical togetherness there remains the natural difference between the pineclad cliffs of the western coast and the drained swamps, now a fertile plain, further east.

EXPLORING THE DEEP SOUTH

East of Mersin, a toll motorway (E24) continues east for 30 km. (19 miles) through lush orchards and groves to Tarsus, birthplace of St. Paul. According to Moslem belief, it was founded by one of Adam's sons, Seth, while according to Greek mythology Pegasos injured his hoof there. The fabulous became less nebulous when Tarsus was the setting for Mark Antony's first meeting with Cleopatra. In Roman days the queen's barge could have sailed right up to the city through a now silted-up lake and the Kydnos river. Cleopatra's Gate is only ruined brickwork, but it is well indicated, as is the well of the house in which St. Paul was born. Originally only 1 meter (3 ft.) deep, the surrounding level has been raised by the rubble of repeated destruction so that the water, much appreciated by pilgrims, is now scooped up by the caretaker from a depth of 10 meters (32 ft.). It was probably to honor the memory of that illustrious citizen that the Eastern Emperor Arcadius made Tarsus the capital of Cilicia in the year 400. The wanderlust that drove St. Paul far and wide must have been endemic, for another native son, Theodore, became Archbishop of Canterbury in 668.

Fragments of Roman baths and temples stand next to a basilica that is now a mosque. Across the road, a medrese houses the small museum with finds going back to the Hittites. Justinian's bridge has been reconstructed as part of the embankment on the eastern outskirts, where there is another Selale, the Tarsus Falls. The Ulu Cami dates from the 16th century. Tarsus was an Arab strongpoint on a fluctuating border and in the 10th century its fleet became the terror of the Eastern Mediterranean. Today, the town of 130,000 inhabitants prospers by more peaceful agriculture.

In the Taurus foothills, 15 km. (9 miles) northwest of Tarsus is another Cave of the Seven Sleepers, only here the Christian neophytes slept for 300 years to escape persecution. On the right bank near the mouth of the Tarsus Çay (Kydnos), the Assyrian King Sardanapal built in the 7th century B.C. the town of Anchiale, while his tomb, according to local tradition, stands at Donuktaş. In fact this is the ruin of a Roman public building, supposed by Gibbon to be the mausoleum of the Emperor Julian.

The motorway passes through the fertile Çukurova Plain and after 5 km. (3 miles) meets the E5 (Route 750) descending south through the wild gorges and passes that form the Cilician Gates. A pleasant excursion is up to the Gülek Pass (1,050 meters, 3,445 ft.), alongside a tributary of the Seyhan River. A road branches left (west) to Namrun, protected by a medieval castle. Longish but worthwhile walks lead to the canyons of the two streams that unite to form the Tarsus River, the ancient Kydnos, in whose ice-cold rapids Alexander the Great caught a severe chill. Pines and junipers carpet the top of the cliff overhanging the road, its menacing sides rearing up to giddy heights. At the end of the pass, note the roughhewn stone tablet, covered with Roman inscriptions. This area was fortified by the Egyptian invader of Turkey, Mehmet Ali, who occupied the Cilician frontier until 1840.

The motorway, briefly uniting E24 and E5, continues east for 37 km. (23 miles) through cotton fields to the South's biggest town.

Adana

Adana, capital of Seyhan province is, with over 2,000,000 inhabitants, Turkey's fifth-largest city and the center of its cotton industry. Osmanli from 1517, it was occupied by the French in the wake of World War II (December 1918), and regained its status as a Turkish city on January 5, 1922.

Credited with its founding have been the mythical Saros and Adanos, the two sons of Uranos (Heaven), also the Hittite King Asitawandas, as well as the Assyrians. Adana is situated on the banks of the Seyhan River. In the 2nd century, Emperor Hadrian gave the city a bridge, the Taşköprü

(Stonebridge), which was restored by Justinian in the 6th century. The bridge is over 300 meters (330 yards) long, and 14 of its original 21 arches are still in place. It also possesses considerable historical significance—it was the sole passageway towards Syria and Palestine. Godfrey of Bouillon and his Crusaders crossed it on the way to Antioch.

The ruling family of the Ramazanoglu left the most lasting mark on the city. They built the Akça Mescit (Small Whitish Mosque) with a fine doorway and mimber, the 14th-century Ulu Cami, and the Eski Cami with a restored minaret. The Kapalı Carsi (Covered Market) features a hamam dating from the 16th century. The Archeological Museum exhibits local Hittite, Assyrian, Babylonian, Hellenistic and Roman finds. At the end of the 19th century, clock towers were all the rage in Turkey: Adana's was put up in 1882.

The construction of the Seyham dam, 16 km. (10 miles) north of the city, has formed a vast artificial lake, a favorite picnic area, and made possible intensive cultivation through irrigation. The main crops are early vegetables, citrus fruit, bananas, tobacco, sesame and flax, but above all cotton, of which about 150,000 tons are produced annually. There is also intensive industrial development. 50 km. (31 miles) south on Route 815 is Adana's port and not particularly attractive beach, at Karataş, ancient Hagarsos, framed by two large lagoons.

Hittite Remains and Crusader Castles

A veritable neo-Hittite open-air museum is to be found in the National Park at Karatepe near Kadirli, 108 km. (67 miles) northeast of Adana via Kozan on Route 815 (slightly less on Route 817 from the Ceyhan junction east). In the 8th century B.C. King Asitawandas built a palace on a hill in the wooded country overlooking the capital of the Danunas in the Ceyhan (not to be confused with the Seyhan) valley. Opposite is a ruined fortress of the same period. The city itself was founded five centuries earlier. Karatepe's bilingual inscriptions, in both Phoenician and Hittite, have provided scholars with invaluable assistance in the deciphering of Hittite hieroglyphics.

On a steep hill in the town of Kozan, 36 km. (22 miles) northwest, rises the fortress in which resided Guy de Lusignan, lord of Cyprus, as well as Leo VI, before Cilicia was conquered by the Egyptian Mameluks in 1375. The bastions are topped by 44 towers; secret passages lead to scary dungeons and huge cisterns provided for prolonged sieges.

Other Crusader castles are at Dumlu, Feke, Kurtlar, Milvan; easiest of access is Cem castle near Kadirli, Flaviopolis of antiquity. Here, archeologists discovered the bronze statue of Hadrian now in the Istanbul Museum. The Ala Cami combines the best features of Roman, Byzantine, and Turkish architectural genius. Anavarsa (Anazarbos), on a mountain ridge east of Route 47 near Kozan, was founded by the Assyrians at the dawn of the last millennium B.C. and has a Byzantine fortress built with Roman materials. The triumphal arch flanked by six Corinthian columns harks back to the 3rd century A.D. The church hollowed out of the rock, Kayakilisesi, predates the earthquake of 526 after which Justinian reconstructed the town. The Church of the Apostles has fallen into a state of disrepair.

Misis (Mopsuestia), 28 km. (17 miles) east of Adana on the motorway, was originally a Hittite settlement, developed by the Romans and the Byzantines. It prospered most from the 12th to the 14th century as the termi-

nal of the caravans from Persia, India and China. The ruins of its Temple
of Apollo and the baths are still in a sort of jigsaw puzzle jumble, but the
local museum houses some beautiful Roman mosaics. The column-strewn
hill affords a good view over the 4th-century bridge restored by Justinian,
who was so happily addicted to improving communications.

The eight towers of 13th-century Yılanlıkale (Castle of the Snakes)
dominate the plain to Ceyhan, 7 km. (4 miles) east. From that small industrial town on the Ceyhan river it is 33 km. (20 miles) on Route 817 to
the port and seaside castle of Yumurtalık, rebuilt by Süleyman the Magnificent above Ayas, one of the oldest Cilician settlements. Yumurtalık is the
terminal of the two 1,000-km. (620 mile) pipelines from the Iraqi oilfields
of Kirkuk.

The motorway continues east to Gaziantep, but at Toprakkale (32 km.,
20 miles) E5 branches south. We shall follow it for an anti-clockwise comprehensive tour of the South, back to this main junction.

South to Antakya (Antiochia)

Just past the crossroads the medieval Armenian fortress of Toprakkale
guards the entrance to the plain of Issos. South of the ruined Roman aqueduct at Dörtyol is the battlefield where the armies of Alexander and Darius
clashed in 333 B.C. Alexander's victory opened the way for the Macedonian
occupation of Syria.

The next turn off to the right (west), leads to a splendid site unfortunately smothered by steel and cement factories: Payas at Yakacık is a uniquely
complete 16th-century Osmanli architectural complex, with a huge caravanserai, mosque, theological school, hamam and covered market round
spacious courtyards, connected by a bridge over the moat with a sea castle,
the Cinkulesi (Tower of the Jinn). Built by order of Selim II in 1574, the
layout is ascribed to the great architect Sinan. Some restoration work has
been carried out—the shops are ready for occupation and the hamam is
functioning—but this has stalled and the caretaker was unable to say why.

Densely wooded rugged mountains force the E5 closer to the coast,
somewhat polluted by industry, and 24 km. (15 miles) on is the busy port
of Iskenderun (Alexandretta). This foundation of Alexander was in antiquity completely overshadowed by Antiocha's natural outlet on the mouth
of the Orontes, Seleukia in Pieria. Destroyed by the Persian Sassanids in
260, Alexandretta's rise dates from the Arab conquest in the 7th century.
Ever since it has shared the fate of Antiochia even giving its name to the
whole province, the Sandjak of Alexandretta, which was incorporated in
the French mandate over Syria after World War I and only returned to
Turkey a few months before the outbreak of World War II. Despite its
fine situation in a deep bay below Kızıl Dağ (Red Mountain, ancient Ana-
mos), the town of 125,000 inhabitants is too industrialized for a pleasant
stay.

Far better for an overnight stop is Uluçinar (Arsuz)—31 km. (19 miles)
along the coast—built over Hellenistic Rosos, whose ruins are partly inside a military camp, partly submerged by earthquakes. 7 km. (4 miles)
further, along a very bad road, are the stumps of the aqueduct which supplied Antiochia in Pieria on a hill overlooking the sea.

The 59 km. (37 miles) from Iskenderun to Antakya climb above the
plain of Issos, outlined by fuel storage tanks, to the Belen Pass, the Syrian
Gates in the Kızıl Dağ. Belen is an attractive village, renowned for its cu-

rative water. From the height of the pass you enjoy a staggering view over the Orontes valley, which is one of the oldest regions of human habitation, as numerous mounds testify.

The first branch right (west) after the descent is the 4 km. (2 miles) to the village of Bakras below the rock of the romantic Crusader castle built on the foundations of a Hellenistic fortress.

Traces left by successive occupants of Antakya go back as far as the 4th millennium B.C. One of Alexander's successors, Seleukos I Nikator, founded the town in around 300 B.C. as one of 16 Antiochias—frequently referred to as Antioch—in memory of his illustrious father Antiochos. (There were five Laodikeas in honor of his mother, four Apameas after his Iranian wife, and nine Seleukias.) Following the example of the Macedonian royal family, the Seleukids were polygamous, but in finance they far outshone them, making millions from the control of the trade routes along excellent roads between Asia and the Mediterranean. Thus they acquired the means to enlarge and embellish Antiochia, which became the third town of the Roman Empire, with 500,000 inhabitants. Famed for its luxury and notorious for its depravity, it was chosen by St. Paul for his first mission to the gentiles and for the creation of the first ecclesiastical organization.

Paganism made its last counter-attack from Antiochia some 300 years later, when Julian the Apostate attempted to revive the ancient gods before his disastrous Persian campaign. Though the senior Orthodox patriarchate, Antiochia's predilection for Arianism and later heresies gravely endangered the unity of the empire. Rising from the ravages of repeated invasions and earthquakes, disputed for hundreds of years by Byzantines and Arabs, Antiochia fell in 1098 to the Crusaders. Under the Norman prince Bohemund and his successors, it became the most powerful of the Latin principalities of the ill-fated Kingdom of Jerusalem, doomed to extinction in less than two centuries. In 1268 Antiochia was occupied by the Mameluks of Egypt, and in 1516 Selim I made it part of the Osmanli Empire. But Antiochia has failed to follow the resurrection of its antique rivals, Rome and Alexandria. Even the Patriarch has left the town whose name he still bears, as with the restoration of Antiochia to Turkey in 1939 he was parted from his flock in Syria where he now resides.

Reduced to 100,000 inhabitants, Antakya's oriental core on both banks of the Asi (Orontes) is ringed by the inevitable modern apartment blocks. Diocletian's proud bridge was replaced by reinforced concrete in 1970 because the Roman brickwork could not withstand the strong current created by the construction of the dam higher up. Several arches of Trajan's aqueduct (Memekli Köprü) span a ravine below Mount Silpios. The great fortress that crowned this mountain from Byzantine times onward was the setting for the most splendid Latin court in the Levant, and was last occupied by Egyptian troops from 1831 to 1840, but only sad broken ramparts extending over several miles remain. The ascent starts 4 km. (2 miles) along Kurtuluş Caddesi, the road to Reyhanlı, on the branch right signposted Altınözü. The last of the 8 km. (5 miles) are very rough going, but certainly worthwhile for the superb view over the town and the Orontes plain from the café.

Also off Kurtuluş Caddesi, but closer to the center, and properly signposted, is St. Peter's Church, its white façade standing out against the background of the reddish rock from which it was hollowed. The Apostle delivered his sermons here to his converts, the first to be called Christians.

In 1967, Pope Paul VI declared a plenary indulgence for pilgrims. The feast of St. Peter and St. Paul is celebrated in the simple bare grotto on June 29, and mass is said the first Sunday of every month. A very unofficial guide entices visitors 200 meters (650 ft.) up a steep path with the intent of selling antique coins out of sight. The nearby Bath of the Sinners features some reliefs.

The Habib Neccar Cami in the center of Kurtuluş Caddesi was originally a church, while the Ulu Cami is an Osmanli construction dating from the 16th century. In Hürriyet Caddesi opposite the Atahan Hotel is the fine loggia of a derelict Latin monastery; its cloister is entered from a side-street, and Orthodox services are held on feast days. There are several mosques in the bazaar quarter, which has remained genuine down to the open drains in the middle of the narrow lanes.

What has been preserved of the ancient glory is now in the Hatay Archeological Museum on the central square on the right bank of the Asi. The most famous statue is a Roman copy of Tyche (Fortune); the lost original belonged to a group sculpted by Eutychides for the recently founded Seleukid capital (296–93 B.C.)—Tyche was seated on a mountain with the river god Orontes at her feet, while Seleukos I and Antiochos I offered wreaths. Outstanding is the collection of magnificent 2nd- and 3rd-century Roman mosaics, most of which once graced the sumptuous villas scattered over the idyllic vale 8 km. (5 miles) to the south. In the cool woods the nymph Daphne was changed into a myrtle bush to escape the amorous advances of Apollo. Even in its present untidy state Harbiye remains a favorite picnic ground, but in antiquity, as Daphne, it was Antiochia's fabulous pleasure resort where waterfalls and groves surrounded Aphrodite's famous sanctuary with its thousand dedicated prostitutes.

Route 825 passes Harbiye on the 57 km. (35 miles) south through barren hills to Yayladağ, the frontier post into Syria on the way to Tripoli and Beirut. Tourist pamphlets mention the formidable Crusader castle of Cursat thereabouts, but there is no indication anywhere of how to reach it.

The Romans lavished special attention on piping in fresh water. For this purpose, they bored the Titus Tunnel, near Samandağ, a splendid beach on the mouth of the Orontes 26 km. (16 miles) southwest of Antakya. The ruins of Antiochia's port, Seleukia in Pieria, now lie some two miles inland. In the precipitous cliffs of Musadağ (Mount Moses), scene of great Armenian suffering during World War I, are numerous rock tombs.

On the Trail of the Hittites

The frontier town of Reyhanlı, 50 km. (31 miles) east on EM 5 (Route 420), the Aleppo road, is surrounded by 183 mounds covering settlements as far back as 3400 B.C. The plain round artificial Lake Amik, which submerged prehistoric pastures and fields when a dam was built across the Orontes, is literally swarming with tumuli, many of which have yet to be explored. Teams have been excavating already at Tel El Cudeyde, Telacana, and Tel Tainat.

It is possible to return from Antakya or even directly from Reyhanlı on inland Route 827 via Kırıkhan and the castle of Trapaosac (Trapaeza), north on Route 825 via Islahiye to the region watered by the Sogutlu and the Hurmas, the two streams eventually merging to form the Ceyhan River.

Kahraman Maraş was the capital of the Hittite Kingdom of Gurgum in the 12th century B.C. Sculpture from this period is displayed in the small museum in the citadel. The Ulu Cami and the Taş Medrese date from the 15th century. Age-old religious hatred, aggravated by modern political antagonism, exploded in a riot on Christmas Day 1978, between Communist Shiites and Nationalist Sunnis, leaving over a hundred dead.

Gaziantep, 82 km. (51 miles) southeast on Route 835, is an industrial center busy with cotton, threads, and oils, while its local artisans maintain the tradition of copperwork. It is also the center of Turkey's pistachio nut production. The wooden mosque of Ahmet Çelebi dates from 1672; the Omeriye looks somewhat more Arabic in origin, and belongs to the 11th century. The former Seljuk medrese houses the town's museum, which contains objects from the sites of Zincirli, Sakçagözü, and Kargamish, plus a remarkable collection of Hittite seals. The fortress that Justinian built here in the 6th century was considerably retouched by the Seljuks, and other Seljuk strongholds abound in the vicinity.

Zincirli, the site of a Hieroglyphic Hittite principality that flourished from the 12th to the 8th century B.C., lies near Fevzipaşa, 10 km. (6 miles) north of Islahiye. The foundations of two citadels, a palace, a temple and numerous reliefs were uncovered, but the most interesting finds are at museums in Ankara and Berlin.

Before the First World War, the future Lawrence of Arabia excavated at a more important neo-Hittite site, Kargamish, for which special permits are required as it lies near the frontier opposite the Syrian city of Djerablus on the Fırat (Euphrates). Sometime around 1200 B.C., following the collapse of the Hittite empire in central Anatolia the rulers of Kargamish regained their independence and prospered until finally succumbing to Sargon II of Assyria in 717 B.C. The bas-reliefs from Kargamish in the Ankara Museum betray a marked Assyrian influence.

The First Latin Principality

Fevzipaşa is only 13 km. (8 miles) south of the E24, and 67 km. (42 miles) west along the E24 is the Toprakkale junction. But once at Gaziantep, it might be as well to continue east, still following the E24, for another 141 km. (88 miles) to Sanliurfa. About halfway, the Fırat is bridged at Birecik, where the World Wildlife Fund is taking care of one of the few known breeding grounds of the Bald Ibis. The birds' return is celebrated each spring.

Local tradition places the birth of the prophet Ibrahim (Abraham) in a cave in Sanliurfa. Reputedly founded by the legendary Assyrian king, Nimrod, in its time it has been occupied by Hurrites, Hittites, Salucides, Romans, Byzantines, Crusaders, Seljuks, and Ottomans, and has been known first as Edessa, then Urfa, and from 1921 as Sanliurfa (meaning glorious Urfa, given this name by Atatürk to commemorate the town's role in defeating the French).

Edessa became known in the West as the first Latin principality in the Levant, and was considered a romantically forlorn Crusader outpost. The capture of Edessa by the resurgent Moslems in 1144 shocked Christianity into precipitating the Second Crusade. The ruined towers of the Crusader citadel still dominate the town.

At the foot of the path that leads to the citadel are two superb mosques: the Halil-ur-Rahman Cami (built in 1211) and the 18th-century Rizvaniye

Cami. The Halil-ur-Rahman Cami is one of the Holy Places of Islam, and as such you must not only remove your shoes but also wash your feet before entering. The nearby Pool of Abraham is crammed with sacred carp, and the whole area is set in lush gardens.

On the way up to the citadel are two caves enshrined as the sanctuaries of the prophets Jethro and Job, places of pilgrimage for the Moslems. They are open to the public except during the month of Ramadan. The citadel, set on a spur of Mount Damlacik, is of Roman and Byzantine origin, and affords a fine view of the town. At its highest point are two Corinthian columns, thought to have been part of the temple of Baal. The ruins of the Throne of Nimrod are also in this area.

The town is full of old winding streets, and its houses have elaborately carved doorways and overhanging balconies. You will notice that the minarets of the various mosques differ widely in style, the most unusual one being that of the Ulu Cami. This was originally the belfry of St Stephen's Church (A.D. 435), and is remarkable for having a clock on top. The Ulu Cami itself is of Seljuk construction and has a large and peaceful courtyard.

Also of interest are the Selehattin Eyyubi Cami (A.D. 900–1200), previously a Christian church built in the Roman architectural style; the Firifirali Cami; the 15th-century King Hassan Cami; the Byzantine Karakoyun aqueduct; the Firuz Bey fountain (Ottoman, from the 18th century); and the remains of the city walls. The modern section of town features an archaeological museum.

East of Sanliurfa lies a region of barren limestone hills known as the Tek Tek mountains. Further on, along an unmarked dirt road into the fringes of the Syrian desert, lie the villages of Sogmator and Suayb. It is advisable to arrange transport to this area with the Sanliurfa Tourist Office. Close to the center of the village of Sogmator are the remains of a temple dedicated to the Sun. Grouped around this, on other hills, are ruined buildings that may once have been temples to other planetary deities. The whole area is littered with fragments of carvings and there are several stones carved with inscriptions. These remains are said to have belonged to the Sabeans, who occupied the area up until the Middle Ages. The track leads on to the "lost city" of Suayb, which flourished under the Assyrians and Romans but was abandoned in the Middle Ages. Much of it is built into the hillside, or underground. Some of the underground caves are still occupied, and are wonderfully cool after the heat of the desert. There are also two ruined Seljuk caravanserai in this area.

Close to the Syrian border is the village of Harran, 45 km. (28 miles) south of Sanliurfa. Genesis 11:31, 32 mentions that Abraham rested here for several years on his way from Ur to Canaan. The present inhabitants live in curious conical-shaped houses. Harran was also the site of the main Sabean temple of the Moon Goddess, Sin. The ruins of the 10th-century Fatimi citadel now stand on the site. The remains of an Arab University built in the 8th century are also here. Purportedly the oldest university in the world, it was destroyed by the Mongols in the 13th century.

PRACTICAL INFORMATION FOR
THE DEEP SOUTH

TOURIST OFFICES. There are tourist offices in the following towns: **Adana,** Atatürk Cad. 13 (tel. 113 23); **Antakya,** Vali Urgen Alanı 41 (tel. 126 36); **Iskenderun,** Atatürk Bul. 49 (tel. 116 20); **Sanliurfa,** Asfaltyol 3 (tel. 24 67).

WHEN TO COME. Along the coast it is pleasant the whole year round. But inland summers can be torrid and winters surprisingly cold, more so the further from the coast you go.

SPECIAL EVENTS. June. Feast of St. Peter and St. Paul, at Antakya on June 29. **September.** Culture and Art Festivities at Adana, continuing into Oct.

HOTELS AND RESTAURANTS

Adana. All the (E) and (M) hotels listed here are air-conditioned, essential in the humid heat. *Büyük Sürmeli* (E), Özler Cad. (tel. 121 944). 170 rooms. Pool. *Divan* (E), Inönü Cad. (tel. 227 01). 116 rooms.
Inci (M), Kurtuluş Cad. (tel. 122 612). 36 rooms. *Koza* (M), Özler Cad. (tel. 146 57). 66 rooms. *Set* (M), Inönü Cad. (tel. 222 73). 42 rooms. *Ağba* (I), Abidinpaşa Cad. (tel. 122 459). 87 rooms. *Raşit Ener* (I), (tel. 119 04). 16 rooms, pool; 2 km. (1 mile) along the Ceyhan road.
Restaurant. *Nihat* (M). At airport.

Antakya. *Atahan* (M), Hürriyet Cad. (tel. 110 36). 28 rooms. Patrons of the roof restaurant opposite can look into the shutterless front rooms; good restaurant. *Divan* (I), Istiklal Cad. (tel. 115 18). 23 rooms.
In **Harbiye,** 8 km. (5 miles) south, a cooler suburb. *De Liban* (M), Dermaşta Mah. (tel. 1054). 36 rooms. *Hidro* (M), Karyer Mah. (tel. 1006). 16 rooms. More pleasant. *Çağlayan* (I), Örgen Cad. 6 (tel. 1011). 13 rooms.
Restaurants. Above and near the waterfalls at Harbiye are several simple but pleasantly situated restaurants.

Belen. *Kamelya* (M), Girne Cad. (tel. 120 41). 44 rooms.

Gaziantep. *Kaleli* (M), Hürriyet Cad. (tel. 134 17). 70 rooms. *Mimar* (I), Hürriyet Cad. (tel. 179 92). 34 rooms. *Türk* (I), Hürriyet Cad. (tel. 194 80). 58 rooms.
Restaurant. *Keyvanbey* (M). Hürriyet Cad.

Iskenderun. *Hataylı* (M), Osmangazi Cad. (tel. 115 51). 60 air-conditioned rooms. *Güney Palas* (I), Beş. Temmuz Cad. (tel. 136 96). 30 rooms. *Hitit* (I), Cumhuriyet Cad. 40 rooms.
Restaurant. *Saray* (M). Atatürk Bul.

Islahiye. *Kent* (I). 32 rooms.

Nizip. *Belediye* (I), Atatürk Bul. 28 (tel. 1684). 33 rooms.

Samandağ. *Diplomat* (M). 32 rooms.

Sanliurfa. *Hotel Harran* (M), Atatürk Bul. (tel. 4118). 54 rooms. Best in town. Fully air-conditioned. Restaurant. *Turban Urfa* (M), (tel. 3520). 53 rooms. Partly air-conditioned.

Soğukoluk. Mountain resort 12 km. (7 miles) southwest of Belen. *Ayvazyan* (M). 40 rooms. *Camlar Oberj* (I). 32 rooms.

Uluçinar (Arsuz). *Arsuz* (M), (tel. 217 82). 102 rooms in two blocks. Beach, pool, excellent service; the most agreeable place to stay on the southern coast.

Camping. Adana. *Raşit Ener,* connected with the motel of the same name, 2 km. (1 mile) east of Adana.

GETTING AROUND. By Plane. There is at least one flight a day between Ankara and Adana (1 hour), and between Istanbul and Adana (80 mins.). Adana is also linked by air with Cyprus (twice a week) and Baghdad (once weekly). There are three flights weekly between Ankara and Gaziantep (80 mins.), two between Istanbul and Gaziantep (105 mins.).

By Train. The *Taurus Express* goes twice a week from Istanbul via Ankara to Adana. East of Ceyhan the line divides into a branch south to Iskenderun, north to Kahraman Maraş, east to Gaziantep—with two branches into Syria—and along the Syrian border to Mardin and into Iraq.

By Car. Route 400 again becomes E24, as along the Aegean coast, at the Mersin bypass to be joined after 30 km. (19 miles) by E5, the main north-south axis from Ankara via the Aksaray junction. 74 km. (46 miles) east of Adana, at the Toprakkale junction, E5 (Route 817) turns south to Iskenderun, Antakya and to two crossings into Syria: the one at Yayladağis the shortest route to Latakia and Tartus, from which a ferry sails three times weekly to Volos in Greece, so that the trip along Turkey's Mediterranean coast can be a one-way drive. E24 (Route 400) continues east, a 245 km. (152 miles) toll motorway from Mersin to Gaziantep. Reduced in width but well surfaced, E24 keeps on straight east to Sanliurfa and Mardin, with several more border crossings south into Syria. Kahraman Maraş is connected by Route 825 with Kayseri, and by Route 850 with Malatya; Sanliurfa by Route 885 and 360 with Diyarbakir.
Car Hire. *Avis* have offices in Adana, Ziya Paşa Bul. 11 (tel. 330 45) and at the airport (tel. 288 81).

By Bus. There are bus and minibus services between all towns.

By Boat. The *Turkish Maritime Lines* regular Mediterranean sailings terminate at Iskenderun.

THE MID-WEST

Of Riches Untold

The coast of Turkey is the treasure-house of Hellenism, while the plateau is the domain of Turkish Moslem civilization. The coast has kept its beautiful sea- and landscapes, while the plateau has been denuded by men and goats and now has the grandiose, unlimited horizons of the steppe. In between is a large region partaking of the cultures of both and often blending them in a happy and original way. But its landscapes are quite different, with gentle fertile river valleys in the north, a delightful lake district in the center, and dramatic mountain ranges in the south.

The dominant power in antiquity was Lydia and its successive conquerors. The capital, Sardis, straddled the Paktolos, whose gold-flecked sand bottom made it known as the river of riches. The panning of the riverbed was indeed in all likelihood the source of the rulers' wealth, which enabled Queen Omphale to buy Herakles as a slave from Hermes, using him not exclusively for labors, but to found the Heraklid dynasty. But according to Herodotos some other of Herakles' numerous sons ventured inland after the fall of Troy and seized Sardis. Traces of their presence, as well as those of the Lydians (six centuries later), have been revealed by a Harvard-Cornell team of archeologists. Their discovery of a prototype bazaar credits the Lydians with the introduction of organized retail trade.

Some 500 years later, Kandaules, the last of the Heraklids, had a beautiful wife called Nyssia, in whom he took great pride, boasting of her beauty to one and all. Overstepping the bounds even of bad taste, he urged Gyges, the commander of his Karian guard, to take a peep at her naked charms.

Inevitably, Gyges was spotted and the outraged queen gave him the singularly easy choice of either killing the indiscreet husband or being killed himself. Gyges married the widow, was duly recognized as king and founded the Mermnad (Hawk) dynasty.

Gyges repulsed the first attack of the Cimmerians who had destroyed Phrygia to the northeast, but was killed in the second onslaught in 652 B.C. The affluent Lydian cities were plundered and razed to the ground; Gyges' grandson Alyattes, however, drove the northern barbarians from Anatolia and restored the greatness of Lydia. He then extended his rule over the Greek towns of Ionia to the Aegean in the west, and to the River Halys, the present Kızılırmak, in the east.

The kingdom reached its height under the fourth and last king, Croesus (563–546 B.C.), the richest man in the world. The court of Sardis was a meeting place for philosophers, for the king "spent his time wisely between warfare, pleasure, and the arts." Solon, the Athenian lawgiver to whom he was showing off his riches, said witheringly: "No man can be called happy before his death." These words, however blighting at the time, were later to save Croesus' life. Misinterpreting a Delphic oracle, which predicted that if he crossed the Halys he would destroy a great empire (it turned out to be his own), he attacked and was defeated by Cyrus (Kyros) the Great at the battle of Thymbreos and thrown back on Sardis; the town was besieged by the Persian armies, and fell. On his way to the stake, Croesus, remembering the words, cried out "Oh Solon! Solon!" When asked what he meant, he told the story, and Cyrus, reminded of the uncertainty of royal glory, spared his defeated enemy's life.

Lydia remained a Persian satrapy until taken by Alexander the Great. After his death, it fell to Antigonos, his lieutenant. Defeated at Ipsos in 301 B.C. by Seleukos I, Antigonos was killed in battle at the age of 84! In around 260 B.C. Sardis became part of the kingdom of Pergamon, whose fate it shared. Under its walls Brutus and Cassius quarreled before marching to Philippi and their death in the final defeat of republican Rome. It became the seat of one of the Seven Churches of Asia Minor. It underwent everything—invasion, sack, plunder, fire, and earthquake, but rose from its ruins until the final destruction in 1402 by Tamerlane.

EXPLORING THE MID-WEST

The E23 (Route 300) from Izmir to Ankara passes through Sart (Sardis) after 87 km. (54 miles). For sightseeing it is, however, preferable to follow the old road further south, winding up the Kavaklidere valley, which has given its name to Turkey's most popular wine, to the Belkave Pass where Kemal Atatürk planned the final attack on Izmir in September 1922, putting an end to the Greek occupation. At ancient Nymphaion, renamed Kemalpaşa in honor of the victor, are the ruins of a Byzantine palace in which the Emperor John III Dukas died in 1254. The first branch right (south) leads to the Karabel bas-relief on the cliffs of Nif, representing a Hittite deity with a bow over the right shoulder. Though the Hittite hieroglyphs stating the god's identity are too worn to be read, they show the extent of the Hittite influence. E23 is joined at Turgutlu, renowned for its cherry festival in June. The wider Gediz valley is a vast orchard and vineyard interspersed with poplars (planted at the birth of a girl as her dowry), but with fewer villages and framed by russet cliffs in the best romantic landscape tradition.

The countryside around Izmir is renowned for its fruit, much of which is dried and shipped abroad. Nearing Sardis, there is also some Indian hemp from which *hashas* (hashish) is produced. Westerners first met with the drug, smoked through a *nargile* or waterpipe, during the Crusades. Tough as the Crusaders were, they dreaded the drug-happy guerrillas who tore open tents to stab the sleepers to death. The few Crusaders who fought off these onslaughts told blood-curdling tales of the *hashasin* or, as they pronounced the word, "assassins."

The broken ramparts on the rugged crag dominate the vast site of antique Sardis, of which only some widely separated areas have been excavated. At the hamlet of Sart, alongside the main road, one is struck by the imaginative reconstruction of the marble court dedicated to the imperial cult, and using as far as possible the original materials, though only a few of the 105 Corinthian columns have been re-erected. At the back are the baths, a large swimming pool with showers, built, like the palaestra, in the 3rd century by the emperors Caracalla and Geta of huge flat rectangles of stone in the town's main Roman revival after the devastating earthquake of A.D. 17.

The adjoining large synagogue is well restored with mosaic floors and marble wall decorations. Next to it ran the paved highway from Ephesus to Susa, once lined by tiny shops backed by a restaurant and bath, the prototype of the oriental bazaar. Across the road, a branch passes some Lydian houses and workshops to end after 2 km. (1 mile) at the famous temple of Artemis on a hill overlooking the Paktolos valley. After the destruction of Croesus' temple by the Athenians during the Ionian Revolt in 498 B.C., Alexander the Great ordered the construction of a splendid new sanctuary, whose grandiose proportions can still be understood from the east side's eight Ionian columns, two of which are intact. There are 20 on each of the long sides, made of huge round stones, placed one on top of the other; the finished shaft was fluted by specialists, and coated over to hide the joints. Sun and rain have stripped them of the coating, and the worn joints are bared; the capital is often held in place by balance alone, at least till the next earthquake. The stadium, covered by a landslide, is now being excavated. Most of the finds are in the Izmir Museum.

If your foray into the interior was restricted to Sardis, there are two ways of returning to Izmir. One is to turn right (south before Salihli on to a minor road connecting with Route 310, along which are some interesting sites in the former domain of the emirs of Aydın. The Ulu Cami in attractive Birgi was built in the 14th century with stones from Greco-Roman Hypapea, which vanished completely. Rulers of Aydın are buried in nearby türbes. Route 310 follows the Küçük Menderes west via Ödemiş till the branch left (south) to Tire, once an important Byzantine town. Old wooden houses surround the Yahsi Bey Cami, now the regional museum. E24 is joined south of Torbalı.

The more conventional way back to Izmir is to turn right (northwest) on to Route 250 to Manisa (Magnesia by Sipylos).

Battles and Myths

A battle which changed the history of the ancient world took place in 190 B.C. on the edge of the alluvial plain below precipitous Manisa Dağ (Mount Sipylos), when Cornelius Scipio, commanding the first Roman army to advance so far east, decisively defeated Antiochos III. Illness prevented Scipio Africanus from being in charge of the actual fighting, but by following his strategy his brother put an end to the astounding military career of the great Carthaginian general Hannibal, who advised the Seleukid monarch. Not only had the momentous struggle between Rome and Carthage been extended to Asia Minor in this world war of antiquity, but the subsequent Treaty of Apamea began the twilight of the Hellenistic kingdoms and made Rome the arbiter of the East.

Manisa was an important stop-over on the Hittite royal road leading to Izmir. At the crossroads of two valleys, the Kum and the Gediz (ancient Hermos), it was to become a key stronghold. Thessalian Magnesia had dutifully contributed a contingent to Agamemnon's army before Troy, but the adventurous band refused to return and founded a new Magnesia by Sipylos in the well-watered plain of the Gediz River, and soon afterwards yet another Magnesia on Meander, further south. Subdued by Gyges in about 670 B.C., Magnesia shared the fate of the Lydian kingdom, was hotly disputed by the successors of Alexander the Great, supported the Seleukids in their struggle against Rome and was finally awarded to Pergamon. Rebuilt by the Emperor Tiberius after the devastating earthquake of the year 17, Magnesia achieved prominence during the Empire of Nikaea. The impressive triple fortifications of the Sandık hill were built on the foundations of the antique acropolis at that period. Occupied in 1313 by the Turkish Emir Surahan, it served as capital of the principality of the Saruhanoğullari. In 1390 it was taken by Bayezit I. Mehmet II the Conqueror spent seven quiet years in Manisa before succeeding his father in 1451. The Greco-Turkish war of 1920–22 gave rise to bloody fighting, as witnessed by several monuments in the neighborhood.

The pleasant modern provincial capital is distinguished by five lovely mosques. Oldest is the Ulu Cami built on 8th-century foundations between 1368 and 1377 by the Emir Ishak Çelebi, a member of the Saruhanoğullari family. Halfway up the fortress hill, the mosque was damaged and restored by subsequent invaders.

An unusual feature are the two places of prayer, one roofless for good weather, the other covered for rainy days. Some of the Corinthian columns with the acanthus leaf design were taken from the surrounding ruins. A few capitals are simply imitations of the classic style; others are Islamic. The wooden mimbar is splendid. The minaret is faced with glazed tiles, in the Seljuk style. Nearby is the türbe of the founder and a medrese. The way to the ruined fortress is a short but stiff climb.

The second mosque was built between 1583–6 by the future Sultan Murat III when he was governor of the province. Embellished with very finely worked marble, glazed tiles, and gilding, the Muradiye is yet another masterpiece of the great architect Sinan. The medrese today shelters the town's Archeological Museum.

A green statue of a Surahan emir on a pink plinth faces the Sultan Cami, built in 1522 in the classical Osmanli style by Ayse Hafize, wife of Sultan Selim I, mother of Süleyman the Magnificent, across the road. The mosque has remained the center of the annual Merkez Efendi festival in April, when you can gain a year's good health by catching a piece of sweetmeat containing 41 different spices, thrown from the minaret (open umbrellas held upside down assist wondrously in the preservation of health). In the bazaar is another fine 15th-century mosque, the Hatuniye, named after

Bayezit's wife, Hatun. A signpost in English points to the 22 sultans' tomb, a well-preserved türbe.

As everywhere in this region, history is complemented by mythology. 5 km. (3 miles) along the road to Karaköy is a small wood, sadly littered with the remains of countless picnics on the banks of an idyllic brook that flows through the trees, splashing down in small waterfalls. Hereabouts was the kingdom of Tantalos, the progenitor of the most intolerably tragic family ever known. The figure of a goddess, cut by a Hittite or perhaps Lydian sculptor into the reddish rock, was long believed to represent Cybele, the Mother Goddess of Asia Minor, but the Greek legend of Niobe, daughter of Tantalos and wife of Amphion, king of Thebes, finally won out. Her overweening pride in her 14 children (seven boys and seven girls) got on the nerves of Leto, herself a boastful mother. She ordered her own son and daughter, Apollo and Artemis, to go forth with bow and arrow and kill all Niobe's children, though some say that two girls were spared. Nothing was left to Niobe but her tears, and Zeus, moved to pity, changed her into unfeeling stone. Even so, the very stone wept, drops of water forever seeping from the rock, and when the wind blows the rock makes a wailing sound, for neither the hand of God nor the passing of time can lessen a mother's sorrow at the loss of a child.

Izmir is 36 km. (26 miles) southwest on Route 565, which follows the Kum Çayı northeast of Manisa to Akhisar, ancient Thyatira, the least important of the Seven Churches of Asia Minor. Road and rail veer north through wooded hills and mountains to Balıkesir, then skirt Kuş Gölü (Lake) to Bandırma on the Sea of Marmara.

From Alaşehir to Ertugrul Gazi

For further exploration of the country in between, it is back to E23. Shortly after Salihli, Route 585 branches off it right (southeast) to Alaşehir, once famous Roman-Byzantine Philadelphia. The much-repaired walls explain how Philadelphia held out against the Turks until the end of the 14th century, but today the three main mosques and the covered bazaar are of greater interest than the remains of the antique theater and of the Basilica of St. John, while nothing can be discerned of the temples of the emperors Tiberius, Caligula, and Vespasian.

Route 585 continues to Denizli, but the 28 km. (17 miles) across the mountains dividing the Gediz and the Büyük Menderes valleys between Sarıgöl and Buldan are rough going. The easier approach to Denizli is via Uşak, 115 km. (72 miles) due east from Salihli on E23. The Hittite town was burnt in about 1180 by the Phrygians and subsequently conquered by the usual sequence of powers. Some of the fiercest fighting in the Greco-Turkish War left few traces of the past, but a factory turns out surprisingly cheap carpets. The vestiges of Flaviopolis near Banaz on E23 east to Afyon (115 km., 72 miles) are of interest only to archeologists. At Selcikler village, near Sivaslı, south on Route 595 to Denizli or Dinar are the ruins of a classical theater.

At 906 meters (2,970 ft.), Usak is only little short of the plateau's average altitude, but the landscape maintains the well-watered fertility of Turkey's Mid-West, so utterly different from the barren limitless spaces of Central and Eastern Anatolia.

Route 240 runs for 113 km. (70 miles) northwards, at first along the Gediz Çayı to the town of Gediz, then northeast across the headwaters of the Kocasu descending, however, to a mere 449 meters (1,473 ft.) at Kütahya. Ancient Kotyaion has vanished, but the Byzantines constructed the inevitable fortress on the dominating hilltop. The local Seljuk rulers enlarged it and added the Vecidiye Medrese (1314), and two small mosques—the Imaret Mescidi, built by Yakup II in 1440 and now used as a library, and the Hidirlik Mescid, built in 1243 by Ibrahim Dinari. Bayezit I married the Seljuk heiress and died a prisoner when Tamerlane temporarily established his headquarters in the town. The Ulu Cami was dedicated to his memory in 1411 by his son Mehmet I. The 19th-century restorers replaced the original wooden columns with marble. The Ishak Fakih Cami dates from 1434 and the Hisarli Cami from 1487. The 16th century saw no slackening in religious building and saw the construction of two baths (Küçük and Balık) as well as covered bazaars.

But fame came only with the forced settlement of Persian craftsmen after Selim I's victorious campaign. Kütahya tiles rivaled those of Iznik, but cobalt blue and milky white were predominant till the 18th century, when Iznik green, turquoise, purple and yellow were added. The local production continues.

The village of Çavdarhisar, 61 km. (38 miles) southwest on Route 240, lies near another famous Roman site, Aesani. Though badly shaken in the 1970 earthquake, the noble temple of Zeus ranks among the best-preserved sanctuaries of Anatolia, and there is also a theater, stadium and arched Roman bridge. Continuing excavations by the German Archeological Institute have unearthed unique payment instructions carved on marble blocks.

Northeast of Kütahya, at a distance of 81 km. (50 miles), in the wide Porsuk valley lies Eskişehir (Old Town) which, except for a few mosques, looks anything but old, displaying all the undistinguished modern characteristics of a prosperous commercial center. Nearby Dorylaion was already centuries old in 1097, when the princes of the First Crusade, fresh from their victory at Nikaea, crushed the united Moslem forces, and the tents of the Moslem commanders fell, with all their treasures, into the hands of the Christians. This victory not only restored Western Asia Minor to the Emperor Alexios I Komnenos, but also opened the Crusaders' way across the Anatolian plateau to the Holy Land. After passing through Pisidian Antiochia (Yalvaç), the Crusaders crossed over the bare passes of the Sultan Dağ chain and proceeded via Philomelion (Akşehir) to Ikonion, which was occupied without resistance.

But 50 years after this triumph of the First Crusade, King Konrad III's German contingent of the Second perished in a massacre rather than a battle close to fateful Dorylaion, when the whole Seljuk army attacked the weary and thirsty dismounted knights. Nine-tenths were killed; Konrad, who had vainly tried to rally his men, and a few survivors fled back to Nikaea, where they were joined by the French of King Louis VII.

North of Eskişehir, in an idyllic valley near Söğüt, is Ertugrul Gazi, where the founder of the Osmanli dynasty resided.

Legal Opium

Up on the plateau, 101 km. (63 miles) south of Kütahya, vast sunflower fields that would have delighted Van Gogh discreetly shield the poppy cultivation round Afyon. Here is the center for the production of opium . . .

under government supervision, however. U.S. narcotic experts and U.N. officials are satisfied that strict supervision of the licensed 200,000 acres in seven provinces of central Turkey has assured that all the opium harvested is shipped to laboratories in the Netherlands and the United States to meet expanding pharmaceutical demand.

Winter can be nasty here, at an altitude of 1,021 meters (3,350 ft.). Afyon's distinguishing landmark is a rock 228 meters (750 ft.) high, crowned by Kara Hisar (Black Fortress), hardly black, but an impressive sight all the same. The rock is sharply silhouetted, jagged and aggressive, provided the wind blows away the smoke of the local cement factory. Credit for building the original fortress is given to the Arzawa, a Hittite tribe, but the present ramparts are Byzantine.

The Ulu Cami dates from 1271. The Imaret Cami, less venerable, is considerably more ornate. An inscription on the Altıgöz bridge that spans the Arpa Çay commemorates the Seljuk conquest. On the main square is a triumphal arch with interesting bas-reliefs celebrating the Turkish victory over the Greeks at Dumlupınar, halfway to Uşak, in 1922. The museum displays an interesting collection of antique coins and some particularly ugly Roman statuary.

Afyon is a starting point for many different excursions, but also an important crossroads. 71 km. (44 miles) northeast on E23 rupestral tombs and Phrygian monuments are scattered round Emirdağ. Seljuk and Osmanli architecture prevail along Route 300 southeast, at Çay (48 km., 30 miles), Bolvadin on a branch 13 km. (8 miles) north, and Sandıklı, off Route 850 to Dinar and the Lake District. The mosque, hamam and imaret at Sincanlı, west on E23, were designed by the great Sinan. Maden Suyu, 26 km. (16 miles) north, produces Turkey's outstanding mineral water.

The Büyük Menderes Valley

The most idyllic transition from coast to plateau is on E24 along the Büyük Menderes (Great Meander) through the orchards and vineyards of Anatolia's most fertile valley. The extensive but not particularly exciting ruins of Magnesia on Meander lie near Ortaklar. Aydın, the provincial capital, a thriving town of 80,000 inhabitants, is graced by the fine 18th-century Baroque Çihanoğlu Cami, the Üveys Paşa Cami, built with material from Tralles, and the Ramazan Paşa Cami at the bazaar. The Archeological Museum is mainly provisioned from Tralles.

The site of Tralles is, however, frankly disappointing; perhaps that is why its position—on a ridge about a mile north—is so badly marked. Three monumental brick arches, a badly ruined theater and some column stumps near a military camp—that's all. Hellenistic Tralles developed a technique which reached the height of fashion in the 18th century—*trompe l'oeil,* or trick painting. The Roman architect Vitruvius describes how Hapathourios, wishing to enlarge the setting of the theater, lengthened the rows of marble columns with copies painted on flat ground.

The 73 km. (45 miles) across the Meander and south to Yatağan, mostly along the Çine River between the ranges of the Batı and Doğu Menteşe (West and East Hinge), are strongly recommended. Not only scenically, but also because of the two branches right (west) to the interesting ruins of Alinda and Alabanda, Karian towns on the edge of minute plains surrounded by heaps of gigantic boulders.

From Aydın E24 follows the right bank of the Meander—which meanders no more—to Sultanhisar, where a left turn will take you to one of the easiest and most rewarding glimpses of ancient Hellenism. Two paved miles into the idyllic hills where the road winds between the considerable remains of ancient Nyssa, lie the well-preserved amphitheater of the city's senate and a theater where some olive trees have been left in the covering layer to add the perfect romantic touch.

The valley's vineyards and orchards varying with cotton and tobacco fields as well as olive groves can support an unusual number of fair-sized towns. Nazilli's inhabitants specialize in cotton fabrics and carpets. Soon after Kuyucak, branch right (south) for the 39 km. (24 miles) to Karacasu and the ruins of Aphrodisias.

Aphrodisias, the City of Aphrodite

Continuing excavations under the direction of Dr. Erim on a National Geographic Society grant are unearthing such a wealth of archeological treasures that the museum, only opened in 1979, is already so full that new finds have to be kept in warehouses. 5th-century B.C. Greek Ninoe, built against the foothills of Baba Dağ (Father Mountain), was dedicated to a local fertility goddess who was later equated with Aphrodite. This led to a change of name and an increase in importance, so that by the 1st century B.C. Greco-Roman Aphrodisias had 60,000 inhabitants. The town flourished under the Romans and Byzantines until the 7th century A.D.

The widely scattered remains are well-signposted. The Baths of Hadrian were discovered by a French archeologist in 1904, and the sculptures and reliefs of its six large halls are now in the Istanbul Archeological Museum. Yet the nearby Agora is still largely unexplored, though the surrounding 12 porticos are clearly discernible. Only since 1961 has a New York University team established the importance of Aphrodisias, especially after the relocation of Geyre, built with and over the ancient marbles. The new village, less picturesque but vastly more hygienic, stands 3 km. (2 miles) east.

The Byzantine wall, 3 km. (2 miles) in circumference, is still intact in places, as is the ancient stadium, where 30,000 spectators in the 1st century A.D. watched athletic events and later gladiators and animal combats. Even better preserved, though 200 years older, are the marble tiers and stage of the theater, a handsome building seating 8,000 people on the eastern slope of the acropolis. Nearby are the theater baths and a recently restored square. Almost complete is the elegant small marble odeon (concert hall) with comfortable dressing rooms. The late-Hellenistic temple of Aphrodite was transformed into a Christian basilica in the 5th century, when the tall Ionic columns with fluted ribbing were moved to form a nave and two aisles. To the south is the Bishop's Palace, while scattered over the fields are porticos, gateways and churches. The Sebasteion, named after the Greek for Augustus, has been uncovered in the town's center; two long parallel porticos converge on a shrine glorifying the Roman emperors. Spectacular reliefs decorated the three-story colonnade.

A surfeit of statues of emperors and empresses fills the Imperial Hall of the Museum, while Aphrodite Hall is full of statues of the goddess, and of her priests and priestesses.

If proceeding further inland, a pleasant alternative is to continue eastwards via Tavas to the junction with Route 330, which leads southeast to Burdur, and northeast over three densely wooded ranges in a fine Alpine setting, before descending to Denizli (77 km., 47 miles) back in the Menderes valley. Route 585 leads to Buldan, a mere 18 km. (11 miles) and an easier approach than from Alasehir. The picturesque settlement clinging to the mountain was Tripolis on Meander, whose ruins lie below some older rock tombs.

Denizli, another prosperous town and important crossroads, was flattened by earthquakes in 1710 and 1899, and the only survivor among the modern broad avenues is the 14th-century Kaleiçi Çarşı (Citadel Market) inside fortifications. Denizli replaced Laodikea on Lykon, founded by the Seleukid Antiochos II in the 3rd century B.C. on the site of Ionian Dispolis, both in turn destroyed by earthquakes. By following a clearly marked branch off the Pamukkale road the hill of Eskihisar is reached, and from here the ruins are visible: a stadium constructed by Emperor Vespasian to which Titus added a theater, odeon and baths. It is hardly worth attempting the last mile of the muddy or dusty track for closer inspection. Laodikea was one of the Seven Churches to whose citizens St. Paul wrote the Epistles emphasizing the union of Christians in the mystical body of Christ. The same theme was elaborated to the Kolossians, whose town, 23 km. (14 miles) east, was levelled by—three guesses—soon after receipt of the Epistles. In between is the 13th-century Ak Han (White Caravanserai); the walls and gate opening on the courtyard mosque are preserved, though the original white marble covering has vanished.

Niagara in Stone

Pamukkale, the Cotton Fortress, is 19 km. (11 miles) north of Denizli. Materialists claim that this name is derived from the peculiar chemical properties of its waters, which are excellent for washing sheep's wool and for making it colorfast. More logical is the poetic vision of the Titan's cotton crop spread out to dry on the sheer mountainside.

An enormous rounded white cliff rises some 100 meters (330 ft.) from the plain to a plateau from which calcareous water cascades and drips from basin to basin, crystalized into dazzlingly white stalactites like some gigantic organ pipes. The miracle of Pamukkale resides neither in the cures produced by the medicinal properties of its hot springs (35°C, 95°F), which provided the Romans with unlimited opportunities for indulging their mania for baths, nor in the incredible resistance of Hierapolis' buildings, which have survived two millennia of destructive earthquakes. The real miracle is the one wrought by Nature herself. The water gushes out from everywhere at once. Fresh drinking water trickles down the slope, and tiny streams of hot thermal water, opaque with calcium carbonate, fan out like veils, carving into the rock, shaping it into small terraces and great basins that quickly overflow. The water duly falls down to the next level, hollowing out a new basin which in turn soon spills over, and so on down to the bottom of the cliff. On the way down, part of the water has become petrified and chalky, glistening with the drops that had slid over the bright white stalactites. This stupendous array forms a staggering spectacle, a fantastic and completely unexpected stack of terraces and curtains of solidified liquid suspended in mid-air.

The silence of the mountain at Pamukkale is broken by the ceaseless murmur of the hot running water that flows along, forming bubbles which burst along the surface of the hollow basins. The wind ripples it, the earth drinks it, and it becomes petrified by its own components.

The motels built round large warm-water swimming pools are decidedly pleasant. The walls of an 11th-century Byzantine castle enclose the Tusan motel, where you can swim right to the edge of the cliff to look over the rim into the vast plain of Denizli to the blue mountains beyond, a wonderful if eerie sensation. The pool of the simple Turizm motel contains ancient columns, steles, and capitals: take care not to bark your shins or dive headfirst onto a slab of antique marble and you can enjoy the new adventure of underwater stalking. Just the other side of the motel are ruins to tour in a more conventional manner.

A terrible earthquake in 1334 spelled the final doom of Hierapolis. The abandonment of the city is thus an occurrence of relatively recent date. Despite repeated tremors, it had remained a sacred city (*hieron*) up to the time of the Crusades and the Seljuk invasions. Hierapolis was founded in 190 B.C. by Eumenes II, King of Pergamon, and reached its heyday following its reconstruction during the reign of Tiberius (A.D. 14–37). The Christian and Byzantine epoch left extensive traces here.

The area covered by Hierapolis, and notably the size of its necropolis, are astounding. Sufferers from rheumatism and arthritis came here to take the cure, some dying here, and most of them enjoyed the kind of wealth that guaranteed a lavish and durable burial monument. The travertine stone, the glory of Rome, was abundant hereabouts, and no expense was spared to import marble from great distances. Vast expanses of marble can also still be seen near the springs of the local waters, which have a high carbonic salt content. At Cindeligi (Plutonium, or Pluto's realm), poisonous gases emanate from the soil. The ancients ascribed the asphyxiating effect of the gases to the presence of malevolent spirits, and the place was guarded by priests whose duty consisted in both warning the passers-by and in assuaging their fears. Two great walls still rise along the main thoroughfare, and empty niches mark the site where the Hall of Statues once stood.

The theater is an outstandingly handsome structure, extremely well-preserved, rivaled only by the one at Aspendos, on the Mediterranean coast. The stage has been restored and the travertine stone seats for 15,000 spectators are ready for a performance.

The most striking feature of the vast site is the monument's incredible solidity. A considerable number of magnificent arches have withstood the ordeals of both time and earthquakes. The city walls rose up behind the theater, and a few of their towers are still discernible. The center, naturally, is taken up by huge thermae, now the museum with finds overflowing into the gymnasium's open space of grandiose proportions made appealing by a brook. The Nymphaion, a 4th-century monumental fountain, has been restored, the slightly earlier temple of Apollo was the outstanding pagan sanctuary, while the Byzantine church marks the site of St. Philip the Apostle's martyrdom. To the south, there are the extensive remnants of another church, one of the earliest Christian ones, dating back to the 1st century A.D.

At either end of the column-lined avenue stand the city gates, still well preserved. The agora was near the southern gate. Beyond the triumphal arch and the 2nd-century baths, transformed into a basilica in the 5th century, is the vast necropolis stretching out for nearly a mile. The huge array of sarcophagi, mausolea, and funerary monuments ranges from the most sumptuous to the modest and discreet, all of them exposed to the mercy of the elements. The custom was for people to be buried with their jewelry and graverobbers, acutely aware of this fact, were able to operate continuously until the last century. Worse yet, the Seljuks, whose religion forbade the representation of the human figure, in most cases defaced the handsome bas-reliefs that originally adorned the tombs.

Some local peasants possess fine collections of old coins, but at the archeological sites touts try to pass off mostly fake coins and artifacts. You have to be very knowledgeable indeed to strike a bargain with the "simple, honest peasant folk."

The Lake District

East of Denizli, E24 rises from the lush Mediterranean valleys of ancient Ionia to the forested hills and mountains of Pisidia. Route 595 branches left (northeast) to Uşak via Çivril (96 km., 60 miles) where, near the junction with Route 825 from Dinar, 21 levels of a prehistoric site from the Neolithic to the Chalcolithic have been excavated below the ramparts and palace of what was probably Hittite Arzawa, destroyed in the 13th century B.C.

The E24 crosses wheat and barley fields before skirting the north shore of Acıgöl (Brackish Lake), the first—but least—of those turquoise green lakes set in a barren landscape broken by vivid patches of irrigated cultivation. The main crop is tobacco. Cows shelter from the strong sun under carob trees, sheep graze on the tufts of greyish grass, and the black goats are apparently content with bare rocks. This southwestern fringe of the Anatolian plateau enjoys a milder climate than further east as forbidding-looking mountains bar the horizon everywhere and give protection from the winter gales. But at an average altitude of 1,000 meters (3,280 ft.) spring and summer are the best times to come to the Lake District: the days are sunny but not too hot, and the nights pleasantly cool. There is snow on the distant Taurus Mountains south and east most of the year.

Early records describe the inhabitants of Pisidia as a "wild, uncivilized tribe, probably driven out of the coastal area by Greek settlers." Sufficiently poor to be spurned by the Persians and Alexander the Great, Pisidia became part of the Seleukid domains and only regained ephemeral independence under Turkish emirs after the breakup of the Seljuk sultanate in the 14th century. Still largely off the beaten track, the Lake District has been spared much of the leveling ugliness of modernity and has preserved, as far as that is possible nowadays, a more serene, traditional way of life that has been lost in the coastal regions.

The local architecture, using wooden beams in red-roofed houses, predominates in Dinar, where a fierce stream tumbles from a steep mountain through orchards of apple and pear trees. 113 km. (70 miles) east of Denizli, this big village is the hub of the region's rail and road network. From here Route 650 goes north to Afyon (107 km., 68 miles), with eastern branches to Yalvaç, Akşehir and Beyşehir; Route 825 heads northwest to Çivril (60 km., 37 miles) and south to Burdur (52 km., 32 miles).

Ancient Arkania Limnae and Byzantine Polydorion were closer to the lake than Turkish Burdur, which lies in a hollow surrounded by low sandy hills 4 km. (2 miles) from Turkey's seventh largest lake. Famous for its attar of roses, the outstanding monument is the Taşoda mansion built by Çelik Paşa in the 16th century. Emir Dündar Bey of the Hamitoğlu dynasty constructed the Ulu Cami 200 years earlier. The Archeological Museum displays artefacts from Hacılar, a settlement mound of nine levels, 24 km. (15 miles) southwest on Route 330: here excavations revealed two-story houses of mud bricks on stone foundations belonging to the Neolithic Period (5,700 to 5,000 B.C.) at levels IX to VI, and cream glazed pottery with bold red ocher motifs of the Chalcolithic period in the upper levels.

The first branch right (west) returns via Yeşilova on Lake Solda to Denizli, while Route 330 continues in a more southerly direction via Tefenni to Gölhisar which offers exactly what the name indicates, an island castle. Albeit ruined, its position in the small lake is very beautiful. On the shore are the agora, theater, stadium and necropolis of ancient Kibyra.

Close to the pointed head of the lake, 12 km. (7 miles) northeast of Burdur, is a branch to the stalactite cave of Insuyu. The mineral water spring at the entrance flows into an underground river forming nine lakes, whose water is so clear that it is barely visible in the half-light, except in the rippling reflections of the vault.

Just beyond is the junction with Route 885 east to Isparta, right in the center of the region, its largest town and at an altitude of 1,049 meters (3,440 ft.) its highest. Roman Baris, in a fertile plain below Akdağ (White Mountain), fell to the Seljuks in 1204 and became in the 14th century the capital of the Hamitoğlu emirate, until the Osmanli conquest in 1381. A quiet and pleasant provincial capital, Isparta is, however, not redolent with roses, as promised by the tourist handouts, nor are the vaunted rose fields much in appearance. Little remains of the Hamitoğlu castle, but the emirs' Çarsi (Market) Cami and Hızır Bey Cami have retained their medieval dignity though they are overshadowed by Sinan's Firdevs Bey Cami built some 200 years later, at about the same time as the Iplikçi (Thread) Cami and the Bedesten (Covered Bazaar). The Museum has various archeological finds and Islamic works, especially illuminated manuscripts.

Ağlasun, 35 km. (22 miles) south on Route 885, lies near the ruined acropolis, agora and 12,000-seat theater of Sagalassos, Roman Pisidia's second town; there are also rock tombs and a Byzantine fortress. Further south are the Seljuk caravanserais of Incidere, Suzus, Bucak and on the descent from the pass, Kirgöz. The gentler landscape heralds Pamphylia on the way to Antalya (146 km., 91 miles, from Isparta).

Eğridir (Eğirdir), 34 km. (21 miles) east of Isparta—over the Davras Dağ, crowned by the ruined acropolis of ancient Prostanna—is the most attractive of the lake towns. Surrounded by rugged, bare mountains, it fills a small promontory jutting into the southern end of the lovely dark-turquoise lake, Turkey's fourth largest. It is connected by a causeway past the Atatürk Park with the Yeşil Ada (Green Island), a tiny islet with some old houses better preserved than the Byzantine chapels. According to local lore, the castle on the tip of the promontory was built by Croesus, but it is more likely that it, the Ulu Cami and the Dündar Bey Medrese were all built by the Hamitoğlu. The many lakeside taverns serve delicious crayfish, and the nearby beach is provided with a restaurant and cabins.

A secondary road follows the Kovada Canal 30 km. (19 miles) south to Kovada Gölü in a National Park, where wild fowl, boar and fox can be hunted the year round among the reeds, pines and cedars. The Zindan Cave, entered by a bridge over a river, is 2,446 meters (8,025 ft.) long.

Eğridir Lake is, except for the northeastern shore, encircled by roads which afford memorable views. West is the village of Barla with a tiled minaret. The road hugs the northern end and turns inland to Yalvaç, near the ruins of Pisidian Antiochia founded by Seleukos I Nikator in 280 B.C. The Temple of Augustus, acropolis and aqueduct must have looked more impressive when St. Paul and St. Barnabus preached here before being driven out to Iconium.

Akşehir (Byzantine Philomenion) is 54 km. (33 miles) northeast. Its name means the White Town and it was the home of Nasreddin Hoca (1208–1284), the outstanding representative of Turkish folk humor. His well-kept tomb is on the large main square and nearby are the 13th-century Taş Medrese and the türbe of Seyit Mahmut. Akşehir has given its name to the easternmost of the large lakes. 131 km. (81 miles) southeast on Route 300 is Konya. At Ilgın, about halfway, and near Çavuşsu Gölü, stands Sinan's splendid complex of mosque, medrese, caravanserai, hamam and harem, built for Lala Mustafa Paşa on the hot springs which have been used for centuries to treat an astounding variety of afflictions.

Route 330 skirts the eastern shore of Eğridir Gölü via Dadil, with its 13th-century caravanserai, before turning inland to Gelendost. Soon after-wards are the crossroads north to Yalvaç, east to Akşehir and south on Route 895—via Şarki Karaağaç with some Seljuk monuments—close to, but unfortunately not on, the eastern shore of Beyşehir Gölü, Turkey's third largest lake. There are only tantalizing glimpses of the light-turquoise water in the ocher setting of the Anatolian plateau. At Eflatun Pınar, the Hittites left their mark with an interesting rock relief. 17 km. (10 miles) south, Route 895 at last converges on the lake at Beyşehir, where the Eşrefoğlu Cami and Medrese are well worth a visit; but the main attraction is the view over the immense sheet of water dotted with 23 islands and islets. No signpost indicates the road to Sultan Alaeddin Keykubat's palace, and one might dispense with the difficult search as only foundations remain of what was the Seljuks' most magnificent residence. What has been saved—mainly some superb tiles—has been taken to the Karatay Medrese Museum in Konya. That town is 94 km. (58 miles) east on Route 330—yes, 330 again, the road numbering is occasionally bewildering.

That leaves the southernmost lake, Suğla Gölü, 36 km. (22 miles) south on Route 895. This road follows the Suğla river to Seydişehir and then the eastern shore of the lake—greatly shrunk in summer—to Bozkır. The shortest way southeast from here to Mut is not recommended, despite the fine mountain scenery, as most of the 138 km. (86 miles) to Ermenek are not asphalted, a regrettable shortcoming at the Faşıkan Geçidi, a 1,540-meter (5,050-ft.) high pass. A gentler highland, sparsely populated and blissfully free of traffic, can be enjoyed for 36 km. (22 miles) on Route 350 east to the junction with Route 705 north near Beloren past reservoirs and canals to Konya (91 km., 56 miles).

The slightly adventurous might continue east on Route 350, though part of the 31 km. (19 miles) is unpaved, but that is no great hardship except after heavy rain. Route 715 is a main north-south axis, which connects not only Konya with Silifke on the coast (262 km., 163 miles) but also prehistory with the struggle for Osmanli domination.

From the Neolithic to the Middle Ages

Going north from the junction with Route 350, after 25 km. (16 miles) is a right (east) turn on to a road which follows a stream for 12 km. (7 miles) to Çumra and Çatalhöyük. The Forked Mound of Çatalhöyük is Turkey's most important Stone Age dig, and one of the most ancient cities ever unearthed. It is certainly the earliest condominium to be discovered: in around 6500 B.C. mud houses were constructed here in groups of 40 to 50 rooms, with a single entrance for better defense. Later dwellings were entered through holes in their roofs. The bigger of the two mounds covered neolithic buildings adorned with mural paintings, including the oldest known landscape. The Mother Goddess and Bull Cult figures are in Ankara's Museum of Anatolian Civilizations.

Karaman, 48 km. (30 miles) southeast from the junction, is today a pale shadow of its late medieval glory under the Karamanoğlu dynasty. The Karamanoğlus, who were the first to use Turkish as the official language, held sway over Konya for well over a century, until finally defeated by Mehmet the Conqueror in 1467. The portals of the Aktekke and Araboğlu Camis are as richly decorated as those of the Konya mosques. The Yunus Emre Cami stands next to the burial place of the poet it is named after, who was the first to write verse in Turkish. The Yeni Hamam is the largest surviving bath of the opulent medieval epoch.

The next 69 km. (43 miles) south cross the Sertavul Geçidi (1,630 meters, 5,350 ft.). It is not 1 km. (as indicated at the left turn) but actually 3 km. (2 miles) of rough, winding track up to the Alahan Monastery, most impressive from below and commanding a splendid view over the Göksu valley. The Church of the Four Evangelists has crumbled away; another church east of the terrace is better preserved. Children sell fossils, but are not a nuisance. From here on, Route 715 follows the Göksu (Green Water) which really is green. 19 km. (12 miles) south is Mut, ancient Klaudiopolis, spreading round the well-preserved 14th-century fortress of four bastions round a keep. The Karaman emirs also left a mosque, a caravanserai and several mausoleums. The remaining 78 km. (48 miles) descend gently through the attractive valley to Silifke.

There is nothing gentle in the easternmost connection between the coast and the plateau. E5 rises so abruptly beyond Tarsus to the Cilician Gates through the Taurus Range on the main axis to Ankara that it lacks the characteristics of the in-between region.

PRACTICAL INFORMATION FOR THE MID-WEST

TOURIST OFFICES. There are local tourist offices in the following towns: **Afyon,** Ordu Bulvar 22 (tel. 32 68); **Aydın,** Çine Cad. 6 (tel. 41 45); **Denizli,** Istasyon Cad. Gar Binası (tel. 133 93); **Eğridir,** Çarşi Içi 15 (tel. 13 88); **Eskişehir,** Iki Eylül Cad. 175 (tel. 172 93); **Isparta,** Gazi Mustafa Mah. (tel. 144 38); **Kütahya,** Yeni Hükümet Konağlı (tel. 26 18); **Manisa,** Doğu Cad. 8 (tel. 25 41).

WHEN TO COME. Spring and summer are best; fall can be pleasant but the countryside is burnt up. Except in the valleys near the coast, as for instance at Sardis, winter is not recommended.

SPECIAL EVENTS. March. Traditional Mesir Festival at Manisa, late March. **April.** Nyssa Festival, with performances in the ancient theater, late April. **May.** Isparta Rose and Carpet Festival, mid-month. **July.** Nasreddin Hoca Festival, Akşehir, early July. **August.** Alaşehir Vintage Festivities, late Aug. **September.** Eğridir Golden Apple-Silver Fish Week, early Sept. Art and Culture Festival at Yalvaç, late Sept.

HOTELS AND RESTAURANTS

Afyon. *Oruçoglu* (M), Bankalar Cad. (tel. 201 20). 40 rooms. Adequate restaurant. *Sağlam* (I). 35 rooms. *Soner* (I). 31 rooms. On E23 to Ankara.

Akşehir. *Hiderlik Dağ* (I). 16 rooms.

Aydin. *Orhan* (I). 28 rooms.

Barla. *Gül Oberj* (M). 18 rooms.

Beyşehir. *Dilayla Motel* (I). 10 rooms. Simple without private showers.

Bozüyük. *Taskin* (I), Ismetinonu Cad. 145 (tel. 1325). 32 rooms.

Burdur. *Cendik Plaj Motel* (M). 24 rooms. On the lake. *Burdur* (I), Gazi Cad. (tel. 2245). 30 rooms.

Denizli. *Altıntour* (M), Kaymakçi Cad. (tel. 161 76). 64 rooms. Good restaurant. *Etemağa* (I), Istasyon Cad. 71 (tel. 145 69). 40 rooms. *Kuyumcu* (I), Delikcicinar Mey. (tel. 137 49). 70 rooms. *Park* (I), (tel. 150 47). 64 rooms. Restaurant.

Eğridir. Both with fine view over lake. *Çinar* (I), (tel. 3250). 19 rooms. *Eğirdir* (I). 18 rooms.
Restaurants. Lakeside fish taverns serve excellent crayfish.

Eskişehir. *Büyük* (M), Sivrihisar Cad. 40 (tel. 121 62). 84 rooms. *Has Termal* (I), Hamam Yolu Cad. 7 (tel. 191 91). 48 rooms. Thermal pool. *Sultan Termal* (I), Sivrihisar Cad. 40, (tel. 183 71). 32 rooms. Thermal pool. *Şale* (I), Inönü Cad. 17 (tel. 147 43). 45 rooms.

Ilica. *Harlek Motel* (I). 33 rooms. Thermal baths.

Isparta. *Bolat* (I), Demirel Bul. 71. (tel. 189 98). 15 rooms.

Karacasu. *Belediye* (I). 10 rooms. No private showers; simple but friendly for overnight stay when visiting Aphrodisias, 13 km. (8 miles) away.
Restaurants. *Blue Trout.* River setting. *Zihni.* Basic, jolly place.

Kütahya. *Gönen* (M), Menderes Cad. (tel. 117 51). 54 rooms. *Gülpalas* 2 (I), Belediye Mey. (tel. 112 33). 59 rooms.

Manisa. *Arma* (M), Doğu Cad. 14. (tel. 1980). 42 rooms. Good restaurant.

Pamukkale. *Beldes* (M), (tel. 1014). 45 rooms. 20 bungalows with small private pools; large pool, dining terrace overlooking the valley. *Mistur* (M), (tel. 1013). 34 rooms. Camp attached; pool. *Motel Koru* (M), (tel. 1020). 120 rooms. Three open and one covered pool. *Pamukkale* (M), (tel. 1024). 31 rooms. Simple. Pool above the ruins of the ancient agora. *Tusan* (M), (tel. 1010). 47 rooms. Pool overlooking the plain.
Konak (I). In refurbished village house at foot of cliff; good Turkish meals served at small pool.

Sahlili. *Alkkent Tesisleri* (I), Tayantköyü (tel. 134 62). 11 rooms. 13 km. (8 miles) east of the ruins of Sardis.

Sandikli. *Kaplica* (I), Belediye Isletmesi (tel. 1420). 32 rooms. Thermal pool.

Tavşanli. *Huzur* (I), Cumhuriyet Mey. (tel. 2126). 48 rooms. Good restaurant.

Uşak. *Ağaoğlu* (I), Ismetpaşa Cad. 62 (tel. 213 99). 28 rooms.

CAMPING. Aydin, *Kervansaray Mokamp.* **Pamukkale,** several camps.

GETTING AROUND. By Train. There are slow services between Izmir, Denizli, Isparta, and Eğridir; and between Izmir, Manisa and Afyon.

By Car. Access by Routes 330 from Muğla, and 350 from Fethiye should be avoided. E23 and E24 cross the region from west to east, with Afyon and Dinar at the main crossroads north and south.

By Bus. There are connections by bus or minibus between all towns.

ANKARA

The Unlikely Capital

At the dawn of the 15th century, the Osmanli Turks occupied most of Asia Minor, as well as much of the Balkans in Europe. Sultan Bayezit I was preparing to lay siege to Constantinople, the dying Byzantine capital, when Tamerlane appeared.

This dreaded warrior, a descendant of Genghis Khan, galloped through history like a horseman of the Apocalypse, known also as Timour Lengh, the cripple. Limping and one-armed, he murdered his way to power as Khan of the Mongols. In 1370, he rode out with his soldiers to conquer the world. His feats were beyond belief: he subjugated all Asia east of the Caspian Sea, invaded Persia, laid waste the Kirghiz Plain, marched on Russia, turned south and attacked India, drove the Egyptians from Syria, and destroyed Baghdad. In the course of 30 years, he wrought havoc throughout the east, leaving a trail of blood and tears in his wake.

It was this savage conqueror who now threatened Asia Minor, and Bayezit I was up in arms. An able soldier, the sultan was called Yıldırım, the Thunderbolt. He had wrested Bulgaria, Macedonia, and Thessaly from the Christian rulers, and in 1396, at the battle of Nikopolis on the Danube, he had slaughtered an army of Crusaders.

Faced with the invincible cripple, the Thunderbolt rightly gave up the siege of Constantinople, and led a huge army against the Mongol enemy, riding headlong against him with an equally large contingent. The clash took place in July, 1402, in the plain below the small town of Ancyra, Enguriye to the Seljuks, which was rendered as Angora by the Europeans who applied the name to the breeding-place of long-haired goats from Tibet.

Much has been written about the defeated, broken-hearted sultan. The poets of Islam sing readily of those forsaken by Allah, who waste away and die. It is known that the Thunderbolt was taken prisoner, and alleged that the ruthless Tamerlane took pleasure in humiliating him, both in body and soul. "He shut him in an iron cage, where Bayezit beat his brains out against the bars." Most authorities, however, agree that the prisoner was treated with the regard due his rank. Bayezit died, probably of a stroke, after eight months of captivity.

His death was followed by one of the most baffling mysteries of all time. With Bayezit out of the way, the door to the west was left wide open. Yet while Europe waited in dread, Tamerlane turned his horse around and rode back with his men to the Mongol plains, perhaps already suffering from the disease that claimed him the following year.

Defeated, the Turks were not long overcome. Half a century later, in 1453, Constantinople fell to Mehmet II, and for 400 years the Osmanli Empire was a great world power.

EXPLORING ANKARA

It is no overstatement to say that Ankara is the work of Atatürk (1881–1938). In 1925, it was a town peopled by 75,000 Anatolians; it is now a capital city of well over 3,000,000. Yet despite the modern appearance, Ankara's history can be traced back some 3,000 years. Legend attributes its foundation to the redoubtable Amazons, but archeologists have decided on a Phrygian origin at the time of the Trojan War, though recent excavations have brought to light even earlier Hittite traces in the citadel.

The usual succession of Lydian, Persian and Macedonian conquerors was rudely interrupted by barbaric Gallic tribes. In 278 B.C. Nikomedes I, King of Bithynia, gave the Galatians a gift of land with Ankyra as capital. Defeated by Attalos I of Pergamon in 229 B.C., the reduced Galatian kingdom subsisted under varying overlords till final annexation by Augustus in 25 B.C.

The derivation of the name is as problematic as the rendering—Ankyra, Enguriye, Angora, Ankara. Perhaps it is Phrygian for ravine, or Greek for anchor; an Egyptian anchor captured in battle featured for some time on the city's coins.

All Turkey is haunted by the presence of Kemal Atatürk, but it is in Ankara, the town he made his city, that it is most strongly felt. One reason why he chose far-off Ankara as the capital of the republic he created, in spite of lack of water, the marshland, the poor communications, and the small population, was his distrust of the Constantinople of the sultans and of Enver Pasha. He wanted a clean break with the recent disastrous past, while the soldier always alert in the statesman rightly saw that where Constantinople was highly vulnerable, Ankara was guarded by its very remoteness.

In answer to his call, tens of thousands of homeless and jobless Turks streamed into the town, mostly on foot, to undertake the building of the new capital. This peaceful army set to work, laid out streets, built houses and, sometimes, lived in them, whenever growing earnings allowed. Slowly, with unshakeable steadfastness and patience, Atatürk shifted the country's center of gravity from Istanbul to Ankara.

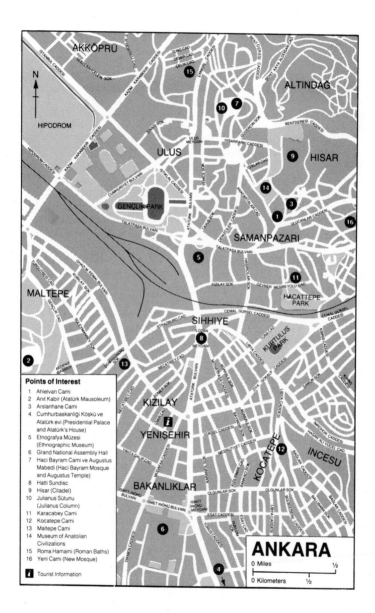

Points of Interest

1 Ahielvan Cami
2 Anit Kabir (Atatürk Mausoleum)
3 Arslanhane Cami
4 Cumhurbaskanliği Köşkü ve
  Atatürk evi (Presidential Palace
  and Atatürk's House)
5 Etnografya Müzesi
  (Ethnographic Museum)
6 Grand National Assembly Hall
7 Haci Bayram Cami ve Augustus
  Mabedi (Haci Bayram Mosque
  and Augustus Temple)
8 Hatti Sundisc
9 Hisar (Citadel)
10 Julianus Sütunu
   (Julianus Column)
11 Karacabey Cami
12 Kocatepe Cami
13 Maltepe Cami
14 Museum of Anatolian
   Civilizations
15 Roma Hamami (Roman Baths)
16 Yeni Cami (New Mosque)

i Tourist Information

ANKARA

0 Miles   ½
0 Kilometers   ½

A grateful people erected many monuments in his honor, more statues in his likeness, and countless streets in his name. Yet the people of Turkey need no reminder to remember him; since his death in 1938, the country is governed in his name, and nothing has been done since without invoking him. The full force of this is nowhere clearer than in Ankara, where the avenues bear the various honorific names bestowed by his grateful countrymen: Kemal, Perfect; Atatürk, the Father of the Turks; and Gazi, the Leader.

Ankara is a rather pleasant city, but without any ostensible style. The large ministries and public buildings lack any memorable features, while the grim realism of the 1930s still prevails even in recent sculptures. But as everything is new, there is nothing incongruous in the drab utilitarianism from which only the new mosques are exempted. Traffic moves smoothly along the wide, tree-lined avenues, except in the old town, the Ulus district, where narrow lanes surround the main sights of Ancyra, some untidy Roman remains, several mosques and the citadel.

From the citadel in the north as well as from the heights of Çankaya in the south there are fine views of the town in between. Round the grounds of the Presidential Palace the embassies are set in pretty gardens, and more gardens with tasteful villas descend from Çankaya to the elegant quarters of Gaziosmanpaşa, Kavaklıdere, and Yukarı Ayrancı. This profusion of green on arid Anatolian hills is another touch of Atatürk who loved trees to the bewilderment of the local people. He laid out parks and surrounded the town with a green belt, where he established a model farm renowned for its yogurt and *ayran*.

No modern capital city has continued to bear the imprint of its creator for so long after his death. Yet, ironically, the town that symbolized the break with Istanbul's Islamic past is now dominated by a huge mosque, modelled on the Süleymaniye, which holds the commanding position in Istanbul. The Kocatepe Cami (Big Hill Mosque), likewise flanked by four minarets, built with Saudi Arabian funds on a small rise in the town center, opened in 1982 and was completed in 1986.

The Highlights

Though neglected on the stereotyped tourist circuit, Ankara nevertheless contains Turkey's outstanding modern monument and, above all, a unique museum of its most distant past. The Atatürk Mausoleum (Anıt Kabir) impressively fuses ancient Anatolian and modern architectural concepts. On a hilltop, it is reached by the marble-paved Lions' Path. To each side are pavilions with remarkable bas-relief carvings. At the far end is a square hemmed in by a colonnade, and in the middle, a towering mast with the Turkish flag floating in the breeze. At the entrance are carved the words: "Beyond all doubt, government belongs to the people." Sailors in white ducks and soldiers in olive drab mount the guard. A monumental stairway leads up to the golden-colored mausoleum, a vast soaring hall lined with brilliant gold mosaics and marble, pierced by seven tall windows. The immensely impressive solitary marble sarcophagus is symbolic, as Atatürk's actual remains rest in the vault below.

The Atatürk Museum, with his personal belongings, objects associated with his life, and mementos from the War of Liberation, is housed in an arcaded wing.

Altındag, a far cry from being the Golden Mountain its name proclaims, turns a slope of neat matchbox houses towards the citadel hill. Fortified by the Galatians, strengthened by the Romans, rebuilt by the Byzantines and maintained by the Seljuks and Osmanlis, the double walls of the Hisar (Citadel) are now crumbling away. Of the former 20 towers, 15 are still standing to various heights. The picturesque ramshackle houses in the warren of narrow lanes within made much use of broken marble columns and slabs taken from the Roman ruins, adding a touch of elegance to a traditional way of life that has long disappeared outside the gates. These gates are fairly intact; the outer, Hisar Kapısı, is topped by an Ilhanli inscription, while near the inner Parmak Kapısı are the best-preserved sections of the fortifications.

At the end of the garden terrace below the Hisar Kapısı is the splendid Museum of Anatolian Civilizations, housed in a 15th-century *bedesten* (covered bazaar) and *han* (inn), harmoniously fitted together. Masterpieces of all the cultures that flourished in the Anatolian heartland are skillfully displayed with English explanations as to Neolithic, Bronze Age, Assyrian, Phrygian, Urartu, Hellenistic, and Roman. There is no overcrowding, though new discoveries are constantly added as many parts of Anatolia provide rich mines for archeologists. Some 30,000 tablets in the cuneiform (wedge-shaped) writing of the Assyrian trade colonies have been found in Boğazkale alone and there are numerous Urartu hieroglyphics.

Fascinating as these finds are, they are overshadowed by the world's most comprehensive collection of Hittite art and crafts, dating back to the dawn of the 2nd millennium B.C. Here is the formal beauty of the art of a hitherto little-known people, whose powerful empire vanished at the time of the fall of Troy, to come back to light in our own century.

Outstanding pieces to look for include a bronze statuette of a bull (c. 2400 B.C.), a limestone Kappadocian idol with two heads (3rd millennium), a ram's head vase (19th century B.C.), a large bull's head cauldron, a three-faced jar (7th century B.C.), and a wreathed portrait bust of the Emperor Trajan (2nd century). A bit forged in about 2000 B.C. is all the more interesting when you remember that the horse was then a new and wild animal, broken in on the Anatolian plains. Looking at it, you might recall the closing lines of Homer's *Iliad:* "And thus were held the funeral rites of Hector, tamer of horses." And there is another huge cauldron with lovely clean lines, upheld by four figures with a hint of the Egyptian—it was found in Gordion, where Alexander the Great cut the legendary knot to fulfil the prophecy. There are small statues, jewels worked in gold and iron, combs and needles. There are, above all, the wonderful bas-relief carvings in stone. While the workmanship of the objects of daily use shows a feeling for proportion and harmony, it is in the higher art of sculpture that we see the Hittite mastery of movement. It is best shown in a small bas-relief whose warriors, brandishing lances under cover of their shields, still bear faint traces of color. Another bas-relief pictures the legend of Gilgamesh, the Babylonian version of the Deluge. The statue of a ruler is intact but for part of a hand and a chip in the beard, finely curled in the Babylonian fashion.

A visit to the Anatolian Museum is an indispensable introduction to the Hittite sites scattered throughout the country.

Temple and Mosques

From Iskitler Caddesi, the ringroad's northern section named after the adjoining district, Irfan Baştuğ Caddesi and Çankırı Caddesi lead through pre-Atatürk Ankara to Ulus Meydanı (Nation Square), the obvious center to start a tour of the old town. To the left of Çankırı Caddesi lie the brick foundations of the 3rd-century Roman Baths and Palaestra, further away on the right, on Hükümet Meydanı, rises the Column of Julian which commemorates that emperor's visit in 362; the 15 fluted drums are topped by a Corinthian capital. Storks still build their nest there, gallantly withstanding the pollution. Facing the column across a fountain is the former Ministry of Finance, white, with pointed arches and blue glazed tiles above the big windows.

On a small eminence beyond, the Haci Bayram Cami was built in the early 15th century of yellow stone and brick, with lavish use of the marble from the nearby Roman ruins and an unusual tiled roof; the glazed Kütahya tiles on the interior walls were added 300 years later. The fine door of the türbe can be seen in the Ethnographic Museum.

The mosque is backed by the remains of the Temple of Augustus. Built in the 2nd century B.C. as a shrine to Kybele, nature goddess of Asia Minor, it passed on to the worship of Artemis. When a law was passed in Rome deifying dead emperors, the Galatians of Ancyra, wishing to show their gratitude for the lenient Roman rule, dedicated the temple to Augustus. Later, the Byzantines turned it into a Christian church. It is now a ruin among many others, but it has a tale worth telling.

Augustus, heir of Caesar, left a testament, a model of clarity and conciseness. In telling words he summed up the achievements of his rule. Both politically and historically, this document was priceless. The emperor's contemporaries mourned his death, revered his memory, and engraved his testament on two bronze tablets meant for his mausoleum, "that all may know." So wrote the Roman historian Suetonius; but the testament itself had disappeared forever, or so it seemed.

In January 1555, Ghislain de Busbecq, entrusted with a mission by the Habsburg Emperor Ferdinand I, arrived in Constantinople. As Sultan Süleyman I was in Amasya, the diplomat followed him there and on his way stopped over in Angora. It may well be that the learned Flemish gentleman, looking at the Roman ruins of Ancyra, did not recognize the long inscription as the testament of Augustus; but he understood its importance, and copied it from what was left of the wall in the old temple once dedicated to the emperor. At that time, nearly all of it was still legible. Scholars have so far listed 350,000 Latin texts inscribed in stone; of them all, the *Monumentum Ancyranum* is the longest, and by far the most important.

Though time has crumbled the stone and worn away most of the writing, a few words here and there, sometimes a whole line, can still be made out.

Small mosques and hamams are scattered through the old quarter below the citadel. Within the Hisar stands the oldest, the small Seljuk Alaeddin Cami, built in 1178. Just outside are the 13th-century Arslanhane Cami, with wooden columns and a tiled mihrab; the Lionhouse Mosque, which took its name from the lion relief on a wall in front; and the Ahielvan Cami with Roman columns and a fine mimbar. Like all the older houses of worship, the 16th-century Yeni Cami (New Mosque) is topped by only one minaret; built by Süleyman's Grand Vizir, Çenabi Ahmet Pasha, on the eastern limit of the old town, supposedly after plans by Sinan, more likely by one of the great architect's pupils, the dark-red porphyry of the walls is enhanced by the white marble mimbar and mihrab.

The New Town

Atatürk Bulvari, Ankara's main artery, starts appropriately below the great man's equestrian statue on Ulus Meydanı and dissects the town from north to south. On the right is the Youth Park, Gençlik Parkı, with its artificial lake, Luna Park, a nightclub facing the railway station, and the opera. To the left, above the intersection with Talatpaşa Bulvari, stands the Ethnographic Museum, which houses a rich collection of folkloric objects, musical instruments, and weapons. Beyond is a complex of public buildings including the Hacettepe Hospital, University, and Park. Above the small park is the Karacabey Cami, built in 1428 on a T-shaped plan, with a rather thick minaret striped in colored glazed tiles. Nearby are the tomb of the founder and the Hamam named after him.

After passing through the railway viaduct, Atatürk Bulvari becomes the principal shopping street of the Sihhiye district with many of the better hotels. To the right is a monumental replica of the Hatti Sundisc, and in the distance, on Gazi Mustafa Kemal Bulvari, the first mosque built in the secular capital, the Maltepe Cami, a handsome building whose large brass-plated dome is topped by two slender minarets.

Left is the small Kurtulus Park with a pond, the Turkish Airlines Terminal and the Kızılay highrise with the largest department store. Visible from afar is the vast Kocatepe Cami, opened in 1982 to the faithful; the sumptuous interior decorations have only just been put into place. To the right extends the governmental district, Bakanlıkar, beginning with the Grand National Assembly Hall at the intersection with Ismet Inönü Bulvari. Higher up, at Kavaklıdere, embassies are surrounded by pleasant gardens. Atatürk Bulvari ends at Çankaya, fittingly before the grounds of the Presidential Palace, next to Atatürk's House, which is open to visitors.

The favorite outing is the nearest, Atatürk's Farm, Atatürk Orman Çiftiğli, at the western outskirts. In 1981, for the centenary of Atatürk's birth, an exact replica of his family home in Thessaloniki, the comfortable pink house of a merchant, was opened to visitors in the large park near the restaurant.

Other cool and shady restaurants are on the Cubuk Dam, 11 km. (7 miles) north, off the airport road. Equally green and suitable for picnics is the country round the Bayındır Dam, 16 km. (10 miles) east, off the Samsun road. The only natural lake in the environs, Göl Bası, 25 km. (16 miles) south on E5, provides swimming from a beach. Elmadağ, 19 km. (12 miles) southwest, is a winter-sport center, but skiing is likewise practised on other nearby mountains.

PRACTICAL INFORMATION FOR ANKARA

TOURIST OFFICES. There are tourist offices at Gazi Mustafa Kemal Bul. 33 (tel. 230 19 11), and at Esenboğa Airport.

WHEN TO COME. The best times of the year to visit Ankara and the surrounding countryside are spring and autumn. Located on a high tableland, Ankara can be bitterly cold in winter and hot in summer.

HOTELS. Our classification departs somewhat from the official list, which hesitates to downgrade an establishment that has had its day. The two top categories are air-conditioned and all have restaurants unless otherwise stated.

Deluxe

Ankara Hilton, Tarhan Cad. 12 (tel. 168 28 88). 363 rooms in 18 stories with fine view.

Büyük Ankara, Atatürk Bul. 183 (tel. 125 66 55). 180 rooms; 14 luxury suites. Swiss management. Three restaurants—the *Rooftop Grill* with dinner-dances, the *Başkent,* and the *Pub.* Casino with slot machines. Heated pool and garage.

Etap Altınel, Tandoğan Meydanı (tel. 231 77 60). 175 rooms. The newest in this reliable chain.

Expensive

Altınısık, Necatibey Cad. 46 (tel. 229 11 85). 55 rooms.

Dedeman, Büklüm Sok. (tel. 11 76 200). 252 rooms. Rooftop nightclub; pool.

Etap Mola, Atatürk Bul. 80 (tel. 117 85 85). 57 rooms. Link in a reliable chain.

Kent, Mithatpaşa Cad. 4 (tel. 135 50 50). 120 rooms. Among Ankara's best, with pleasant and helpful staff. Lunch in its excellent restaurant (Turkish specialties) and go to its Oriental Salon for coffee and *ceyif* (rest). In the busiest part of town.

Marmara, Atatürk Orman Çiftiğli. 51 rooms. Located at a farm on the outskirts; has large public facilities; restaurant serves Turkish specialties.

Stad, Istiklal Cad. 20 (tel. 310 48 48). 217 rooms.

Tunalı, Tunalı Hilmi Cad., Kavaklıdere (tel. 167 44 40). 54 rooms. In diplomatic quarter and rather expensive.

Moderate
In the Center of Town

Apaydın, Bayındır Sok., Yenişehir (tel. 133 22 25). 50 air-conditioned rooms.

Bulvar Palas, Atatürk Bul. (tel. 117 50 20). 177 rooms. Good value; restaurant with Turkish specialties.

Ergen, Karanfil Sok. 48 (tel. 117 59 06). 60 rooms. New.

Erşan, Meşrutiyet Cad. (tel. 118 98 75). 64 rooms.

Keykan, Fevzi Çakmak Sok. (tel. 231 80 70). 50 rooms.

Sultan, Bayındır Sok., Yenişehir (tel. 131 59 80). 40 rooms.

In the Ulus Quarter

Ercan, Denizciler Cad. 36 (tel. 310 48 90). 40 rooms. No restaurant.
Güleryüz, Sanayi Cad. 37 (tel. 310 49 10). 42 rooms. No restaurant.
Hitit, Hisar Park Cad. (tel. 310 86 17). 45 rooms.
Yeni, Sanayi Cad. (tel. 310 47 20). 66 rooms.

Inexpensive
In the Center of Town

Akman, Itfaiye Meydani, Tavus Sok. (tel. 324 41 40). 49 rooms. No restaurant.
Anıt, Gazi Mustafa Kemal Bul. (tel. 229 21 44). 92 rooms.
Bannak Onur Sok., Maltepe (tel. 231 80 40). 42 rooms, 27 with shower.
Öztürk, Talatpaşa Bul. (tel. 312 51 86). 42 rooms.

In the Ulus Quarter

Efes, Denizciler Cad. (tel. 324 32 11). 40 rooms. No restaurant.
Olimpiyat, Esdost Sok. (tel. 324 30 88). 65 rooms. No restaurant.
Paris, Denizciler Cad. (tel. 324 12 83). 31 rooms. No restaurant.
Safir, Denizciler Cad. (tel. 324 11 94). 28 rooms. No restaurant.

Elmadağ. Turban Elmadağ Lodge (M), (tel. 411 68). 10 rooms. Rustic mountain lodge.

RESTAURANTS. The most fashionable restaurants are those in the best hotels and those up at Çankaya. There is a good choice in the adjoining embassy quarter and in the center of town. For cool outdoor meals in the heat of summer, often with dancing at night, the environs are pleasant. Scattered throughout the center of town are numerous tasty kebab places, mostly clean and very cheap.

Expensive

Altınnal, Cinnah Cad. 67 (tel. 138 44 64). At Çankaya.
China Town, Köroğlu Sok. 19, Gaziosmanpaşa (tel. 127 71 50).
RV, Tarhan Cad. 13 (tel. 127 43 44). In Kavaklıdere, embassy quarter.
Washington, Bayındir Sok. 28 (tel. 117 89 64). Central, at Kızılay.

Moderate

Altınkupa, Selanik Cad. 33 (tel. 17 71 27). Central.
Anadolu Cicek Pasajı, Izmir Cad. 18 (tel. 18 45 75). Central.
Ay-Sa Turistik Tesisleri, at Golbasi, shortly after the branch off from E5 to Haymana. Has evening dancing.
Bizon, Çankaya Cad. 14 (tel. 39 25 88). At Çankaya.
Hülya, Hoşdere Cad. 199 (tel. 38 29 61). At Yukari Ayrancı.
Italyan, Hoşdere Cad. 200 (tel. 138 09 35). At Yukarı Arancı.
Kafdağı Lokantasi, Çubuk Dam. Dancing at night.
Kanyon, Hoşdere Cad. 193 (tel. 138 09 08). At Yukarı Ayrancı.
Liman, Izmir Cad. 11 (tel. 230 27 05). For seafood; central.
Merkez Lokantasi, Atatürk Orman Çiftliği, (tel. 213 17 50). At farm on outskirts, with dancing at night.

Milka, Atatürk Bul. 185 (tel. 118 66 77). In Kavaklıdere, embassy quarter.

Panorama, Çankaya Cad. 28 (tel. 139 17 50). At Çankaya.

Piknik Pub, Inkılap Sok. 7 (tel. 18 44 58). At Kızılay.

Pizza Pino, Tunalı Hilmi Cad. 111 (tel. 26 77 80). In Kavaklıdere.

Ulker, Yunus Sok. 10 (tel. 38 32 97). Small but excellent; at Çankaya.

Villa Restoran, Negis Sok. 10 (tel. 27 28 24). Also at Çankaya.

Inexpensive

Set Kafeterya, Emek Ishani. Self-service in highrise department store with large terrace.

CAMPING. *Kervansaray Susuzköy Mokamp* (capacity 400), on the Istanbul highway, 20 km. (13 miles) from Ankara.

GETTING AROUND. By Plane. Some international airlines continue from Istanbul to Ankara, a 50-minute flight. THY has at least eight flights daily; there are frequent flights to provincial capitals. A taxi to the airport costs approximately $7.

By Train. Istanbul–Ankara Blue Train (Mavi Tren) day train takes 7½ hours; *Anatolia Express* night train with sleeping car. From Izmir an express runs three times weekly taking about 12 hours; daily regular service.

By Car. Main highway Istanbul–Ankara 458 km. (284 miles). Route 200 and E23 from Bursa, 319 km. (235 miles); E23 from Izmir, 583 km. (362 miles); E5 from Adana; four-lane highway from Aksaray, 486 km. (302 miles). Exits from the Ankara ringroad to the main Anatolian highways.

Car Hire. *Avis,* Tunus Cad. 10/5, Bakanlıklar (tel. 125 17 25), and at the airport. *Hertz,* Atatürk Bul. 169/F (tel. 118 84 40), and at the airport.

By Bus. Frequent cheap private coach services between Istanbul and Ankara. The city buses are the best organized in Turkey, complemented by minibuses along the outer arteries.

NIGHTLIFE. Nightlife in Ankara is fairly lively and expensive in the main hotels; also at the *Gar Gazinosu,* Istasyon Meydani, which serves late suppers; *Baskent,* Büklüm Sok. 4; and *Mon Amour,* Ghazi Mustafa Kemal Bul. 30.

Somewhat less sophisticated are the *Pino,* Cinnah Cad. 188; *Sehrazat,* Sümer Sok. 20; *Sergen,* Çankaya Cad. 30; *Yeni Sureyya,* Bestekar Sok.; *Kulup Feyman* and *Tuna,* Atatürk Bul.; *Karavan, Lalezar,* and *Yakut,* Ghazi Mustafa Kemal Bul.; *Yıldız,* Gençlik Park.

The *Set* in the Kızılay highrise stays open at night with music.

For more serious entertainment, only the Opera is of interest for those not knowing Turkish.

SHOPPING. In Ankara there is no big covered bazaar as in Istanbul. The main shopping area is Kızılay, with several department stores on Atatürk Bulvari, the largest one being in the highrise.

The *Turkish Handicraft Association,* Selanik Cad., sells jewelry, embroidery, kilims, etc. In the Samanpazarı district below the Hisar are cheaper souvenir shops where bargaining is possible. Not a practice for the elegant boutiques in the main hotels, on upper Atatürk Bulvari and Tunalı Caddesi in Kavaklıdere.

USEFUL ADDRESSES. Embassies. *United States,* Atatürk Bul. 110 (tel. 126 54 70); *Canada,* Nenehatun Cad. 75, Gaziosmanpaşa (tel. 127 58 03); *Great Britain,* Şehit Ersan Cad. 46/A, Çankaya (tel. 127 43 10).

Travel Agents. *American Express,* Celikkale Sokak 12/B, Yenişehir; *Gentur,* Atatürk Bul. 103; *Wagons-Lits/Cook,* Ziya Gokalp Cad. 20/A (to book sleeping car on night trains).

Airlines. *British Airways,* Atatürk Bul.; *Pan Am,* Atatürk Bul. 53; *THY,* Zafer Meydani.

Churches. *Catholic,* St. Paul (in the Italian embassy), Kavaklidere, Atatürk Bul. 118, mass on Sun. at 10 and 11 A.M. *Protestant,* Kızılılırmak Cad. 20, Sun. service at 11 A.M. *Synagogue,* Birlik Sokak near Ulus Anafartalar Cad.

Useful Phone Numbers. Traffic police, 131 75 75. Ambulance, 311 95 55. Railway Station Information, 11 06 20. Esenboğa Airport Information, 12 28 20.

CENTRAL ANATOLIA

The Ancient Heartland

History has a way of coming full circle over long stretches of time. This middle region of the enormous Asia Minor rectangle was the centerpiece of the Hittite Empire in the 2nd millennium B.C., and of the Seljuk Empire in the 13th century A.D. Today it is the center of the modern Turkish Republic in a political as well as physical sense, as it is dominated by the capital, Ankara, creation of the republic's founder, Kemal Atatürk.

As a close neighbor of Mesopotamia, the cradle of civilization, this vast region shared in the vital prehistory of mankind. Çatalhöyük, settled first around 7000 B.C., became one of the world's first towns just 500 years later. Since then, Central Anatolia has been the homeland of many tribes and nations, a historical battleground as well as a melting pot of East and West. Transition from the nomadic to a more settled way of life was the rule rather than the exception up to modern times, as recurring tribal invasions destroyed established cultures with monotonous barbarity, assimilated them, to fall in their turn to succeeding conquerors. Frontiers remained nebulous, as there are few natural boundaries on the interminable Anatolian plateau. Even the Taurus mountain chain in the south and higher chains to the southeast proved insufficient barriers.

The dense forests of antiquity were thinned for thousands of years till they succumbed finally to the goats of medieval invaders. The ensuing steppe could support only a sparse population, but in the last 50 years an ever increasing part has been converted to wheat growing. Yet much of the tawny plateau of an average height of 1,000 meters (3,500 ft.) is still an arid plain, slashed by ravines and with a huge salt lake in the middle. Near the scattered mountains—often extinct volcanoes—the rare rivers have been dammed up into artificial lakes. The climate is harsh, with extremes of temperature, especially in the north.

Hattis and Hittites

The Paleolithic Period is represented by axe heads and flint stones found, inter alia, in the Maltepe district of Ankara; the Neolithic Period by artifacts from Çatalhöyük, which flourished further in the Chalcolithic when it was joined by Alisar. Both continued throughout the Bronze Age, while the simple pottery developed into spouted vessels and figurines, and jewelry made its appearance with gold diadems and necklaces.

The people who had progressed to this fairly sophisticated culture were the Hattis, whose symbol was the bronze sundisc surrounded by radial lobes representing the planets. A monumental modern replica at Sihhiye in Ankara commemorates this advanced notion of the solar system. Sargon of Akkad (2334–2279 B.C.), the world's first empire builder, extended his rule from Mesopotamia over the silver-rich mountains of Anatolia, but towards the end of his reign 17 subject Hatti princes revolted and regained their independence. Yet from about 2000 B.C. on, the princes ruling the main city states—Hattushash (one symbol of the cuneiform script is rendered as "sh" as well as "s," so it could be Hattusas too), Kanesh, Kushara, and Zalpa—encouraged trade with the great Mesopotamian towns, from which they derived considerable taxes. In this Period of Assyrian Trade Colonies, donkey caravans brought textiles, arms and other commodities to Anatolia in exchange for metals, especially silver. The imported goods were unloaded at trade colonies (*karum*) outside the princely towns and distributed throughout Anatolia. Sometimes the karum surpassed the original town in importance, but all flourished for about 200 years. In around 1800, Anitta, King of Kushara, a town not yet located, conquered one city state after another, and forming an Anatolian Confederacy called himself King of Kings (Rabum Rabum). The glory was shortlived in practice but the name lived on.

The Indo-European Hittites from the steppes beyond the Black Sea entered Anatolia via the Caucasus around 2000 to become a dominant factor at the time of Anitta. The Hattis bowed to the superior forces, but absorbed the Hittites in their own culture. Not only was the Hittite capital Hattushash named after the conquered, but the entire land was referred to as the Land of the Hattis. Not for the last time in history, the parvenu conquerors sought legitimacy by tracing their descent from the most prominent of the conquered. Anitta was the obvious choice for a respectable ancestor, so that from his death in about 1740 a royal line was established to Labarna who ascended the throne in 1680. This outstanding monarch is considered the founder of the Old Kingdom and his name became the title of succeeding kings. His son Hattushilish I (1650–20) extended his dominions into Syria, his grandson Mushilish I conquered and plundered Babylon, but on his return fell victim to a palace plot and was assassinated. There followed a confused period of dynastic power struggle, uprising and famine, while the Mitanni, an Indo-Iranian tribe, grew powerful in the South.

King Telipinush (1525–1500) put a temporary stop to the rot and issued a famous decree—preserved in full—to restore law and order. But on his death the whole of the ancient East was plunged into chaos and darkness by the invasion of new tribes. The Old Kingdom came to an end for all practical purposes. The last scion of the royal line was killed in 1375 by Shupiluliuma who himself ascended the throne. He defeated the Mitanni king, but married his daughter to the latter's son to form a buffer state against the Assyrian and Egyptian empires. Tutankhamun's widow asked for and obtained one of his sons in marriage, but the Hittite prince was murdered at the Egyptian border. This led to a war which ended with Shupiluliuma's conquest of Damascus. His grandson Mushilish II succeeded in 1335, defeated the Assyrians, put down revolts by his uncles and became the founder of the New Kingdom. Though he spent his life on the battlefield, he also wrote a prayer that the plague should spare the Land of the Hatti, not a bad piece of literature for the period. He prayed in vain, for he succumbed to the plague in 1306, leaving his son Muvattali a vast empire.

A clash with Egypt became inevitable as both tried to absorb the Mitanni buffer state. The Hittite army of 4,500 war chariots and 1,700 foot soldiers met the Egyptians of Ramses II at Kadesh on the river Orontes. Both sides claimed victory, both armies retreated with great losses, and the war ended with the favorable Treaty of Kadesh, signed in 1280 by Hattushilish III, a fine soldier and skillful diplomat. After his death the decline of the New Kingdom followed the familiar pattern of family strife, with the final blow being delivered by the invasion of barbaric tribes in the Aegean migration.

From the Sea People to Atatürk

Like the Hittites, the Luwians, often called the Sea People, came from the Pontic steppe, but entered Anatolia from the west, where the great bulwark of Troy had just been destroyed by the Achaeans. The main Luwian tribe, the Phrygians, had assisted the Trojans, and by 1180 had left an unprecedented trail of destruction from the lower Danube to the main Hittite towns. Their burning marked the end of the Bronze Age. Some Neo-Hittite principalities survived in the south till the 8th century. They were also called Hieroglyphic Hittite states, as their records were written exclusively in this script.

From the 12th to the 8th century the center of the stage was held by the Phrygians in a loose confederation. They built their settlements over the towns they had destroyed, but as they kept no records little is known about them until the end of the period when they had become sufficiently important to be mentioned in the Assyrian archives. Midas of the golden touch became king in 738, to end his reign by being defeated in 695 by the Cimmerians who had advanced from the Caucasus. The Lydians (of the far west) drove the Cimmerians out of Anatolia, and before long the Persians arrived (546), a blessing in disguise as they kept relative peace for the next two centuries. This ended in 334 with the advent of Alexander the Great and the war between his successors, when the fierce Galatians settled round Ancyra and proceeded to attack their richer neighbors until eventually contained by Attalos I of Pergamon. Attalos III handed over parts of Central Anatolia to Rome and the rest was subdued by the Roman generals.

Though the Pax Romana which extended into Byzantine times provided the longest peaceful interlude the region had ever known, it also became a provincial though prosperous backwater. Happy are those who have no history, and there was but little till the Arab invasion of A.D. 642 when it restarted with a vengeance. The Arabs only raided, but the Seljuk Turks conquered. After the battle of Manzikert in 1071, they advanced across the Anatolian plateau. Twenty-six years later Ikonion became Konya, when Kilic Arslan I made it the capital of the Sultanate of Rum which extended over most of Anatolia. The greatest of the sultans, Alaeddin Keykubat (1219–36), left his mark in numerous magnificent buildings. Only seven years later his successor Keykavus II was defeated by Genghis Khan near Erzincan, whereupon the Seljuk dominions disintegrated into competing emirates, mostly dependent on the Ilhanid Mongols of Iran. In this time of decay, Mevlana Celaleddin inspired Islamic thinking from Konya till his death in 1273.

From their emirate in the northwest, the Osmanli dynasty directed their main thrust against the remnants of the Byzantine Empire, suffered its first great defeat at the hands of Genghis Khan's grandson Tamerlane but, unlike the Seljuks, quickly recovered and completed the conquest of Central Anatolia with the occupation of Kayseri in 1515. Though not exactly enjoying a Pax Osmanliana, it became a backwater once again, minus the ancient prosperity. In 1919 Mustafa Kemal Pasha launched the resistance at the Congress of Sivas; from then on history has been made again in Central Anatolia.

EXPLORING CENTRAL ANATOLIA

The E5 from Istanbul to Ankara hugs the north shore of Lake Sapanca, then bypasses Adapazarı, repeatedly damaged by earthquakes and continues 115 km. (72 miles) via Düzce and Kaynaşlı to Bolu. The province of Bolu bears the name of its capital. Once part of the Hittite Empire, it became, after the death of Alexander the Great, the kingdom of Bithynia, whose capital, Claudiopolis, is today called Bolu. (Mut, in the south between Silifke and Karaman, also went by the name of Claudiopolis.) Within the town the Ulu Cami and the hamam were built by order of Bayezit I. Kızılcahaman in the woods, 110 km. (68 miles) before Ankara, is a pleasant place for a stopover.

An Empire Rediscovered

Top priority for sightseeing in Central Anatolia goes to the great sites of the Hittite Empire contained within the Boğazkale–Alacahöyük–Yazılıkaya triangle, 181 km. (112 miles) northeast on Route 190, then 29 km. (18 miles) right east.

There are several references to the Sons of Hit in the Old Testament and Egyptian records in cuneiform script mention Hittite kings. The treaty of Kadesh is engraved on memorial stelae at Karnak in the languages and scripts, cuneiform and hieroglyphic, of the opponents. There were likewise letters of the Pharaoh commenting on the treaty.

Yet for almost three millennia an empire and its culture had fallen into oblivion till, in 1812, a German traveler named Burckhardt found at Hamath, in Syria, a stone tablet bearing hieroglyphics different from the Egyptian ones. In 1839, a Frenchman, Charles Texier, finally stumbled on the ruins of Boğazkale, with its stone carvings and bas-reliefs. An Englishman John Hamilton discovered Alacahöyük, but only his countryman Henry Sayce suggested in 1879 that the Hittites of the Bible had at last been located.

Great Britain and Germany competed for the conduct of the excavations. The latter prevailed, and Hugo Winckler started in July 1906. After only one month he unearthed the letter written by Ramses II, thus confirming beyond doubt that Boğazkale was indeed ancient Hattushash. Excavations were interrupted by World War I, but sufficient tablets, incised with sharp implements while the clay was soft, had come to light to show that documents of a political nature were in the cuneiform Akkadian script used in the Assyrian trade colonies, while the bulk was in unknown hieroglyphics. In 1915 the Austrian scholar Hrozny deciphered them, opening up a wealth of information about religion, law, and customs. Excavations were resumed in 1934 and are continuing. Some 30,000 tablets have been listed, and from an unknown people the Hittites have emerged as one of the best documented of early antiquity.

Although of small physical stature—probably under five feet—the Hittites were muscular and strongly-built. Their diet included bread, honey, cheese, vegetables and fruit, but this didn't mean that they were necessarily vegetarians at heart. The Hittite kings and nobility had the privilege of eating both fish and meat, and this distinction may well have been one of the ways of pointing up the difference between the Hittites and the indigenous population. Their society was sharply divided into free men and serfs, and the sovereign who ruled over the federation of principalities and was also its high priest, becoming a god himself after death; yet on important matters he had to consult his council. The king's mother occupied the second place, the queen only the third, relative positions which reappeared some 3,000 years later in the Osmanli Empire. Succession was vested in the eldest son; the other princes ruled conquered cities. In so warlike a nation, national service was, of course, compulsory, The war chariots, holding two bowmen and a driver, were accompanied by foot soldiers.

Religion was a tolerant polytheism, with Hatti and, later, Hurri deities admitted to the Hittite pantheon. Subsequent mythologies may have derived their symbolism from the Hittite set of creeds. For example, there were Runda, the god of hunting, and Tarhund, the god of the tempest. Compare these with the Etruscan Tarchuna and with the Taraxippos of the Greeks, who set up statues of this god at the starting line in stadium chariot races. Then, too, there were the Universal Mother, who eventually became Kybele, and Kupapa, the god of victory, whose attributes are reflected in those of his Hellenic female counterpart, the goddess Nike. And there may well be many points in common between the mischief-making god Telepinu, the perpetrator of all manner of joyous tricks—he specialized in banquets for the gods—and Dionysos, whose practical jokes set his fellow Olympians' teeth gnashing.

The Hittite Sites

The three most important Hittite sites in the area—the capital Hattushash as well as the temples, bas-reliefs and tombs of Yazılıkaya and Alacahöyük—can easily be seen on one excursion. This unique combination merits a visit both by those interested in archaeology and by history buffs who like a first-hand encounter with the dawn of civilization.

Accommodation at Boğazköy, the village below the main ruins, is practically nonexistent, but there are two motels at Sungurlu, 29 km. (18 miles) back on Route 190. The small Archeological Museum at the village entrance retains only what was not considered worthy of the Museum of Anatolian Civilizations in Ankara.

Hattushash was occupied as early as the 3rd millennium B.C. and might even have become the capital of the Hatti Federation. Anitta described its fall and put a curse on any future king residing there. This did not prevent Labarna from choosing it once again as capital, because of the excellent defensive position in a valley framed on both sides by rivers. The walls of brick on stone foundations, reinforced by large cut stones and surmounted by towers, were 6 km. (4 miles) in circumference. Following the abrupt end of the Hittite empire at the beginning of the 12th century, the city was burned by the Phrygians, who built a new one which was eventually occupied by the Persians.

The tour of the ruins can be exhausting; save your strength for the most important places. When you've gone round the ramparts of the lower city, the first ruins to the right as you go up toward the citadel are those of Temple I, dedicated to the Storm God. Hattushash had five temples, all patterned on an identical model. Like the Babylonian temples, they consisted of small rooms arranged around a paved courtyard roughly 215 by 520 meters (700 by 1,700 ft.) square. The only difference between the temples lay in the means of access to the sanctuary in which the statue of the divinity was enshrined. In Babylon, the people were allowed to contemplate the statue from a courtyard through the small open gates of an intermediary chapel. Hittite temples were designed so that it was necessary to run a sort of obstacle course to reach the sanctuary, and the god's statue was not placed facing the entrance—rather, it stood to one side. It is therefore reasonable to conclude that the Hittites regarded religion as something reserved for only a select few, who were admitted into the innermost shrine, and that the people had a right only to an indirect form of participation in religious rites or ceremonies.

The rooms opening out from the courtyard were doubtless administrative offices and archives, at least in Temple I. It is more difficult to reconstitute the exact circumstances for the other four temples. Temple I stands on a terrace overlooking some of the public buildings; to the north and east of it lay private residential buildings, parts of which have been dug out. They were occupied by a thriving colony of Assyrian merchants and traders.

The second most important ruins are those of the citadel, or Büyükkale, reached by a modern stairway which has replaced the ancient ramp. On the terrace atop the sheer cliff stood the royal palace, probably several stories high, with a large hall, perhaps the throne room, on the second floor. The citadel's outbuildings include storage rooms where the archives were kept; here, in 1906, thousands of stone tablets were found, mute but eloquent survivors of the plundering Phrygians.

Continuing up the hill, you come first to the eastern side of the fortified wall of the upper city, with its Royal Gate (Kral Kapısı). It is here, and also on the south, that the ramparts are most impressive. They consist of two parallel walls connected by the two main gates, the latter in themselves being formidable bastions. The overall concept of this defense set-up, plus the other military installations, prove that the Hittites had attained a higher level of perfection in warlike, political, legislative, and judicial matters than in art, literature, and religion.

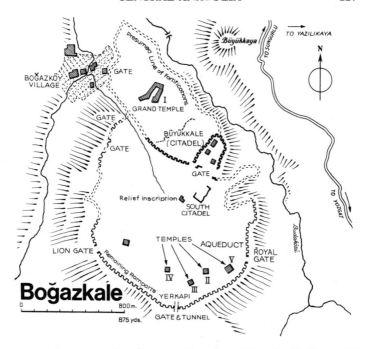

Now follow along the ramparts. The ruins of Temples V, II, and III lie to your left. Beyond is the entrance to a tunnel (Yerkapi) leading to the base of the wall outside. The ruins of Temple IV are to the north. Beyond, at the end of the pathway that runs the length of the ramparts, rises the well-preserved Gate of the Lions.

The open-air rock sanctuary of Yazılıkaya lies about 2 km. (1 mile) northeast of Hattushash. A large entrance portal opens onto a natural crevice forming a narrow passageway through the rocks and emerging onto a small circular open space—the shrine proper. The rocky walls of the passageway are decorated with bas-reliefs illustrating various personages, and the figures increase in size as you approach the shrine. On the wall beyond, facing each other, are the carved figures of the god Teshub and the goddess Hepatu. They were the two main divinities of the Hurri religion, assimilated by the Hittites, who built this sanctuary around 1300 B.C. In order of increasing size, from the outside in, the figures represent warriors, genies, and minor gods (on the left) and goddesses. As you emerge from the passageway, note the second, smaller passageway on your left: at the end are several more bas-reliefs representing, among other people, King Tudhalia IV (13th century B.C.), probably protected by Sharruma, the same god who appears directly behind the goddess Hepatu in the main sanctuary.

The site of Alacahöyük, 36 km. (22 miles) northeast, has been inhabited from the Chalcolithic to the Post-Hittite periods. Some scholars assert that here might be Anitta's lost Kushara. Continuing excavations have brought to light 15 levels of four different cultures, beginning with 13 rectangular burial chambers. There the Hatti kings had been laid to rest with golden diadems, belts, necklaces and other jewelry, silver combs, mirrors and drinking vessels beside funerary artifacts, all now in the Ankara Museum.

A later temple in typical Hittite style was entered through the Gate of Sphinxes, likewise in Ankara, with concrete casts *in situ*. The Egyptian style of the two sphinxes indicate the empire period. The double-headed eagle, the emblem of the Hittite as of so many succeeding empires, appears on the inside wall. Bas-reliefs depict a royal couple worshipping a bull, the sacrifice and the sun goddess Arima. A modern tower affords a view of the entire site.

At Eskiyapar (5 km., 3 miles) gold and electrum objects of the Early Bronze Age were found. At Pazarli, 52 km. (32 miles) northeast, a mound revealed levels from the Early Bronze Age to a Phrygian citadel.

Intrepid amateurs of pottery might brave the unpaved 31 km. (19 miles) south from Boğazkale to Yozgat, founded in the 18th century, but for once only A.D. and not B.C. The Çapanoğlu Cami and the adjoining Süleyman Bey Cami date from this period. Another 45 km. (30 miles) southeast lie the remains of Alisar, a Chalcolithic village of wattle-and-daub houses on a hill where over the centuries an urban culture flourished. The variety of pottery types, mainly dark grey and red ware, is unique in Anatolian archeology. The bones of the dead were preserved in vases and placed in shaft-graves below the stone foundation of the houses. Returning on E23 resist the temptation 34 km. (21 miles) before Ankara to take a look at the village of Hasanoğlan, which gave its name to a rare silver idol. The Early Bronze Age figure, c. 2300, its head covered with a gold mask, was— together with five gold and silver pins—the only find and duly delivered to the Ankara Museum.

For Hittite fans, the Gavur Kalesi (Fortress of the Infidels) rock bas-reliefs depict two figures in front of a poorly-preserved goddess. Near Ikizce, 40 km. (25 miles) south of Ankara on the Haymana road.

Amasya

Çorum on Route 785 is located 68 km. (42 miles) northeast of Sungurlu, on the site of antique Nikonia. There are several Osmanli monuments, especially the Ali Paşa Hamam, the 13th-century Ulu Cami, restored during the 19th century, and the Inayet Cami, of more recent construction.

Route 180 due east reaches Amasya, one of Anatolia's most attractive towns, after 94 km. (58 miles). Ancient Amaseia, capital city of the Pontic kingdom described in the chapter dealing with the Black Sea, clustered around the ancient fortress built high on a rock overlooking the valley of the Yeşilırmak. According to the geographer Strabo, who was born here, the city had been founded by the Amazon queen Amasis. The Seljuks moved in fairly early, in 1071, after their victory at Manzikert, followed by the Mongols in the 13th century until Bayezit I's conquest in the beginning of the 15th. On the right bank of the Yeşilırmak, a palace, the Saray Düzu, was built for the heirs to the throne, who often acted as governors and even retained the office after their accession. Only the outer walls and baths remain.

The türbe of Torumtay, dating from 1266, is characteristic of the Seljuk style. The nearby Gök (Blue) Medrese, built by Torumtay, is now a museum, displaying among other things the mummies of its founder and other Mongol Ilhanid rulers of the town. The angles of the portal are supported by cylindrical abutments. In the little street opposite stands a mosque (1430) bearing the name of its builder, Mehmet I's vizir, Yorguç Paşa.

Amasya's local dignitaries appear to have been deeply concerned over their own final resting places. Both sides of the town's main street are lined with tranquil little türbes containing the mortal remains of such dignitaries as Prince Sehzad, Halifet Gazi, Mehmet Paşa, and Sultan Mesut.

The Sultan Bayezit Cami is a much bigger mosque, built in 1486. It stands out on a terrace shaded by plane trees along the banks of the Yeşilırmak. Its mimbar and mihrab are made of marble, and the blue tiles have quotations from the Koran.

The venerable Burmalı Minare Cami (1242) is perhaps a bit over-restored. One of its outstanding features is its fluted minaret that, despite the restorations, has managed to retain a distinctive air of originality. The Fethiye Cami close by, started as a Byzantine church and became a mosque in 1116, while the Timarhane hospital dates from 1309.

Even though the river is badly polluted take a stroll on its tree-lined bank to enjoy the picturesque frontage of overhanging houses opposite and the old bridges. The restored 19th-century Hazeran Mansion houses the Fine Arts Gallery. The Alçak Köprü bridge has a new span, but still rests on its original arches. The Kuş Köprü has a poetic name meaning "Bridge of the Birds." The Kapı Ağası Medrese (1488) is now the School of Arts and Crafts. At the citadel, the inevitable *kale* of every townsite that has had to withstand the centuries of warring attacks, only a few bits of wall remain upright. It is a short but steep climb up the cliff face to Kral Mezarlari, well-preserved rock tombs of the first four Pontic kings, impressively floodlit at night. More of them can also be seen at Aynalı Mağara north, on the left bank of the Yeşilırmak: its name signifies "mirror grotto," because it literally shines in the rays of the sun.

Halfway between Amasya and Tokat, at Turhal, turn right (south) on to Route 190 to Zile. From the fortress above the restored Uli Cami, built in 1296, you can gaze out on the scene of Caesar's victory over the Pontic king. This was the battle that inspired Caesar's celebrated and terse message to the Roman Senate: *"Veni, vidi, vici"* (I came, I saw, I conquered). Although perhaps never actually uttered by Caesar, these words were contained in a letter that he wrote to his friend Amintius describing his victory in Asia over Pharnakes II, the son of Mithridates VI Eupator.

Near Tokat, 114 km. (71 miles) southeast of Amasya on Route 180, a Bronze Age cemetery was unearthed at Horoztepe. Thereabouts was Komana, the Place of Hymns, a temple state ruled by a High Priest. It became Roman Comana Pontica, and was contracted by the Seljuks to Tokat, when they moved the town 8 km. (5 miles) in the 11th century. Their hilltop fortress with 28 towers is now a crumbling ruin, but not the Garipler Cami or the fine Gök (Blue) Medrese, at present a museum full of tiles, Byzantine frescoes and geometrical designs. The mausolea are likewise of Seljuk origin; those of Elbukasim and Halef Gazi, Acikbas, Nurettin Sentimur, and Sumbul Bab. The Hatuniye, a school and mosque dating from 1485, was built in memory of Bayezit II's mother. The Ali Paşa Cami is of more recent construction. A Seljuk bridge spans the Yeşilırmak.

54 km. (33 miles) northeast, Niksar, once Roman Neo-Caesarea, possesses two 12th-century monuments, the Ulu Cami and the Yağıbasan Medrese within the Byzantine-Osmanli citadel.

Sivas

From Tokat, it is 102 km. (63 miles) southeast to Sivas, where a park now covers the original Hittite settlement on the central hill. Hellenistic Sebasteia became an important trading center under the Romans, a position it long preserved on the crossroads of the caravans from Baghdad and Persia. Capital of the Danishment emirs from 1142 to 1172, it fell successively to the Seljuks, Mongols and Osmanlis, and suffered badly from Tamerlane's hordes in 1400. Sivas was the setting for the congress convened by Mustafa Kemal Pasha in September, 1919, which decided the liberation of Turkey, then partly occupied. Today the meeting hall and the room in which Atatürk lived constitute the Inkilap Museum (Museum of the Revolution).

A beautifully carved portal topped by two intricately wrought open-work brick and tile minarets in the façade are all that remain of the splendid Çifte Minare Medrese built in 1271 by the Seljuk Vizir Semsettin Mehmet. It may have touched off a rash of competition, because in the same year another vizir, Muzaffer Burucirci, likewise founded a medrese. Efficiently restored, it now houses a small museum; the founder's mausoleum is decorated with lovely blue tiles. These unfortunately have mostly disappeared from the school of a third vizir, Sahip Ata, though it is still called the Gök (Blue) Medrese.

The Şifaye started as a hospital in 1217, when portals and their adornment were a matter of supreme importance. This one is a particularly handsome example, and the mosaics in the interior are also exquisite. The Sultan Keykavus Türbe, in the Şifaye, is a symphony in faience. The mosques, on the other hand, are Osmanli, except the 12th-century Danishment Ulu Cami, whose minaret, with its ribbon of enameled tilework, dates from the 14th century. The Yeni Cami has been recently restored. The façade of the Güdük (Squat) Minare is made of marble, a material conspicuous for its scarcity in Anatolia. A han (inn) is named after its founder, Behram Paşa, and a hamam bears the name of the lead roofing that covers it—Kurşunlu.

At Kangal, 13 km. (8 miles) northeast, hot springs feed a thermal pool, where 10 cm.-long fish thrive at a temperature of 36°C (97°F). The water possesses curative qualities for skin diseases and rheumatism.

Çankırı, 130 km. (80 miles) north of Ankara on Route 765, was Galatian Gangrea in the 3rd century B.C. On the hill is a ruined 11th-century Byzantine fortress where the great Seljuk Alaeddin Keykubat founded a hospital, the Taş Mescit (Small Rock Mosque), in 1235. The strikingly situated Ulu Cami was designed by Sinan himself.

As for local color, the shepherds wear a cloak (çoban), a cylinder of handwoven raw wool, with no openings except for the head. The şadouf, used for dipping water from wells, is a straight stick with a shaft to which the dipper is attached, and with a counter-weight at the other end of the shaft.

South into Mysticism

Once past the green belt with which Atatürk surrounded Ankara, E5 leaves Lake Gölbası to the right. After 31 km. (20 miles), Route 280 branches left (east) through endless wheatfields in an apparently empty countryside, intersected by tawny hills and ridges, shading from ocher through red to lavender. A huge grain silo, Anatolia's new architecture, dominates the village of Bala at an altitude of 1,370 meters (4,500 ft.). The road drops to the Seljuk bridge over the Kızılırmak, the ancient Halys, which King Croesus so rashly crossed somewhere near here. The branch right (southwest) arrives after 18 km. (11 miles) at the Hirfanli Dam which has formed an elongated artificial lake. After another minor artificial lake on the left, Kırşehir (181 km., 112 miles) can, but should not, be bypassed. An important agricultural center, Kırşehir presents the usual Anatolian tumbletown blend: old and new houses side by side, plus a scattering of Seljuk monuments. The inevitable Alaeddin Cami—Keykubat's of course; the Caca Bey Cami built in 1272 as an astronomical observatory; and the Ahi Evran Cami, with the türbe of the founder of the Ahi brotherhood. The religious thinking of this sect exercised considerable influence for several centuries. Before the juncture with Route 280 stands the türbe of the poet Aşık Paşa, built during the Mongol occupation.

Beyond Mucur, Route 765 branches right (south), the shortest road (68 km., 42 miles) to Nevşehir. After 20 km. (12 miles) you arrive at Hacıbektaş, where a religious sect was founded by Haci Bektaş Veli in the 13th century. His teachings were based on a synthesis of Sunnism and Shiism blended with an admixture of Christianity. The dervishes of this sect also acted as almoners for the Janissaries and gradually came to exert considerable political power. In fact, their influence survived the liquidation of the Janissaries in the 19th century, but was finally eradicated by Atatürk. The monastery that belonged to Haci Bektaş' disciples is still standing, and he is buried in a türbe here.

Back on Route 280 you recross the Kızılırmak and soon see the great volcanic cone of Mount Erciyes, ancient Argeus, rising above Kayseri.

Origin of Monasticism

Never conquered by Alexander the Great, Cappadocian Mazaka became in 257 B.C. Eusebeia, capital of another hellenized kingdom, annexed by the Emperor Tiberius only in A.D. 17, when it changed name once again to Caesarea. In 329 a son was born to the Professor of Rhetoric in the provincial capital, and named Basilius. He studied in Constantinople and Athens, where he was joined by a fellow Cappadocian, Gregorius, son of the Bishop of Nazianzos. On his return to Caesarea Basilius followed his father's profession, but soon became convinced of the need for spiritual perfection, which he sought in the monastic settlements of Egypt and Syria. He then withdrew to Annesi—Greek for Comfort, in his case exclusively spiritual—in Pontus, where he applied his Rules which are still observed by Orthodox monks with hardly any alterations. In 370 he became Bishop of Caesarea and spent his considerable inheritance on the establishment of a charitable institution, which cared for the poor and the sick. Though himself in bad health, he personally looked after the poorest of the poor, the lepers, still finding time for preaching and writing his doctrinal works. The Eucharist Liturgy bears his name and he is one of the Four Doctors of the Church. He died on January 1, 379, and as St. Basil entered Christian tradition as bringer of joy and gifts.

Gregorius had joined Basilius at Annesi, was consecrated Bishop of Sasima, but chose to assist his father as coadjutor. At the Council of Constantinople he defended Orthodoxy in the famous Five Theological Speeches, which earned him the epithet of Theologian and contributed largely to the condemnation of the Arian heresy. He was appointed Patriarch by Theodosius the Great, but had to resign after one month because of the hostility of the Egyptian and Macedonian bishops. He retired to Arianzos where he died in 389. He, too, is a Doctor of the Church.

Basilius' charitable foundation became the nucleus of Byzantine Caesarea. After being occupied in the middle of the 6th century by the Persian Sassanid King Shah Sapur, the Emperor Justinian protected Caesarea by a citadel and strong ramparts. Continuously attacked by the Arabs from the 7th to the 9th century, Caesarea was occupied by the Seljuks and became Kayseri, passed briefly to the Danishments in 1075, back to the Seljuks, followed by the Mongols and the Mameluks of Egypt. The last important Anatolian town to be integrated into the Roman Empire, it was again the last in the Osmanli Empire almost exactly 1,500 years later.

Kayseri

At an altitude of 1,054 meters (3,458 ft.), the undistinguished modern town of 350,000 inhabitants has spread far beyond the Justinian walls, whose crumbling remains are scattered over a wide area. Only the northern section has preserved some cohesion, resembling a Roman aqueduct seen from the inside. But the citadel, a rectangle 800 by 200 meters (875 by 220 yards) was strengthened by Sultan Alaeddin Keykubat in 1224 and again by the Osmanlis after the conquest by Sultan Selim I in 1515. Mehmet II added a mosque and a pretty fountain. Two Seljuk lions guard the gate in the 3-meter-thick blackish ramparts, reinforced by 18 towers, all sufficiently intact for a circuit on the catwalk. The Covered Bazaar across the road displays some good rugs, gold and silver jewelry, besides garlic-redolent *pastirma,* a local specialty.

The adjoining double-domed Ulu Cami was built by a Danishment Emir, Melik Mehmet Gazi, in 1142 in the Anatolian basilical style and contains a finely carved wooden mimber. The cylindrical minaret features a mosaic design of tiles. Continuing round the citadel clockwise, the Kurşunlu Cami—which takes its name like so many others from the lead-covered cupola—has recently been restored in the small Atatürk park. Built in 1518 by Ahmet Pasha after the design of Sinan Pasha, this small provincial mosque is far from representative of the genius of the greatest Osmanli architect who left his birthplace, a nearby village, at the age of 19 never to return, though he lived to be 100.

Behind the park, the Giyasiye Medrese, the first medical school in Anatolia—earlier than any in medieval Europe—is joined by a passage to the Sifahiye Medrese, a hospital. Both were built in 1205 from legacies left by the daughter of Sultan Giyassedin Keyhusrev I; the main gate is exquisitely decorated. Higher up Cumhuriyet Bulvari, the town's main artery, the Haci Kılıç Cami and Medrese, built in 1249 by the Vizir Abdul Kasim, are entered by handsomely wrought portals. Facing the citadel, the Vizir Sahipata established in 1267 the single-floor Sahabiye Medrese round an open courtyard. The geometrical carvings are among the finest of the late Seljuk period.

Sultans, sultanas, princesses and vizirs vied with each other throughout the 13th century to leave their imprint on Kayseri, not with sumptuous palaces, but for the glory of Allah, charity or the rest of their earthly remains. These three motives are piously combined in the outstanding group of buildings, the Hunad Hatun Cami, Medrese and Türbe. The persuasive influence of Seljuk spouses, mothers and daughters was demonstrated by the wife of the greatest sultan. The courtesy title "Noble Lady" of this Georgian princess refers, however, to birth rather than character, as Hunad Hatun was suspected of having poisoned Alaeddin Keykubat when he was about to disinherit their son. Once Giyaseddin Keyhusrev II was safely enthroned, the queen-mother might have constructed the religious complex in 1237 in atonement. The mosque is in the basilical style, with a finely decorated main gate and double arches. The first instructor at the Medrese, now an Ethnographical Museum, was Burhaneddin Tirmizi, teacher of Mevlana Celaleddin. The octagonal tomb is encircled by a double band of elegant geometrical designs. The austere interior is distinguished by a rare Seljuk stone mihrab and holds three sarcophagi. Hunad Hatun's is of white marble, ornated with the finest Sulus calligraphy.

The main hamam, next door—a large, square room centered on a pool, surmounted by a brick cupola—is still in use. The Tourist Office is nearby. The black-domed Mosque of Industry, entered through handsome gates, was constructed at the beginning of the religious revival in the 1960s.

Numerous Seljuk kümbets (mausolea) are scattered along Cumhuriyet Bulvari. In 1247 three rival vizirs prepared for the uncertain future by constructing the cylindrical Sırçalı (Crystal) Kümbet, named after the tiles of the vanished decoration; the Çifte (Twin Vault) Kümbet, octagonal under a cone-shaped roof; and the Ali Kafer Kümbet. The Kasbek Kümbet is the oldest, but the best-known is the Döner (Turning) Kümbet of Sultan Shah Cihan, so called as the conical roof supposedly fits upon the 12-sided structure so lightly that it might be turned by any breeze. All the panels are decorated with bas-reliefs, among others the Tree of Life, as popular with Seljuks as the double-headed eagle above lions.

Across Cumhuriyet Bulvari, the Archeological Museum relies mainly on finds from Kültepe. Close by is the Seyid Burhaneddin Kümbet. The boulevard narrows on climbing into the foothills of Mount Erciyes, which has given its name to the local university. A pleasant villa suburb has risen over the site of ancient Eusebeia, followed by barren slopes which miraculously supply the wherewithal for countless beehives, whose excellent honey is sold on the roadside. Journey's end is at the ski-club (2,125 meters, 6,972 ft.), whence a chairlift ascends to the eternal snows round the peak (3,916 meters, 12,848 ft.), the best ski run so far south.

Trade Colonies and Caravanserais

22 km. (14 miles) northeast of Kayseri along Route 260 to Sivas, turn left for 2 km. (1 mile) to the village of Karahöyük near Anatolia's largest city mound, Kültepe, the Ash Hill from the vast amount of ashes covering the charred remains of the palace and the uppermost of several levels of Kanesh. Inhabited from the 4th millennium B.C. on, Kanesh became a powerful city around 2,500. Five hundred years later, with Assyrian trade caravans passing through Anatolia, the trade colony (karum) of Kanesh flourished behind its single wall, attached to the double fortifications of the upper town. Though most of the 15,000 cuneiform Kültepe Tablets, Anatolia's oldest, deal with commercial transactions, there is also a certain

amount of family correspondence, which has changed remarkably little over 4,000 years.

Palace and karum, after nearly 2,000 years of alternate prosperity and destruction, disappeared finally with the Romans. Only foundations are left *in situ,* the rich finds from the excavations, alabaster idols, statuettes and painted pottery are in the Ankara and Kayseri Museums.

Fraktin is 78 km. (48 miles) south from Kayseri, via Develı which features a Seljuk mosque (1281) and the Seyid Şerif Kümbet (1276). The Hittite rock monument, the Yazılıkaya—which means "Inscribed Rock" and is therefore given to several sites—depicts on the left bas-reliefs of a shrine flanked by figures in tunics and wearing precursors of the Phrygian bonnet; on the right the storm god, King Hattushilish III and his wife, according to the hieroglyphic inscription.

Kervansaray is a Palace for Caravans, and no less did the Seljuk and Osmanli rulers provide throughout their empires. Three of these remarkable *hans* (inns) stand within a day's journey from Kayseri. 46 km. (28 miles) along the Sivas road, Alaeddin Keykubat built the Sultan Han, one of the most handsome in Anatolia. Behind the thick walls of a formidable rectangle (42 by 29 meters, 138 by 95 ft.), the travelers and their beasts found ample space for a rest. The Seljuk hans conform to the same pattern, distinguished by the two unusually high arches supporting the dome of the obligatory mosque. Near Bunyan, 42 km. (26 miles) northeast on Route 300 to Malatya, the Vizir Celaleddin Karatay in 1255 gave his name to a han. The tomb of the founder is decorated with fine reliefs. At Incesu, 35 km. (22 miles) southwest on Route 805 to Niğde, Kara Mustafa Pasha provided his caravanserai not only with a mosque and baths, but also with a bazaar.

19 km. (12 miles) further south, in view of a saltlake shimmering on the left, Route 767 branches right (northwest) into a moonscape more intriguing than the moon itself, because in a setting without parallel on this planet man's ingenuity has triumphed over nature for almost 2,000 years, bending the hostile surrounding to his own ends.

Cappadocia (Kappadokia)

Known as Katpatuka by the Assyrians, this massive isolated table land, subject to extreme temperatures, was famed for its horses, mules and sheep. A superficially hellenized Persian kingdom, it extended from Galatia in the north to the Taurus Mountains in the south, and prospered under Ariarathes V Eusebes Philopator (The Pious Father-Loving, 163–130 B.C.), who transferred his allegiance from the Seleukids to the Romans. When his widow Nysa murdered her five sons to keep the rule in her hands, the Pontic kings and later the Romans intervened until Cappadocia was incorporated into the Empire in A.D. 17.

Today Cappadocia designates the triangle formed by Kayseri, Nevşehir and Niğde. Frequent eruptions of Erciyes and Hasan Dağ covered considerable parts of this triangle with tufa, a thick layer of mud and ashes, over which lava spread at various stages of hardening. Erosion by rain, snow and wind created "fairy chimneys," surrealistic shapes of cones, needles, pillars and pyramids, often topped by an ingeniously balanced slab. Earthquakes and gigantic subsidences molded valleys, rivers long since vanished slashed rifts into the fragile tuff. Depending on the consistency of the exposed rocks, the indentations have been more or less violent, with utterly fantastic results. To the infinite variety of forms, oxidization added an improbable range of colors, from the off-white of Göreme through yellow, pink, red and russet to the violet-grey of Ihlara.

But these spell-binding rocks which have sheltered the persecuted for so long have lately been revealed as no less dangerous to their inhabitants than their most ruthless enemy. For generations villagers at Karain have suffered painful deaths, known throughout the area as the Karain agony. These have finally been diagnosed as a cancer epidemic, caused by the pale yellow rock. Karain and a similarly affected village nearby have been declared natural disaster areas and the villagers have been evacuated; a fate which seems to them no less an evil than the disease.

But a few improbable villages carved from the rocks are still inhabited, while the holes that riddle the cliff bases shelter the occasional anachronistic troglodyte.

Anchorites in Wonderland

The first use made of the inaccessible pinnacles was for military purposes, when the Hittites hollowed fortresses into the friable cliffs. The Persians as well as subsequent dominant powers preserved this original defense set-up, but the weird world in between seemed singularly unattractive for peaceful settlement, at least of the normal kind.

St. Basil favored and organized communal monasticism, but recognized the merit of stricter asceticism. It was thus in 373, while he held the see of Caesarea, that the first recluse in search of solitude carved a cave dwelling into the malleable rock, his only tool a stout stick. The simplicity of construction set a fashion which quickly led to the formation of anchorite colonies, combining the individuality of meditation with communal work on the fertile volcanic soil wherever there was a patch of level ground. But the worship of God always remained uppermost, so that rock chapels and churches proliferated, especially in the Göreme Valley. This later Turkish name, meaning "Can't See," became poignantly justified with the first Arab attack in 642. Large numbers of Christians sought refuge in the hide-out, even tunnelling into the earth in their search for safety. Successfully, because several underground cities, with populations of up to 60,000, remained hidden from the ruthless invaders. After the emperors of the Isaurian dynasty had finally repulsed the Arabs 200 years later, churches were again hollowed out above ground, in contemporary Byzantine architectural styles, decorated with geometrical paintings. With the restoration of the images by the Empress Theodora, the churches were adorned with increasingly ambitious frescoes, rivalling the rocks outside in unusual color schemes. Counting all the chapels and shrines at Göreme, the magic number of 365 might well have been achieved, so that masses could be said at a different altar every day of the year. A much greater number was certainly hollowed out of the rocks in all the retreats combined. Ironically, ecclesiastical art climaxed in the 11th century, just when the Christian era was drawing to a close. Yet Christian communities, religious as well as secular, persisted under tolerant Seljuk and Osmanli rulers up to the exchange with the Moslems of Greece in 1922.

The Frenchman Lucas wrote the first report about the hitherto unknown rock churches in 1705. Charles Texier and John Hamilton passed through Cappadocia in the 1830s before exploring Boğazkale, starting the fashion of books and paintings depicting a fantasy come true.

Churches, Citadels and Cities

Ürgüp is the geographical and touristic center from which to explore the "villages of the realm of the dead." The hotels might, however, be booked out by tours, which also provide the transport essential within so wide an area. The private motorist should consider hiring a guide through the local tourist office, about $20 per day. Expert advice, in fluent if slightly over-enthusiastic English, helps in programming the sites according to the time available.

Sightseeing begins in some hotels straight from the windows, which open on a cataclysmic scenery. A serrated white cliff is riddled with man-made holes whose fragile masonry walls have often crumbled away, stripping the dwelling of their protective screens; not unlike the aftermath of some terrorist bombing, when the interior of houses are laid bare. But here the troglodytes simply remove the mess and dig deeper into the rock. The caves as well as some giant cones and chimneys in the nearby villages are still inhabited.

7 km. (4 miles) northwest, the valley of Göreme, which by itself warrants a visit to Cappadocia, is the only one within walking distance—by the hardy at a pinch. Near the ticket office for the "Open-air Museum" is a parking lot, as before all the main sites which open from 8:30 to 5.

The oldest rock church dates from the 4th century, but no frescoes are earlier than the 8th, when the geometrical designs applied directly to the rockface gradually gave way to scenes from the New Testament and the lives of the more popular saints painted on plaster, which provided the flat surface for more sophisticated motifs. The steep rock to the left of the entrance housed a six-story convent, kitchen and refectory below, a cruciform chapel on the third, with the cells of the nuns connected by tunnels above; large millstones lay ready to block the narrow passages in time of danger. Opposite is a monastery on the same plan, close to the Elmalı Kilise, the Church with the Apple, probably named after a vanished orchard. Relatively new, only 12th century, the polychrome scenes from the life of Christ on a dark-blue background have been restored under the auspices of U.N.E.S.C.O. like those in the other main churches. But to prevent defacing and mutilation by man, a more insidious danger than time or humidity, these churches have to be kept locked and are opened only to groups or by special permission.

At the rear of the outcrop of rocks, the Barbara Kilise is decorated with early, red designs and 11th-century frescoes of St. Barbara above the baptistry font. The Yılanlı (Serpent) Kilise might be named after St. George's dragon or the serpent coils round the damned. A bevy of saints adorns the two sections, one barrel-vaulted, the other flat-roofed, accessible from a kitchen by a narrow passage; St. Thomas and local St. Basil flank rather surprisingly a half-female, half-male figure. The 11th-century Karanlık (Dark) Kilise—bring a flashlight—is lit only through a small orifice in the narthex, reached by a spiral staircase from a refectory. The frescoes are among the finest, especially the Christ, in vivid colors on a dark-blue background, in the center of the main apse. The Çarıklı (Sandal) Kilise, named after the footprint below the Ascension fresco, is distinguished by four domes over the three apses, separated by two columns. The figures are large and elongated, the colors warm. Shrines and habitats of sorts line the narrowing valley to the head, where sightseeing bears an uncanny resemblance to mountaineering.

Outside the fenced-in site, near the car park on the right side of the road to Avcılar, is the largest and most interesting church, the 10th-century Tokatlı (Knocker) Kilise. Probably named after a knocker, a more likely implement than the one in the official handout's translation "Church with the Buckle." The dominant colors in the narthex are red and green, while dark blue prevails in the three apses. The usual cycle from the Annunciation to the Resurrection is complemented by scenes from the life of St. Basil. The restoration has left blanks where the original had disappeared, a practice laudable for the purist, but less appreciated by the tourist.

A path to the right leads to the Church of the Madonna, while the 11th-century El Nazar Kilise, with polychrome frescoes, stands in a nearby orchard. The 12th-century Saklı (Hidden) Kilise, fittingly difficult to find and discovered only in 1958, has been carved out of the rock in no recognizable style.

In the vicinity of the troglodyte village of Avcılar are five more rock churches, including the Sergeants Cave, dedicated in the 10th century to St. John, hollowed into the semicircular cliff of Çavuşin. Zelve, to the right, is a close second to Göreme, but the ghostly white of the ravines and caves deepens in this monastic complex to a hellish red. At the entrance rises a small minaret, as fairly recently the central ridge divided the valley into a Christian and Moslem sector, mosque and church hewn out of the same rock back to back. The Moslems remained only briefly in sole occupation after the Christians were expelled in 1922; rockfalls necessitated complete evacuation in the 1960s.

Avanos, on the north bank of the Kızılırmak, abounds with tourist shops selling onyx jewelry and pottery. Here was the northernmost point of the supermarvel's triangle till the opening up of the underground city of Özkonak, 20 km. (12 miles) northwest, which has been hailed as the eighth Wonder of the World, as it supposedly sheltered 60,000 refugees. Being somewhat off the most convenient circuit, it is omitted by conducted tours, which have plenty of scope in the two others, more extensively cleared of rubble and electrically lit. The remaining five towns located so far are not yet accessible.

The return along the western branch traverses vineyards that produce excellent grapes and a pleasant white wine. After the Seljuk Sarı Han, the Yellow Caravanserai, in ruins but for the fine portals, every bend in the road reveals stunning views of the rock citadels. First prize to Uçhisar (Castle of the End), an extraordinary honeycombed escarpment that dominates the horizon. The village stands at the edge of an awesome erosion basin of fairy chimneys and other Cappadocian phantasmagoria. The smaller citadel of Kale (Fortress) rises from a terrace above the village, while the higher Sap Kalese is a 300 meters (984 ft.) ridge. Both were strongholds of feudal chiefs in the Middle Ages and may be climbed by rather strenuous interior staircases. 7 km. (4 miles) before Ürgüp, the citadel of Ortahisar (Median Castle) is hewn out of a gigantic serrated sugarloaf. Here, too, it is possible to climb to the railed-in top, but the cave dwellers have been removed to safer accommodations below.

The road south from Ürgüp passes Mustafapaşa, restored as the center
of a new tourist development area; then the Monastery of St. Stephen near
the village of Cemil; the mosque and mausoleum at Taşkinpaşa; before
following the willow-shaded Soğanlı River into the valley of this name (50
km., 31 miles). Why it is called "Of Onions" is a mystery none of the inhabitants seems able to solve; there are, moreover, no fields of this useful
plant, nor are the 60 rock churches distinguished by that shape. Three
shrines may be singled out for a visit: the Tahtalı (Framed) Kilise, from
the bands framing the damaged frescos; the Karabaş (Blackhead) Kilise,
no disparagement to the skin texture of the saints, but a darkening of their
haloes from the candle smoke; and the Canavarlı (Monster) Kilise, after
St. George's dragon.

Depending on the state of exhaustion—and several Soganlı churches
necessitate steep climbs—sightseeing may be maximized by taking on the
return the first branch left, 23 km. (14 miles) to Derinkuyu. While in the
rock churches and dwellings man made use of nature, he succeeded in
mastering a hostile environment by constructing the underground cities.
The Greek historian Xenophon mentions Cappadocian underground
dwellings as early as 401 B.C., but only under the impetus of the Arab raids
from the 7th to the 10th centuries did human ingenuity create this amazing
underworld, with ominous overtones of the shape of things to come. Eight
spacious floors, each offering accommodation for 20,000 people, were
carved into the bowels of the earth, a labyrinth of chapels, dormitories,
stores and cellars, where the descent to the next level is often difficult to
make out. The narrow entrance, sealed off by a millstone-shaped rock, was
uncovered only in the 1950s. A central airshaft assures perfect ventilation
all the 120 meters (394 ft.) so far opened up. As for the remaining 20 floors
proudly claimed by local guides, to see is to believe. Sloping corridors and
steps connect the floors, self-contained but for cemeteries and kitchens,
spaced on every second; smoke was not allowed to escape, for fear of be-
traying the hideout. The tuff guaranteed an equitable dryness, subsidiary
ventilation ducts kept the air as fresh on the lowest as on the highest level;
interior wells provided water.

The 10 km. (6 miles) tunnel north to the underground city of Kaymaklı
has not yet been unblocked, but the easily accessible three floors should
not be missed, to deepen the admiration for such feats of engineering.

Nevşehir and Beyond

Nevşehir, ancient Nissa, 20 km. (12 miles) north on Route 765, the region's largest town, clings to the slopes below a ruined Seljuk fortress.
Likewise from the 13th century is the Kaya Cami, but the town owes its
prosperity to the Grand Vizir Damat Ibrahim Pasha, who endowed his
birthplace in 1726 with yet another Kurşunlu (Lead-domed) Cami, surrounded by medrese, hospice and library. The solid square houses, built
of the light local stone, often stand in pleasant gardens.

If Cappadocia was the sole goal of the trip, the quickest return to Ankara is north via Hacıbektaş. Pink and white mushroom rocks are scattered
along Route 765 the 19 km. (12 miles) to Gülşehir, where the Vizir Kara
Mehmet Pasha constructed a rare Osmanli Baroque complex, mosque,
medrese, hamam and six fountains, next to some Byzantine ruins. 14 km.
(9 miles) left (west) are the Tuzla salt mines which supply most of Anatolia.

With a little more time to spare, it is certainly worthwhile to take Route 300 southwest of Nevşehir for the 73 km. (45 miles) to Akarsay. Of the three caravanserais along this part of the Seljuk Empire's main artery, the Oresin and Alay Hans feature the usual handsome portals, but only Alaeddin Keykubat's Ağzikara Han, on the left side 15 km. (9 miles) before Aksaray, has been restored to a semblance of the splendor when it was opened in 1239.

4 km. (2 miles) further west, after the Mamasın Reservoir formed by the damming up of the Melendiz, a tree-shaded brook, the road left (southeast) returns into fairyland. The first violet gray fairy chimneys appear at the village of Selime, where Selime Sultan is buried in an octagonal türbe. The frescoes in the three-naved, barrel-vaulted basilica are late Byzantine, in black and orange tones. The left branch at the road fork leads to Guzelyurt, where yet another large concentration of rock needles and pillars is being opened up; a partly unpaved road connects thence eastward with Route 765, south of Derinkuyu. For the time being the right branch suffices, as in the Valley of Ihlara (34 km., 21 miles) man has once again combined with nature in the approved Cappadocian tradition. The Melendiz has carved a rift into the tuff cliffs, which rise sheer up to 1,150 meters (3,773 ft.), pierced not by a mere 365 but thousands of churches, chapels and caves. The best view can be obtained from the restaurant terrace, from which 285 easy steps descend the wall-like rock to the bottom of the canyon, a green gash in the barren highland below Mount Melendiz (2,935 meters, 9,629 ft.). Byzantine Peristrema is still idyllic with poplars and wild olive trees shading the slow-moving water, along which the 20 main churches are crumbling away. The Sümbüllü (Hyacinth) Kilise is singled out for its poetic name, but its frescoes are as badly defaced as in all the other churches, mainly by Greek graffiti and thus, sad to say, by Christians before their expulsion in 1922.

Thanks to the Melendiz, which loses itself in the salt marshes of the Tuz Gölü, Aksaray is surrounded by an oasis in the baked plain. Not quite up to the standards of Pisa's Leaning Tower, the Eğri (Crooked) Minaret, a reddish brick structure, has leant alarmingly for almost as long, since 1236, over the low houses on the river banks. The main monuments date from the 15th century, the Ulu (Great) Cami dominating the main square, the Ibrahim Bey and Zinciriye Medreses.

The Aksaray bypass is one of Anatolia's main road junctions, of E5 (Route 750) north-south from Ankara to the Mediterranean near Adana with Route 300 east-west from Kayseri to Konya. The 214 km. (133 miles) north to Ankara are mainly a four-lane highway, skirting for the first 125 km. (78 miles) the immense expanse of the Tuz Gölü in the very center of Anatolia. The salt lake is almost dry in summer, leaving a shimmering residue much whiter than the notorious North African shotts, but becomes a seemingly limitless sheet of shallow water after the winter rains. The 69 km. (43 miles) south to the junction with Route 330 from Niğde cross featureless steppe, but another 42 km. (26 miles) further on, at Ulukısla, the monotony is at last broken by the towering peaks of the Taurus Range, when E5 rises to the Gülek Pass (Gates of Cilicia) before the winding descent to the Mediterranean.

It would be hard to tell the difference between steppe and desert, at least in summer, for the 142 km. (88 miles) of Route 300 southwest to Konya. At the outskirts of the Aksaray oasis, the branch right (northwest) stops after 18 km. (11 miles) at Yeşilova, where the five levels of the Acemhöyük excavations start in the early Bronze Age and finish with the charred mud walls of the two 13th-century B.C. palaces on a hill.

There is one more oasis, round another Sultan Han (39 km., 24 miles), needless to say built by the indefatigable Alaeddin Keykubat in 1229. It looms most impressively from afar, as the towers have been expertly restored. Then there is literally nothing till the junction with four-lane Route 715 in the fertile fields round Konya.

Niğde and Southwest

The quickest connection from Cappadocia to the Mediterranean is Route 765 south from Derinkuyu for 50 km. (31 miles) to Niğde. The steppe is, for a change, riddled with volcanic blisters till the green valley flanked by volcanic peaks, where Hittite Nahita eventually emerged as Seljuk Niğde. The town flourished in the 13th century when Sultan Keykubat built the Alaeddin Cami. It proudly bears its three domes, exquisitely pure in line, but it is more famous for the human figures on the portal. A century later, the Mongol Sungur Bay constructed another mosque, whose portals are distinguished by unusual Gothic features (rose window, etc). The inevitable fortress looks down from the heights; it's the earliest Seljuk monument, dating from the end of the 11th century. Subtle lacy stone carvings adorn the Hüdavent Hatun Türbe (1312), and the charming white medrese (Akmedrese, 1409), built by the Karaman princes, is now a small regional museum.

9 km. (5 miles) northwest is the 10th-century church of Eski Gümüş, featuring exceptionally well-preserved frescoes; the adjoining monastery is hollowed out of the rock. 14 km. (9 miles) south along Route 330 the small town of Bor possesses, naturally, an Alaeddin Cami, a 16th-century covered bazaar and bath, but more interesting is the Roman aqueduct, pool and hot springs at Tyana nearby, which is now Kemerhisar and was the Hittite's Tuvana.

Route 330 joins E5 (Route 750) southeast, to branch off again west through the endless steppe to Ereğli, ancient Heraklea of Cappadocia, where the First Crusade was victorious in 1097, while Christian reinforcements suffered crushing defeats by the Seljuk and Danishment Turks in 1101. The massacre of a French contingent was quickly followed by the slaughter of a larger Franco-German army, accompanied by the Dowager Margravine Ida of Austria who, according to legend, became the mother of the Moslem hero Imad ad-Din Zengi, grandfather of Saladin; however, it is more likely that she was trampled to death in the panic.

At Ivriz, 12 km. (7 miles) southeast in the Taurus foothills, the neo-Hittites carved remarkable reliefs of a fertility god and a king. Then it is 148 monotonous km. (92 miles) to Konya, the only relief afforded by the deep-green uncanny lake of Karapınar in an extinct crater and later on a vast marsh to the south, providing excellent grazing for huge herds of cattle.

Konya

Anatolia's holy city lies at an altitude of 1,017 meters (3,350 ft.) in a large, well-watered oasis 262 km. (163 miles) due south of Ankara. With well over 2,000,000 inhabitants, it is Turkey's fourth largest town, its industrial suburbs sprawling ever wider into the surrounding orchards.

One unappetizing explanation of the etymology of Konya's name drags in Perseus and the slaying of Medusa, whose severed head he nailed to a pillar, thereby creating an ikon of sorts, whence the name of Ikonion. But most accounts have Perseus stashing the hideous trophy away in his pack, and hauling it out only in order to terrify his enemies. Though perhaps not the first town to emerge from the Flood, as claimed in Phrygian myths, the excavations in the Alaeddin hill in the center of town are proof of the site's occupation as early as the 7th millennium B.C. A Hittite settlement was followed by an important Phrygian town. When St. Paul and St. Barnabus were expelled from Antiochia of Pisidia, they made their way to Claudiconium (renamed in honor of the Emperor Claudius) and delivered sermons there in the years 47, 50 and 53. The prosperous Roman city hosted one of the first church councils, in 235. Reverting to the plain Greek name, Ikonion suffered Arab raids from the 7th to the 9th centuries, was taken by the Seljuks and promoted capital by Kılıç Arslan I in 1097 after the fall of Nikaea to the First Crusade. The reign of Alaeddin Keykubat (1219–36) was the time of glory, soon followed by the disintegration of the Sultanate of Rum, domination by the Karamanoğlu dynasty and incorporation into the Osmanli Empire by Mehmet the Conqueror in 1467.

Mevlana the Great Mystic

Celaleddin (Jalal al-Din) was born in present-day Afghanistan in 1207, son of a renowned theologian who fled with his family before Genghis Khan's hordes and after wandering for ten years accepted the invitation of Sultan Alaeddin Keykubat. Celaleddin, then 22, studied the philosophies and religions of the cosmopolitan and tolerant Seljuk capital, until 1244, when he came under the influence of Şems of Tabriz, a mysterious, unorthodox and wild preacher, and became a mystic. Şems taught that love transcends the mind and that intellect is narrow and restrictive. Their relationship has been likened to that between Socrates and Plato, but Celaleddin became totally dependent on his moral and spiritual guide—whose name means Sun, the sun of enlightenment, symbol of humanity and embodiment of God—and entered a period of ecstasy, poetic creativity, immersion in music and in the *sema,* mystic whirling.

When Şems disappeared, probably murdered, Celaleddin gave vent to his passionate sorrow in a collection of odes, the *Divan-e Şems-e Tabriz,* forming part of the *Divan-e Kebir* of 40,380 couplets. The fervid lyrical verses are considered to be the first sonnet sequence in world literature. The slightly shorter *Mesnevi* was, like his other work, dictated in Persian to a disciple Hüsameddin, while Celaleddin was performing the *sema* to the accompaniment of a reed flute, an expression of lament for Şems. It is the only philosophical system formulated in poetry that ranks close to the Koran in Islamic literature, and earned the great mystic the Persian title of Mevlana (Grand Master), to which Rumi was added to evoke the Sultanate extending over the lands of the Second Rome.

Mevlana's monastic Sufism maintains that man is not only God's creation, but also God's reflection, and that the individual who loves is part of God. Whoever has temporarily parted from God yearns to return. Reason is nought compared to love. This unique synthesis of poetry and philosophy viewed formal institutions as restrictive and wished to transcend national as well as religious divisions.

Mevlana was a firm believer in the virtues of music and of its corollary, the dance, as a means of abandoning oneself to God's love and freeing oneself from earthly bondage. He considered the whirling pattern of motion as being both the exterior representation of the sphere and the interior representation of the soul's state of agitation. It is of course by this more spectacular external aspect that the world has come to know of the existence of the *mevlevi* dervishes, if not of the theologian himself and his teachings.

Mevlana died on December 17, 1273, and was succeeded by Hüsameddin Çelebi, followed in turn by Mevlana's son, Sultan Veled, who organized the dervish order.

The *tekke* (monastery) and türbe of Mevlana are situated at one end of Konya's main avenue, Mevlana Caddesi. A blue band adorned with Arabic inscriptions runs round the conical drum of turquoise glazed tiles, a startling yet pleasing color combination visible from far away. The small lead-topped domes set over the dervishes' cubicles form an honor guard around the garden with its marble flagstones leading up to the entrance. There are 18 flagstones, the mystic number of the sect. The *tekke* became a museum in 1927, but Mevlana's tomb has remained a place of worship, in a profusion of carved woodwork, gold and silver work, tiles, calligraphic ornamentation, precious rugs and rich fabrics. Vivid reconstructions illustrate the founder's and the dervishes' way of life in their former cells.

The square room that you enter first is the Koran reading room. On the walls hang framed examples of distinguished calligraphy, including one specimen executed by a great devotee of this art, Sultan Mahmut. The translation of the quotation above the silver door would be: "He who enters incomplete here will leave complete." On the right and left lie the tombs of the most illustrious disciples, those who were closest to Mevlana, 65 in all. The tomb of his eldest son reposes next to his own.

In one of the showcases containing the manuscripts that the founder dictated as the inspiration came to him are the first 18 verses of the *Mesnevi*, written in his own hand. The intricately wrought chandelier has 18 branches. The mausoleum itself dates from the 13th century, while the rest of the monastery was built later.

Mevlana's enormous tomb rests on a pedestal. At its head are his black turban and the curious cylindrical headgear of the sect. Two silver steps lead up to the platform; they are the sacred stairway. Believers press their faces against it as a sign of devotion. A brocaded cover embroidered with gold thread and weighing almost 50 kg. (90 lb.) covers the biers of Mevlana and his son. They used to be covered by the rug that now hangs on the wall in the back. Sultan Mehmet II was responsible for the extraordinary cover that has replaced the rug. At the foot of the tomb, the coffin of Mevlana's father stands vertical, his white funerary turban on top. The quotations from the Koran are embedded in the sarcophagus with the exquisite precision and mastery of technique that characterize Seljuk art at its best.

The opulence of the wall decorations defies description. In the music room, the ceiling cross-beam has a chain of marble links hanging from it. These links are carved out of a single block and the attached ball has been wrought with typical Seljuk artistry, allowing for a second ball inside, completely detached, on which the artist carved four of Mevlana's verses.

The Rite of the Whirling Dervishes

This famous ceremony symbolizes man's love for God; extremely detailed and specific directions govern every slightest pattern and gesture in this ritual dance, the ultimate purpose of which is to effect a mystic union. The instrumentalists and singers sit opposite the floor on which the dancers perform. The Sheik's pole stands at one end, and an imaginary line connecting this pole with the center of the entrance to the room represents the most direct route to union with God. This line must never be crossed. The Sheik incarnates Mevlevism, and is the representative of the Islamic faith at the ceremony. The pole is red, which is the color of union and ceremony.

The dervishes' ritual starts with a gathering for prayers and meditation in the room off the music room in the monastery. The narrative portion of the ritual begins when the musicians, the dancers, and the Sheik enter the great hall through the wrought-iron door and have taken their places. The flutes intone a melody expressing the desire for mystic union, and this is the signal for the whirling dances to begin. In the center of the floor the Sheik and the dervishes whirl three times to the rhythm of the music.

The dervishes' costumes are symbolic: the conical hat represents a tombstone, the jacket is the tomb itself, and the skirt is the funerary shroud. The right side of the room represents the known, tangible world; the left is the unknown and invisible part of it.

Each whirling dance consists of three stages: the first is the knowledge of God; the second, the seeing of God; and the third, union with God. At the end of the first stage, the Sheik returns to his pole and the dervishes resume their places. The main part of the ritual now commences. The dervishes remove their jackets, signifying that they are thus shedding earthly ties and escaping from their graves. While this is going on, the Sheik performs certain steps near the pole, and each dancer proceeds to follow him. The leading dervish passes in front of the Sheik and kisses his hand. Each man in turn then presents himself to the Sheik, and a new whirling dance starts up. As they whirl, the dervishes extend their right hands in prayer, while their left hands point toward the floor. The symbolic meaning of these gestures is that "what we receive from God, we give to man; we ourselves possess nothing." As the dervishes whirl, they also rotate around the room like the astral bodies. Their whirling motion is the symbol of the rotation of the universe in the presence of God. It is also the means of attaining that form of ecstasy that leads to the soul's bliss and a full awareness of the divine presence. The leading dervish directs the patterns of the other dancers, who follow the gestures he makes with his feet and head.

In the final part of the dervishes' dance, the Sheik, incarnating Mevlana, joins the dancers and whirls in their midst. When he finishes, he slowly returns to the pole, and the dances end.

The annual commemorative rites, mainly the *sema* accompanied by mystical music, as well as a symposium on Mevlana's life and philosophy, last for a week culminating in the Nuptial Night of December 17, when Mevlana found union with God. Two galleries run the length of all four sides of the music room; the lower one is for the men, the upper one reserved for the ladies, who are screened off by a wooden latticework partition.

Viewing Moslem Art

The Selimiye opposite was started by the heir to the throne in 1558, when he was governor of Konya, and finished after he had become Sultan Selim II. The style is reminiscent of the Fatih Cami in Istanbul, with soaring arches and windows surrounding the base of the dome. To the right of Hükümet Caddesi, the central avenue leading from Mevlana's Tekke to the hill of the ancient acropolis, now the Alaeddin Tepe, the Şerafettin Cami was begun by the Seljuks and completed by the Osmanlis. The ravages of time and fire necessitated extensive restoration in the mid-19th century. Further back is the Şems Cami and Türbe, while almost across the road stands Konya's oldest mosque, the Iplikcı (Thread) Cami, dating from 1202, evocative of the Arab style.

The Alaeddin Cami crowns the hill that now bears the name of the great Seljuk ruler, who in 1220 finished the construction started by Sultan Mesut I, 70 years earlier. Designed by an architect from Damascus, the mosque is of the Syrian style, unusual for Anatolia. Recent extensive restorations preserved the original magnificence, setting off the lovely 12th-century pulpit against the forest of 42 columns taken from Roman temples. The decagonal türbe in the courtyard contains the remains of Kılıc Arslan and seven subsequent Seljuk rulers. Most of the hill is taken up by a park and a café that affords good views of the town. Below are the scanty remains of the Seljuk palace, two venerable stumps of walls. The city has somehow deemed it expedient to throw an unsightly concrete shelter over them.

Across the circular Alaeddin Bulvari there beckons one of the world's most exquisite portals, the intricately carved marble entrance of what is left of the Karatay Medrese, the theological seminary founded by Emir Celaleddin Karatay in 1251. No better setting could have been chosen for the Ceramics Museum, as the dome is lined with tiles, blue predominating on white, and the effect is one of dazzling brilliance. The frieze is in an excellent state of preservation, while the hunting scenes on the rare figurative tiles from the Kubadabat Palace at Beyşehir show the influence of Persia on Seljuk art. Each student was assigned a small cubicle. For their astronomy courses they had only to scan the heavens through the dome's central opening, which also provided light for the study hall. In the middle of the room, a fountain spills into the basin, and "the gentle sound of the water soothed the future scholars' minds and hearts, while the lightly shaded blues of the tiles roundabout were restful to their eyes." Many inscriptions covered the walls as an ever-present reminder of the fragility of human judgment and of the condition of mankind's knowledge.

An anti-clockwise walk along Alaeddin Bulvari leads to another splendid portal of geometric and floral designs, opening into the 13th-century Ince Minare Medrese (Slender Minaret Seminary), decapitated by lightning. This is the Museum of Stone and Wood Carvings, featuring amongst others representative bas-reliefs of the Seljuk period. Further along is the Sırçalı Medrese, opened in 1242 as a school for Islamic jurisprudence. The lavish tile decoration provides a dignified frame for the Museum of Funerary Monuments. The small Catholic Church of St. Paul next door proves that Konya has remained as tolerant as in its Seljuk heyday.

On the opposite side of the Sırçalı are Roman catacombs and a mosaic, on the way to Larende Caddesi where another magnificent portal is all that remains of the 13th-century Sahip Ata complex, next to the Archeological Museum. Exhibits start from the Bronze Age, but the main displays are from Ikonion and Claudiconium; outstanding is a 3rd-century B.C. marble showing the 12 labors of Herakles. Close by, the Ethnographical Museum continues the story of this very ancient town with Islamic art, and the emphasis is on embroidery, carpets, rugs, keys and weapons.

Carpets and rugs still provide the main interest in the bazaar, off lower Hükümet Caddesi. Though today hardly justifying Marco Polo's comment that here were "the most beautiful carpets in the world," colors and designs are pleasing. The bazaar is flanked by the Aziziye Cami, dating from 1676, with two short minarets topped off by a kind of loggia with a Florentine flavor. This mosque dates from the Osmanli period, as do the Kapı Cami and the Piri Paşa, nearby. Among the numerous lesser mosques is the Hatuniye Cami of 1213, and among the many türbes are those of Ali Gav, Fakih Dede, Kalender Baba, Kesikbaş, Pir Hüsseyin Bey and Ulaşbaba. The Koyunoğlu Museum at Topralık Caddesi has private collections on Natural History and Anatolian Civilizations as well as Ethnographical objects.

By the four-lane beginning of Route 715 to Ankara is yet another of those fabulous Seljuk portals, the entrance to the ruined Horozlu Han. At Sille, 8 km. (5 miles) northwest, St. Helena, mother of Constantine the Great, built in 327 a small church which was restored in the last century. Frescoed rock chapels overlook the shores of a tiny artificial lake.

Phrygia

94 km. (57 miles) southwest of Ankara, plus 12 km. (7 miles) after branching right (north) off E23, close to the village of Yassıhöyük are the remains of Gordion, which was inhabited from 6300 B.C. to A.D. 189. When it was the Phrygian capital the royal palace stood on the low hill, while the town spread from below the fortified terrace to the banks of the Sakarya. The surrounding plain is pimpled with some 90 tumuli, the largest covering the Tomb of King Midas. A well-lit tunnel, some 70 meters (230 ft.) long, has been cut through the mound to the burial chamber (6.20 by 5.15 meters, 20 by 17 ft.), framed with cedar and juniper beams. When the tomb was opened, the skeleton of a rather short man, aged about 60, lay on a large table. The funeral artifacts and bronze fibulae were taken to the Ankara Museum of Anatolian Civilizations; the small local museum displays only a minor miscellany of pottery and copper objects.

Besides the Phrygian bonnet, inexplicably chosen as a symbol of the French Revolution, we owe to the Phrygians two well-known expressions: the Gordion Knot and the Midas Touch. A poor farmer named Gordios fulfilled an oracle predicting that the first man to enter the gates of the ancient city would become its ruler. In renamed Gordion the new king dedicated in gratitude a chariot to the gods, tying the yoke and shaft together with a knot so stout that another oracle could safely declare that whoever was to rule Asia would have first to untie it. Alexander the Great found the challenge irresistible and, deviating from his march of conquest in 334 B.C., he resolutely sliced through the knot with his sword blade.

Midas, son of Gordios, succeeded in 738 B.C. According to Herodotos, he preferred Pan's flute to Apollo's lyre. Considerably put out, the god of music caused donkey's ears to sprout from Midas' head. Not unnaturally, the unfortunate king strove to conceal his deformity. His barber was sworn to silence, which the loquacious ancester of Figaro circumvented by digging a hole in the ground; after whispering his terrible secret to the earth, he filled in the hole. Reeds sprang up on the spot and murmured in the breeze, "King Midas has asses' ears."

Having learned nothing from this encounter with the Olympians, Midas entertained Dionysos, who promised in return for hospitality to grant a wish. Midas rashly asked that everything he touched be transformed into gold. No sooner said than done. But though richer than Croesus, he was starving as even his food turned to gold. Dionysos prescribed a plunge into the Paktolos to get rid of this over-generous gift. Since that time the river has been flowing with gold, to the joy of the Lydians downstream. Defeated by the Cimmerians in 695 B.C., Midas committed suicide, supposedly by drinking bull's blood, an unusual end to an unusual life.

Further along E23, 136 km. (84 miles) from Ankara, including the 16 km. (10 miles) left (southeast) to Ballıhissar, is the site of ancient Pessinos, another temple-state, where the priest-kings celebrated the elaborate pageantry connected with the worship of the Earth-Mother Kybele and her companion Attis, who had been assimilated to immeasurably old Anatolian deities. Their temple is as ruined as the rest of this Phrygian cult center.

Closer to Eskişehir, 115 km. (71 miles) south via Seyitgazi, Midas Şehri, the oddly named City of Midas, offers only a tenuous connection with the Phrygian king. A third Yazılıkaya—not to be confused with the more famous Hittite rock monuments—consists of Phrygian inscriptions and rock tombs.

PRACTICAL INFORMATION FOR
CENTRAL ANATOLIA

TOURIST OFFICES. There are local tourist offices in the following towns: **Kayseri,** Hunat Camii Yani (tel. 192 95); **Kırşehir,** Aşıkpaşa Cad. (tel. 1416); **Konya,** Mevlana Cad. 21 (tel. 110 74); **Nevşehir,** Lale Cad. 22 (tel. 1137); **Niğde,** Istiklal Cad. (tel. 112 61); **Sivas,** Vilayet Konağı (tel. 135 35); **Ürgüp,** Kayseri Cad. 37 (tel. 10 59).

SPECIAL EVENTS. June. Konya Rose Festival, early in the month; Tourist Festival at Nevşehir, late in the month. **August.** Hacıbektaş Commemoration Ceremonies, mid-August. **September.** Ahi Evran Festival at Kırşehir, early September; Hittite Festival at Çorum, mid-September. **October.** Folk Poets' Contest, horse races and javelin throwing at Konya, October 20–30. **December.** Mevlana Commemoration Ceremonies at Konya, early December.

WHEN TO COME. Spring and fall are best, though the climate of the plateau is dry and fairly sunny throughout the year, which relieves the heat of summer and the cold of winter.

HOTELS AND RESTAURANTS. Standards in this region have risen dramatically over the last few years, with new establishments offering excellent value and comfort. Others are still very basic with unpredictable plumbing, but the rewards of visiting this area are great.

Aksaray. *Ihlara* (M), Kiliçaslan Mah. (tel. 118 42). 64 rooms. In town. *Orhan Ağaçh* (M), (tel. 149 10). 87 rooms and mini-suites; pool. At the intersection of E5 and Route 300.

Amasya. *Turban Amasya* (M), Emniyet Cad. (tel. 4054). 34 rooms. On the banks of the Yeşilirmak.

Avanos. *Venessa* (M), Orta Mah. (tel. 1201). 72 rooms. At the bridge over the Kızılırmak. *Zelve* (M), Kenan Evren Cad. (tel. 1524). 25 rooms. The new hotels *Irmak, Epok, Altinyaze, Büyük Avanos,* and *Erkoy* are all of a high standard.

Boğazköy. *Asikoğlu* restaurant has 8 hotel rooms, simple but clean.

Bolu. *Koru* (E), Ömerler Köyü. (tel. 2528). 128 rooms. Motel, on the slopes of Bolu Dağ. *Emniyet* (M), Ayrilik Çeşmesi Mey. (tel. 12075). 27 rooms, 21 with shower. Motel. *Kaytur* (M). 70 rooms. Mountain lodge at 2,100 m. (6,890 ft.) near the Bolu Dağ peak. *Yurdaer* (M), Hürriyet Cad. 1 (tel. 2903). 50 rooms. *Çizmeci* (I), Kiliçaslan Köyü (tel. 1066). 30 rooms, 20 with shower. Motel. *Menekşe* (I), Hürriyet Cad. 1 (tel. 1522). 45 rooms, in town.

Cihanbeyli. *Agabeyli Çeşmebası Motel* (M). Between Ankara and Konya.

Çorum. *Turban Çorum* (M), Inönü Cad. 80 (tel. 185 15). 59 rooms. *Kolağası* (I), Inönü Cad. 97 (tel. 119 71). 46 rooms.

Gülsehir. *Belediye Motel* (I). 8 rooms. *Gülsehir,* (M) 20 rooms. A new hotel set in pretty surroundings on outskirts of town.

Haymana. *Cimcime* (M), Kemalpaşa Cad. 25 (tel. 1072). 34 rooms. *Saraçoğlu* (I), Hamam Sok. 4 (tel. 1057). 36 rooms, no private showers.

Kartalkaya. 2,200 meters (7,218 ft.) altitude; cable lift, wintersports. *Turban Köroğlu* (E). 270 rooms; indoor pool, disco. *Kartal Oberj* (M), (tel. 3572). 80 rooms. Pool.

Kaynaşli. *Kaynaşlı Motel* (I). 16 rooms. Restaurant.

Kayseri. *Hattat* (M), Istanbul Cad. 1 (tel. 193 31). 70 rooms. *Turan* (M), Turan Cad. 8 (tel. 119 68). 70 rooms. Both have good restaurants. *Terminal* (I), Istanbul Cad. 76. 18 rooms, 10 with shower. Also possible are—*Divan, Ipek Palas, Kent, Sinan,* all (I).
Restaurants. *Cumhuriyet,* Mayis Cad. *Iskender Kebap Salonü,* Mayis Cad. 5.

Kizilcahamam. *Çam* (M), (tel. 1065). 39 rooms. Superbly situated in Milli Park. Thermal pools and top class restaurant. *Hotel Kaplica* (M) is comfortable and friendly with restaurant, bar, and adjoining thermal pools.

Konya. *Konya* (M), Mevlana Alanı (tel. 210 03). 29 rooms. Thermal bath, sauna. *Ozkaynak Park* (M), Otogar Karsısı (tel. 133 770). 90 rooms. *Sema* (M), Yeni Meram Yolu (tel. 171 510). 30 rooms. Off center, good restaurant. *Dergah* (I), Mevlana Cad. (tel. 111 197). 43 rooms, 35 with shower. *Otogar* (I). 33 rooms, 27 with shower. At bus terminal. *Şahin* (I), Hükümet Alanı (tel. 113 350). 44 rooms.

Restaurants. Try the local specialties: *tandir kebab, etli pide* (meat pizza) and *peynirlipide* (cheese pizza). *Fuar* (M), Konya Fuari (Luna Park). Pleasant outdoor dining. *Konak Lokantasi* (I). *Merkez* (I), near Hükümet Meydanı. *Catal,* (I) Mevlana Cad. Simple and good.

Nevşehir. *Göreme* (M), Bankalar Cad. 16 (tel. 1706). 72 rooms. Closed mid-Oct. to mid-Mar. *Hisar* (M), (tel. 3857). 28 rooms. Close to bus station. *Orsan Kapadokya* (M), Kayseri Cad. (tel. 1035). 80 rooms. Pool. *Lale* (I), Belediye Yani (tel. 1797). 28 rooms. *Viva* (I). Kayseri Cad. (tel. 1326). 24 rooms.

Niğde. *Merkez Turist* (I). 32 rooms.

Ortahisar. *Motel Paris* (I), Aksaray Mev. (tel. 1099). 25 rooms. Pool, restaurant.

Pinarbaşi. *Yağlıcı Tur-Tes* (M), (tel. 1010). 15 rooms. Restaurant; on route 300, east of the town.

Sivas. *Köşk* (M), Atatürk Cad. 11 (tel. 111 50). 44 rooms. *Sultan* (I), Belediye Sok. (tel. 129 86). 30 rooms, 7 with bath. *Belediye, Belgin, Kent, Konyak, Talat* and *Tirkec* are (I) hotels along Atatürk Cad.; all have showers, but are mainly remarkable for the number of fittings not working. **Restaurant.** *Cicek.*

Suluova. *Saraçoğlu Muzaffer Turistic Tesisleri* (I). 15 rooms. Restaurant.

Sungurlu. 30 km. (19 miles) from Boğazkale. *Hattuşaş* (I). 30 rooms, 12 with shower. Very simple. *Hitit Motel* (I), Ankara Samsum Yolu (tel. 1409). 16 rooms with bathrooms. Gardens. Swimming pool.

Tokat. *Plevne* (I), Gaziosmanpaşa Bul. 71 (tel. 2207). 18 rooms, 12 with shower. *Turist* (I), Cumhuriyet Mey. (tel. 1610). 30 rooms, 5 with shower. Even less comfort.

Uçhisar. *Kaya* (M). Uçhisar Istanbul (tel. 1007). 60 rooms. Pool, good restaurant; stunning views. Club Méditerranée members have priority.

Ürgüp. *Büyük* (M), Kayseri Cad. (tel. 1060). 49 rooms. Lovely view. *Turban Motel* (M), (tel. 1490). 160 mini suites. Pool; near village. *Belde* (I), Dumlupinar Cad. 10 (tel. 1970). 23 rooms. Restaurant. *Hitit* (I), Dumlupinar Cad. 54 (tel. 1481). 15 rooms. Excellent restaurant and hospitality. *Hotel Ozata* (I), Atatürk Bul. 56 (tel. 1981). 32 rooms. Good standard.

Maria (I), Kayseri Cad. 10 (tel. 1487). 8 rooms. Well run by friendly Dutch owner.

Restaurant. *Haneden* (I), Nevshir Yolu Uzeri (tel. 1266). The chef, Ozcan, cooks excellent local specialties. *Sinasos* (I), Mustafapaşa (tel. 9). 14 rooms. *Tepe* (I), (tel. 1154). 36 rooms. Restaurant; away from village, on a hill as name indicates.

Efes, Europa, Göreme and *Turist* are pensions; most rooms have showers.

Yozgat. *Yılmaz* (M), Ankara Cad. 14 (tel. 111 07). 44 rooms.

Zara. *Bozali* (M). 14 rooms. Useful for an overnight stop.

CAMPING. On Ankara-Istanbul E5,*Kurt Boğazi Baraji Camping*, 50 km. (31 miles), near the dam, with pool; *Yayla Mokamp*, 110 km. (63 miles).

Konya, *Turizm Dernegi Kampi*, behind city stadium. **Nevşehir,** *Göreme Kervansaray Mokamp*, 2 km. (1 mile). **Ortahisar,** *Paris Kamp*. **Uçhisar,** *Koru Mokamp*. **Ürgüp,** *Cimenli Tepesi Camping*, with big swimming pool. *Hotel Eyfel.* Camping, pool.

GETTING AROUND. By Plane. *THY* operates the following flights: Istanbul—Ankara (50 min.), eight flights daily; Izmir—Ankara (1 hour), twice daily; Ankara—Kayseri, three times weekly; Istanbul—Konya, twice weekly.

By Train. An express train links Ankara and Kayseri daily; and there is a diesel train between Istanbul and Konya, also daily. The rail route between Kayseri and Konya is very round-about and slow: the bus is quicker.

By Car. Motoring in this region can provide some spectacular scenery and a lot of adventure. Roads in some parts have stabilized surfaces, i.e. bad ones. You can count on dust in the summertime and mud in the rainy season. Gas stations tend to be rather far apart in the remoter areas. Another vital thing to bear in mind is that if you drive in the Taurus Mountains, on narrow, winding stretches you may find yourself face to face with oncoming trucks.

By Coach. There are daily services between Ankara and all provincial centers. At Ankara's long-distance coach station, competition between the private bus companies for customers is keen.

TOURS AND EXCURSIONS. By Bus. Organized tours are undoubtedly the most comfortable way of seeing Anatolia: they are the easiest means of visiting all the sights within a particular area and, moreover, the guide can smooth away a lot of irritants, among which the language problem looms large. *Trek Travel,* Aydede Cad. 10, Taksim, Istanbul (tel. 155 16 24) organizes trekking, horseback riding and cycling trips to Cappadocia, as well as to remoter places. Trek Travel's U.K. agent is *Turkish Wildlife Holidays,* 8 The Grange, Elmdon Park, Solihull, West Midlands B92 9EL (tel. 021–742 54 20).

For details of daily guided tours from Ankara to Cappadocia and Hittite Empire sites such as Boğazkale, consult the tourist office in Ankara.

By Taxi. The Göreme valley can be visited by taxi from either Nevşehir or Ürgüp.

THE BLACK SEA

The Wilder Shore

The north coast rivals the southern in scenic beauty but lacks its infinite variety of historical remains and also the guaranteed sunshine. Though the climate is temperate, skies are often overcast and it may rain for days on end even in summer, especially in the eastern parts below the Giresun Dağları and the Karadeniz Dağları. These gently curved massifs link into the mighty Pontic Mountains, now called the North Anatolian Mountain Chain (Kürey Anadolu Sira Dağları), rising to 3,937 meters (12,917 ft.), which stops the rainclouds from penetrating into the arid interior. The wet weather has prevented the development of beach resorts, but has favored the cultivation of hazelnuts, maize, tea and tobacco on the lush coastal plains and hills.

An adequate highway hugs the sea, past numerous, easily accessible but largely ignored beaches, for most of the coast from Karasu to the Russian border. This long and lovely ocean drive is connected by several branches north to E5 and E23, the main Anatolian West–East axis. Accommodation is, except in the main towns, still very simple.

In the 7th century B.C. the well-watered coast of the Euxinos Pontos (Black Sea, Kara Deniz in Turkish) was settled by Megarian and Miletian colonists, who joined the Athenian Alliance 200 years later. But the interior, where 22 different languages were current, was dominated by the feudal Iranian nobility, and also comprised the autonomous temple-state of Komana (now Tokat), ruled by Kybele's High Priest and served by 6,000 temple slaves. In the War of Succession after Alexander's death, a lesser

Persian city-dynast, octogenarian Mithridates II Ktistes (the Founder) established his dynasty in Amaseia (Amasya) in 302 B.C. His successors gradually extended their rule over the petty Hellenistic and Anatolian states along the coast. Pharnakes I transferred the capital to Sinope (Sinop) in 183 B.C. The superficially hellenized Pontic kingdom preserved a Persian religious and social structure, and the monarchs even claimed a spurious descent from the Great Kings, indulging also for good measure in Egyptian-style brother-to-sister marriages.

Mithridates V Euergetes occupied Phrygia and Cappadocia, while his son, Mithridates VI Eupator (c.115–63 B.C.) not only expelled the Roman armies from Asia Minor and massacred 80,000 Italian civilians, but he even advanced into Greece and seriously contested Rome's influence. For 30 years Rome's greatest generals, Sulla, Lucullus and Pompey, fought successive campaigns to drive him back to his homeland and to suicide. His son, Pharnakes II, temporarily restored Pontus by skilfully playing on the rivalry between Pompey and Caesar, but the latter finally carved up the kingdom, which was incorporated into the Roman Empire in 63 B.C. From then on it shared the fate of Anatolia, except for the 250 years of the Komnenos Empire of Trebizond (Trabzon) at the end of the Middle Ages.

EXPLORING THE BLACK SEA COAST

Some of the western ports on the Black Sea Coast are best reached by ship, though the sea can be very rough even in summer. The beach resort of Şile, dominated by a ruined Genoese castle, is 71 km. (44 miles) northeast from the Bosphorus Bridge. Route 020 continues eastward with occasional branches to the coast, the most important from Kandıra—once famous for its amazons, now for its yogurt—to the pleasant fishing villages of Kerpe and Kefken. Route 020 turns south to Adapazarı, which can be reached more quickly on the E5 from Istanbul. After this inevitable detour, the coast is rejoined at Karasu, another fishing village, whence Route 010 hugs the coast, with only minor deviations, all the way east to the Russian border.

Akçakoca, 240 km. (149 miles) from Istanbul, bears the name of the Osmanli general who conquered Bithynia between 1326 and 1330. Under the now familiar ruined Genoese castle stretches a long sweep of sand beach. The next castle ruin is, for a change, Byzantine, at a second Ereğli. Through one of the three grottoes in the vicinity, Herakles descended to the underworld to accomplish the worst of his labors, fetching Kerberos (Cerberus), Hades' three-headed, hundred-eyed watchdog. The huge iron foundry, like the one 65 km. (40 miles) east at Zonguldak, is based on Turkey's largest coal mines, served by the western part of the coast's most important port. Infinitely more attractive are the expertly restored old timber houses at Safranbolu, inland on Route 750 or 755.

Imperial Rome left some traces at Hisarönü, ancient Filyos, and slightly inland at Bartın, more at Amasra (76 km., 47 miles), which is named after Amastris. This nephew of the Persian Great King Darius I realized the advantage of the two harbors divided by a rocky promontory, now crowned by the ramparts of a Byzantine citadel. A church of the same period has been converted into the Fatih Cami. The next 166 km. (103 miles) follow the coast east, past fine sand beaches, to Inebolu. Then comes a rather difficult stretch of 158 km. (100 miles) via Abana—whose excellent beach awaits easier access—to Sinop; parts of the road are still under construction.

Route 785 inland is a better alternative, though it climbs over two passes, of 1,315 meters (4,315 ft.) and 1,210 meters (3,970 ft.), in the densely wooded Küre mountains, on the 95 km. (59 miles) to Kastamonu. Once the seat of Byzantine bishops and the capital of the independent Seljuk Isfendiyaroğlu emirate in the 13th century, it owes, oddly enough, much of its reconstruction, in the early 15th century, to the Mongol hordes led by Tamerlane. The castle, on its low hilltop, still has a few massive towers. There is no shortage of mosques—Atabey, Isfendiyar, Ibn Neccar (its beautifully carved doors are in the town museum), Yakup Ağa, and so on. By far the most beautiful is Mahmut Bey Cami, a 14th-century wooden mosque in the nearby village of Kasaba. In town, the Karanlık Bedesten, the 16th-century covered bazaar, is still going strong. In the building which houses the town museum Atatürk announced, in 1926, the abolition of the fez.

On Route 030 northeast to the coast stood a second Pompeiopolis. (The first was near Mersin.) An old stone bridge with five arches crosses the Gökırmak (Blue River), hence the present name, Taşköprü (Stone Bridge). Nearby, at Ev Kaya, is an interesting 6th-century B.C. rock tomb, with colonnades and a frieze.

Tobacco Land

The return to Sinop is through tobacco fields, which take the place of wheat, corn and flax. Vast forests cover a good third of the province. The sheltered port of Sinop—as Sinope, successively the capital of Pontos and Paphlagonia—was reputedly founded by the Amazons, like so many other towns. The historical authenticity of Queen Sinova, who gave her name to the town, is confirmed by Hittite texts. The ruins of a Hellenistic temple to Serapis can be seen near the Municipal Park, marking the birthplace of the Cynic philosopher Diogenes (c. 400–325 B.C.), who brought the Hellenistic quest for peace of mind to the fore. He scarcely professed any philosophical doctrines, but preached the disregarding of conventions and uninhibited freedom of action, to the point of making love in public like a dog—*kyon* in Greek, hence cynic. The citadel was built by the Hittites, though its present layout dates from Mithridates IV, who ordered its reconstruction in the 2nd century B.C.

Alaeddin Keykubat, so prominent on the shores of the "White Sea," built, in 1214, the mosque that bears his name. The splendid mihrab was sent to the Museum of Islamic Art, in Istanbul, after the collapse of the rounded vault. The Alaiye Medrese, now a museum, was built in 1262 by the Grand Vizir of Keykubat, Süleyman Pervane. Of interest too are the tombs of the great families—Isfendiyaroğlu, in the courtyard of the Alaeddin mosque; and Candaroğlu, Ibrahim Bey Türbe. There are also the touchingly small mosques or *mescit* of Saray and of Fetih Baba, both built in 1339; the Çifte Hamam built in 1332; and a Byzantine church, Balat Kilise, dating back to the same century. A walk through the town reveals many small mosques, tombs, and fountains.

For outings, you can drive to the hilltop of Seyyit Bilal, for the view; to Zeytinlik, for a picnic; to the beaches of Ruya and Ak Liman Köyu,

where the forest grows right down to the shores of the island-studded sea.
All around are pleasant beaches with excellent seafood restaurants, none
better than at Gerze, 32 km. (20 miles) on the coastal highway southeast.
At Bafra, 120 km. (75 miles), near the mouth of Turkey's longest river,
the Kızılırmak (Red River), thermal springs supply a 13th-century
hamam; the complex of mosque, medrese and mausoleum dates from the
15th century.

Bafra, Samsun and Merzifon form a triangle that may be called the
Turkish tobacco region, with maize and delicious peaches as secondary
crops. Cattle, buffalo and geese mysteriously prefer the paved highway to
the lush meadows, yet are less emaciated than their cousins on the Anatolian plateau. Tobacco leaf and cigarettes, farm produce, caviar and fish
are shipped from Bafra and Samsun.

The triangle's inland point, Merzifon, lies at the junction of the
west–east Route 100 to Amasya and the main Ankara–Black Sea highway,
Routes 785 and 795 to Samsun. Nothing remains of ancient Phazemon,
but the Osmanli Çelebi Sultan Mehmet Medrese and the Kara Mustafa
Paşa Cami are noteworthy. Route 795, winding down the foothills of the
Canik Dağları, affords lovely views over the coastal plain and the sea.

Samsun is the most important Turkish Black Sea port, and rapidly
growing. Founded by the Miletians in the 7th century B.C., the remains
of ancient Amisos lie at the outskirts of the modern town. It is the birthplace of the War of Independence. Mustafa Kemal had set sail from Istanbul with an army inspection order rashly signed by the Sultan. By the time
the hapless monarch was made to see his blunder, it was too late—the
dauntless rebel was on the high seas, with the paper that was to open to
him the door of the army. His faith and his powers of persuasion did the
rest. To all intents and purposes, the Turkish Republic can be considered
to have been born in Samsun on May 19, 1919. (May 19 is a national holiday in Turkey.) In honor of its great man the town put up a monument,
opposite the government house; it is one of the finest in the country. The
villa in which he stayed after his landing is open to the public. The Archeological Museum displays finds from Amisos and Dündar Tepe; there is
also an interesting ethnographical section. The mosque in the bazaar dates
from the 14th century, but the 19th-century Büyük Cami is more impressive.

Though there is a long sweep of sandy beach little use is made of it,
as the waterfront is taken up with port installations, railway yards, a fair-
ground and ungainly shacks.

At Havza, halfway between Samsun and Amasya, the house which
lodged Mustafa Kemal has been turned into a museum. The small town
also boasts a library containing a few valuable manuscripts, and some rock
tombs nearby. Fine carpets are woven at Ladik.

From Samsun to Trabzon

The coast road leading from Samsun to Trabzon winds between the sea
and plains covered with hazelnut bushes, fruit trees, and vast cornfields
bending to a soft wind. Minarets watch over long stretches of beach, big
empty spaces for the lonely swimmer. Inland, the mountains rise up and
offer wonderful views.

After crossing the Yesilirmak (Green River), past Terme the densely wooded foothills of the mighty Giresun Dağları come ever closer to the sea and amid the luxuriant green the coast is lined with fishing villages.

At Ünye, 93 km. (58 miles), ancient Oenae, the remarkable 18th-century town hall vies with the sea caves, called Fokfok, a breeding place for seals. 3 km. (2 miles) beyond is the splendid beach of Çamlık. Outside Ordu are traces of the 5th-century B.C. Greek settlement of Kotyora on the beach at Bozzukale; the port itself is dominated by a once-replendent 18th-century basilica. The Güzelyalı beach is 2 km. (1 mile) along the road to Giresun, ancient Kerasous, whence the Roman general Lucullus brought the cherry (cerasum) back to Europe. Giresun spreads over a cape below a ruined Byzantine fortress; some ramparts still rise from the cliffs to guard the tomb of Seyyit Vakkas, whose part in the battle led to the taking of Kerasous by the Turks. The ruins of a temple on the island facing the town are attributed to the queens of the Amazons.

The landmark of Tirebolu, ancient Tripolis, is a Byzantine tower. Between the pleasant fishing ports of Görele, Vakfıkebir and Akçaabat (Hermanossa), the road turns inland up the densely wooded hills, affording splendid views into the narrow vales that separate the ragged peaks of the Anatolian Range. A last bridge over one of the numerous mountain streams on the 351 km. (217 miles) from Samsun leads to Trabzon, the Trebizond of old.

Among Trabzon's other claims to fame, it was here that the great cry of "Thalatta!" ("the Sea!") went up from the troops of Xenophon. In 401 B.C. Cyrus the Younger was defeated and killed at Kunaxa near Babylon. The 10,000 Greek mercenaries in the leaderless army refused to surrender to King Artaxerxes, but after agreeing to an honorable retreat the Greek leaders were treacherously murdered by a satrap. Led by a young Athenian officer called Xenophon, the Greeks started out on the seemingly hopeless trek to the Black Sea coast, without supplies. An endless column of wounded and hungry men trudged through deserts, over mountains and around enemy towns. After told and untold dangers and hardships, they at last got safely to the Black Sea, at Trapezos. On his retirement at Corinth, Xenophon wrote the story of the march north across Anatolia in the second part of his *Anabasis,* usually translated as *Inland Journey.*

Trapezos (Table) was, like so many Black Sea towns, founded by the Miletians in the 7th century B.C. Only briefly part of the Pontic kingdom, the entire coast prospered during the Pax Romana, but its moment of glory came during the decline and fall of the Byzantine millennium. After the occupation of Constantinople by the Crusaders in 1204, Alexios, grandson of the last Komnenos Emperor, Andronikos I, established his dynasty at the Black Sea port, where his successors retained their independence for some 250 years by playing off their powerful Moslem neighbors against one another. But in 1461 Mehmet the Conqueror swept the token empire off the map of Asia and put a crescent on the domes and bell-towers, together with a coat of whitewash over the often lovely frescoes.

The best-known Byzantine monument, at the entrance to Trabzon, is the church of St. Sophia, built in the 13th century, and today a museum. Set on a green hill overlooking the bay, its fine frescoes, long hidden under a hard layer of plaster, have recently been uncovered by a team of Scottish archeologists.

A short distance away is the Gülbahar Hatun Cami, with the tomb of its founder, the mother of Sultan Selim I, finished in 1514. Iskender Paşa Cami was built in 1529, but lost the characteristics of early Osmanli mosques in subsequent alterations. The tomb of this governor of Trabzon is in the courtyard. He likewise constructed the Taş Han and a hamam still in use. Another 16th-century mosque, the Erdoğlu Bey Cami, stands on the way to Atatürk's summer pavilion, now a museum in a pretty garden, 6 km. (4 miles) south.

The citadel, which has held out against so many sieges, is still imposing, situated between two ravines. The ramparts were restored after the Turkish conquest, but the remains of the Byzantine palace are insignificant. The old church of Panaghia Chrysokephalos, the Virgin of the Golden Head, is in the middle part, the Orta Hisar; made over into a mosque, the Fatih Cami, it still has the trace of the old basilical plan, in spite of later tamperings. The Yeni Cuma Cami was in the early 13th century the church of St. Eugene; the three naves in a row are cut through by an upper nave to form a Latin cross. Kudreddin Cami, consecrated as St. Philip in the 14th century, became the cathedral after the Osmanli victory. Küçük Ayvasil, dating from the 7th century, is the oldest church and still dedicated to St. Ann.

During World War I, the Tsar of Russia was to pay a visit to Trabzon, occupied by his forces. A palace was built for his reception, in a style "combining Turkish architecture and western decoration." The Republic turned it into a girls' school, which did nothing to improve matters. More in style is the 16th-century Bedesten, the covered bazaar of the jewelers and merchants of valuable goods, joined by an arch to the Çarşı Cami, the city's largest mosque, built in 1839.

The most rewarding site is the monastery of the Virgin at Sumela, 54 km. (33 miles) southwest along E390 to Gümüşhane and Erzurum, turning left after Maçka. The most important Byzantine monument in the region, it is now abandoned and crumbling away in the hollow of a sheer cliff some 350 meters (1,000 ft.) above the valley floor, at an altitude of 1,188 meters (3,900 ft.). 93 steps ascend to a labyrinth of courtyards, corridors and chapels. Founded by Blessed Barnabas to house a miraculous icon of the Virgin painted by St. Luke, the venerated shrine was completely rebuilt by Alexios III, as he had been crowned there in 1340—as depicted in the frescoes of the main church in the grotto. Tolerant sultans further added to the sanctuary's treasures and the frescoes were restored in 1740. Before the expulsion of the Greeks in 1922, the monks hid the icon of the Virgin in a neighboring chapel, and in 1930 the Turkish government allowed the transfer of the relic to the new monastery of Sumela in Greek Macedonia.

The Zigana Geçidi (Pass), 2,025 meters (6,645 ft.), is a stunning rift between two different worlds, in appearance as in way of life. Leaving below the lush damp green of the coastline, E390 climbs steeply upwards through misty forests to descend, on the south side, to the low brushwood and yellow dust of the endless arid Anatolian plateau. Here shepherds move with the changing seasons between highland and lowland pastures, dotted with makeshift huts and grazing flocks.

Towards the Soviet Border

The 189 km. (117 miles) northeast along the coast from Trabzon to
Hopa are scenically the loveliest. The densely wooded slopes of the Karadeniz Dağları sometimes tumble straight into the sea, but are more often
broken by intensely green tea plantations and rice paddies, thriving in the
mild, humid climate. Women wearing bright striped shawls as aprons are
picking tea from early May to the end of October. Occasional tea factories
exude black smoke, the only pollution on the coast. The men have a well-
deserved reputation as cooks and are employed in restaurants and pastry
shops all the way to Istanbul.

Rize (76 km., 47 miles), the tea capital, rises steeply from the sea to
a ruined Genoese castle. The outstanding building is the 16th-century
Islam Paşa Cami. Route 925 via Ikizdere and Ispir provides a scenic but
risky alternative connection to Erzurum. 22 km. (13 miles) inland from
Ardeşen is the unusually attractive village of Çamlıhemşin, a good center
for walks in the mountains and trout-fishing. The Kackar Dağ is for more
ambitious mountaineering, requiring a guide.

Fındıklı, at the mouth of two streams, is surrounded by tea plantations.
Continuing under huge cliffs, past waterfalls and sandy coves, you reach
Hopa, a bustling frontier town, journey's end for the Turkish Maritime
Line boats as well as for cars. For the remaining 22 km. (13 miles) to the
Russian border—which is open at Sarp—a special military permit is re-
quired.

Route 950 climbs over the Cankurtaran Geçidi, a mere 690 meters
(2,260 ft.) southeast through dense forests to Borçka, then follows the
Çoruh River through wild, unspoilt landscape to Artvin. This remote provincial capital lies below a cliff crowned by a ruined castle. A new road
is opening from Ardahan to Artvin via Savsat. The south route via Ar-
danuç is very tough, ideal for 4-wheel drive. Allow four hours for this section.

PRACTICAL INFORMATION FOR
THE BLACK SEA COAST

TOURIST OFFICES. There are local tourist offices in the following
towns: **Akçakoca,** Santral Sok. 2 (tel. 1554); **Giresun,** Vilayet Konağı (tel.
3560); **Ordu,** Belediye Binası (tel. 171 00); **Samsun,** Irmak Cad. (tel. 112
28); **Sinop,** Iskele Meydanı 2 (tel. 5837); **Trabzon,** Taksim Cad. 31 (tel.
358 33).

WHEN TO COME. Spring and summer are best, though even then it
rains a lot; temperatures remain moderate throughout the year.

SPECIAL EVENTS. May. Aksu Festivities at Giresun, late May. **July.**
Samsun Folk Dance Festival, throughout the month.

HOTELS AND RESTAURANTS

Akçakoca. *Sezgin Pansiyon* (I), Tevfik Ileri Cad. (tel. 1162). 10 rooms. No private showers. *Tezel Pension* (I), (tel. 1115). 9 rooms. On private beach. The home cooking here is recommended.

Amasra. *Nur Aile Pension* (I), Camli Cad., Kücukköy (tel. 1015). 18 rooms, 3 showers.

Artvin. *Kultur Palas* (I). 18 rooms.

Bafra. *Belediye Motel* (I), Çetinkaya Köprü Yani (tel. 1524). 12 rooms.

Gerze. *Köşkburnu Turistik Tesisleri* (I). 22 rooms. Beach, restaurant.

Giresun. *Aksu Motel* (I). 1 mile east. *Giresun* (M), Atatürk Bul. 7 (tel. 3017). 29 rooms.

Görele. *Sahil* (I). 20 rooms, 10 showers.

Hopa. *Papilla* (I) Ortahopa Cad. (tel. 2641). 36 rooms. Beach, good fish restaurant. Hot water in all rooms.

Kastamonu. *Arslan* (I). 36 rooms, 18 with shower.

Of. *Caykent* (M), Cumhiriyet Cad. (tel. 2424). 27 rooms, most with sea views. Quiet part of town.

Ordu. *Gülistan* (I). 12 rooms. On sea but no beach. *Kervansaray* (I). 40 rooms. *Turist* (I), Atatürk Bul. (tel. 14273). 40 rooms.
Restaurant. *Gongur* is the leading restaurant.

Rize. *Keles* (M), Palandoken Cad. 2 (tel. 14612). Good standard. *Turist* (I), Atatürk Bul. (tel. 114 46). 30 rooms. With the best restaurant in town.

Samsun. *Turban Samsun* (E), Sahil Cad. (tel. 107 50). 116 rooms and suites. Pool, tennis. *Burç* (M), Kazimpaşa Cad. (tel. 154 80). *Terminal* (I). 44 rooms. With restaurant. *Vidinli* (I), Kazimpaşa Cad. (tel. 160 50). 60 rooms. Restaurant.

Şile. *Değirmen* (M), (tel. 1048). 73 rooms. On beach. Restaurant. *Kumbaba* (M), (tel. 1038). 40 rooms. On beach.

Sinop. *Melia Kasım* (M), Gazi Cad. (tel. 4210). 57 rooms. *Hotel 117* (I). 34 rooms. On the waterfront.
Restaurant. *Liman Lokantasi* (M). At the harbor.

Tirebolu. *Ayana* (I). 20 rooms, 10 showers.

Trabzon. *Özgür* (M), Kibris Şehitler Cad. 29 (tel. 113 19). 45 rooms. Best hotel in town. In central square. Good rooftop terrace restaurant. *Horon* (I), Sira Mağazalar 125 (tel. 111 99). 42 rooms, 22 showers. *Usta*

(I), Telegrafhane Sok. 3 (tel. 121 95). 72 rooms. Rather bland but comfortable.

Restaurants. *Belediye Sahil Lokantasi* (M), on seafront. *Boztepe Piknik Gazinosu* (M), on a hill in the suburbs. Highly recommended is *Çanli Alabalk* (M), located 1½ miles west of town center on the main road. The baked, grilled, fried, and boiled fish dishes are the specialties. *Trabzon* (I), in the main square, is decorated in log cabin style. Also in the square, and cheaper, is *Üzungöl* (I).

Üniye. *Çamlık Motel* (I). 13 rooms. Also camping; in pinewood by the sea. *Kumsal Otali* (I), Golevi Köyü (tel. 4490). 11 rooms. On the beach. *Urer* (I). 29 rooms. Noisy, on coastal road.

Restaurant. *Park* (I). Good fish; on seafront.

Zonguldak. *Ay* (I), Gazipaşa Cad. 61 (tel. 113 10). 40 rooms. *Otel 67* (I), Fevipaşa Cad. 1 (tel. 167 67). 23 rooms.

CAMPING. The camp sites listed here are all located on beaches. **Akçakoca,** *Tezel Camping,* small private beach, less than 1 km. (half a mile) from town. Overlooks sea. *Esentepe Camping,* 4 km. (2 miles) to the west of town. **Şile,** *Akkaya Camping,* 90 km. (56 miles) from Bosphorus Bridge; *Kumbaba Camping,* 71 km. (44 miles) from Bridge. **Trabzon,** *Uzunkum Camping,* 4 km. (2 miles) to the west of town. There is also a campsite off the E390 road between Trabzon and the Sumela monastery, just after Maçka.

GETTING AROUND. By Train. The *Eastern Express* goes from Isanbul via Erzurum to Kars; thence by bus to the coast. There are also services between Ankara and Zonguldak, and Ankara–Kayseri–Amasya–Samsun (a long, roundabout way; better take the Ankara–Samsun bus).

By Plane. *THY* has flights from Ankara to Samsun and Trabzon.

By Car. Route 010 along the coast is described in the text. Recommended access roads are: 020 from Istanbul to Şile and Kandıra; 805 from Izmit to Kandıra; 850 from Adapazarı to Karasu; 855 from Düzce to Akçakoca; 750 from Ankara to Zonguldak, with the 755 branch to Amasra; 765 from Çankırı via Kastamonou to Inebolu and 785 to Sinop; 795, the main Black Sea highway from Ankara via Çorum to Samsun. The fully paved access further east is E390 from Erzurum to Trabzon. All other north/south roads are risky. They are muddy most of the year and iced over in the winter. There are a fair number of filling stations. Super-grade petrol is now available in most parts.

Cars may be shipped on the *Turkish Maritime Lines* boats. Small private craft also make the journey, but getting the car on board may be more than your nerves can stand.

By Bus. There are bus and minibus connections to all centers.

By Boat. The easiest way to travel here, though it is by no means luxurious, is on *Turkish Maritime Lines'* somewhat antiquated boats which can serve as inexpensive floating hotels. The Istanbul-Trabzon round trip takes six days, sailing weekly all year round. From mid-June to mid-September a weekly six-day cruise goes as far as Trabzon. Boats also stop at small ports all along the west coast up to Abana and beyond. There are *Turkish Maritime Lines* offices in all ports.

THE EASTERN PROVINCES

Discoveries for the Adventurous

The big attractions in the eastern part of Turkey are Mount Ararat, the Nemrut Dağ, and Lake Van. The town of Van has developed into a resort in the midst of a magnificent unspoilt landscape; the other two are only for the adventurous who scorn the well-trodden paths. Organized tours will save a lot of rugged moments, but even the best tour leader is powerless during the frequent violent earthquakes. A geological fault runs right across Eastern Anatolia, and earthquakes have destroyed over 300 towns and villages in the last 50 years, killing some 45,000 even in this sparsely populated region. Most of the victims froze to death, as the worst tremors occur during the bitter winters.

From the Hittite, Greek and Roman ruins, the Byzantine, Seljuk and Osmanli religious architecture of Central Anatolia, it is in every respect a long way to the sparse Hurri remains, the imposing Urartian fortresses, and the distinctive Christian churches of Eastern Anatolia. Although this region, located between the Byzantine and Iranian empires, underwent the influence of both to a certain extent, it nevertheless produced from the 9th to the 12th centuries a highly original architecture.

The basilical floor plan that prevailed in the western part of the country was early abandoned in the eastern part to make way for a central structure featuring domes topped off with the characteristic conical roof. Exteriors are generally simple and solid, in striking contrast with the highly ornate and intricate interiors. The inside niches, secondary rooms, and even the apse itself are built right into the great walls, the very thickness of which conceals the partitioning. The core of the walls is quarry rock, and the interiors and exteriors are covered with carved stone. The outer surfaces are embellished with arcades and occasionally with designs in relief.

Peoples Old and New

In about 1275 B.C. an Indo-European tribe infiltrated the land of their Hurri cousins. These Urartians gradually established a chain of emirates from the Caucasus to Syria, uniting against Assyrian predominance in a confederation under a paramount king in around the year 900. After the Assyrians destroyed the first capital, Arzashku, so thoroughly that the location at Mollakent can only be surmised, King Sarduri I (840–830) founded a new dynasty and capital. Tushpa—now Van—prospered under his successors until Sarduri II (760–735) was defeated in a revival of Assyrian expansion and driven back to the gates of his capital, where a palace revolt placed Rusas I (735–713) on the throne. Rusas III committed the fatal mistake of allying himself with the Assyrian arch-enemy against Babylonia and the nascent power of Media. A raid by the barbaric Scythians tipped the scale; most of Urartu was annexed by the Babylonians, the eastern part going to the Medes, who propelled yet another Indo-European tribe into the Anatolian embroilment. The Hayks, called Armenians by the Greeks in a confusion with the Aramaeans, were after the fall of Babylonia incorporated into the 13th Persian satrapy, which eventually became part of the Seleukid dominions.

After the battle of Magnesia in 190, the Satrap Artaxias declared himself with Roman connivance King of Armenia. In the Urartian tradition, the founder of the next dynasty, Tigran I, moved his capital from Artaxata south to Tigranakert. Tigran II joined his father-in-law Mithridates VI of Pontus in resisting Roman domination of Asia Minor, but his capital was taken by Lucullus in 69, and he was decisively defeated by Pompey in 66 B.C.

In A.D. 303, St. Gregory the Illuminator converted Tiridates III, who decreed Christianity as the official state religion. A break with Persia ensued. Rome and Persia settled their conflict in 387 by dividing Armenia.

The dispossessed Armenian princes had been granted estates, where they were joined by large numbers of their former subjects, fleeing southwest before the Seljuks. The last scion of the Bagratid dynasty ruling Armenia was killed by the Byzantines in 1079. A distant relative, Roupen, then founded a principality between the Taurus Mountains and the Mediterranean coast that aided the Crusaders in exchange for the latter's assistance in maintaining their independence.

From 1236 to 1405 Eastern Anatolia was in the hands of the Mongols, and then was fought over by the Turkoman Black and White Sheep clans, to become once again the battlefield of neighboring powers. Persia's claims on Turkey were taken over by Russia in the 18th century. Russian incursions were quickly repulsed, and though Erzurum and Van were occupied in 1916, the Treaty of Alexandropol of 1920 restored the pre-World War I frontiers.

EXPLORING THE EASTERN PROVINCES

Eastern Turkey is under martial law, following the Kurdish uprising which began in Diyarbakir in the 70s. Visitors will find that traffic is stopped for random searches by police and soldiers. Identification papers are very seldom demanded of tourists, but it is advised that you have your travel documents with you at all times.

You will find the local people very friendly; they often invite visitors to drink tea with them. The somewhat off-putting sport of stone-throwing practiced by young children and adolescents can be discouraged with a determined *Yok* (No); Turkish adults on the scene will also help reprimand the young miscreants.

The least strenuous way to visit this region is by flying from Ankara to the various provincial capitals, of which only Diyarbakir and Van are connected with one another by Turkish Airlines. Motoring across the vast Anatolian plateau seems justified only in transit to Iran, and then best in an organized tour with all bookings made beforehand. Bear in mind that because of extremes in temperature, snow, ice or dust and sheer travel-weariness, a trip that at home would be just an average lap in a journey can begin to feel like hard labor.

Though the shortest road route from Sivas to Erzurum is along the E23 (486 km., 302 miles), most motorists will prefer the longer but scenically greatly superior detour via the Black Sea coast. The E390 from Trabzon to Erzurum crosses the Zigana Mountains to Gümüşhane on the southern slopes. Once of considerable importance on the ancient Silk Road traveled by Marco Polo, this is a town on the move in the most unfortunate sense: frequent earthshifts have reduced the pleasing architecture of the old parts to uninhabitable ruins. At the next road junction, partly paved Route 885 branches right (south) over the formidable Kösedaği Geçidi (1,910 meters, 6,266 ft.) to Erzincan, with the emphasis on the spectacular to the neglect of safety. Storms burst in these mountains so suddenly that even the locals can be caught unaware. Bells—a relic of the distant Christian past—toll a warning whenever the wind blows up.

Better keep to E390 southeast, the easiest passage through the North Anatolian Mountain Chain. Xenophon and the Ten Thousand probably followed it in the opposite direction. Seljuk Kale (Citadel), duly menacing, is passed before the road goes over the Vauk Dăgı Geçidi (1,875 meters, 6,150 ft.) to Bayburt, 195 km. (121 miles) from Trabzon and 72 km. (44 miles) from the junction with E23 at Aşkale. Satala, near Baiburt, was the Roman legions' remotest outpost on the Armenian border.

The other equally spectacular but unpaved ascents from the coast cannot be recommended (which will appear to those disregarding the advice something of an understatement), with the exception of the 64 km. (40 miles) from Hopa near the Soviet frontier to Artvin.

On E23, 255 km. (158 miles) from Sivas to Erzincan, the sidetrip to Divriği, Byzantine Tephrike, breaks the monotony. But the 100 km. (64 miles) after turning south (right) at Zara are so awful that the long roundabout by either Routes 850 and 260 or, for once, by rail from Sivas are preferable. The 13th-century Seljuk fortress and an even older mosque are within its enclosure walls. The Ulu Cami and the hospital next to it also date from the 13th century. The northeast portal, or Taç Kapısı (Crown Gate) is richly carved. Both of these are exceptionally lovely works of architecture and it is too bad that Divriği is still so hard to reach.

Erzincan and Erzurum

The Mongols crushed the Seljuks in the fertile upper Euphrates valley near Erzincan in 1243. But even more than by battles, the town suffered

by earthquakes, the most devastating in December 1939 leaving some
39,000 dead. No wonder nothing remains of particular interest. However,
33 km. (20 miles) further on lie the Altıntepe diggings, a necropolis in
which Urartian funerary artifacts have been discovered. Turkish archeologists have also unearthed here the remains of a palace and temple.

Erzurum, the region's capital and largest town, lies at an altitude of
1,980 meters (6,500 ft.). Under its earlier name of Theodosiopolis, this was
one of the eastern bastions of Byzantium for many centuries. After the
7th century, the Byzantines managed to wrest it from the Arabs on recurrent occasions, during the periods of strife that rent the Moslem world
asunder—the struggle for the caliphate and the wars between the Ommey-
yads and the Abbassids. The Armenians gained a foothold here around
the year 1000, but the city fell to the Seljuks after the battle of Manzikert
(1071). The etymology of the city's present name is *arz* (world), *er Rum*
(of the Roman).

An early 19th-century traveler was impressed by the amount of brisk
trading carried on, and by the warehouses full of goods on their way from
and en route toward India and Persia. He counted 100,000 inhabitants,
including "2,500 schismatic Armenians, 1,600 Catholics, 400 Greeks, and
the remainder Turks" (J. MacCarthy, *Dictionnaire de geographie*, Paris,
1841). Now entirely Turkish, the population has almost trebled.

The Ulu Cami, built in 1179, is distinguished by seven wide naves and
a fine colonnaded courtyard. Nearby lies the Byzantine citadel, with its
own mosque and minaret, bright with gleaming tilework, its walls intact.
Noteworthy are the splendidly carved portal of the Çift Minareli Medrese,
built in 1253, as well as the truncated minaret of the Yakutiye Medrese,
dating from the early 14th century. The first of these two Koranic colleges
was built by Alaeddin Keykubat, as was the Hatuniye Türbe, the mausoleum of his daughter. Among the other mausolea, the most interesting is
the circular Emir Sultan Türbe. The exhibits in the Archeological Museum cover several millennia. Skiing during the long winter is only 6 km.
(4 miles) away on a good road, at Inis Boğazı in a fine Alpine setting.

Three Ways to Kars

The best and shortest road from Erzurum to Kars, 211 km. (131 miles),
is E23 running east through Pasinler, epicenter of the 1983 earthquake
that left some 2,000 dead, to Horasan, then northeast on Route 080 to
Karakurt, and north to Sarıkamış, to continue parallel to the railway.
Near Andereköy rises Mecinbert castle, and from Karakurt you can take
another sidetrip to see Cangili church, venerable Armenian relics both.

There are two other ways of getting to Kars, but both require courage
and strong axles. Your extra time and trouble will be amply rewarded by
the landscape's wild beauty, which is virtually untouched, and by the various stops to be made along the way. Route 950 climbs northeast to Artvin,
where it veers east to Ardahan then Route 965 south to Kars. These 480
km. (298 miles) can only be considered in the summertime and it is advisable to investigate the road's state of repair before plunging ahead.

You will gain some idea of the inaccessibility of this entire region by
remembering that, throughout the Middle Ages, it was never occupied by
conquerors. Although neighboring powers often claimed nominal sovereignty, for all practical purposes the local Armenian princes—an interminable succession of Davids of Tayk—enjoyed complete autonomy, punctu-

ated now and then by punitive expeditions fitfully organized by their overlords. It is difficult but infinitely rewarding to explore the Torum and Çoruh River valleys, with their gorges, peaks, and the meticulously tended fields. About 23 km. (14 miles) beyond Tortum on Route 950, take the trail off to the left leading to Haho (a two-hour hike), where, in the 10th century, one David of Tayk built a Georgian monastery, which is now a mosque.

Another rewarding walk is that from Ösk to Vank for a look at another monastery from this same period. Although local farmers are using it as a storehouse, the building is in a remarkably fine state of preservation. Take time for another halt at the end of Lake Tortum (an exquisite gem), where you can marvel at the Tortum Cay waterfalls from the opposite side of the road. Some 23 km. (14 miles) farther on, another foot trail (right side of the highway) leads to the village of Ishan, where you will find the 10th-century cruciform Church of the Mother of God, which was damaged in World War I. Notice the lovely bas-reliefs on its outside walls. Near Yusufeli, 10 km. (6 miles) east from Route 950, are two more churches: the 10th-century Georgian Dört Kilise to the southwest, and Parhal, near Sarıgöl, to the north.

From the Yusufeli branch, Route 950 is paved through the Çoruh gorges—to the greater appreciation of the spectacular views—before reaching the crossroads 11 km. (7 miles) south of Artvin's mighty fortress.

Continue east (right) along the Çoruh's tributaries, where churches and monasteries are scattered in the forests and on unlikely precipices to Ardahan, a garrison town that was occupied by the Russians until 1921. The remaining 94 km. (58 miles) to Kars are unpaved, but not lacking in interest.

The middle road from Erzurum is 278 km. (172 miles) long and frequently in bad shape. It branches off the Artvin road after Tortum. Oltu, the next town, was the capital of the Tayk princes, whose castle rises above a church and some mosques.

Kars

Ever since the Byzantines forced the last Armenian prince to resign in 1064, Kars has been coveted by invaders from east and north. Consequently, the city's history is that of the successive sieges it has withstood. In the 11th century, the Seljuks expelled the Byzantine garrison. Tamerlane then impressed his bloody mark. The vicissitudes of the Russo-Turkish wars caused it to fall into the hands of the tsars on three different occasions during the 19th century—in 1828, 1855, and 1877. The irresistible tides of the Turkish war of independence swept it back under Turkish domination in 1921. Kars has its own local tradition of heroism—for five months during the Crimean War, a Turkish garrison of 15,000 men held out here against 40,000 tsarist troops.

Kars is the center of a thriving farming community, noted for its butter and other dairy produce. The solid wheels of excellent cheese are distributed throughout Turkey. Kars is rather forbidding, a typical frontier town, cold and greyish, high up at 1,788 meters (5,866 ft.) on a wide plateau at the mercy of the winds. An old Georgian fort overhangs it from a high rocky vantage point, jutting out over the Kars River that winds around its base. The heap of grey rock beneath that looks like a millstone is the Armenian church. Its interior is embellished with circular niches representing the Twelve Apostles. Originally dedicated to the Holy Apostles in the 10th century, this church was converted into the Kümbet Cami by the Seljuks, reconsecrated by the Russians at the end of the 19th century and is now a museum.

The old and new parts of town stretch out on either side of the river, forming its upper and lower levels. The old bridge between them is of Seljuk origin. A weekly train runs from Kars to one of the two border crossings into the Soviet Union. Along the 79 km. (49 miles) of unpaved road are Armenian monuments, including the 10th-century Argina basilica and the Tiknia castle.

Up to the time of the devastating Mongol invasion, Ani (Aniköy) was the chief Armenian town. 46 km. (28 miles) along a paved road, Ani stands within sight of the Soviet machine-gun towers across the border, a military permit is required which can be obtained in Kars. No photography is permitted. The great wall that used to defend the city lying between two deep ravines is still impressive, but of the "thousand and one" churches of what was a great capital with 20,000 inhabitants, scarcely half a dozen remain standing. Two rivers wind their boiling black waters around what is virtually a ghost town.

Pick you way through weeds and thistles to the remnants of the Georgian Church (early 13th century); the Church of St. Gregory of Gagik, which was built in the year 1000; the Church of the Holy Apostles (built just a few years later); and the Church of Gregory of Abugamrentz (10th century). The cathedral was originally Armenian, became a Seljuk mosque in 1064 (50 years after its building), and was restored to Christendom in the 13th century by the Georgians. The Church of St. Gregory of Honentz dates from 1215: note the truly remarkable mural decorations in the interior. Clinging to the heights overlooking the Arpa River, the Menucer Mosque also emphasizes the Armenian influences. Take the climb up to the first citadel, and continue on to the second, at the far edge of town, where the two gorges converge. The Church of Our Lady is built out on a promontory above the tumbling waters of the gorge.

Excursions might be made to the 10th-century Horomotz monastery, 16 km. (10 miles) northeast; to the Bagnair monastery, also 10th-century, 23 km. (14 miles) west; and to the Magasbert fortress. Give the shockabsorbers a rest and stretch your legs for a change. A trip north to Lake Çıldır is most rewarding, both scenically and culturally; the road is paved only as far as Arpaçay.

Mount Ararat

181 km. (112 miles) east of Erzurum, after crossing the Tahir Geçidi (2,471 meters, 8,105 ft.), E23 arrives at the remarkably unremarkable provincial capital Ağrı. It hardly justifies its name—ache or pain—which might more aptly be applied to Turkey's highest mountain, Mount Ararat. "In the six hundredth year of Noah's life, in the second month, the seventeenth day of the month, the same day were all the fountains of the great deep broken up, and the windows of heaven were opened" (Genesis VII:11). That was the Deluge. "And God remembered Noah . . . and the waters assuaged . . . And it came to pass in the six hundredth and first year, in the first month, the first day of the month, the waters were dried up from off the earth; and Noah removed the covering of the ark, and looked, and behold, the face of the ground was dry" (Genesis VIII:1, 13). The survivors

had just landed on top of the Ağrı Dağ. Connoisseurs of wine will also find this a pious pilgrimage, for it was here on the slopes of this mountain that Noah discovered the grapevine.

On either side lie two small settlements, both of which suffered in the earthquake of 1976. Igdır to the north is easily accessible from Horasan over paved Route 080, thence Route 975 for 51 km. (31 miles) due south over the western spurs of Mount Ararat to connect with Doğubayazıt, 95 km. (59 miles) east of Ağğrı on E23. The lofty peak of Mount Ararat, an extinct volcano, soars up to 5,165 meters (16,945 ft.) and is snow covered even all summer, a magnificent sight on the arid plateau.

There are many ancient accounts of an all-destroying flood, and of the heroic efforts of a single man, divinely inspired, to escape its consequences. The two versions of the Book of Genesis (the Yahwist, from the 7th century B.C., and the Sacerdotal, from the 6th century B.C.) both provide a complete and concordant account of the Deluge. A Chaldean priest named Berossus, in the 3rd century B.C., bequeathed to posterity a similar report (based on Eusebius of Caesarea), in which Noah appears as Xisuthros and Jehovah is called Chronos (Father Time of Greek mythology). Tablets deciphered from among those found in Ashurbanipal's library at Nineveh (7th century B.C.) recount the Epic Gilgamesh, whose ancestor Utnapishtim (none other than Noah himself) duly constructed an ark when ordered to by the god Ea. The Babylonians likewise have handed down an almost identical version. The tradition—or the legend, unless, of course, all this is historical fact—of the Deluge and the ark is known even in China. Scientists agree that during the 4th millennium B.C., a veritable cataclysm may have occurred, accompanied by rains and floods.

As early as 1876 James Bryce, an Englishman, discovered "amid blocks of lava, a piece of wood about four feet long and five inches wide, which had obviously been shaped by means of a tool". Fragments of ancient timber, embedded in the ice, have been brought back by ark-hunting expeditions, but radiocarbon dating tests proved inconclusive. A boat had been shown by satellite photos to be embedded in a glacier at 3,810 meters (12,500 ft.); similar objects were observed by pilots from low-flying aircraft. But after examining one of these "boats" on the spot, it turned out to be nothing more than a freak formation in the strata. Yet expeditions by Christian fundamentalist groups are constantly making new claims.

Potential mountain-climbers have to obtain permission from the Turkish military authorities because of the proximity of the Soviet frontier; then brave three zones of increasing unpleasantness, of spiders, snakes and bears, in addition to the difficulties of the ascent, suspicious military patrols, snowstorms, avalanches, and divers technical problems. Despite this impressive array of local hindrances, horses and guides are for hire at Igdır, Aralık and Doğubayazıt. From the last-named don't miss the Ishak Pasha Saray, 6 km. (4 miles) up a hill. It is a fairytale castle and mosque set in spacious courtyards, built by a local chief in a fantastic mixture of Georgian, Persian and Osmanli styles in the 18th century, and with a spectacular view. The magnificent view from this romantic conglomeration ranges over the valley to the western spur of Ararat. Across a chasm, but accessible by road, are extensive 2,800-year-old Ururtian ruins and a 500-year-old Osmanli mosque.

Lake Van

Turkey's largest lake, 3,738 sq. km. (1,443 sq. miles), is divided into two unequal parts: the main southern body of deep water encircled by steep, rocky shores, and the shallow northern section, connected by a fairly narrow passage. Vaguely triangular, with an eastward tilt, the lake extends at a height of 1,720 meters (5,643 ft.). Thus it is no wonder that the mighty peaks in the south are resplendent with sun even in the hot summers, while the volcanic cones in the west, facing the arid plateau and ridges in the east, compose a grandiose frame, comparable to the Dead Sea, despite the difference in altitude. A further similarity consists in the high salinity, due to sulphur springs within the lake, at 100 meters (328 ft.) along the shores, double that towards the center. Sodium carbonate and sodium sulphate have rendered the water too brackish for irrigation, but the former is the main natural resource, extracted in several somewhat basic plants for use in detergents. A small member of the carp family, the *darekh,* has, however, adapted to the saline environment. Fishermen come up from the Black Sea in March and April to catch this slight but tasty fish. Swimming in the soft water is pleasant, but beaches along the rocky shores are few and far between.

The landscape roundabout is forbiddingly barren and desolate, the result of a landslide that occurred sometime in the tertiary epoch. In the wintertime fierce storms can suddenly occur. The scattered lakeside settlements are by no means safe from the water's fury. In the 19th century, a flash flood completely inundated a number of localities, including Arsis and Kale, which have remained under water. There is no known outlet for Lake Van's excess liquid. Within five years, the fluctuations in its water level can vary as much as 3 meters (10 ft.). Added to this are violent earthquakes; a particularly destructive shock in 1976 left more than 4,000 dead in the Muradiye district just north of the lake. The scheme of things here is far beyond the ordinary human scale.

One of the claims to fame of the region are the Van cats, a rare breed now, but famous and much in demand in the West. They have long white fur, very short legs and traditionally one blue and one yellow eye!

In 840 B.C. King Sarduri built the formidable fortress of Tushpa on the steep cliff that rises from a narrow promontory 90 meters (295 ft.) to a plateau. Steps—fortunately considerably less than the 1,000 of local handouts—ascend to the citadel. A path branches right to Urartian tombs in the sheer southern rockface below a cuneiform inscription in honor of King Xerxes, incised almost 400 years later. The Persians, like all subsequent conquerors, occupied the fortress and continued the Urartian tradition of rock memorials in Chaldean or neo-Assyrian cuneiform. The crumbling ramparts are still impressive, but as so often in these parts, it is the view from such a vantage point that makes the steep climb worthwhile. The lower part of the ruins is accessible from behind a mosque further inland.

As capital of Vaspurakan, Van nestled below the southern cliff, gradually spreading to the lake shore till it became the main town of Turkey's far southeast. Totally destroyed by the Russians in 1917, the melancholy jumble of foundations cannot be sorted out; only two vaguely restored mosques, one 13th-century Black Sheep, the other 16th-century Osmanli, rise from the marshland, which makes the visit somewhat squelchy, but provides excellent grazing for the sheep appropriate to romantic ruins. The irrigation ditch alongside seems excessively effective, as the beach at its mouth can only be reached through patches of mud, even in the height of summer.

No more recommendable is the beach of black volcanic sand extending from the fortress rock's north side to the port, as the water is polluted by a mixture of town sewers and ferryboat tar. Though the ground here is less marshy, no hotels have been built on the shore, which is particularly regrettable because of the splendid view over the lake against the backdrop of the fortress.

Van now lies 7 km. (4 miles) inland from the port, 5 km. (3 miles) from the fortress. The largest building of this town of 100,000 inhabitants is a mosque which dwarfs the small but well-arranged Archeological and Ethnographical Museum. The museum is open Tuesday through Sunday 9–12 and 1–6, and mainly exhibits Urartian finds. Van's mainstreet is lined with shops selling local artifacts, especially *kilim* at very reasonable prices; and hotels offering an adequate choice to accommodate the rapidly increasing number of tourists. The Toprakkale mound at the northern outskirts has been closed after being excavated for almost 100 years; all the finds are in the Museum. Further Urartian and subsequent foundations on top of the hill beyond are likewise out of bounds, as part of a reafforestation scheme round a small reservoir.

Route 975 skirts Lake Van north to Erciş (92 km., 57 miles), then turns northwest to Patnos (55 km., 34 miles), the closest town for a visit to the battlefield of Manzikert, now Malazgirt, where Christianity lost Asia Minor to Islam.

On the road between Van and Gevaş a particularly striking Türbe of the Seljuk period stands on the shore of Van Gölü (Lake Van). It was built by Izzaldin for Princess Halima. West of here, en route to Tatvan, you will see the black tents of nomads' encampments.

Leaving Van southward, the road climbs the Kurubaş Geçidi (2,260 meters, 7,415 ft.), affording splendid views over the oasis at the lake round the town, then descends to the Dönemeç Valley, dominated by Çavuştepe (25 km., 15 miles), an 8th-century B.C. Urartian fortress of finely dressed stone on a hill, which has contributed a fair share of the exhibits in the Van Museum. A second Urartian fortress can be seen on the hill opposite; it is occupied by the military and is not open to the public. Continuing eastward along the reservoir, Hoşap Castle (57 km., 35 miles) looms over a chasm the river has cut through the rocks. Built in 1643 by Sari Sulayman, a Kurd of the Mahmudis, to "protect" (i.e. ransack) caravans, strong walls ascend the forbidding cliff to the palace, two mosques, three baths and the dungeon. A Farsi inscription can be seen above the impressive entrance gate. It is advisable to bring a flashlight with you as there are no lights within the castle.

Route 975 then rises via the Güzeldere Geçidi (2,730 meters, 8,957 ft.) southeast to where the road forks at Bağıslı, 161 km. (100 miles) from Van. Route 400 branches 75 km. (47 miles) east, below Buzul Dağ (4,119 meters, 13,510 ft.) to Esendere on the Iranian border; and 44 km. (27 miles) southwest to Hakkari, the small provincial capital with a fine medrese under the medieval citadel. The next 73 km. (45 miles) follow swift streams through lovely mountain scenery to Çucurca on the Iraqi border. Even bigger and better are the Cilo and Sat Mountains in the Hakkari Dağları (Mountain chain) further east. This inaccessible fastness became the refuge of the Nestorian heretics after their condemnation by the Council of Ephesus in 431. Not yet opened up for tourism, oil drilling is already in progress.

As a four-lane highway, Route 300 follows the shore south of Van to Gümüşdere (15 km., 9 miles), locally called Edremit, the nearest beach and not much at that. At the landing stage of Gevaş (41 km., 25 miles), below an eating place of sorts, motorboats wait till the required number of passengers—between 12 and 17—is assembled to chug the 4 km. (3 miles) to the Islet of Akdamar, where in 921 King Gagik built a monastery and the splendid Church of the Holy Cross. Of the former only traces remain among some wild olive trees, but the bas-reliefs on the church's outer walls are well preserved, clearly showing the Byzantine influence in the medallions of saints and kings, but following the Persian Sassanid model in the larger scenes, mostly of animals. The wall paintings in the upper and lower church, divided by a few steps, are barely recognizable. At Adlicevaz there is a small chocolate-colored mosque and a Seljuk castle which affords beautiful views of Lake Van. Also of note are the remains of the Urartian castle of Haldi.

The next 106 km. (65 miles) continue westward between the lake and the peaks of the Kavuşsahap Dağları (2,985 meters, 9,790 ft.) to Tatvan, starting point of the train and car ferries to Van. Even if the spectacular drive around the lake is not completed, it is recommended to undertake the first 38 km. (24 miles) north to Ahlat below the Nemrut Dağ (2,828 meters, 9,280 ft.), an extinct volcano with an unusual amount of vegetation round the crater lake—not to be confused with its famous namesake near Kahta. Eski (Old) Ahlat is now a ghost town, but in the 12th century it was the capital of a Seljuk principality that dominated the Van basin. There are the remains of several Seljuk buildings, including the Ulu Kümbet, the Bayındıt Türbe, the Hassan Paşa Kümbet and the Cifte Kümbet. There are also inscribed tombstones that date from the 12th century.

The remaining 103 km. (64 miles) are in the shadow of the loftiest Van peak, Süphan Dağ (4,058 meters, 13,313 ft.), past a small lake of a particularly high salinity,indicated by its name, Sodalı Gölü, to Ercis.

25 km. (16 miles) southwest is Bitlis, a green oasis at over 1,545 meters (5,070 ft.) among towering mountains and set on a tributary of the Tigris. The polygonal towers of the Byzantine citadel rise above the Şerefhan Medrese, the 12th-century Ulu Cami and Gökmeydanı Cami, to which the Osmanli added the Şerefiye Cami in the 16th century. There are many old houses in the town with Armenian inscriptions above the doors.

Siirt, 93 km. (58 miles) south, flourished under the Abbasid Caliphs, when the 12th-century Ulu Cami, the 13th-century Asakır Çarşı Cami and the Cumhuriyet Cami, distinguished by beautifully carved wooden portals, were built.

84 km. (52 miles) west, the citizens of Muş pray in the Seljuk Alaeddin Paşa and Hacı Şeref mosques below the remains of a 6th-century Byzantine citadel. 118 km. (73 miles) further west on Route 300, is Bingöl, guarded by another medieval fortress. The name means a thousand lakes, to be taken with more than the usual pinch of salt. Admittedly there are some glacier lakes in the surrounding mountains, but they seem rather insignificant, roughly halfway between Turkey's largest natural and artificial lakes. The Keban Dam on the Upper Fırat (Euphrates) has created an enormously elongated sheet of water bridged by Route 300 west to Elazığ, 142 km. (88 miles). The town is only about 100 years older than

the lake, over which an ancient Harput fortress on the mountain top commands a splendid view.

Diyarbakır and Mardin

Diyarbakır signifies in Arabic "City of the Bakır tribes," and these tribes renamed Hurri-Mitanni Amida. After absorption into the Assyrian empire, interrupted by a century of Urartu domination, followed by the now familiar succession of Medes, Persians and Macedonians, Diyarbakır came under successive domination by Romans, Sassanids, and Byzantines. Then came the Moslems, including the Ommiads, the Abbassids and the Marwanids, who battled with one another for possession of the city, a period that was punctuated by occasional but redoubtable reoccupations by the Byzantines. Absolutely everybody was after this place—the Turkomans, the Ortokids, the eastern and western Seljuks. Next came the Mongolian hordes. Finally, Selim I made it Osmanli and it settled into a relatively calm period.

Diyarbakır's triple walls of black basalt were originally constructed by the Emperor Constantius in 349. The current walls were erected by the Seljuks in 1088, and the Mardin and Urfa gates were added in 1145 and 1183 respectively. On the whole they are still in good shape along their entire length of 5.5 km (3 miles) encircling the old town. Of the original 72 towers 67 still stand. The strongest defense towers are near the main gates: the Bab El Rumi, also called the Urfa Gate; Ulu Badan (Great Bastion); Bab El Tell; Bab Yeni. The best view over the Dicle (Tigris) can be obtained from the Fort of the Goat; it is possible to make a circuit inside the ramparts, except for the elevated northeast corner, where the sad remains of the Artakid palace surround a dry octagonal pool. Much more interesting is the Ulu Cami complex in the center. This converted basilica with Corinthian columns dates in its present form from the 12th century, but the buildings surrounding the large courtyard present a mixture of several styles, up to Osmanli Rococo. The Hassan Paşa Kervanseray is still used by shops; adjoining are the Mesudiye Medrese and the Zinciriye Medrese, now the small local museum, where the exhibits cover a period of some 4,000 years.

Indicative of the sectarian division of the few remaining Christians are the three old dilapidated churches, tucked away behind houses and walls in the maze of lanes. The largest, the Syrian Church of Mary, even imposes the Moslem custom of taking off the shoes. There are also an Armenian-Gregorian and a small Jacobite church.

Not to be missed is the drive past the house built for Atatürk's visit in 1937 and across the Tigris over the Abbassid bridge for a splendid view over the ramparts. This is the dusty approach to the sprawling Tigris University on the river's barren left bank, but the return to the large modern suburbs can be made over a paved road and new bridge.

The most widely-accepted hypothesis has always been that the cradle of humanity lay in the area between the Tigris and the Euphrates, with the concomitant rise and fall of various civilizations. Some scholars boldly claim that this was the site of the earthly paradise, the Garden of Eden. However, the scene as it looks today does not bear much resemblance to the one described in the Old Testament, afflicted as it is by drought, dust, and stark stretches of rough country. Yet irrigation is gradually restoring vegetation, already sufficient to warrant a Watermelon Festival at Diyarbakır.

Mardin lies 94 km. (58 miles) southeast on Route 950. Its ancestor, Marida, was no less important in the Hurri-Mitanni and Assyrian empires, though often threatened by neighboring Amida and Nisibis. The Roman citadel with its frontage of 730 meters (800 yards) was reputedly impregnable as neither the Seljuks in the 12th century nor the Mongols in the 13th managed to capture it. The only victor here was Tamerlane, at the tail-end of the 14th century. And when he returned to Mardin in 1401 in an attempt to crush the revolt of his own brother, Isa, this time the citadel resisted even Tamerlane. The citadel is at present closed to the public due to local unrest.

England had its War of the (Two) Roses; the Turks, in the 15th century, had a War of the Two Sheep (the *ak,* white, *kara,* black). This particular area served as the battleground for their rivalry, with Mardin—situated on the slopes of a hill dominating the vast plain—of great strategic importance. Except for the citadel, all outstanding buildings are Islamic. The Latifiye Cami was built in 1371; the Seljuk Ulu Cami, dating from the 11th century, was restored in the 15th and disfigured in the 19th; the Sultan Isa Medrese (1385) is remarkable for the exquisite stone carvings and exedra, unfortunately marred somewhat by the presence of telegraph wires. The local museum, adjacent to the Sultan Isa Medrese, is worth a visit. Its courtyard shelters tombstones inscribed with cuneiform writings. The stately Kasım Paşa Medrese dates from the following century. There are assorted medreses, mosques, and türbes—especially those of Zeynel Mirza and Imam Abdullah, noteworthy for their delicate ornamentation—and a 17th-century covered bazaar.

Route 955 southeast to the junction with E24 passes after 7km. (4 miles) the large Jacobite Monastery of Deyrulzaferan, the spiritual center of the Christian Syriac sect, the members of which speak Aramaic, said to be the language spoken by Jesus and his disciples. Aramaic is used in the inscriptions above the doors of the adjoining church and in the church's missals. Visitors can attend the Sunday service, and a guide will gladly show you around the lovely monastery. E24 hugs the Syrian border past the ruins of Dara and the frontier fortress of Anastasiopolis, founded by the Emperor Anastasius in the 6th century. Road and railway cross into Syria at Nusaybin, ancient Nisibis, mentioned in Assyrian inscriptions some 3,000 years ago, and constantly fought over as witnessed by a Roman triumphal arch and a castle. An early church stood over the tomb of St. Sergius. The border crossing at Şenyurt, due south, though closer, is less frequented.

The Tur Abdin plateau lying northeast of Mardin, near Savur, was a prominent stronghold of Christianity as early as the 4th century. The Syrian church founded a large number of monasteries here, some of which were occupied up until the early 1900s. The Midyat area farther on contains several interesting churches dating from the 8th to the 12th centuries—in Salah, the Mar Yakub; near Arnas, the Mar Kyriakos and the Mar Azaziel; in Kakh, El Hadra; and the 5th-century Mar Gabriel monastery, near the village of Kartmen.

Malatya and Nemrut Dağ

Malatya lies in a fertile plain at the foot of the Anti-Taurus, a welcome change in the endless steppe extending from Kayseri to Elazig. The prosperous but uninteresting market town developed on its present site only after 1838. It is 7 km. (4 miles) west of Hittite Milid, now Aslantepe, and 19 km. (12 miles) southwest of Roman Melitene, Eski Malatya. Milid became a Hurri principality, an Assyrian dependency, a vassal of Urartu. Abandoned after the Cimmerian incursion in the 7th century B.C., the excavations at Aslantepe have yielded precious finds from ancient Hittite settlements, notably bas-reliefs and the foundations of the palace of the 8th-century B.C. Assyrian king, Sargon II. After an interval of some 700 years, the Romans established a legion headquarters at Melitene, which was later fortified by Justinian and promptly taken by the Persians.

Occupied by the Arabs in 640, Malatya was plundered and burnt down with monotonous regularity by Byzantines and Moslems until the advent of a Christian adventurer who was miraculously delivered from his Seljuk besiegers by the opportune arrival of the First Crusade. Then, in 1243, came an incredible switching-over of alliances. When the Mongols laid siege to the city, it was jointly defended by Christians and Moslems! Traces of the double wall of Eski Malatya can still be seen. The Ulu Cami in the town center is a handsome edifice of Seljuk origin.

Last, but certainly not least, there remains the uniquely rewarding excursion up the 2,150-meter (8,205-ft.) Nemrut Dağ, only advisable between May and October. The easiest but, of course, most expensive visit is by helicopter from Adıyaman, where accommodations are better. Minibuses also run from there, but the usual starting point for the drive up is Kahta on Route 360, 41 km. (25 miles) east of Adıyaman, within easy driving distance from Gaziantep, Kahraman Maras, Malatya and Sanliurfa. *Warning:* The arrival of parties to share the cost of a car often fails to materialize, with days lost in waiting. The ascent should ideally start at 2 A.M. to reach the summit for sunrise and return before the fierce midday heat. Minibuses climb the 52 km. (32 miles) north to within 1 km. (½ mile) below the east terrace of the sepulchral mound—50 meters (165 ft.) high and 150 meters (492 ft.) in diameter—which tops the cone-shaped pinnacle of Nemrut Dağ. The stupendous spectacle compensates for the extremes of heat and cold as well as the absence of shade and water. If you do not wish to see the sunrise on the mountain top, a car can be arranged with assistance from the Sanliurfa tourist office for a day trip to the site, thus avoiding the need to stay overnight at Kahta as well as the crowds and the cold morning air.

Antiochos I Kommagenes (69–34 B.C.) conceived the megalomanic idea for the colossal statues. Seated in hieratic attitudes on thrones on three vast terraces, they are 8 to 9 meters (26 to 30 ft.) high. The inscription reads: "I, Antiochos, caused this monument to be erected in commemoration of my own glory and of that of the gods." It was inevitable that through the centuries such vainglory should fall prey to the forces of erosion, to thunderbolts (unleashed by jealous gods?), to earthquakes, and to the ravages of time itself. The Olympian gods and goddesses, Tyche, Herakles and, of course, Antiochos himself, have been decapitated. Their gigantic heads, combining the Greek harmony of features with oriental headgear and hairstyles, have been set upright on the ground and arranged around the incredible tumulus.

Antiochos I is almost certainly concealed beneath. So far, extensive explorations by archeologists have failed to bring to light any passageway, if indeed one exists. Despite the elaborate precautions observed, all attempts at excavation have caused cave-ins. The experts hesitate to persist lest the whole extraordinary monument collapse. It's something of a feat just to have uncovered the statues and heads. In 1926 a thunderstorm brought the last one crashing down—ironically enough, it was the head of Tyche, the goddess of fortune.

It is obvious that a veritable army of slaves must have toiled like ants for many years to heap up this pyramid of small rocks on a mountain top, just to perpetuate the name of a master drunk with his own power. Now, two millennia later, the miracle of discovery has resuscitated the extraordinary array, and the world is at least aware that this man lived and dreamed his dreams of grandeur.

Should even this stunning display of human vanity be insufficient reward for the discomfort of access, the same Texan who was attempting to recover Noah's Ark also claims to have discovered the foundations of the Tower of Babel near Nemrut Dağ.

As the ascent is strenuous enough even in the cool of the morning, the other sights are better left for the return journey. They are sufficiently remarkable even after those unique white colossi round the ocher-pink cone. Least impressive is the Gerger Castle at the end of a bad road following the dammed-up Fırat (Euphrates) upstream. So turn back towards Kahta after Karadut, right past Narince to Eski (Old) Kahta, near Eski Kale, ancient Arsameia of Nymphaios. Across the Seljuk bridge over the Kahta (Chalkinas) River, Antiochos I had a stunning relief of his father Mithridates being greeted by Herakles carved into the rock. Higher up are Anatolia's most copious rock inscriptions providing information about the Kommagene dynasty, while on the mountaintop are the foundations of Arsameia's acropolis with colored floor mosaics. Below, a hall has been hollowed out of the rocks. Across the river, Yeni Kale (New Castle) was built by the Mameluks over a smaller Kommagene fortress.

Cross the Kahta by the Cendere Köprü, a single span with two tall columns on one end and one on the other, built by the Roman Emperor Septimus Severus in the 3rd century A.D. The 35-meter (115-ft.) high funerary tumulus of Antiochos' queen or perhaps the royal family was once surrounded by 18 columns topped by animal sculptures. The only one still standing bears the Roman eagle, albeit monocephalic, its "other head having been gnawed away by the starving centuries."

The Euphrates valley to the south will be flooded by the Karakaya Dam, with an output of 1,800,000 kW., and 180 km. (112 miles) downstream near Samsat, by the Atatürk Dam, with an output of 2,400,000 kW., now under construction. This project will irrigate some 1.8 million hectares (4.4 million acres) of semi-desert, but submerge what is probably the cradle of civilization. Intensive excavations are being carried out all through the region. Successive remains of every conqueror—Hittite, Assyrian, Persian, Anatolian, Byzantine, Roman and Timourid—have piled up within the 5-km. (3-mile) ramparts of the Kommagene capital Samasota, now Samsat, birthplace of the Roman poet Lucianus, 38 km. (24 miles) southeast of Adıyaman. Only 5 km. (3 miles) from that town, at Pirin, are the remains of Roman Perrhe: walls, reliefs and the foundations of a palace. In 208 caves the progress of civilization can be traced from cave man to the Middle Ages.

PRACTICAL INFORMATION FOR
THE EASTERN PROVINCES

TOURIST OFFICES. There are local tourist offices in the following towns: **Adıyaman,** Hükümet Konağı, Zemin Kat (tel. 1008); **Diyarbakır,** Lise Cad., Onur Apt. 24 (tel. 121 73); **Elazığ,** Istasyon Cad. 35 (tel. 165 72); **Erzurum,** Canal Gürsel Cad. (tel. 156 97); **Gürbulak,** at the Turco-Iranian frontier post (tel. 9); **Hakkari,** Belediye Binası; **Kars,** Ortakapı Mah. Faikbey Cad. (tel. 2300); **Van,** Cumhuriyet Cad. 127 (tel. 120 18).

WHEN TO COME. The weather is extreme: bitterly cold in winter (especially at the higher altitudes), scorchingly hot in summer. Winds and rains can be torrential. Late spring and early fall are best. All hotels offer reduced prices in the off season (October to May).

SPECIAL EVENTS. July. Malatya Apricot Festival. **September.** Diyarbakır Watermelon Festival, late in the month.

HOTELS AND RESTAURANTS

Adıyaman. *Antiochos Motel* (I). 43 rooms. Restaurant. *Arsemia Motel* (I), (tel. 2112). 12 rooms. Restaurant; on road to Nemrut Dağ.

Ağri. *Divan, Gök* and others even worse.

Ardahan. *Turistik.* 16 rooms.

Bitlis. No hotel of any standard, but *Turistik* is cheap and very basic. 18 rooms. If you want ethnic Turkey, this is it.

Diyarbakır. None are air-conditioned, despite the summer heat. *Demir* (M), Izzetpaşa Cad. 8 (tel. 123 15). 39 rooms. *Diyarbakır Büyük* (M), (tel. 158 32). 72 rooms. Facing the ramparts. *Turistik* (M), Ziyagökalp Bul. 7 (tel. 126 62). 54 rooms. Pleasant garden restaurant round fountain. *Cantürkler* (I). 41 rooms. Restaurant. *Derya* (I), Inönü Cad. 13 (tel. 149 66). 28 rooms. *Saraç* (I), Izzetpaşa Cad. 16 (tel. 123 65). 35 rooms.

Doğubeyazit. *Isfahan* (I), Eminiyet Cad. 48 (tel. 1139). 60 rooms. Sauna. *Sim-Er Turistik Tesisleri* (I), (tel. 1601). 63 rooms. Magnificent view of Mt. Ararat. Both these have restaurants, mainly frequented by Eastern Anatolian Tours and truck drivers on the way to Iran. *Yılmaz* (I). 17 rooms. Very simple. *Ishakpasa* (M), Emniyet Cad. 10 (tel. 1243). In center of town. Very clean and friendly.

Elazığ. *Beritan* (M), Hürriyet Cad. 24 (tel. 144 84). 70 rooms. Restaurant. *Büyük* (M), Harput Cad. 9 (tel. 220 01). 90 rooms. Restaurant. **Restaurant.** *Altınşiş Lokantası* (I). *Bisyuk Pasaj* (I), Belediye Cad. Exceptional pizzas, country yogurts and ayrans.

Erzincan. *Urartu* (M), Cumhuriyet Mey. (tel. 1561). 58 rooms. *Evcan* (I). 25 rooms.

Erzurum. *Büyük* (E), Alirevam Cad. (tel. 165 28). 50 rooms. Restaurant; newest and best in its category. *Oral* (M), Terminal Cad. (tel. 197 40). 90 rooms. *Efes* (I), (tel. 170 81). 46 rooms. *Polat* (I), Kazimkarabekir Cad. (tel. 116 23). 60 rooms.
Restaurant. *Tufan* in the center.

Hakkari. *Turistik* Very basic. *Calli* Better standards. Good restaurant. Somewhat suspect plumbing.

Ilıca. 15 km. (9 miles) west of Erzurum on E23. *Turistik* (I). 16 rooms, 4 showers.

Kahta. *Nemrut Tür Motel* (M), Adiyaman Kahta Yolu (tel. 863). 100 rooms. Small pool. Good value. *Komegana* (I), Eski Kahta Yolu 1 (tel. 92). 15 rooms. No private showers. *Merhaba* (I). Atatürk Bul. (tel. 1970). 28 rooms.

Kars. *Temel Palas* (I). 20 rooms. *Yılmaz* (I). 36 rooms. Still the only reasonable hotels in Kars. Clean if somewhat shabby rooms.
Restaurant. *Samdan* (I), Atatük Cad. 3 (tel. 4647). Oasis for good cooking.

Malatya. *Kent* (I), Atatürk Cad. 151 (tel. 121 75). 51 rooms. *Sinan* (I), Atatürk Cad. 14 (tel. 129 07). 54 rooms.

Mardin. *Bayraktar* (I). 41 rooms.

Muş. *Turistik* (I). 30 rooms. Some showers. *Zengök* (I). 42 rooms, 24 showers.

Nemrut Dağ. *Zeus.* On mountainside. Comfortable and ideal for seeing summit at sunrise or sunset.

Nusaybin. *Nezirhan Motel* (I) 35 air-conditioned rooms. Pool; on Syrian border. The Deyrulzaferan monastery also provides accommodation.

Pasinler. *Kale* (I). Germeli Köyü Mev. (tel. 1425). 36 air-conditioned rooms. Pool, restaurant.

Siirt. *Erdef* (I). Cumhuriyet Cad. 9 (tel. 1081). 30 rooms, 16 showers.

Tatvan. *Van Gölü* (I). 22 rooms, 8 showers. Pleasant hotel on lakeside of shabby town. Set in gardens. Owned and operated by shipping line.

Van. Van has some of the best accommodations in this region. Pleasant local wine, St. Emilion red and white, at present uniformly labeled 1976. *Büyük Urartu* (E), Hastane Sok. 60 (tel. 206 60). 75 rooms. New and the best. *Akdamar* (M), Karabekir Cad. 56 (tel. 181 00). 75 rooms, 6 suites. Good food, roof dining room and terrace. Fraying slightly. *Büyük Asur* (I), Cumhuriyet Cad. (tel. 187 92). 46 rooms. Highly recommended. *Caldı-*

ran (I), Sihke Cad. (tel. 127 18). 48 rooms. *Efes* (I). 48 rooms. *Tekin* (I), Küçükcami Civari (tel. 130 10). 52 rooms.

Restaurants. *Altin, Kosk,* and *Solen.*

CAMPING. Camping alongside the road is not recommended in the Eastern Provinces, mainly because of the security regulations. If you need to consult the police, it is best to go to the nearest Military Gendarma post. There are however several official campsites on the approach road to Van.

GETTING AROUND. By Plane. *THY* has flights between Istanbul and Erzurum (1 hr. 40 mins.) daily; between Ankara and Erzurum (70 mins.) daily; between Ankara and Elaziğ (65 mins.) four times weekly; between Ankara and Malatya (55 mins.) three times weekly; between Ankara and Diyarbakır (70 mins.) daily; between Ankara and Van (1 hr. 25 mins.) on Wed., Fri. and Sun., and calling at Diyarbakır (2 hr. 10 mins.) on Mon. and Thurs.

By Train. The *Eastern Express* runs daily: Istanbul–Haydarpaşa–Erzurum–Kars; also Istanbul–Haydarpaşa–Muş—Tatvan, and on by ferry to Van, whence the train continues to Teheran (Iran). The *Southern Express* runs four times a week: Istanbul–Haydarpaşa–Sivas–Malatya–Kahraman Maraş or Gaziantep.

By Car. E23, Anatolia's main west–east axis, is now paved from Istanbul via Agri to the Iranian border. to Ağrı, but the last 130 km. (80 miles) stretch to the Iranian border leaves a lot to be desired. Route 965 south from Ağrı to Patnos is unpaved for the first 32 km. (20 miles) but easy going for the remaining 196 km. (123 miles) to Van, mainly Route 280. The two other principal west–east connections, Route 300 from Kayseri via Elaziğ to Van; and E24 from Sanliurfa along the Syrian and Iraqi border, are perfectly adequate. The extension of E24 is still highly adventurous between Uludere and Hakkari, but paved again from there to the Iranian border at Esendere. This is a controlled military area. If you do not pass the control point before 4 P.M. it is likely that you will have to stay until the following morning. The Suvarihalil Pass (2,470 m. high) and the Tanintanin Pass (2,230 m.) make this an excellent scenic drive. On all these mountain routes the extreme winters and spring thaws break up the road surfaces, even asphalt roads. By June these routes are usually graded, and potholes in asphalt roads have been filled. However, if summer is late in coming maintenance can be set back weeks, so be prepared for possibly slow progress. Route 885 is the only fully paved north–south axis from Erzincan via Elaziğ to Diyarbakır, prolonged by Route 950 to E24 and the Syrian border. For connections with the Black Sea, see the previous chapter.

By Bus. There are daily nonstop motorcoaches from Istanbul and Ankara to all major towns and points in between. Very comfortable considering the price. New Mercedes are used on many routes. Most bus stations are located outside the main towns they serve. Ticket offices within the towns provide a mini-bus service to the depots. It is advisable to shop around for a bargain 24 hours before your journey. A variety of prices are offered by the towns' stores for the same excursion. The store which provided you with a ticket will ask you to return 30 minutes before departure time and will then take you to the bus station and see you safely on to the bus. On arrival at your destination you can either make your own way into the town or take a taxi or Dolmush, both of which are readily available.

Most towns are also connected by Dolmush (shared taxi or minibus). This service is less convenient than the regular bus, as it only departs when the vehicle is full and makes frequent stops.

By Boat. Besides the twice-weekly Tatvan–Van rail ferry, often delayed especially for trains from Iran, there are car ferries in both directions twice daily. A ferry to Erciş is planned.

MOUNTAIN CLIMBING. The Cilo and Sat mountain ranges lie in the southeast spur of Turkey, in the province of Hakkari, between the borders of Iran and Iraq. They have nearly 20 glaciers and over 100 peaks of different heights, covered with snow all the year round. Icy lakes are scattered among the mountain tops, most of which are over 3,505 meters (11,500 ft.) high. The most awesome peak in the Cilo chain is the Gelyaşım (4,135 meters, 13,566 ft.). The Sat Mountains, further to the south, are also renowned for their lakes and valleys, which are a preserve of wild goats or ibex of Anatolia, the forebears of our tame goats, together with sheep, bears and other wildlife.

198 km. (123 miles) south from Van on Route 6 is Yüksekova, the starting point for mountain climbers, whether on pony, donkey, or muleback.

1) **Sat Mountains.** Leaving Yüksekova toward Piskasir, and following the mountain ridges to the village of Bay, you will come to the lake of Bay in 12 to 14 hours (guide required).

2) **Cilo Mountains.** Starting point is the gendarmerie post of Zap, 18 km. (11 miles) from Hakkari. The high plateau of Mercan is followed by the even higher plateau of Serpil, where there are lodgings of sorts. From the eastern glacier of the Gelyaşım it is possible for a hardy climber with a guide to scale one of the most majestic but difficult mountains in Anatolia.

Continuing southeast toward the village of Istazin, you come to the lake of Sat. From there you go down, through the Beraga Pass, towards the village of Oramar (at 1,454 meters, 4,770 ft.) and the ruins of Zir to your right; after visiting Zir, continue northwest to the village of Medi; then the cleft between Mount Kisara (3,572 meters, 11,719 ft.) and Mount Samdi (3,461 meters, 11,354 ft.), until you reach Hakkari. This excursion may last a week or more.

For information and permits apply to the *Turkish Mountaineering Club* (Dagcılık Federasyonu), B.T.G.M., Ulus Işhanı, A Block, Ulus, Ankara.

VOCABULARY

Turkish-English Tourist Vocabulary

A Brief Introduction to Turkish Spelling and Pronunciation

Turkish is written in the Latin alphabet with some diacritic marks which modify the sound to suit Turkish phonetics. Of the 29 letters six do not exist in English, these are ç, ğ, ı, ö, ş, and ü, while the characters q, w, and x do not exist in Turkish, though they may appear in some foreign names. Most consonants are pronounced much the same as their English equivalents, except—

    c as **j** in jam
    ç as **ch** in chair
    g as **g** in good
    ğ silent, but lengthens the preceding vowel, thus *dăğ* is pronounced
daa
    s as **s** in sun, as ss within a word, thus *hisar* and not the anglicized
hissar
    ş as **sh** in shine

Vowels are pronounced as follows:
    a as **u** in gun
    e as **e** in pen
    ı (undotted i) somewhat as **a** in portable (the *schwa* sound)
    i as **i** in it
    o as **o** in Oscar
    ö as **i** in bird
    u as **u** in pull
    ü no English equivalent, as **u** in French tu

Each letter keeps the same sound wherever its place in the word. The letter ğ has a capital Ğ but never starts a word. The undotted ı and the dotted i are separate vowels whose distinctions are strictly observed in pronunciation and spelling. In names t increasingly replaces the Arab d, p the b, and ü the u. Thus Murat instead of Murad, mihrap for mihrab, Abdül for Abdul, though the older forms are still in use, especially for historic personalities. A and e are sometimes interchangeable, thus Alaattin as well as Alaeddin, Beyazıt and Bayezıd.

Contrary to Indo-Germanic languages, the possessive case is taken by the noun and not the name, thus Mosque of Ahmet becomes Ahmet of Mosque, Ahmet Camii. But as after an adjective the nominitive Cami is used, Ulu Cami (Great Mosque), this case has been generally adopted throughout this Guide for simplicity's sake—Cami, Dağ (Mountain), Saray (Palace), etc. There is no danger of misunderstanding, even if official maps and handouts usually add the suffix. Exceptions had to be made for Bulvarı (Boulevard), Caddesi (Street), Meydanı (Square), and Sokakı (Alley), which hardly ever appear as Bulvar, Cadde, Meydan or Sokak; in addresses they are always abbreviated to the first three letters. Names of streets and public buildings may be spelled separately or in one word, the latter being more common; thus, Sultanahmet Cami (i) rather than Sultan Ahmet, Talatpaşa Caddesi rather than Talat Paşa.

As there seems no point in providing phrases to which the answer will not be understood, the following Vocabulary has been kept to the essential minimum, but there is a larger glossary for words recurring frequently in place names, as they convey a useful series of pointers.

General

Hello, Greetings	Merhaba
Good morning	Günaydın
Good evening	Iyi akşamlar
Goodnight	Iyi geceler
Goodbye	Allaha ısmarladık (said by the person leaving)
	Güle güle (said by the person remaining behind)
How are you?	Nasılsınız?
I am well	Iyiyim
Please	Lütfen
Thank you	Teşekkür ederim/mersi
Yes	Evet
No	Hayır
There is/not	Var/yok (used to express the availability or unavailablity of something)
Excuse me	Özür dilerim/affedersiniz
Big	Büyük
Great, exalted	Ulu
Little, small	Kücük
Much, very	Çok
New, recent	Yeni
Old, ancient	Eski
Hot	Sıcak/kızıgın
Cold	Soğuk

Numbers

1	bir	10	on	90	doksan
2	iki	11	on bir	100	yüz
3	üç	20	yirmi	101	yüz bir
4	dört	30	otuz	200	iki yüz
5	beş	40	kırk	300	üç yüz
6	altı	50	elli	1000	bin
7	yedi	60	altmış	2000	iki bin
8	sekiz	70	yetmış		
9	dokuz	80	seksen		

Colors—often used in place names

White	Ak
Whitish	Akça
Black	Kare/siyah
Yellow	Sarı

Blue	Mavi
Skyblue	Gök
Green	Yeşil
Red	Kızıl/kırmızı
Grey	Gri/külrengi

Time and Days

When?	Ne zaman?	What time is it?	Saat kaç?
Today	Bugün	At what time?	Saat kaçta?
Yesterday	Dün	Sunday	Pazar
Tomorrow	Yarin	Monday	Pazartesi
Morning	Sabah	Tuesday	Salı
Afternoon	Ögleden sonra	Wednesday	Çerşambe
Evening	Akşam	Thursday	Perşembe
Night	Gece	Friday	Cuma
One hour	Bir saat	Saturday	Cumaresi

Traveling

Airport	Hava alanı	Where is it?	Nerede?
Altitude	Rakim	Is it far?	Uzak mı?
Bus	Otobüs	Dining car	Vagon-restoran
Intercity bus station	Otogar	Sleeping car	Kuşet
Landing place, quay	Iskele	First class	Birinci mevki
Population	Nüfus	Second class	Ikinci mevki
Port	Liman	Attention	Dikkat
Railway station	Gar	A good hotel	Iyi bir otel
Station	Istacyon	A restaurant	Bir lokanta
Ticket	Bilet	Repair garage	Bir tamirci
Town center	Şehir merkezi	Tourist office	Turizm bürosu
Train	Tren		

At the Hotel

A room	Bir oda	Key	Anahtar
One person	Bir kisi	Porter	Kapıcı
Two people	Iki kişilik	Waiter	Garson
With bathroom	Banyolu	Napkin	Peçete
What is the price?	Fiatı nedir?	Breakfast	Kahvaltı
Hot water	Sıcak su	Coffee	Kahve
An extra bed	Ilave bir yatak	Tea	Çay
Toilet	Tuvalet / hela	Milk	Süt
Laundry	Çamaşir hane	Sugar	Şeker
Dry cleaning	Kuru temizleme	Come in	Giriniz
The bill / check	Hesap		

Note: Menu and other food words are in the Food and Drink chapter

At the Garage

Gas (Petrol)	Benzin normal/süper	Change of oil	Yağlama
Gas station	Benzin istasyonu	Tire	Lastik
Oil	Motor yağı	Brakes	Frenier

Spark plugs   Bujiler   It does not work   Çalışmıyor

Shopping

How much is it?	Bu ne kadar?	Cigarettes	Sigara
It is very expensive	Çok pahalı	Cigars	Puro
I don't like it	Beğenmedim	Stamps	Damgalamak
Postcard	Kartpostal		

In Town

Bank	Banka	Boulevard	Bulvar
Church	Kilise	Square	Alan / Meydan
Consulate	Konsolosluk	Street	Cadde
American	Amerikan	Narrow street	Sokak
British	Ingiliz	Road	Yol
Mosque	Cami	Park	Park
Museum	Müze	Quarter	Mahalle
Police station	Karakol	Theater	Tiyatro
Bridge	Köprü	Telephone token	Jeton

Glossary of Useful Words

Ada	Island
Ağa	Big landowner
Agora	Market in ancient towns
Akropolis	Upper town in antiquity
Bahçe	Garden, park
Bayram	Religious festival
Bedestan	Covered bazaar
Burnu, burun	Cape, headland
Cami	Mosque
Çan, çanlık	Pine, pinegrove
Çay	Brook, stream
Dağ	Mountain
Dağlar	Mountain range
Deniz	Sea
Divan	Council of State, council chamber
Fuar	Fair
Gazi	Leader
Gecit	Mountain pass
Göl, gölü	Lake
Haci	Respected pilgrim to Mecca
Hamam	Bath
Han	Old Inn
Harabe (abr. Hrb.)	Ruin
Hastane	Hospital
Hisar	Citadel
Hoca	Moslem teacher
Höyük	Mound, tumulus
Ilıca	Hot spring, spa
Imam, Molla	Moslem clergy
Imaret	Hospice

Irmak, Nehri or Nehir	River
Kale	Fortress
Kapalı Çarşi	Covered market
Kapı	Gate
Karayolu	Highway
Kavşak	Crossroads
Kaya	Rock
Kervansaray	Caravanserai
Kilim	Woven rug
Kilise	Church
Konak	Mansion
Körfez	Gulf, bay
Köşk	Kiosk, pavilion
Köy	Village
Kule	Tower
Kulüp	Club
Kümbet	Dome, vault, mausoleum
Kumla	Sandy beach
Mağara	Cave
Manastir	Christian monastery
Medrese	Theological school
Merkez	Center
Mescit	Small mosque
Mihrab	Niche indicating direction of Mecca
Mimber	Pulpit in mosque
Minare	Minaret
Müezzin	Summoner to prayer
Pazar	Bazaar
Plaj	Beach
Şadirvan	Fountain
Sahil	Shore, coast
Saray	Palace
Şehir	Town
Şelale	Waterfall
Stele	Inscribed stone monument
Tekke	Dervish monastery
Tepe	Hill, mound
Türbe	Mausoleum, tomb
Ulema	Theologian
Vilayet	Province
Yeniçeri	Janissary
Yürük	Nomadic Turkoman

INDEX

Index

MAP OF TURKEY

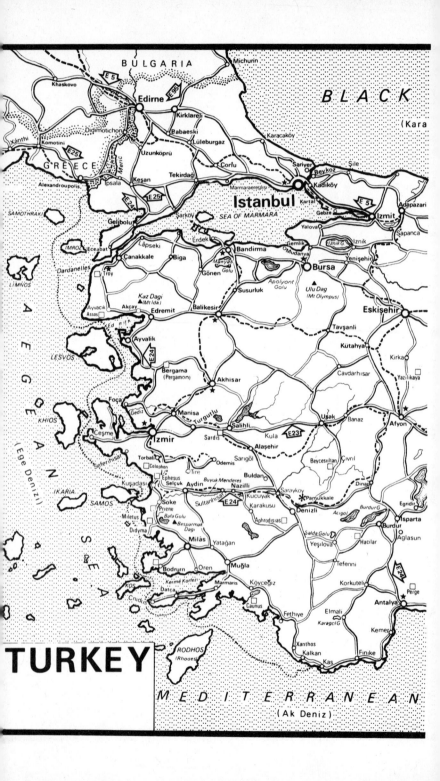

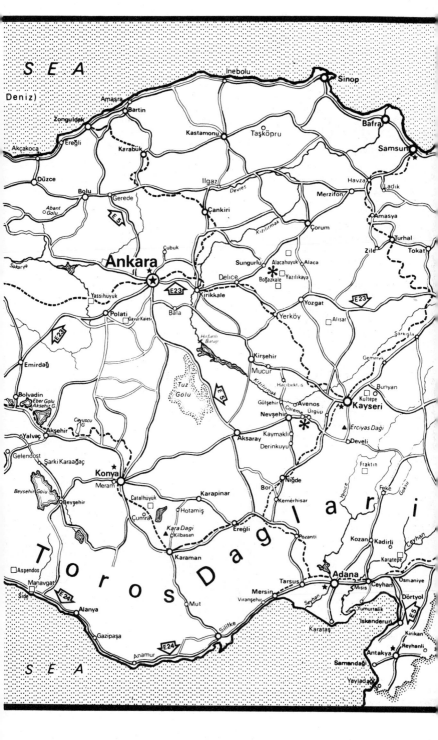

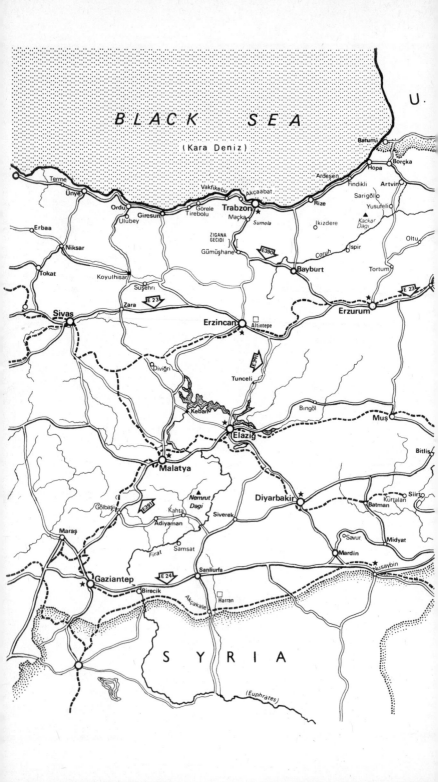

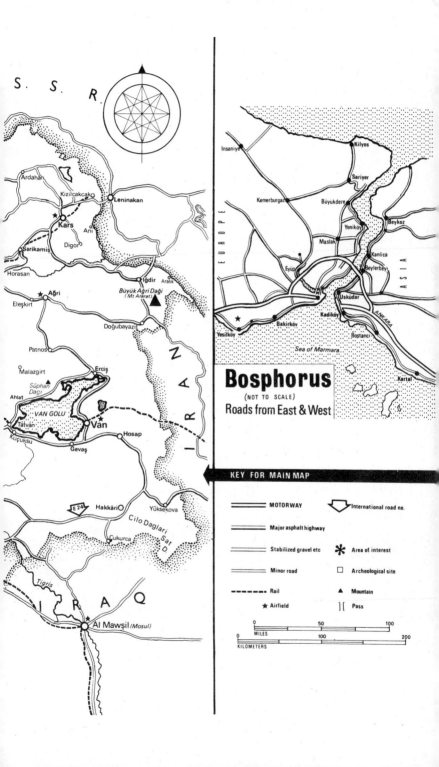

Bosphorus

(NOT TO SCALE)

Roads from East & West

KEY FOR MAIN MAP

═══════ MOTORWAY	⬭ International road no.
─────── Major asphalt highway	
─────── Stabilized gravel etc	✳ Area of interest
─────── Minor road	☐ Archeological site
┈┈┈┈┈ Rail	▲ Mountain
★ Airfield	][Pass

MILES 0   50   100

KILOMETERS 0   100   200

Fodor's Travel Guides

U.S. Guides

Alaska
Arizona
Atlantic City & the
  New Jersey Shore
Boston
California
Cape Cod
Carolinas & the
  Georgia Coast
The Chesapeake Region
Chicago
Colorado
Dallas & Fort
  Worth

Disney World & the
  Orlando Area
Florida
Hawaii
Houston &
  Galveston
Las Vegas
Los Angeles, Orange
  County, Palm Springs
Maui
Miami, Fort Lauderdale,
  Palm Beach
Michigan, Wisconsin,
  Minnesota

New England
New Mexico
New Orleans
New Orleans (Pocket
  Guide)
New York City
New York City (Pocket
  Guide)
New York State
Pacific North Coast
Philadelphia
The Rockies
San Diego
San Francisco

San Francisco (Pocket
  Guide)
The South
Texas
USA
Virgin Islands
Virginia
Waikiki
Washington, DC
Williamsburg

Foreign Guides

Acapulco
Amsterdam
Australia, New Zealand,
  The South Pacific
Austria
Bahamas
Bahamas (Pocket
  Guide)
Baja & the Pacific
  Coast Resorts
Barbados
Beijing, Guangzhou &
  Shanghai
Belgium &
  Luxembourg
Bermuda
Brazil
Britain (Great Travel
  Values)
Budget Europe
Canada
Canada (Great Travel
  Values)
Canada's Atlantic
  Provinces
Cancun, Cozumel,
  Yucatan Peninsula

Caribbean
Caribbean (Great
  Travel Values)
Central America
Eastern Europe
Egypt
Europe
Europe's Great
  Cities
Florence & Venice
France
France (Great Travel
  Values)
Germany
Germany (Great Travel
  Values)
Great Britain
Greece
The Himalayan
  Countries
Holland
Hong Kong
Hungary
India, including Nepal
Ireland
Israel
Italy

Italy (Great Travel
  Values)
Jamaica
Japan
Japan (Great Travel
  Values)
Jordan & the
  Holy Land
Kenya, Tanzania,
  the Seychelles
Korea
Lisbon
Loire Valley
London
London (Great
  Travel Values)
London (Pocket Guide)
Madrid & Barcelona
Mexico
Mexico City
Montreal &
  Quebec City
Munich
New Zealand
North Africa
Paris
Paris (Pocket Guide)

People's Republic of
  China
Portugal
Rio de Janeiro
The Riviera (Fun on)
Rome
Saint Martin &
  Sint Maarten
Scandinavia
Scandinavian Cities
Scotland
Singapore
South America
South Pacific
Southeast Asia
Soviet Union
Spain
Spain (Great Travel
  Values)
Sweden
Switzerland
Sydney
Tokyo
Toronto
Turkey
Vienna
Yugoslavia

Special-Interest Guides

Health & Fitness
  Vacations
Royalty Watching

Selected Hotels of
  Europe

Selected Resorts and
  Hotels of the U.S.
Shopping in Europe

Skiing in North America
Sunday in New York